Fodor's

MAINE COAST

2nd Edition

Where to Stay and Eat
for All Budgets

Must-See Sights
and Local Secrets

Ratings You Can Trust

Fodor's Travel Publications   New York, Toronto, London, Sydney, Auckland
www.fodors.com

FODOR'S MAINE COAST
Editor: Debbie Harmsen

Editorial Production: Astrid deRidder
Editorial Contributors: Stephen and Neva Allen, John Blodgett, Lelah Cole, Sherry Hanson, Mike Nalepa, Mary Ruoff, Laura V. Scheel, George Semler
Maps & Illustrations: David Lindroth, *cartographer*; Bob Blake and Rebecca Baer, *map editors*
Design: Fabrizio LaRocca, *creative director*; Guido Caroti, Siobhan O'Hare, *art directors*; Tina Malaney, Chie Ushio, Ann McBride, *designers*; Melanie Marin, *senior picture editor*; Moon Sun Kim, *cover designer*
Cover Photo: (Schoodic Point, Acadia National Park): Susan Cole Kelly
Production/Manufacturing: Angela L. McLean

2nd Edition

ISBN 978-1-4000-1904-5

ISSN 1554-5830

SPECIAL SALES

This book is available at special discounts for bulk purchases for sales promotions or premiums. Special editions, including personalized covers, excerpts of existing books, and corporate imprints, can be created in large quantities for special needs. For more information, write to Special Markets/Premium Sales, 1745 Broadway, MD 6-2, New York, New York 10019, or e-mail specialmarkets@randomhouse.com.

AN IMPORTANT TIP & AN INVITATION

Although all prices, opening times, and other details in this book are based on information supplied to us at press time, changes occur all the time in the travel world, and Fodor's cannot accept responsibility for facts that become outdated or for inadvertent errors or omissions. So **always confirm information when it matters,** especially if you're making a detour to visit a specific place. Your experiences—positive and negative—matter to us. If we have missed or misstated something, **please write to us.** We follow up on all suggestions. Contact the Maine Coast editor at editors@fodors.com or c/o Fodor's at 1745 Broadway, New York, NY 10019.

PRINTED IN THE UNITED STATES OF AMERICA
10 9 8 7 6 5 4 3 2 1

Be a Fodor's Correspondent

Your opinion matters. It matters to us. It matters to your fellow Fodor's travelers, too. And we'd like to hear it. In fact, we need to hear it.

When you share your experiences and opinions, you become an active member of the Fodor's community. That means we'll not only use your feedback to make our books better, but we'll publish your names and comments whenever possible. Throughout our guides, look for "Word of Mouth," excerpts of your unvarnished feedback.

Here's how you can help improve Fodor's for all of us.

Tell us when we're right. We rely on local writers to give you an insider's perspective. But our writers and staff editors—who are the best in the business—depend on you. Your positive feedback is a vote to renew our recommendations for the next edition.

Tell us when we're wrong. We're proud that we update most of our guides every year. But we're not perfect. Things change. Hotels cut services. Museums change hours. Charming cafés lose charm. If our writer didn't quite capture the essence of a place, tell us how you'd do it differently. If any of our descriptions are inaccurate or inadequate, we'll incorporate your changes in the next edition and will correct factual errors at fodors.com immediately.

Tell us what to include. You probably have had fantastic travel experiences that aren't yet in Fodor's. Why not share them with a community of like-minded travelers? Maybe you chanced upon a beach or bistro or B&B that you don't want to keep to yourself. Tell us why we should include it. And share your discoveries and experiences with everyone directly at fodors.com. Your input may lead us to add a new listing or highlight a place we cover with a "Highly Recommended" star or with our highest rating, "Fodor's Choice."

Give us your opinion instantly at our feedback center at www.fodors.com/feedback. You may also e-mail editors@fodors.com with the subject line "Maine Coast Editor." Or send your nominations, comments, and complaints by mail to Maine Coast Editor, Fodor's, 1745 Broadway, New York, NY 10019.

You and travelers like you are the heart of the Fodor's community. Make our community richer by sharing your experiences. Be a Fodor's correspondent.

Happy Traveling!

Tim Jarrell, Publisher

CONTENTS

CLOSE UPS

MAPS

ABOUT
THIS BOOK

Our Ratings

Sometimes you find terrific travel experiences and sometimes they just find you. But usually the burden is on you to select the right combination of experiences. That's where our ratings come in.

As travelers we've all discovered a place so wonderful that its worthiness is obvious. And sometimes that place is so unique that superlatives don't do it justice: you just have to be there to know. These sights, properties, and experiences get our highest rating, **Fodor's Choice**, indicated by orange stars throughout this book.

Black stars highlight sights and properties we deem **Highly Recommended**, places that our writers, editors, and readers praise again and again for consistency and excellence.

By default, there's another category: any place we include in this book is by definition worth your time, unless we say otherwise. And we will.

Disagree with any of our choices? Care to nominate a place or suggest that we rate one more highly? Visit our feedback center at www.fodors.com/feedback.

Budget Well

Hotel and restaurant price categories from ¢ to $$$$ are defined in the opening pages of each chapter. For attractions, we always give standard adult admission fees; reductions are usually available for children, students, and senior citizens. **AE, D, DC, MC, V** following dining and lodging listings indicate when American Express, Discover, Diner's Club, MasterCard, and Visa are accepted.

Restaurants

Unless we state otherwise, restaurants are open for lunch and dinner daily. We mention dress only when there's a specific requirement, and reservations only when they're essential or not accepted.

Hotels

Hotels have private bath, phone, TV, and air-conditioning, and operate on the European Plan (aka EP, meaning without meals), unless we specify that they use the Continental Plan (CP, with a continental breakfast), Breakfast Plan (BP, with a full breakfast), Modified American Plan (MAP, with breakfast and dinner), or are all-inclusive (AI, covers all meals and most activities). We list facilities but not if there's a charge for them.

Many Listings
★ Fodor's Choice
★ Highly recommended
⊠ Physical address
✛ Directions
🕮 Mailing address
🕾 Telephone
🖷 Fax
⊕ On the Web
✍ E-mail
🖃 Admission fee
☉ Open/closed times
🖶 Credit cards

Hotels & Restaurants
🏨 Hotel
🛏 Number of rooms
ᾧ Facilities
🍽 Meal plans
✕ Restaurant
ᾨ Reservations
✕🏨 Hotel with restaurant that warrants a visit

Outdoors
⅄ Golf
⚠ Camping/No Rooms

Other
☾ Family-friendly
⇨ See also
⊠ Branch address

Essentials

Please see the Essentials section in the back of the book for travel essentials for the entire Maine Coast; city- and area-specific basics end each chapter.

WHAT'S WHERE

THE SOUTHERN COAST 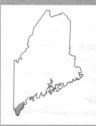	The Southern Coast is Maine's most visited region. Despite the cold North Atlantic waters, beachgoers enjoy the area's miles of sandy expanses, which invite long walks and provide sweeping views of lighthouses, forested islands, and the wide open sea. The towns along the shore cater to summer visitors with shops. Kittery, the Yorks, and the Kennebunks have much to offer of historical interest, while the boisterous towns of Old Orchard Beach and York Beach feature Coney Island–like amusements, cotton candy, blinking neon, and carnival rides.
GREATER PORTLAND 	Maine's largest and most cosmopolitan city, Portland deftly balances its historic role as a working—and still-thriving—harbor with its new identity as a center of sophisticated arts and shopping, innovative restaurants, and stylish accommodations. The city has an active and varied cultural scene, with strong local music, numerous theater groups, plenty of impressive art galleries and venues, and a grand art museum. In the warmer months the city comes alive with outdoor concerts, performances, blooming garden parks, and a twice-weekly farmers' market.
THE MID-COAST REGION 	North of Portland, from Brunswick to Monhegan Island, the state's geography begins to defy traditional compass-point parameters. The craggy coastline swirls and winds its way around pastoral peninsulas. Dozens of lighthouses stand watch atop rock-strewn bluffs. And calm waters welcome pleasure boats, sailing sloops, and solitary kayakers. Historically, the area prospered in maritime trade; today it's known for rest, relaxation, and exploration. Its villages boast maritime museums, antiques shops, and beautiful architecture, and a wealth of antiques shops.
PENOBSCOT BAY 	The Penobscot Bay region combines lively coastal towns with dramatic natural scenery. Camden is one of Maine's most picture-perfect towns. With nearby Rockland, the two towns make up the general headquarters of the famed historic windjammer fleet. These dramatic wooden schooners are a common sight in the bay; cruises of various lengths are available. For another remarkable view, head to the top of Camden's Mt. Battie to gaze at the surrounding hills that tumble down into the sea. Farther up the coast, Belfast stands out with its beautiful waterfront, and Searsport is known as the "Antique and Flea Market Capital of Maine."

THE BLUE HILL PENINSULA 	Life on the Blue Hill Peninsula is decidedly more peaceful than in the coastal areas to the south, driven not by tourist attractions and activities but by its sheer natural beauty. At home here is the inquisitive explorer who seeks entertainment and enchantment in the outdoors. Artists and art lovers have long been attracted to the area for that very reason, and galleries are far more plentiful than shops selling lobster T-shirts and lighthouse curios. The entire region is ideal for biking, hiking, kayaking, and boating. For many, the Blue Hill Peninsula defines the silent beauty of the Maine Coast.
ACADIA NATL. PARK & MT. DESERT ISLAND 	Mount Desert Island is home to Acadia National Park—Maine's most heavily visited attraction. Travelers come by the millions to climb (mostly by car) the miles of 19th-century carriage roads leading to the stunning peaks and vistas of the island's mountains. Each curve of the road reveals breathtaking scenes of cliff and rock set amid the surrounding bays. Hikers and cyclists enjoy a less-crowded experience on off-road jaunts and trails. In the northeast quadrant is Bar Harbor, filled with tourists and all the accompanying attractions; the smaller towns of Southwest Harbor and Bass Harbor reveal quieter characters. Wherever you go, ever present is the peak of Cadillac Mountain, heralded as the first place in the nation to see the sun rise. ·
WAY DOWN EAST 	Many people believe that the *real Maine* exists only above Mount Desert, up past the heavily trod tourist draws of the south. Way Down East unfurls in thousands of acres of wild blueberry barrens, congestion-free coastlines, and a tangible sense of rugged endurance not found elsewhere. Outdoor enthusiasts can amble or paddle through pristine expanses of numerous wildlife refuges, state parks, and preservation lands. The impact of nature's hand is felt strongly, and it is the vulnerability of the land here to the winds, the winters, and the immense tides that makes the area so strikingly beautiful.

QUINTESSENTIAL
MAINE COAST

Lighthouses

Maine's long and jagged coastline is home to more than 60 lighthouses, perched high on rocky ledges or on the tips of wayward islands. Though modern technology in navigation has made many of the lights obsolete, lighthouse enthusiasts and preservation groups restore and maintain many of them, and often make them accessible to the public. Some of the state's more famous lights include Portland Head Light, commissioned by President George Washington in 1790 and immortalized in one of Edward Hopper's paintings; Two Lights, a few miles down the coast in Cape Elizabeth; and West Quoddy Head, on the United States' most eastern tip of land. Some lighthouses are privately owned and others accessible only by boat, but plenty are within easy reach and are open to the public, some with museums and tours.

Fishermen

Fishermen are to Maine as farmers are to the Midwest. Commercial fishing is a big part of the state's economy, and much of it is driven by hardy individuals or small family outfits who often go to work in the wee hours of the morning. It's a tough gig—working conditions vary with the weather; boats, traps, and nets require a lot of care; regulations must be met; and the catch can be feast or famine. Yet the rugged men and women who ply the coast live their heritage with pride and determination. The lobster boat is beautiful in its simplicity, a classic study in form following function, and it's the working waterfront of coastal towns and villages that makes a visit to the Maine Coast worthwhile.

Counting all its nooks, crannies, and crags, the Maine Coast would stretch for thousands of miles if you could pull it straight. All that space hides great heritage, food, and ideal places for relaxation.

Shellfish

Maine will forever be famous for its delectable lobsters, but it would be a shame to visit the state without trying one of its other, equally delicious shellfish. Maine shrimp are smaller than the more familiar cocktail variety, yet sweeter and perfect in a salad. A variety of clams, including the perennial favorite littleneck, is readily available in waterfront markets such as Portland's Harbor Fish Market. Steam them in large pots until they open, then dip in drawn butter. A cousin to the clam, mussels are sweet enough to eat without butter. Scallops here are especially tender. Try them fried and dipped in tartar sauce, or sautéed as an appetizer. Crabmeat is best eaten in a toasted hot dog roll with a minimum of mayonnaise and a leaf of green lettuce.

The Idyllic Shore

A large sign greets drivers coming into the state as they cross over from New Hampshire: MAINE: THE WAY LIFE SHOULD BE. Indeed. Though the suburbs are growing, life for the most part along the coast is far removed from the chaotic crowd scene of large urban areas. This simple-life vibe is especially apparent along the water's edge. Imagine standing on the shore, waves washing the sand rhythmically, as seagulls float and cry above. From offshore come the clang of bell buoys, keeping time with the waves, as a lone lobstermen pulls his traps one by one into his chugging boat. The breeze carries the scent of salt mixed with a hint of diesel-boat fuel and brine-soaked wharf wood. With a little luck, there's a weathered Adirondack chair nearby to plunk down into for the remainder of the day, and a B&B behind it for the night's stay. What more could one ask for?

IF YOU LIKE

Art

Inspired by the state's quiet graces, artists for generations have been migrating to the Maine Coast. This has made art a cottage industry of sorts here. Painters such as Winslow Homer, Edward Hopper, and the Wyeths have put Maine scenes on their most famous canvases, while the functional beauty of the state's potters is among the best anywhere.

Portland has some fine repositories for art. In the **Portland Museum of Art** hang two of Homer's best-known coastal Maine paintings. The museum also owns or displays more than 20 works from the artist, as well as pieces by Monet, Picasso, and Renoir. Unique in New England is the **Museum of African Culture,** also in Portland, devoted exclusively to sub-Saharan African tribal arts. Its collection includes wooden masks and bronze figures. Farther up the coast, the owner of **Gypsy Moose Glass Co.** gives glassblowing demonstrations in Gouldsboro.

Visitors who come to Maine to create their own art have plenty to paint or photograph. **Monhegan** and **Vinalhaven** islands are well-known destinations for painters attracted to the power that exists where land meets sea. Photographers flock to the region during foliage season in the fall; at other times of the year they focus their lenses on classic New England architecture, colorful lobster buoys, and the mighty windjammers.

Beachcombing

There is nothing at all fancy about beachcombing. All you need is a pair of comfortable shoes, a relaxed gait, and an appreciation for the simple things in life—a trio of which most any visitor to the Maine Coast has in abundance. One thing to note is that some beaches have restrictions on whether you can take away shells and other flotsam and jetsam. Keep an eye out for posted rules, or ask a local what you can or cannot take home with you.

Plenty of secluded coves and rocky beaches on Maine's famously rugged coastline await exploration. The best time to wander is after the tide has gone out, when the retreating water has left behind its treasures. Early spring is an especially good time to see sand dollars washed upon beaches. **Popham Beach** or the sandy expanse at nearby **Reid State Park** are two especially good choices. Farther south, don't miss **Old Orchard Beach.**

The best part of beachcombing is that you never quite know what to expect to find at your feet. Sea glass—nothing more than man-made glass worn smooth from its seaward journeys—is a common find. You'll also find leftovers from dining seagulls, who drop sea urchins and other shellfish from up high to crack open, then swoop down before another gull has a chance to steal dinner.

Bicycling

Long-distance cyclists have long favored Maine's byways for their terrain, stunning vistas, and ease of navigation. Biking in Maine is especially scenic in and around Kennebunkport, Camden, Deer Isle, the Penobscot Bay area, and the Schoodic Peninsula. But most any town offers easy access to windy, hilly, and often tree-lined roads that meander through towns and villages that you might otherwise pass by. It's a great way to see small working farms and classic New England architecture.

The carriage paths in **Acadia National Park** are especially ideal for cycling, with many

miles of off-road trails providing finer and more intimate views than the roads open to traffic. For a cardio workout, ride the road to the top of **Cadillac Mountain** and then gaze out in every direction to the surrounding coast, islands, and bays. For more-adventurous riders, many ski resorts, such as **Camden Snow Bowl** (⇨ Chapter 4), allow mountain bikes during the summer months.

If your stay in Maine includes Portland, put your wheels to the paved **Eastern Prom Trail** (⇨ Chapter 2). It extends from the edge of the Old Port to East End Beach, then to Back Bay for a 6-mi loop, before returning.

U.S. 1, the major road that travels along the Maine Coast, is only a narrow two-lane highway for most of its route, but it is still one of America's most historic highways, a sort of Appalachian Trail on a highway. As a result, this road is very popular in spring, summer, and fall with serious long-distance bike riders. Bicyclists should ride carefully and look out for motorists who may be looking out for a glimpse of the sea.

The Maine government publishes many maps and routes for cyclists; printable versions of these maps, as well as general cycling information, are available on the Web at ⊕ www.exploremaine.org/bike.

Sailing

Maine's maritime history is rich, going back nearly 400 years, and a good portion of the early colony's wealth came from its prowess in shipbuilding. Before the advent of steam engines, tall, graceful, and speedy wooden schooners called windjammers were built to transfer goods for trade throughout the seas of the world markets. These ships were strong yet lightweight, and relied on the power of the winds and the sharp eye of the sailors who guided them.

Though modern technology put an end to the building of these beauties for commerce, the advent of recreational boating gave windjammers an entirely new purpose. The **Penobscot Bay** region is famous for its mighty fleet of windjammers—a good portion of them original, aged, and retired from their 19th-century workloads. The drama of their majestic sails unfurled in the wind is a common sight in the harbors of the area. Their hulls have been redesigned to house passengers for overnight trips; the cruising season starts in mid-May and continues into fall foliage season.

Each year in late June, **Windjammer Days,** a weeklong festival in Boothbay, brings dozens of members of the fleet to gather for a floating parade in the harbor. A cruise on one of these elegant vessels is an ideal way to truly appreciate the beauty of the Maine Coast. Some day trips are also available; check with the **Maine Windjammer Association** (☎ 800/807–9463; ⊕ www.sailmainecoast.com) for details.

Shopping

The Maine Coast has a surprisingly vibrant shopping scene, running the gamut from lobster T-shirt tourist traps to fine-art galleries, from local pottery studios to high-end and world-famous furniture makers. Many small-town main streets have been rejuvenated thanks to storefronts that cater to tourists. Be advised that the best shopping areas tend to concentrate in the corridor from Kittery to Bar Harbor.

The world headquarters of **L.L. Bean** put the town of Freeport on the shop-

IF YOU LIKE

ping map, and it's now shopping central for the state. The L. L. Bean store has expanded greatly over the years, taking over separate buildings that once housed other shops. There are plenty of stores to check out, many of them factory outlets such as **Cuddledown of Maine** and **Polo Ralph Lauren.** For fine-furniture aficionados, there's world-renowned **Thos. Moser Cabinetmakers.**

The **Old Port,** the heart of downtown Portland, is filled with specialty shops and assorted galleries in the area of Exchange Street, while more touristy stores proliferate along the waterfront's Commercial Street. Independent bookstore lovers will revel in the stacks of **Longfellow Books,** and **Abacus** has long been known for its one-of-a-kind artisan jewelry. Try delicious Maine-made mustards, jams, jellies, sauces, and other foodstuffs at **Stonewall Kitchen.**

Whale-Watching

Few things speak of the great deep blue unknown like a whale, and any sighting of these magnificent creatures is dramatic and not soon forgotten. Fortunately, the cold waters off the Maine Coast are the perfect summer feeding ground for a variety of whales, including finbacks, humpbacks, minkes, and even the occasional rare blue whale and the endangered right whale.

The whale-watching season varies by tour skipper, but generally is contained between the months of April and October. No matter which part of the coast you visit—even far east (called "Down East"), near New Brunswick, Canada—there is a tour available from a not-too-distant port. Tour lengths vary typically from two to five hours, as boats chug within 20

miles of the coast. Whale-watching vessels have plenty of open deck space for photo ops, plus covered areas for inclement weather or those with underdeveloped sea legs. Most also offer basic meal items and bottled drinks.

A whale sighting is not always a sure bet, though some skippers boast good track records, but there are other things likely to be seen, including seals, dolphins, and various oceangoing birds. No matter; the experience of being on the sea in such a way is a good way to spend a few hours during your coastal tour.

A few companies to sign on with for spotting these mighty creatures are **Cap'n Fish's Boat Trips** in Boothbay Harbor, which has both whale- and puffin-watching adventures; **Bar Harbor Whale Watching Co.,** with its three-hour excursions via catamaran; **Old Port Mariner Fleet,** based in Portland and also offering fishing trips; and **Island Cruises,** which departs from Head Harbour Wharf in Wilson's Beach and allows passengers to spot whales while aboard a lobster boat.

GREAT ITINERARIES

HIGHLIGHTS OF THE MAINE COAST

Much of the appeal of the Maine Coast lies in its geographical contrasts, from its long stretches of swimming and walking beaches in the south to the cliff-edged, rugged rocky coasts in the north. And not unlike the physical differences of the coast, each town along the way reveals a slightly different character. This sampler tour will provide you with a good taste of what the Maine Coast offers; allow the individual chapters to invite you along other trails on the way.

Day 1: The Yorks

Start your trip in York Village with a leisurely stroll through the seven buildings of the Old York Historical Society, getting a glimpse of 18th-century life in this gentrified town. Spend time wandering amid the shops or walking the nature trails and beaches around York Harbor. There are several grand lodging options here, most with views of the harbor. If you prefer a livelier pace, continue on to York Beach, a haven for families with plenty of entertainment venues. Stop at Nubble Light for a seaside lunch or dinner. *See Chapter 1.*

Days 2 & 3: Ogunquit

For well over a century, Ogunquit has been a favorite vacation spot for those looking to combine the natural beauty of the ocean with a sophisticated environment. Take a morning walk along the Marginal Way to see the waves crashing on the rocks. In Perkins Cove, have lunch, stroll the shopping areas, or sign on with a lobster boat cruise to learn about Maine's most important fishery— the state's lobster industry supplies more than 90% of the world's lobster intake. See the extraordinary collection at the

Ogunquit Museum of American Art, take in a performance at one of the several theater venues, or just spend time on the beach. *See Chapter 1.*

Day 4: The Kennebunks

Head north to the Kennebunks, allowing at least two hours to wander through the shops and historic homes of Dock Square in Kennebunkport. This is an ideal place to rent a bike and amble around the backstreets, head out on Ocean Avenue to view the Bush estate, or ride to one of the several beaches to relax awhile. *See Chapter 1.*

Days 5 & 6: Portland

You can easily spend several days in Maine's largest city, exploring its historic neighborhoods, shopping and eating in the Old Port, or visiting one of several excellent museums. A brief side trip to Cape Elizabeth takes you to Portland Head Light, Maine's first lighthouse, which was commissioned by George Washington in 1790. The lighthouse is on the grounds of Fort Williams Park and is an excellent place to bring a picnic. Be sure to spend some time wandering the ample grounds. There are also excellent walking trails (and views) at nearby Two Lights State Park. If you want to take a boat tour while in Portland, get a ticket for Casco Bay Lines and see some of the islands that dot the bay. *See Chapter 2.*

Day 7: Bath to Camden

Head north from Portland to Bath, Maine's shipbuilding capital, and tour the Maine Maritime Museum or have lunch on the waterfront. Shop at boutiques and antiques shops, or view the plentitude of beautiful homes. Continue on U.S. 1 north, through the towns of Wiscasset and Damariscotta, where you may find

NEW HAMPSHIRE

Searsport

Mt. Desert Island

Bar Harbor

Camden

Penobscot Bay

Blue Hill Bay

ACADIA NAT'L PARK

Wiscasset

Damariscotta

Bath

Muscongus Bay

Portland

Casco Bay

Kennebunk

Kennebunkport

Ogunquit

The Yorks

ATLANTIC OCEAN

yourself pulling over frequently for outdoor flea markets or intriguing antiques shops. *See Chapter 3.*

Days 8 & 9: Camden

Camden is the picture-perfect image of a seaside tourist town: hundreds of boats bobbing in the harbor, immaculately kept antique homes, streets lined with boutiques and specialty stores, and restaurants serving lobster at every turn. The modest (by Maine standards, anyway) hills of nearby Mt. Battie offer good hiking and a great spot from which to picnic and view the surrounding area. Camden is one of the hubs for the beloved and historic windjammer fleet—there is no better way to see the area than from the deck of one of these graceful beauties. If you're an art lover, save some time for Rockland's Farnsworth Art Museum and the Wyeth Center. *See Chapter 4.*

Days 10 & 11: Mount Desert Island/ Acadia National Park

From Camden, continue north along U.S. 1, letting your interests dictate where you stop (or head south to explore the Blue Hill Peninsula, *see Chapter 5*). Once you arrive on Mount Desert Island, you can choose to stay in Bar Harbor, the busiest village in the area, or in the quieter Southwest Harbor area; either way, the splendor of the mountains and the sea surround you. Several days are easily spent exploring Acadia National Park, boating or kayaking in the surrounding waters, and simply enjoying the stunning panorama. *See Chapter 6.*

GREAT ITINERARIES

MAINE MARITIME HISTORY TOUR

Maine's maritime leanings extend well back into the early 17th century, and while many things have changed, the sea—via lobstering, fishing, and tourism—is still the backbone of the state's economy and culture. This tour gives the traveler a glimpse of how the sea has influenced the people, towns, and industries along the coast of Maine to create the delightful and diverse region it is today. ■ TIP➔ You can squeeze the Bath-to-Rockland portion into one day, and Searsport into one day as well if you want to do the trip in just six days.

Days 1 & 2: Portland

A thriving, working harbor since the 17th century, Portland has maritime history written all over it. Take a step back in time at the Fish Exchange, where the day's catch is unloaded and auctioned off to worldwide markets just as it was centuries ago. For a more refined maritime experience, head to the Portland Museum of Art to see the impressive collection of sea-inspired art by such greats as Edward Hopper and Winslow Homer. Lighthouses still play an integral role in keeping Maine's coast safe and navigable. Visit Fort Williams Park and Two Lights State Park, in Cape Elizabeth, to see the area's most famous lighthouses. For a more intimate view of the sea, try a boat cruise from Portland to the nearby islands in Casco Bay. *See Chapter 2.*

Days 3 & 4: Bath to Rockland

From Portland, head north to Bath, Maine's present shipbuilding capital. The Bath Iron Works, which once built tall-masted wooden schooners, now builds destroyers for the U.S. Navy. Spend some time at the Maine Maritime Museum and Shipyard to get a sense of the area's previous prowess in the shipping industry. Wander the streets of Bath to see the grand mansions of 19th-century sea captains (many of which are now elegant B&Bs).

Head north on U.S. 1 to Wiscasset, a village that gained great wealth in the shipbuilding industry as evidenced by its stunning array of grand sea captains' and merchants' homes. Tour the Nickels-Sortwell house (1807) to get a glimpse of the wealth these seafaring businessmen enjoyed. Continue on to Damariscotta, another town that found success in shipbuilding. From here, take a detour down Route 130 to the Pemaquid Peninsula. At the end of Route 130, Pemaquid Point Lighthouse has stood watch since 1827. Adjacent to the light is the Fishermen's Museum, which has a fascinating display illustrating Maine's 400-year-old fishing industry. *See Chapters 3 and 4.*

Days 5 & 6: Rockland/Camden

Make your way north from Damariscotta to Rockland, where you can tour the Farnsworth Art Museum and Wyeth Center, an excellent place to see maritime-inspired artworks. The fascinating Maine Lighthouse Museum, also in Rockland, displays many lighthouse and Coast Guard artifacts as well as other maritime memorabilia. You can—and should—take a one-day or overnight cruise on a historic windjammer from either Rockland or nearby Camden. Time spent aboard one of these graceful schooners is the ideal way to see the coast. *See Chapter 4.*

Days 7 & 8: Searsport

Farther up U.S. 1 is the town of Searsport, Maine's second-largest deepwater

Searsport

1

Blue Hill Bay

Camden

Penobscot Bay

1

Rockland

Wiscasset

Damariscotta

Bath

Muscongus Bay

1

Pemaquid Point Lighthouse

NEW HAMPSHIRE

Portland

Fishermen's Museum

ATLANTIC OCEAN

port and a haven for both maritime history buffs and antiques treasure hunters. The relationship between the two is not accidental—world-traveling 19th-century sea captains, a good many of whom made their homes here, constantly brought back goods and gifts from Europe to fill their houses. You never know what kind of gem you can find in one of the multitude of antiques shops and outdoor flea markets. A treasure of another sort exists here as well: the Penobscot Marine Museum is a multibuilding complex brimming with fascinating sea history. Several hours can be easily spent here. *See Chapter 4.* ■TIP→Weekend traffic heading to the Maine Coast along its feeder roads, I–95 and U.S. 1, can be brutally frustrating, especially at the tollbooths. If you travel midweek instead (or outside of peak season), you won't find yourself nearly as stymied.

WHEN TO GO

Despite long winters, Maine's dramatic coastline and pure natural beauty welcome visitors of all tastes year-round. Be aware that black-fly season, from mid-May to mid-June, can rile even the most seasoned outdoorsfolk. Also note that many smaller museums and attractions are open only for high season—from Memorial Day to mid-October—as are many of the waterside attractions and eateries.

Memorial Day is the start of the migration to the beaches and the mountains, and summer begins in earnest on July 4. This is the high season for the Maine Coast, when many smaller inns and hotels from Kittery on up to the Bar Harbor region fill up early on the weekends. Larger hotels will have more vacancies, but it's still a good idea to book in advance in some of the more popular locales.

Fall, with its fiery foliage, is when many inns and hotels are booked months in advance by leaf-peeping visitors. As green disappears from the leaves of deciduous species, a rainbow of reds, oranges, yellows, purples, and other vivid hues appears. The first colors emerge in mid-September in northern areas; "peak" color occurs at different times from year to year. Generally, it's best to **visit the northern reaches in late September and early October** and move southward as October progresses.

All leaves are fallen by Halloween, and hotel rates drop significantly until ski season begins around Thanksgiving. Late October until late November is the hunting season for deer (using firearms) in most areas; those who venture into the woods should wear bright orange clothing.

Winter (November–April) is the time for downhill and cross-country skiing. Maine has several major ski resorts. Along the coast, bed-and-breakfasts that remain open will often rent rooms at far lower prices than in summer.

The third Sunday in March is Maine Maple Sunday. Farms throughout the state open their doors to visitors to watch sap turn into golden syrup and sample the sweet results.

Climate

In winter, coastal Maine is cold and damp; inland temperatures may be lower, but generally drier conditions make them easier to bear. Snowfall is heaviest in the interior mountains, up to several hundred inches per year in northern Maine. Spring is often windy and rainy. Coastal areas can be uncomfortably humid in summer, though nights are usually cool. Autumn temperatures can be quite mild in southerly areas well into October.

Forecasts Weather Channel Connection (☎900/932–8437 95¢ per minute from a Touch-Tone phone ⊕www.weather.com).

The following are the average daily maximum and minimum temperatures for Portland.

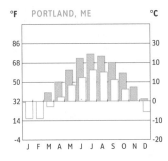

ON THE CALENDAR

WINTER	
January	Warm up with chili, hot cocoa, and toasted marshmallows next to a bonfire at **WinterFest** (January 26–27) in Stonington, then chill out while ice-skating.
March	Held the third Sunday of the month, **Maine Maple Sunday** is when syrup producers throughout the state open their doors to share the spring rite of syrup making with the public.
May	Birders flock to Whiting every spring migration for the **Down East Spring Birding Festival** (May 25–28).
June	Stately old tall ships parade the bay during **Windjammer Days** (June 24–28) in Boothbay Harbor. Climb aboard one of these fine sailing vessels during the grand sail parade.
SUMMER	
July	Guests can participate in the **Great Schooner Race** (July 1–6) in Penobscot, when more than two dozen tall ships and their skippers compete against one another. Celebrate an important part of coastal Maine's heritage at the **Native American Festival and Maine Indian Basketmakers Market** in Bar Harbor on July 7. Watch members of the Wabanaki tribe demonstrate their work and sell their fine handmade baskets. Blues bands from around the country converge in Rockland for the **North Atlantic Blues Festival** (July 14–15). One of the most beautiful of all wooden sailing boats is celebrated during **Friendship Sloop Days** in Rockland (July 19–21), during which you can watch sloop and rowboat races. Enjoy clams fried, steamed, and in clam cakes at the immensely popular **Yarmouth Clam Festival** (July 20–22).
August	Ten tons of Maine's most famous crustacean are prepared and consumed at the **Maine Lobster Festival** in Rockland from August 1–5, where the Maine Sea Goddess, a prom queen of sorts, receives her coronation. Held Way Down East in Machias, the **Wild Blueberry Festival** (August 17–19) has pie-eating and baking contests, music, and food courts.
FALL	
September	Catch Maine's windjammer fleet at the **Wooden Boat Sail-in with Maine Windjammers** (September 9–15) in Brooklin, when the harbor fills with these wonderful old schooners.
November	The **Maine Literary Festival,** in Camden the first weekend of November, celebrates authors who write about Maine.
December	Santa arrives by boat during **Christmas by the Sea,** in Camden, Rockport, and Lincolnville the first weekend of December.

The Southern Coast

WORD OF MOUTH

"Ogunquit is blessed with a wide, clean, white-sand beach that goes on for miles. The water is pretty cool, but some don't seem to mind. There are often tidal pools along the beach that are a bit more tolerable temperature wise."

—Zootsi

By Laura V.
Scheel

MAINE'S SOUTHERNMOST COASTAL TOWNS—Kittery, the Yorks, Ogunquit, the Kennebunks, and the Old Orchard Beach area—reveal a few of the stunning faces of the state's coast, from the miles and miles of inviting sandy beaches to the beautifully kept historic towns and carnival-like attractions. There is something for every taste, whether you seek solitude in a kayak or prefer being caught up in the infectious spirit of fellow vacationers. The Southern Coast is best explored on a leisurely holiday of two days—more if you require a fix of solid beach time.

North of Kittery, long stretches of hard-packed white-sand beach are closely crowded by nearly unbroken ranks of beach cottages, motels, and oceanfront restaurants. The summer colonies of York Beach and Wells brim with crowds and ticky-tacky shorefront overdevelopment, but nearby, quiet wildlife refuges and land reserves promise an easy escape. York evokes yesteryear sentiment with its acclaimed historic district, while upscale Ogunquit tantalizes stylish and sporty visitors with its array of shops and a cliff-side walk.

More than any other region south of Portland, the Kennebunks—and especially Kennebunkport—provide the complete Maine Coast experience: classic townscapes where white clapboard houses rise from manicured lawns and gardens; rocky shorelines punctuated by sandy beaches; quaint downtown districts packed with gift shops, ice-cream stands, and visitors; harbors with lobster boats bobbing alongside yachts; rustic, picnic-tabled restaurants specializing in lobster and fried seafood (aka lobster pounds in Maine lingo); and well-appointed dining rooms. As you continue north, the scents of french fries, pizza, and cotton candy hover in the air above Maine's version of Coney Island, Old Orchard Beach.

EXPLORING THE SOUTHERN COAST

Although the Southern Coast makes up just a mere portion of Maine's many thousands of miles of shoreline, it offers an incredible variation of sights to discover. The best way to explore the region is by car—taking the time to sidetrack on inviting byways. Summer traffic may be demanding and an inconvenience, but the beauty and diversity of Maine is worth a little patience. (Note that Amtrak, coming from Boston, does make a seasonal stop at Old Orchard Beach, but service is infrequent.)

This chapter begins just across from the New Hampshire border in Kittery, the "Gateway to Maine," and heads in a general northward direction. Many of the sites and towns are off the main thoroughfares of U.S. 1 and I–95; you can decide how quickly you want to pass from one town to the next. From Kittery, a brief northwestward trip will bring you to pastoral South Berwick, then back to the coastal towns of the Yorks, Ogunquit, and Wells. The town of Kennebunk is slightly inland, while its sister town of Kennebunkport is right on the water. Old Orchard Beach is a quintessential frolicking beach town.

GREAT ITINERARIES

IF YOU HAVE 3 DAYS

A three-day trip to the Southern Coast can give you a good taste of the different flavors of the region. Start your trip in **South Berwick.** Here you can tour the historic home of author Sarah Orne Jewett and the grand Hamilton House. From South Berwick, follow Route 236 east to Route 91, back to U.S. 1 in York. Take Route 1A and explore the historic sites of **York Village.** Continue the few miles to **York Harbor,** a good place to spend the night. On your second day, follow the Shore Road (Route 1A) and stop in lively **York Beach,** where you can swim, bowl, or play arcade games until after dark. Continue north on Route 1A and spend the night and the next day in **Ogunquit.** Here you can walk the Marginal Way, and spend several hours perusing the shops of both Perkins Cove and the village of Ogunquit. If you're visiting in summer, save some time to relax at Ogunquit Beach.

IF YOU HAVE 5 DAYS

Start your first day in **Kittery,** an area rich in history and natural beauty, as well as a shopper's mecca. If the weather cooperates, bring a picnic, a kayak, or your walking shoes for a full day of enjoying the vistas and trails of Ft. Foster. From here, follow the three-day itinerary above. On Day 5, leave Ogunquit, and continue on U.S. 1 into **Wells,** a town known for its 7-mi stretch of pristine beaches. There are several opportunities for bird- and nature-watchers at Beach Plum Farm as well as the Wells Reserve and the Rachel Carson National Wildlife Refuge. Follow scenic Route 9 to the Kennebunks, a good place to spend the night. If you have more time, visit historic homes and museums, as well as the shops in **Kennebunkport's** busy Dock Square, or, if you like the sights and sounds of a carnival-on-the-beach atmosphere, take coastal Route 9 north from the Kennebunks to **Old Orchard Beach.**

WHEN TO GO

As with most of the Maine Coast, the Southern Coast is highly popular in summer. Crowds converge and gobble up rooms and dinner reservations at prime restaurants. Even so, July, August, and September are the best months to vacation in Maine. The weather is warm, and every town has its share of summer festivals, outdoor concerts, and gatherings. In July and August, most roads are extremely busy (don't expect speedy jaunts down U.S. 1), campgrounds are filled to capacity, and hotel rates are high. Midweek tends to be a little quieter than weekends.

The brilliance of fall foliage brings another round of visitors to the state; often the off-season rates revert back to their summer heights, but even then, it's not quite as crowded as summer. The prime time for leaf peeping here is usually the first week of October (check the state's weekly updated site: *www.mainefoliage.com*).

Many accommodations and restaurants stay open throughout the year, though they do have limited hours come winter. In the off-season, rates are lower, and you won't be waiting in line anywhere.

ABOUT THE RESTAURANTS

Maine produces well over 90% of the world's lobsters, so it's no surprise that a good portion of its restaurants feature the state's mascot on their menus. Creative chefs have gone well beyond the traditional steamed variety with seemingly endless ways to prepare the dish. Fortunately, the area's restaurants, while almost always giving a nod to the famous crustacean, do not limit themselves to it. Many places specialize in local seafood, and given that Maine has more than 5,000 miles of shoreline, there is plenty of it to choose from. Restaurants range from the casually eclectic to the formal prix fixe—and everything in between. You won't find many international restaurants (except Asian), but most menus make explorations into the flavors of other cultures.

ABOUT THE HOTELS

The variation in lodgings along the Maine Coast has a lot to do with individual zoning laws. Towns like the Kennebunks, York Harbor, and Ogunquit have a much higher number of small inns and bed-and-breakfasts, while York Beach, Old Orchard Beach, Wells, and Kittery seem to be filled with one hotel-motel complex after another. U.S. 1 is famous (or infamous, depending on how you look at it) for its rampant commercialism, and its lodging options usually show it. A stay in one of the restored mansions will cost you quite a bit more than a night at a sprawling hotel, but almost all lodging establishments offer off-season price reductions and special package rates. Minimum-stay requirements are common for weekends and July through Labor Day. Expect to pay the most in Kennebunkport, Ogunquit, and the Yorks.

WHAT IT COSTS					
	¢	$	$$	$$$	$$$$
RESTAURANTS	under $7	$7–$10	$11–$17	$18–$25	over $25
HOTELS	under $60	$60–$99	$100–$149	$150–$200	over $200

Restaurant prices are for a main course at dinner, excluding sales tax of 7%. Hotel prices are for two people in a standard double room in high season, excluding service charges and 7% tax.

SOUTHERN & INLAND YORK COUNTY

KITTERY

55 mi north of Boston; 5 mi north of Portsmouth, New Hampshire.

One of the earliest settlements in the state of Maine, Kittery suffered its share of British, French, and American Indian attacks throughout the 17th and 18th centuries, yet rose to prominence as a vital shipbuilding center. The tradition continues; despite its New Hampshire name, the Portsmouth Naval Shipyard is part of Maine and has been one of the leading researchers and builders of U.S. submarines since its inception in 1800. The shipyard has the distinction of being the oldest naval

IF YOU LIKE

ANTIQUES

The north–south corridor of U.S. 1 may be irritatingly slow moving for some in the summertime, but if you're more interested in moseying and poking in and out of antiques shops, then the traffic won't bother you a bit. The stretch of U.S. 1 from just north of Kittery all the way to Scarborough, just south of Portland, is so packed with antiques shops that it would take days for scrutinizing shoppers to make the trip. There are antiques "malls," abrim with the offerings of many dealers; towering and often tipping aged barns filled with all manner of items, right up into the haylofts; individual shops with particular specialties; and several outdoor flea markets that fill parking lots in summer. You can find everything from retired lobster traps (it is Maine, after all) and maritime antiques to European furniture, quilts, kitsch, and glass.

BEACHES

Few places can claim mile after mile of smooth sandy beaches, ideal for walking, sunbathing, or contemplating life's mysteries, the way the Southern Coast of Maine can. This is a haven for beachgoers, provided you don't mind cooler-than-average water temperatures (it's fine after you get in, really). Punctuated by harbors, the occasional rocky ledge, and the distant views of lighthouses and islands, the beaches of this region are grand and plentiful.

shipyard continuously operated by the U.S. government and is a major source of local employment. It's not open to the public, but those on boats can pass by and get a glimpse of its national significance.

Known as the "Gateway to Maine," Kittery has come to more recent light as a major shopping destination thanks to its complex of factory outlets. Flanked on either side of U.S. 1 are more than 120 stores, which attract hordes of shoppers year-round. For something a little less commercial, head east on Route 103 to the hidden Kittery most people miss: the lands around **Kittery Point.** Here you can find hiking and biking trails and, best of all, great views of the water. Pepperell Cove, the harbor at Kittery Point, is said to be the first commercial port in Maine to thrive in the salt cod trade. With Portsmouth, New Hampshire, across the water, Whaleback Ledge Lighthouse, and the nearby Isles of Shoals, the town of Kittery is a truly picturesque and idyllic place to pass some time. Also along this winding stretch of Route 103 are two forts, both open in summer.

WHAT TO SEE

Built in 1872, **Ft. Foster** was an active military installation until 1949. Now a town park, the 88-acre area is ideal for picnics (barbecue grills are all over) and explorations into the rocky crevices along the beach. There are also numerous walking trails, swimming areas, and special spots from which to windsurf and kayak. ⊠*Pocahontas Rd., Kittery Point* ☎*207/439–3800* ⊠*$10 per car.*

Built in 1690 to protect the mouth of the Piscataqua River, **Ft. McClary** is particularly notable for its 1812 hexagonal blockhouse (open for touring with admission to the park). The fort, which successfully countered pirates, American Indians, the French, and the British, sits on a scenic harbor and has ocean views. ⊠*Rte. 103, Kittery Point* ☎*207/439–2845* ⊕*www.state.me.us/doc/parks* ⊠*$2 (suggested donation)* ⊙*Memorial Day–Labor Day.*

For a glimpse into Kittery's three centuries (and continuing) of naval history, visit the **Kittery Historical and Naval Museum.** It has a curious exhibit of artifacts and photographs, and even a lighthouse lens on display. ⊠*U.S. 1 at Rogers Rd.* ☎*207/439–3080* ⊠*$3; $6 family* ⊙*June–Oct., Tues.–Sat. 10–4.*

One of the most elegant houses in America, the **Lady Pepperell House** was built in 1760, as it claims above the doorway, which is framed by two glorious two-story fluted pilasters. Set just past Ft. McClary, this was meant to be the grandest mansion in the Piscataqua Valley, as befits "a lady." The immensely rich widow of Sir William Pepperell—one of the J. Paul Gettys of his day—Lady Mary retained the honorary title bestowed on her husband's family owing to his great exploits during the French and Indian wars. Although private and not open regularly for tours, the house may be visited a few times during the year—make inquiries in town. ⊠*Rte. 103, Kittery Point.*

> ## SOUTHERN COAST TOP 5
>
> ■ Step back in time at the Hamilton House.
>
> ■ Dig into Maine's best doughnuts at Congdon's.
>
> ■ Stay at a luxurious Kennebunkport inn.
>
> ■ Head out on a lobster boat excursion to glimpse one of Maine's largest industries—and take home some of the catch!
>
> ■ Chomp into a famous frankfurter at Flo's Steamed Hot Dogs.

WHERE TO EAT

$$–$$$ ✕ **Warren's Lobster House.** A local institution, this waterfront restaurant specializes in seafood and has a huge salad bar. The pine-sided dining room leaves the impression that little has changed since Warren's opened in 1940. Dine outside overlooking the water when the weather is nice. ⊠*U.S. 1 and Water St.* ☎*207/439–1630* ⊟*AE, MC, V.*

$–$$$ ✕ **Cap'n Simeon's Galley.** The nautical-theme dining room may have one of the best views in the area. Look out to the pier, nearby lighthouses, islands, and historic forts while you sample any number of fresh seafood or steak options, from fried oysters and boiled lobster to fresh haddock and New York sirloin. It's a popular place for a hearty Sunday brunch, with everything from lobster quiche to specialty pancakes rounding out the menu. On Saturday nights there's live musical entertainment in the lounge. ⊠*90 Pepperell Rd. (Rte. 103)* ☎*207/439–3655* ⊟*D, MC, V* ⊙*Closed Tues. and Columbus Day–Memorial Day.*

$–$$$ ✕ **Chauncey Creek Lobster Pound.** From the road you can barely see this
★ restaurant's red roof hovering below the trees, but chances are you can see the cars parked at this popular spot amid the high banks of the tidal river. The menu has lots of fresh lobster items and a raw bar with locally harvested offerings like clams and oysters. Bring your own

beer or wine if you desire alcohol. In season, it's open daily for lunch and dinner. ⊠*Chauncey Creek Rd., Kittery Point* ☎*207/439–1030* ⊟*MC, V* ⊗*Closed Nov.–Apr.*

WHERE TO STAY

$$$–$$$$ 🏨**Portsmouth Harbor Inn & Spa.** Renovations have added a bit more
★ decadent luxury to this property, formerly the Inn at Portsmouth Harbor, but the antique beauty of the place remains the same. The brick Victorian was built in 1889 on the old Kittery town green. It overlooks the Piscataqua River and Portsmouth Harbor. An easy walk over the bridge takes you to nearby Portsmouth, New Hampshire. English antiques and Victorian watercolors decorate the inn, and most rooms have water views. Special spa packages are available. **Pros:** Easy walk to historic Portsmouth, most rooms have harbor and water views, spa treatments available on-site. **Cons:** Rooms are on the second and third floors, up steep stairs; antique home's rooms are not huge (though bright and uncluttered, with high ceilings). ⊠*6 Water St., 03904* ☎*207/439–4040* 🖷*207/438–9286* ⊕*www.innatportsmouth.com* ⤴*5 rooms* ⚒*In-room: VCR, Wi-Fi. In-hotel: spa, no kids under 16, no-smoking rooms, no elevator* ⊟*MC, V* ⊗*BP.*

$$–$$$$ 🏨**Enchanted Nights B&B.** This three-story Victorian is about as amply dressed as a painted lady can be; sitting rooms and guest rooms are chock-full of unusual antique furniture, draped in frilly fabrics and pillows, and adorned with floral wallpaper and bed coverings. Some rooms have painted skylike ceilings, complete with stars, clouds, and a sliver of moon to encourage the kind of respite conjured up by the inn's name. Those who want space to spread out will love the finest room of all: the Bella, in the adjacent carriage house. It has vaulted ceilings, a whirlpool tub for two, a fireplace, and lots of privacy. If you love a particular piece of furniture, ask about it: chances are it's for sale. **Pros:** Good base for exploring both Portsmouth, New Hampshire, and the southern Maine region; vegetarians and animal lovers (pets encouraged) feel at home. **Cons:** Two rooms share a bath, spaces feel a little tight with all the Victorian flourishes and furniture, rooms accessed via steep stairs. ⊠*29 Wentworth St. (Rte. 103), 03904* ☎*207/439–1489* ⊕*www.enchanted-nights.org* ⤴*8 rooms, 6 with bath; 1 apartment* ⚒*In-room: refrigerator (some), DVD (some), VCR (some). In-hotel: no-smoking rooms, some pets allowed, no elevator* ⊟*AE, D, MC, V* ⊗*BP.*

SPORTS & THE OUTDOORS

With all the water around—the Piscataqua River and the Atlantic Ocean meet here—it's no wonder that outdoor recreation in Kittery revolves around marine pursuits. For a lively historical boat tour narrated by the captain himself, take a trip with **Captain & Patty's Piscataqua River Tours** (⊠*Rte. 103, Kittery Point* ☎*207/439–8976*). The hour-plus-long trips leave the dock seven times daily; get tickets at the dock. For private off-shore fishing trips, scenic cruises, whale-watching, or scuba charters, sign up with **Seafari Charters** (⊠*7 Island Ave.* ☎*207/439–5068* ⊕*www.seafaricharters.com*). Head out on the Piscataqua River and the ocean to find striped bass and bluefish with **Tidewater Fishing Charters**

(⊠ *Pepperell Cove, Kittery Point* ☎ *207/439–1914*). Half- and full-day charters are available for up to three people.

SHOPPING

Kittery has more than 120 outlet stores. Along a several-mile stretch of U.S. 1 you can find just about anything, from hardware to underwear. Among the stores are Crate & Barrel, Eddie Bauer, Jones New York, Esprit, Waterford/Wedgwood, Lenox, Ralph Lauren, and J. Crew. Find store locations, discounts, and events within the **Kittery Outlets** (⊠ *U.S. 1* ☎ *207/439–4367 or 888/548–8379* ⊕ *www.thekitteryoutlets.com*) by contacting the outlet association; also, look for brochures in nearby restaurants or tourist centers. **Kittery Trading Post** (⊠ *U.S. 1* ☎ *207/587–6246 or 888/587–62463* ⊕ *www.kitterytradingpost.com*) rivals Freeport's L.L. Bean for camping, fishing, boating, and other types of outdoor accoutrements. In business since 1938, the company continues to grow and offers various outdoor seminars and instruction.

EN ROUTE If you're continuing on to the Berwicks, take Route 101 north from U.S. 1 and relax amid farmland on your way to South Berwick. If you want to stay along the coast, skip the Berwicks and head straight to the Yorks by taking beautiful Route 103 from Kittery Point, a drive of about 6 mi.

THE BERWICKS

14 mi northwest of Kittery via Rtes. 236 (or 101) and 91.

For a brief stay or just a passing detour westward from the coast in Kittery, the several towns that make up the Berwicks—North Berwick, South Berwick, and Berwick—reveal many of the pleasant pastoral byways that originally attracted its 17th-century settlers. Most of the activity is in the little town of South Berwick, a somewhat artsy little enclave amid the farmland and just next to the border of New Hampshire (it seems that many of its residents spend more time in nearby Portsmouth than elsewhere in Maine). The main street is a busy thoroughfare and popular travel route for interstate trucks, but its sidewalks are lined with practical shops set in stately brick buildings and its quaint layout bespeaks its New England setting. It's a great place to spend a morning or afternoon, sampling some of its good restaurant offerings and exploring the nearby historical homes and state park.

WHAT TO SEE

Fodor'sChoice
★
Set on a bluff overlooking the Salmon Falls river, a palatial Georgian Colonial known as the **Hamilton House** was part of author Sarah Orne Jewett's Revolutionary War novel, *The Tory Lover*. The mansion, with four immense chimneys, dormer windows, and a mansard roof, was built in 1785 by shipbuilder Jonathan Hamilton to receive noted guests (including John Paul Jones) in regal splendor. In 1898 Mrs. Emily Tyson and her stepdaughter purchased the home and, with the help of their friend Sarah Orne Jewett, resurrected and decorated the place in a combination of Colonial and Victorian styles. If touring the innards of old homes doesn't interest you, come here to explore the grounds; they're simply spectacular. Beautifully kept gardens look out over the

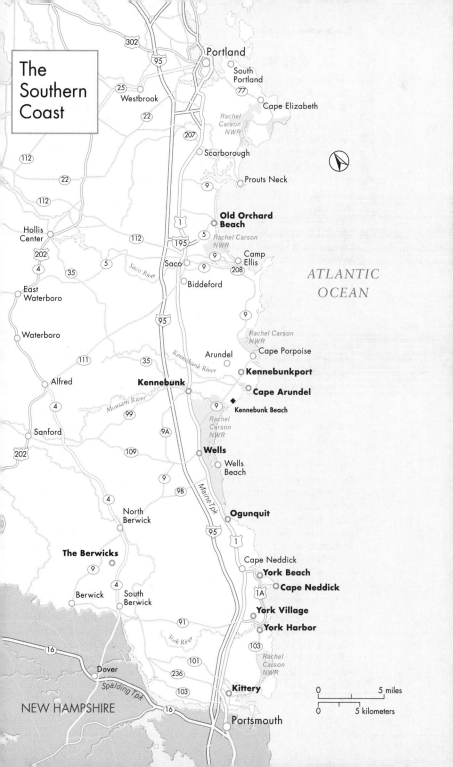

The
Southern
Coast

302

95

Portland

Westbrook

25

South
Portland

77

Cape Elizabeth

22

207

Rachel
Carson
NWR

Scarborough

112

9

Prouts Neck

22

112

**Old Orchard
Beach**

1

Hollis
Center

202

112

5

195

Rachel Carson
NWR

Camp
Ellis

4

35

5

Saco River

Saco

9

208

ATLANTIC
OCEAN

East
Waterboro

Biddeford

9

Waterboro

95

9

111

Rachel Carson
NWR

Cape Porpoise

35

Kennebunk River

Arundel

Kennebunkport

Alfred

Kennebunk

Cape Arundel

4

Mousam River

99

9

◆
Kennebunk Beach

Sanford

9A

Rachel
Carson
NWR

202

109

Wells

9

Wells
Beach

4

9B

Maine Tpk

North
Berwick

Ogunquit

95

1

The Berwicks

Cape Neddick

9

York Beach

Berwick

4

South
Berwick

1A

Cape Neddick

York Village

91

York Harbor

103

York River

Rachel
Carson
NWR

16

101

Dover

236

103

Spalding Tpk

Kittery

NEW HAMPSHIRE

16

Portsmouth

0   5 miles

0   5 kilometers

Maine's Beloved Sarah Orne Jewett

"Tact is, after all, a kind of mind reading."–Sarah Orne Jewett

Maine has had its share of famous authors, resident and visiting, who have heralded both the natural and the physical spirit of the state itself in their literary works. Horror guru Stephen King makes his home in Bangor; Harriet Beecher Stowe wrote *Uncle Tom's Cabin* while living in Brunswick; and poet Henry Wadsworth Longfellow grew up in Portland. But few are as endearingly held among Maine's literary greats as Sarah Orne Jewett, born the daughter of a country doctor and his wife in South Berwick in 1849.

Sarah Orne Jewett grew up privileged yet not out of reach of those within the rural farming community of 19th-century Maine; often she accompanied her father on house calls throughout the area, and many accredit her skills of quiet observation and sensitivity to these trips in the doctor's horse and buggy. Known for her sketches of rural life, Jewett is seen as a true daughter of Maine in the way that she beautifully and lovingly portrayed the intimate and poignant moments of her fellow citizens. Most famous are her novels *The Country Doctor* (1884) and *The Country of Pointed Firs* (1896), though she published dozens of short stories and poems throughout her writing career. Nowhere else in literature are there more endearing portraits of small-town life as in *The Country of Pointed Firs*; within her words you can nearly smell the sea air as it mingles with the scent of pines and clearly visualize the colorful characters that make up the pages within her stories.

After she published her novel *The Tory Lover* (1901), based on the wealthy Hamilton family who lived in nearby South Berwick, a review in the *Lewiston Journal* magazine section from that year summed up her writing skills aptly: "So strong and true are the pictures drawn of life...they come to Maine readers with a sort of familiarity, born of the tales of those troublous times handed down from their forefathers. Her readers feel a nearness to these men and women which makes them forget that more than a century separates them."

Jewett never married though she had a long and loving friendship with the widow Annie Fields, with whom she spent many years traveling and socializing with other literary greats of the day, including Willa Cather, William Dean Howells, Henry James, Rudyard Kipling, and Harriet Beecher Stowe. A serious carriage accident in 1902 precipitated the end of her writing career and her eventual death in 1909. Sarah Orne Jewett's writing remains as a picture of the quintessential Maine known in the hearts and minds of Maine residents, both past and present.

tidal Salmon Falls river below, where first owner Hamilton built ships, filled them with goods, and sailed straight to England from his front yard. The Embargo Act of 1807 ended his trade and, hence, his fortune quite abruptly. Picnickers and hikers are welcome on the grounds, year-round from dawn to dusk, free of charge. Held within the formal gardens, **Sundays in the Garden** offers a summer concert series ranging from classical to folk music. ⊠*40 Vaughn's La., South Berwick*

☎*207/384–2454* ⊕*www.historicnewengland.org* ✉*$8* ⊙*House tours June–mid-Oct., Wed.–Sun. 11–4.*

The **Sarah Orne Jewett House,** a sturdy Georgian-style home, dates to 1774 and reflects the shipbuilding wealth of its time. Sarah Orne Jewett was born in the house in 1849, lived elsewhere for a time, then came back to her house of birth to reside with her sister for the remainder of her life. The view from her desk in the top-floor hall looks down on the town's major intersection, which indeed gave her material for her novels, including *The Country of the Pointed Firs.* Now a museum, the house contains period furnishings. Jewett's bedroom remains as she left it. To reach the Sarah Orne Jewett House, follow Route 236 until you reach the center of South Berwick; at the division of Routes 236 and 4, look for signs; the home is right in the center of town. ✉*5 Portland St., South Berwick* ☎*207/384–2454* ⊕*www.historicnewengland.org* ✉*$5* ⊙*June–mid-Oct., Fri.–Sun. 11–4.*

Vaughn Woods, a 250-acre preserve along the banks of the Salmon Falls river, is a perfect place for a picnic or stroll. Its many nature trails wind amid pine and hemlock forests. The river was of prime importance to early settlers, and it was here that the nation's first water-powered sawmill was built. Local legend says that among the ships that carried supplies and the harvested timber downriver and to the sea, one called the *Pied Cow* unloaded the first cows to inhabit Maine in 1634. ✉*28 Oldsfields Rd., South Berwick* ☎*207/384–5160* ⊙*Memorial Day–Labor Day, daily dawn–dusk.*

WHERE TO EAT & STAY

$$–$$$$ ✕**Lodge Restaurant at Spring Hill.** With a waterfront seat alongside Salmon Falls river, this location is hard to beat. The menu mixes a good amount of land and seafood; there's a bit of everything from salmon to filet mignon, and haddock to, yes, even Wiener schnitzel. ✉*117 Pond Rd., South Berwick* ☎*207/384–2693* ▭*D, MC, V* ⊙*Closed Mon. and Tues. No lunch.*

$$–$$$ ✕**Pepperland Café.** Think upscale diner without the neon, chrome, and swivel chairs for this popular spot in downtown South Berwick. Brick walls alternating with those painted a deep red add to the warmth of the scattering of tables and pillowed couches. The lunch menu gives the greatest nod to the diner culture with blue-plate favorites such as hot meat-loaf pie or bangers and mash; dinner gets a bit more sophisticated with options like the ancho-and-cardamom-dusted grilled tuna loin. The Sunday brunch offers up a tasty mix of classics like chicken fried steak and eggs or a crab-cake Benedict. The owners strive to use local produce and meats whenever possible. The bar is a favorite among local micro and Belgian beer fanciers. ✉*279 Main St., South Berwick* ☎*207/384–5535* ▭*MC, V* ⊙*Closed Mon. No dinner Sun.*

$ ▤ **Academy Street Inn.** Antiques, family photos, and a collection of sleds
★   and snowshoes adorn the interior of this grand 1903 home, within walking distance of the historic Sarah Orne Jewett home. Inside is all warm wood, a blending of Arts and Crafts and Mission styles, with colorful touches of rich fabrics and textiles. Its location on the New Hampshire border is convenient for exploring both southern Maine

and New Hampshire. Rates include big breakfasts served in the formal dining room. Rooms are comfortably furnished and spacious; some have the added decadence of claw-foot tubs for a good soak. **Pros:** Exquisite and authentic historic lodging, very reasonable rates, walk to town center. **Cons:** One room's bathroom is a few paces down the hall (though private), rooms are upstairs (no elevator). ⊠ *15 Academy St., South Berwick 03908* ☏ *207/384–5633* ⬭ *5 rooms* ⬭ *In-room: no phone, no TV (some). In-hotel: no kids under 10, no-smoking rooms, no elevator* ⊟ *AE, MC, V* ⏱ *BP.*

NIGHTLIFE & THE ARTS

In July, the Hamilton House presents **Sundays in the Garden** (⊠ *40 Vaughan's La.* ☏ *207/384–2454* ⬭ *$8*), a series of Sunday afternoon concerts ranging from blues to folk and jazz. Picnicking is encouraged on the ample lawn; concerts begin at 4.

SHOPPING

Tiny but filled with tempting, bulging shelves to peruse, the **SoBo** (⊠ *241 Main St.* ☏ *207/384–8300*) is a used-book store–coffee shop. It's definitely a long way from Manhattan and perhaps that's the point. Pick up copies of former neighbor Sarah Orne Jewett's famous books to get you in the mood for further Maine travels.

EN ROUTE **For an appealing drive back toward the coast and the Yorks, follow Route 236 east out of South Berwick until it meets with Route 91, which branches off to the left. The less-than-10-mi winding road leads you past farmland, exquisite antique homesteads, and marshland views meandering from various tidal rivers. When you get to U.S. 1, head north to the York area.**

THE YORKS, OGUNQUIT & WELLS

The Yorks—York Village, York Harbor, York Beach, and Cape Neddick—are typical of small-town coastal communities in New England and are smaller than most. Many of their nooks and crannies can be explored in a few hours. The beaches are the big attraction here.

Not unlike siblings in most families, the towns within this region reveal vastly different personalities. York Village and York Harbor abound with old money, picturesque mansions, impeccably manicured lawns, and gardens and shops that cater to a more staid and wealthy clientele. Continue along Route 1A from York Harbor to York Beach and soon all the pretense falls away like autumn leaves in a storm—it's family vacation time (and party time), with scores of T-shirt shops, ice-cream and fried-seafood joints, arcades and bowling, and motor court–style motels. Left from earlier days are a number of trailer and RV parks spread across the road from the beach—in prime real estate that must have developers and moneyed old-timers in pure agony.

North of York Beach, Cape Neddick blends back into more peaceful and gentle terrain, while Ogunquit is elegant high-spirited tourism to the hilt. With its walkable village filled with restaurants, shops, and

B&Bs, Ogunquit is a prime resort destination. Farther north on U.S. 1 is Wells, a town seemingly lost in the commercialism of the main route yet blessed with some of the area's best beaches.

YORK VILLAGE

About 6 mi north of Kittery on Rte. 103 or Rte. 1A via U.S. 1.

As subdued as the town may feel today, the history of York Village reveals a far different character. One of the first permanently settled areas in the state of Maine, it was once witness to great destruction and fierce fighting during the French, Indian, and British wars; towns and fortunes were sacked yet the potential for prosperity encouraged the area's citizens to continually rebuild and start anew. Colonial York citizens enjoyed great wealth and success from fishing and lumber as well as a penchant for politics. Angered by the British-imposed taxes, York held its own little-known tea party in 1775 in protest. Then in the late 1700s, the first cries for independent statehood from ruling Massachusetts were heard here, though these would not be answered until the next century.

The actual village of York is quite small, housing the town's basic components of post office, town hall, a few shops, and a stretch of impressive antique homes. It feels more lived in than touristed, though the various museums of the York Historical Society are well worth a visit. Sharp-eyed American history buffs may notice something amiss with York's Civil War Monument. After the war, it was common for towns to erect a statue of a Civil War soldier to honor the local boys who served and died, and York was no exception. The statue sent to York, however, was most likely meant to be shipped much farther south—the image is of a Confederate soldier. Legend says that the citizens of York, acting in accordance with their frugal New England Yankee nature, refused to pay the extra money required to switch the statue for the correct one. That lost Confederate soldier still stands today in York Village, though no one seems to know where the Union statue ended up.

WHAT TO SEE

Most of the 18th- and 19th-century buildings within the **York Village Historic District** are clustered along York Street and Lindsay Road; seven are owned by the Old York Historical Society and charge admission. You can buy tickets for all the buildings at the **Jefferds Tavern** (⊠ *Rte. 1A at Lindsay Rd.*), a restored late-18th-century inn. The **Old York Gaol** (1720) was once the King's Prison for the Province of Maine; inside are dungeons, cells, and the jailer's quarters. Theatrical jailbreak tours are staged Friday and Saturday nights. The 1731 **Elizabeth Perkins House** reflects the Victorian style of its last occupants, the prominent Perkins family. The Historical Society also gives guided walking tours (or simply take the self-guided tour as you go through each of the seven buildings) and a popular Decorator's Show House held each July and August. ☎*207/363–4974* ⊕*www.oldyork.org* ⊠*All buildings $10* ⊙*Mid-June–mid-Oct., Mon.–Sat. 10–5.*

In an effort to keep traffic down, ease parking woes, and keep visitors (and locals) happy, the trolleys of the **York Trolley Company** make daily loops through York Village, York Harbor, out to Nubble Lighthouse, and all the way to Short Sands Beach in York Beach. In addition to regularly scheduled stops, you can take narrated sightseeing tours, trips to Ogunquit and Perkins Cove, and trips to the shopping outlets in Kittery. Day passes are available for about $8 (cheaper than beach parking!). Route maps can be picked up nearly everywhere in York and at the chamber of commerce. ☎207/748-3030 ⊕*www.yorktrolley.com.*

York is the headquarters and processing center of **Stonewall Kitchen.** You've probably seen their smartly labeled jars of gourmet chutneys, jams, jellies, salsas, and sauces in specialty stores back home. The company's attractive complex houses the company store, a bustling café and take-out restaurant, a viewing area of the cooking and bottling processes, and stunning gardens. Café tables are set outside and the store is brimming with wares that would make Martha Stewart proud. Sample all the mustards, salsas, and dressings that you can stand, or have lunch at the café. Takeout is available during store hours; lunch is served daily 11–3; Sunday is brunch day. ⊠*Stonewall La. just off U.S. 1, next to information center* ☎207/351-2719 ⊕*www.stonewall-kitchen.com* ⊘*Mon.–Sat. 8–8, Sun. 9–6.*

WHERE TO EAT

$$$$ ✕**Foster's Downeast Clambake.** Save your appetite for this one. Specializing in the traditional Maine clambake—a feast consisting of rich clam chowder, a pile of mussels and steamers, Maine lobster, corn on the cob, roasted potatoes and onions, bread, butter, and Maine blueberry crumb cake (phew!)—this massive complex provides entertainment as well as belly-busting meals. You can also opt to have clambake fixings shipped to your home or have a special event catered. ⊠*5 Axholme Rd.* ☎207/363–3255 or 800/552–0242. ⊟*AE, MC, V.*

SHOPPING

With its eclectic showing of housewares, casual women's clothing and jewelry, baby items, and unusual tokens for the home and garden, **Daisy Trading Company** (⊠*388 Rte. 1* ☎*207/363–7941*), is a feast for shoppers. You can't miss the bright yellow building and mélange of eye-catching products outside, on Route 1 close to the entrance to York Village. Bring a basket for Saturday morning shopping at the **Gateway Farmers' Market** (⊠*Rte. 1*), held at the Greater York Region Chamber of Commerce visitor center. Beginning at 9 AM, you'll find a variety of local fresh produce as well as flowers, artisan bread, homemade soaps, and many specialty foods. It's a good place to gather the means of a nice beach picnic. Guess the theme at **Gravestone Artwear** (⊠*250 York St. [Rte. 1A]* ☎*207/363–0000*), where you'll find items adorned with Colonial, Victorian, and Celtic gravestone carving designs. There are also crystals, gravestone rubbing supplies, books, and candles. Watercolors, mixed media, oils, photography, and more make up the featured art at **Village Gallery** (⊠*244 York St. [Rte. 1A]* ☎*207/351–3110*), where many local artists are represented.

YORK HARBOR

Approximately 3 mi north of York Village via Rte. 1A.

Just a few miles from the village proper, York Harbor opens up to the water and offers many places to linger and explore. The harbor itself is busy with boats of all kinds, while the harbor beach is a good stretch of sand for swimming. Much more formal than the northward York Beach, and much quieter, the area retains a bit more exclusive air.

WHAT TO SEE

The waterfront **Sayward-Wheeler House** was built in 1718. In the 1760s, Jonathan Sayward, a local merchant who had prospered in the West Indies trade, remodeled and furnished the dwelling. By 1860 his descendants had opened the house to the public to share the story of their Colonial ancestors. The house, accessible only by guided tour, reveals both the simple decor of the 18th century and the more opulent and elaborate furnishings of the 19th century. ⊠ *79 Barrell La., York Harbor* ☏ *207/384–2454* ⊕ *www.historicnewengland.org* ☏ *$5* ☺ *June–mid-Oct., 1st and 3rd Sat. of month 11–5; tours on the hr 11–4.*

WHERE TO EAT

$$$–$$$$ ✕ **Dockside Restaurant.** On an island, overlooking York Harbor, this restaurant is ideally situated. With the water in such close proximity, it's no surprise that there's plenty of seafood on the menu, but also such treats as beef tenderloin and duckling. Start with the rich lobster and scallop crepe or an order of local Maine oysters. ⊠ *Harris Island Rd. just off Rte. 103* ☏ *207/363–2722* ⊟ *D, MC, V* ☺ *Closed Mon. (except July and Aug.) and late Oct.–May.*

$$$–$$$$ ✕ **Harbor Porches.** Eating here is actually very much like sitting on someone's porch—assuming that someone has a lot of money and can afford extravagant views over York Harbor. Wicker chairs at linen-covered tables fill the space and are surrounded by large windows. There is a lot of local seafood on the menu, as well as rack of lamb and steak. For lunch try one of the interestingly prepared sandwiches or wraps. The Maine crab-cake appetizer is worth a try, as is the lobster bisque. Jeans and sneakers are not allowed at dinner. It is open for breakfast, lunch, Sunday brunch, and dinner. ⊠ *Stage Neck Rd.* ☏ *207/363–3850* ⊟ *AE, D, DC, MC, V* ☺ *Closed 2 wks in Jan.*

WHERE TO STAY

$$–$$$$ ✕ ▣ **York Harbor Inn.** A mid-17th-century fishing cabin with dark tim-
★ bers and a fieldstone fireplace forms the heart of this inn, while several wings and outbuildings have been added over the years, making for quite a complex with a great variety of styles and appointments. The rooms are furnished with antiques and country pieces; many have decks overlooking the water, and some have whirlpool tubs or fireplaces. The nicest rooms are in two adjacent buildings, Harbor Cliffs and Harbor Hill. The dining room ($$$–$$$$; no lunch off-season) has great ocean views. For dinner, start with Maine crab cakes and then try the lobster-stuffed chicken breast, or the scallops Dijon. Ask about various packages and Internet specials. **Pros:** Many rooms have harbor views, close to beaches and scenic walking trails, some luxury

appointments. **Cons:** Rooms vary greatly in style and appeal, many rooms accessed via stairways (no elevator). ✉*Rte. 1A, Box 573, York Harbor 03911* ☎*207/363–5119 or 800/343–3869* 🖷*207/363–7151* 🌐*www.yorkharborinn.com* *54 rooms, 2 suites* *In-room: Wi-Fi. In-hotel: restaurants, bar, executive floor, no-smoking rooms, no elevator* *AE, DC, MC, V* *CP.*

$$$$ **Edward's Harborside.** This turn-of-the-20th-century B&B sits on the harbor's edge and is a two-minute walk from the beach. Rooms have private baths (there are three additional rooms without baths that can be combined to make suites for families), are spacious, and have big windows to take in the water views. One room has a large whirlpool tub. There is a very homey feel here; throughout the inn are photos of the various family members' weddings and other gatherings. **Pros:** Grand water views and access to deep-water dock, close to beach. **Cons:** Most rooms located up steep stairs, third-floor rooms are smallish and share bath. ✉*Stage Neck Rd., Box 866, York Harbor 03911* ☎*207/363–3037* 🖷*207/363–1544* 🌐*www.edwardsharborside.com* *7 rooms* *In-room: Wi-Fi. In-hotel: no kids under 8, no-smoking rooms, no elevator* *MC, V* *BP.*

$$$–$$$$ Fodor's Choice ★ **Chapman Cottage.** Set proudly atop a grassy lawn is this impeccably restored inn, named for the woman who had it built as her summer cottage in 1899. The luxuriant bedspreads, fresh flowers, antiques, and beautiful rugs only hint at the indulgence found here. Innkeepers Donna and Paul Archibald spoil their guests with sumptuous breakfasts, afternoon hors d'oeuvres, port, sherry, and homemade chocolate truffles, all prepared by Paul, a professionally trained chef. Most rooms have fireplaces and whirlpool tubs; all are spacious, bright, and airy. It's a five-minute walk to either York Village or the harbor, but you may never wish to leave. What used to be an off-season hobby is now a year-round, ambitious little restaurant that serves dinner Wednesday–Sunday ($$–$$$), as well as offers a tasty tapas menu; a great accompaniment to the wine/martini bar. **Pros:** Beautifully restored historic lodging, luxury appointments, and attention to detail. **Cons:** No water views, most rooms located on upper floors (and no elevator). ✉*370 York St., 03911* ☎*207/363–2059 or 877/363–2059* 🖷*207/351–3242* 🌐*www.chapmancottagebandb.com* *6 rooms* *In-room: no phone, Wi-Fi. In-hotel: restaurant, bar, no kids under 12, no-smoking rooms, no elevator* *AE, D, MC, V* *BP.*

$$$–$$$$ ★ **Inn at Tanglewood Hall.** The inn's artfully painted floors, lush wallpapers and meticulous attention to detail are the fruits of a former designation as a designers' showcase home. This 1880s Victorian "cottage," as these mansions were humbly called back in the day, is a haven of elegance and comfort, set back among trees and stunning perennial gardens. Rooms are individually decorated though all share decadently rich coloring and fabrics, high ceilings, and many large windows; some have fireplaces. **Pros:** Elegant and authentic historic lodging, serene setting amid gardens and grand trees, short walk to beaches and nature trails. **Cons:** No water views, most rooms located on upper floors (no elevator). ✉*611 York St., 03911* ☎*207/351–1075* 🖷*207/351–1296* 🌐*www.tanglewoodhall.com* *6 rooms* *In-room: no phone, no*

TV, refrigerator (some), Wi-Fi. In-hotel: no kids under 12, no-smoking rooms, no elevator ☰*AE, MC, V* ⏉⊙⏉*BP.*

$$–$$$$ ⌂**Dockside Guest Quarters.** This is the kind of place that people return to year after year. Set on its own private peninsula bordering York Harbor and the ocean, the complex consists of the main inn as well as a series of buildings that house standard rooms and suites with kitchenettes. Adirondack chairs are thoughtfully placed by twos around the spacious lawn, with plenty of space for privacy if desired. Many hours could be spent on the wraparound porch enjoying the views. Rooms are adorned with antiques and simple white bedspreads; some have fireplaces and most have outdoor decks. **Pros:** Secluded, waterfront location with boating access, ample green space for strolling or lawn games. **Cons:** Rooms in outer buildings not as charming as those in the main house, not an in-town location. ✉*Harris Island Rd., 03909* ☎*207/363–2868 or 800/270–1977* ⎙*207/363–1977* ⊕*www.docksidegq.com* ⇲*13 rooms, 6 suites, 6 studios* ♿*In-hotel: bicycles, water sports, restaurant, public Wi-Fi, no-smoking rooms, no elevator* ☰*D, MC, V* ⊙*Closed Dec.–Mar.* ⏉⊙⏉*BP.*

SPORTS & THE OUTDOORS

For a good beachcombing exploration and a jaunt across York's beloved Wiggly Bridge, take the **Shore Walk.** You can start at various spots—either from Route 103 alongside York Harbor (there is minimal parking here, but you'll know it when you see the bridge), or from the George Marshall Store in York Village (140 Lindsay Rd.).

KAYAKING Take to the water in a guided kayak trip with **Harbor Adventures** (⌂*Box 345, York Harbor 03911* ☎*207/363–8466* ⊕*www.harboradventures. com*). Choose from harbor tours, full-moon paddles, half-day trips, and even a luncheon paddle; prices start around $32. Departure locations vary. Bicycle tours are also offered.

BIKING **Berger's Bike Shop** (✉*241 York St. No. 1, York* ☎*207/363–4070*) rents all manner of bikes for local excursions.

FISHING **Captain Tom Farnon** (✉*Rte. 103, Town Dock No. 2, York Harbor* ☎*207/408–1194*) takes passengers on lobstering trips, weekdays 10–2. **Fish Tale Charters** (✉*85 Bog Rd., York Harbor* ☎*207/363–3874* ⊕*www.maineflyfishing.net*) takes anglers on fly-fishing charters out of York Harbor. **Rip Tide Charters** (✉*1 Georgia St., York* ☎*207/363–2536* ⊕*www.mainestriperfishing.com*) goes where the fish are—departure points vary, from Ogunquit to York and Portsmouth, New Hampshire. They specialize in fly-fishing and light tackle for stripers, mackerel, and bluefish. **Seabury Charters** (✉*Town Dock No. 2, York Harbor, York* ☎*207/363–5675* ⊕*www.yorkme.org/seaburycharters*) offers two trips daily aboard the *Blackback*. The first trip is from 7:30 AM to noon; the second is from 12:30 to 5 PM. There are no trips Monday or Thursday. Walk-ons are welcome if space allows. **Shearwater Charters** (⌂*Box 472, York Harbor 03911* ☎*207/363–5324*) offers spin or fly-casting charters in the York River and along the shoreline from Kittery to Ogunquit. Bait-fishing trips are also available. Departure spots depend on time and tides. **Tidewater Sportfishing Charters** (✉*Rte. 103,*

Town Dock, York Harbor ☎207/363–6524) specializes in light tackle and fly-fishing for striped bass and bluefish.

HIKING &
WALKING

For a peek into the Rachel Carson National Wildlife Refuge, take the 2-mi **Brave Boat Harbor Trail,** which is one of the few walking trails available in the refuge. It's a prime bird-watching area. Look for Brave Boat Harbor Road just off Route 103 for trail access and parking.

EN ROUTE

Continue along Route 1A from York Harbor to York Beach. The waterfront mansions eventually give way to seaside trailer parks, 1950s-style resort motels, and stunning sections of rocky shores and beaches.

YORK BEACH

6 mi north of York Harbor via Rte. 1A.

Like many shorefront towns in Maine, York Beach has a long, long history of entertaining summer visitors. Take away today's bikinis and boom-box music and it's easy to imagine squealing bathers adorned in the full-length bathing garb of the late 19th century. Just as they did back then, visitors today come here to eat ice cream, enjoy carnival-like novelties, and indulge in the sun and sea air.

York Beach is a real family destination, devoid of all things staid and stuffy—children are meant to be both seen and heard here, and that's part of what gives the area its invigorating feel. Just beyond the sands of Short Sand Beach are a host of amusements, from bowling to indoor minigolf and the Fun-O-Rama arcade.

WHAT TO SEE

Head out a couple of miles on the peninsula to see **Nubble Light,** said to be one of the most photographed lighthouses on the globe. Set out on a hill of rocks, the lighthouse is still in use. Direct access is prohibited, but an informational center shares the 1879 light's history. Find parking at Sohier Park, at the end of Nubble Road, as well as rest rooms and plenty of benches. ⊠*End of Nubble Rd., off Rte. 1A.*

Between the zoo and the carnival rides, it's sometimes hard to distinguish the wild animals from the kids at **York's Wild Kingdom.** Combination tickets can be purchased to visit the zoo and the amusement park, and discounts are available for kids under 10. There are extensive picnic areas, paddleboats, elephant shows, and plenty of other amusements. The zoo has an impressive variety of exotic animals and is home to the state's only white Bengal tiger. ⊠*U.S. 1, also entrance from Short Sands Beach area, York* ☎207/363–4911 ⊕*www.yorkzoo.com* ☜*$14 zoo only; $18.50 zoo and rides* ☉*Late May–Sept.*

WHERE TO EAT

$$–$$$$ ✕**Fox's Lobster House.** This place is a little pricier than your average fried-seafood joint (then again, few are cheap), but its location is ideal—right up by Nubble Light and with grand views of the ocean beyond. The place gets packed, but the scenery should make the wait quite bearable. You can get takeout or dine inside with table service.

For the most ambitious appetite, see if you can tackle the 3-pound baked stuffed lobster. In addition to the regular offering of seafood, choose from steaks, chicken, and pasta; save room for the homemade blueberry pie. ⊠ *End of Nubble Rd.* ☎ *207/363–2643* ♙ *Reservations not accepted* ⊟ *MC, V* ⊘ *Closed Nov.–Apr.*

$$$ ✕**Mimmo's.** Water views can be had from some tables at this casual but very busy spot on Long Sands Beach. The menu is Italian, with lots of pastas to choose from and classics such as eggplant parmigiana. If you can't get enough seafood, try the *coastazurro,* with shrimp, haddock, calamari, and mussels sautéed with garlic. No alcohol is served, but diners can bring their own. For dinner, reservations are a good idea. ⊠ *Long Beach Ave. (Rte. 1A)* ☎ *207/363–3807* ⊟ *AE, MC, V.*

$–$$ ✕**The Goldenrod.** If you wanted to—and you are on vacation—you could eat nothing but the famous taffy here, made just about the same way today as it was back in 1896. The famous Goldenrod Kisses, made to the tune of 65 tons per year, are a great attraction and people line the windows to watch the process. Aside from the famous taffy, this eating place is family oriented, very reasonably priced, and a great place to get ice cream from the old-fashioned soda fountain. Breakfast is served all day while the simple lunch menu doubles as dinner; choose from sandwiches and burgers. There is even penny candy for sale for, yes, a penny apiece. ⊠ *Railroad Ave.* ☎ *207/363–2621* ⊟ *AE, MC, V* ⊘ *Closed Columbus Day–late May.*

WHERE TO STAY

$$$–$$$$ ✕🏨**Union Bluff Hotel.** Although this hotel had to be rebuilt after a devastating fire, the face of the massive, turreted structure remains very similar to its mid-19th-century beginnings. Things are quite a bit more modern these days, but its original grandeur is still evident. Many of the rooms have endless ocean views from private balconies; those that don't are so close that you can still smell the sea air. Rooms don't have a lot of antique character but they feature all the amenities of contemporary hotels, with standard, comfortable furnishings. You couldn't get much closer to all the activity of Short Sands Beach, which is just steps away. The pub serves lunch and dinner daily and has a late-night menu; the restaurant ($–$$$) is open for breakfast and dinner. **Pros:** Many spectacular, uninterrupted ocean views; hotel located right in the midst of the York Beach action. **Cons:** Rooms lack any charm or character befitting of inn's origins (but the views!), not for those looking for a quiet getaway. ⊠ *8 Beach St., 03910* ☎ *207/363–1333 or 800/833–0721* ⊕ *www.unionbluff.com* ⟿ *36 rooms, 6 suites in main inn; 21 rooms in adjacent motel* ♿ *In-room: refrigerator, Wi-Fi. In-hotel: restaurant, bar, no-smoking rooms* ⊟ *AE, D, MC, V.*

$$$$ 🏨**Inn at Long Sands.** You can't stay much closer to the beach than this, and most rooms have private balconies from which to enjoy the view of Long Sands Beach. The inn is in the milder area of York Beach, a mile or so from the downtown action. Rooms are simply decorated and comfortable, with such touches as wallpapered walls and four-poster beds. The front porch is a great place for people-watching. It's worth getting breakfast (not included in the room rate) in the on-site restaurant—try the rum raisin French toast or one of their well-stuffed omelets. The little café is also open nightly for dessert and coffee. **Pros:** Private balconies open out to ocean views, great spot for beach lovers, close to downtown attractions. **Con:** Street and people noise from below may be audible. ⊠ *125 Long Beach Ave. (Rte. 1A), 03910* ☎ *207/363–5132 or 800/927–5132* ⊕ *www.innatlongsands.com* ⇲ *8 rooms* ⚙ *In-room: refrigerator, Wi-Fi. In-hotel: room service, restaurant, no-smoking rooms, no elevator* ⊟ *AE, MC, V.*

\$–\$\$ **Katahdin Inn.** This is the kind of place that is much like visiting family: you feel at ease enough to sit on the front porch (which overlooks the ocean) in your bathing suit, settling in for an evening of board games and—not everyone's favorite thing—sharing the bathroom. Nonetheless, this vivid yellow 19th-century inn sits on the edge of a residential area (many of the neighboring homes are aged Victorian vacation beauties), faces the ocean, and is a short walk to all the action of York Beach. Most of the rooms—on the small side but with high ceilings—have water views and each, is adorned simply with white bedspreads and floral wall coverings. It's simple, affordable lodging at its best, where the ocean and the area attractions ought to stand out with more flourish. Coffee is served in the morning; most guests start the morning watching the sunrise over the sea. **Pros:** Direct waterfront location, walk to beach and to town attractions, reasonable rates. **Cons:** Most rooms share bathrooms, upper-floor rooms accessed via steep stairs. ⊠ *11 Ocean Ave., 03910* ☎ *207/363–1824* ⊕ *www.thekatahdininn. com* ⇲ *9 rooms, 2 with bath* ⚙ *In-room: no a/c, no phone, no TV, refrigerator. In-hotel: no-smoking rooms, no elevator* ⊟ *MC, V.*

NIGHTLIFE & THE ARTS

Inn on the Blues (⊠ *7 Ocean Ave., York Beach* ☎ *207/351–3221*) is a hopping blues club that attracts national bands.

SHOPPING

There is no shortage of souvenir shopping here. Be sure to get some Goldenrod Kisses—Maine's famous saltwater taffy, made the same way today as it has been for more than a century—at the **Goldenrod** (⇨ *see Where to Eat & Stay, above*). If you need new flip-flops, a sweatshirt, or a bathing suit to brave the waters of the ocean, you'll find plenty to choose from. Route 1A is the main drag, with smaller, alleylike streets running perpendicular to it; the center of town is easily walkable.

CAPE NEDDICK

4 mi north of York Beach via Rte. 1A, just north of York on U.S. 1.

Cape Neddick is one of the more peaceful of York's villages, running from the water (and Route 1A), along U.S. 1 between York and Ogunquit. Not heavily developed, the town has many modest residential homes, with a sprinkling of businesses catering to both locals and visitors. There are a few restaurants and inns, but no distinct downtown hub. The views are a nice combination of water, pastoral, and wooded landscapes.

WHAT TO SEE

Mount Agamenticus Park. Maintained by the York Parks and Recreation Department, this humble summit of 692 feet above sea level is said to be the highest peak along the Atlantic seaboard. That may not seem like much, but if you choose to hike to the top, you will be rewarded with incredible views that span all the way to the White Mountains in New Hampshire. If you don't want to hoof it (though it's not very steep), there is parking at the top. The Nature Conservancy has chosen the site as very significant owing to the variety of unusual natural flora and fauna. To get here, take Mountain Road just off U.S. 1 in Cape Neddick (just after Flo's Steamed Hot Dogs) and follow the signs. The area is open daily, with no charge. It's a popular place for equestrians and cyclists as well as families and hikers. ⓓ *York Parks and Recreation Department, 200 U.S. Rte. 1 S, York 03909* ☎*207/363–1040.*

WHERE TO EAT & STAY

$$$–$$$$
★
✕ **Clay Hill Farm.** Set on 30 acres of pastoral farmland, this is a popular place for elegant weddings. It also has a long-standing reputation for excellence. If you can bear to forgo the lobster crepe—a scallion crepe wrapped around fresh Maine lobster, caramelized onions, and spinach served over toasted almond rice pilaf and drizzled with Newburg sauce—inquire about the intriguing nightly chef's special. An extensive wine list complements the menu, and there is a pianist in the dining room Wednesday through Saturday nights in season. Get a table by a window and you'll be treated with quite an avian showing—the restaurant property has been named a bird refuge by the National Wildlife Federation. Jeans and sneakers are not allowed. ✉ *220 Clay Hill Rd.* ☎*207/361–2272* ⚑*Reservations essential* ▭*AE, D, MC, V.*

$$–$$$$
✕ **Frankie & Johnny's Natural Food Restaurant.** If you've had about all the fried seafood and calories you can stand for one day, try this casual little spot that focuses on healthy—but tasty—meals. Choose from a variety of vegetarian dishes as well as seafood, poultry, and meat options. The toasted peppercorn seared sushi-grade tuna, served with coconut risotto on gingered vegetables, is excellent. You're welcome and encouraged to bring your own libations. ✉*1594 U.S. 1, Cape Neddick* ☎*207/363–1909* ▭*No credit cards* ◷*No dinner Mon.– Wed., no lunch.*

★ ¢
✕ **Flo's Steamed Hot Dogs.** Yes, it seems crazy to highlight a hot dog stand, but this is no ordinary place. Who would guess that a hot dog could make it into *Saveur* and *Gourmet* magazines? But there is something grand about this shabby, red-shingle shack that has been dealing dogs since 1959. The line is out the door most days, but the operation is so efficient that the wait is not long at all. Flo has passed but her granddaughter keeps the business going, selling countless thousands of hot dogs each year. Be sure to ask for the special sauce—consisting of, among other things, hot sauce and mayo (you can take a bottle of the sauce home, and you'll want to). ✉*1359 U.S. 1* ☎*No phone* ▭*No credit cards* ◷*Closed Wed.*

$–$$$
▥ **Country View Motel & Guesthouse.** Set back along one of U.S. 1's less-hectic sections is this appealing little motel—it looks more like an inn than what you usually envision as a motel. There are a few rooms in

the main house and the rest are in the adjacent motel complex. It's clean, pretty, and in a good central location for exploring the Yorks and Ogunquit, which are just miles away. Suites sleep up to four people and have full kitchens. **Pros:** Central location between Ogunquit and Yorks, ample grounds provide picnic areas and gas grills. **Cons:** Not an in-town location, no water views or beachfront. ✉ *1521 U.S. 1, 03902* ☎ *207/363–7160 or 800/258–6598* ⊕ *www.countryviewmotel. com* ⌐ *19 rooms, 3 suites* ⌂ *In-room: kitchen (some), refrigerator, Wi-Fi. In-hotel: pool, some pets allowed, no-smoking rooms, no elevator* ⊟ *MC, V* ⦿ *CP.*

SPORTS & THE OUTDOORS

FISHING   Offering a host of various fishing and kayak guided tours is **Eldredge Bros. Fly Shop** (✉ *1480 U.S. 1* ☎ *207/363–9269 or 207/363–9279* ⊕ *www.eldredgeflyshop.com*). Fishing trips are in fresh- or saltwater; kayak trips come in all types. Rod-and-reel rentals are also available.

GOLFING   For a challenging 18-hole round, head to the **Cape Neddick Country Club** (✉ *1480 U.S. 1* ☎ *207/361–2011* ⊕ *www.capeneddickgolf.com*), where the public is welcome. Greens fees start at $50.

KAYAKING   Hop on one of the regularly scheduled guided kayak trips with **Excursions/Coastal Maine Outfitting Co.** (✉ *U.S. 1* ☎ *207/363–0181* ⊕ *www. excursionsinmaine.com*). You can cruise along the shoreline or sign up for an overnight paddle. Reservations are recommended. Kayaks and other boats are available for rental.

SHOPPING

Home furnishings with an antique feel are the specialty of **Jeremiah Campbell & Company** (✉ *1537 U.S. 1* ☎ *207/363–8499*). Everything here is handcrafted, from rugs, decoys, furniture, and lighting to glassware. The shop is closed Wednesday. Quilt and fabric lovers will delight in a visit to **Knight's Quilt Shop** (✉ *1901 U.S. 1* ☎ *207/361–2500*), where quilts and everything needed to make them—including instructional classes—can be found. For a huge selection of glassworks, pottery, and jewelry, stop at **Panache Gallery of Fine American Crafts** (✉ *1949 U.S. 1* ☎ *207/646–4878*).

EN ROUTE   You have two options when continuing on to Ogunquit: travel north on Route 1A, which will merge with U.S. 1 and take you into downtown Ogunquit; or, for a slower, more winding, scenic jaunt, take a right just out of York Beach onto Shore Road. You'll pass impeccable homes and get frequent glimpses of the rocky coast before ending up just shy of Perkins Cove; continue to the village of Ogunquit by turning left at the end of the road.

OGUNQUIT

10 mi north of the Yorks via Rte. 1A and 1 or Shore Rd.

A resort-village in the 1880s, stylish Ogunquit gained fame as an artists' colony. Today it has become a mini Provincetown, with a gay population that swells in summer. Many inns and small clubs cater to a primarily gay and lesbian clientele. For a scenic drive, take Shore Road through downtown toward the 100-foot Bald Head Cliff; you'll be treated to views up and down the coast. On a stormy day the surf can be quite wild here.

The **Ogunquit Trolley** is one of the best things that happened to this area. Parking in the village is troublesome and expensive, beach parking is costly and often limited, and so it's often just easier to leave your car parked at the hotel. The trolley begins operation in May and stays in service until Columbus Day. The fare is $1.50 (at each boarding) and kids under 10 ride free with an adult. Stops are numerous along the route that begins at Perkins Cove and follows Shore Road through town, down to Ogunquit Beach, and out along U.S. 1 up to Wells (where a connecting Wells trolley takes over for northern travel). Maps are available wherever you find brochures and at the chamber of commerce Welcome Center on U.S. 1, just as you enter Ogunquit from the south. *Box 2368, Ogunquit 03907* 🕾 *207/646–1411.*

WHAT TO SEE

For a look at Ogunquit's colorful past, including its early days as a thriving art colony and its maritime history, visit the **Ogunquit Heritage Museum.** Exhibits in the Winn House, which itself dates to 1785, also focus on Colonial architecture. ✉ *86 Obed's La.* 🕾 *207/646–0296* ⊕ *www.ogunquitheritagemuseum.org* 🖾 *Donations accepted* ♥ *June–Sept., Tues.–Sat. 1–5.*

The small but worthwhile **Ogunquit Museum of American Art,** dedicated to 20th-century American art, overlooks the ocean and is set amid a 3-acre sculpture garden. Inside are works by Henry Strater, Marsden Hartley, Winslow Homer, Edward Hopper, Gaston Lachaise, Marguerite Zorach, and Louise Nevelson. The huge windows of the sculpture court command a superb view of cliffs and ocean. ✉ *543 Shore Rd.* 🕾 *207/646–4909* ⊕ *www.ogunquitmuseum.org* 🖾 *$7* ♥ *July–late-Oct., Mon.–Sat. 10:30–5, Sun. 2–5.*

★ **Perkins Cove,** a neck of land connected to the mainland by Oarweed Road and a pedestrian drawbridge, has a jumble of sea-beaten fish houses. These have largely been transformed by the tide of tourism to shops and restaurants. When you've had your fill of browsing and jostling the crowds, stroll out along the **Marginal Way,** a mile-long footpath between Ogunquit and Perkins Cove that hugs the shore of a rocky promontory known as Israel's Head. Benches along the route give walkers an opportunity to stop and appreciate the open sea vistas, flowering bushes, and million-dollar homes.

WHERE TO EAT

$$$$ ✕ **Arrows.** Elegant simplicity is the hallmark of this restaurant in an
Fodor's Choice 18th-century farmhouse, 2 mi up a back road. Grilled salmon and
★ radicchio with marinated fennel and baked polenta, and Chinese-style duck glazed with molasses are typical entrées on the daily-changing menu—much of what appears is dependent on what is ready for harvest in the restaurant's abundant 1-acre garden. The Maine crabmeat mousse and lobster risotto appetizers, and desserts such as strawberry

shortcake with Chantilly cream, are also beautifully executed. The accolades are continual: *Gourmet* magazine rated this small-town restaurant 14th of the 50 best restaurants in the country. ⊠*41 Berwick Rd.* ☎*207/361–1100* ☜*Reservations essential* ▤*MC, V* ⊙*Closed Mon. and mid-Dec.–mid-Apr. No lunch.*

$$$–$$$$ ✕**Bintliff's Restaurant.** The lounge is inviting with velvet chairs and
★   couches, but it's the food and the extensive wine list that bring people back again and again. Steaks are a specialty here, but don't overlook the other intriguing entrées. One recommendation is the Eggplant Napoleon, combining crispy eggplant, tomatoes, braised onions, fresh mozzarella, roasted red peppers, and marinated portobello mushrooms. This is also one of the best spots around for Sunday brunch and breakfast. ⊠*335 Main St.* ☎*207/646–3111* ☜*Reservations essential* ▤*AE, D, MC, V.*

$$$–$$$$ ✕**98 Provence.** Country-French ambience provides a fitting backdrop for chef Pierre Gignac's French fare. Begin with the duck foie gras or country-style rabbit pâté, and follow it up with a cassoulet or medallion of veal tenderloin with a wild-mushroom cream sauce. Locals and visitors both rave about the consistent excellence of this favorite. ⊠*104 Shore Rd.* ☎*207/646–9898* ☜*Reservations essential* ▤*MC, V* ⊙*Closed Tues. and mid-Dec.–early Apr. No lunch.*

¢–$$ ✕**Amore Breakfast.** One could hardly find a more-satisfying, full-
★   bodied breakfast than at this smart and busy joint between Ogunquit and Perkins Cove. Amid a lighthearted mix of enamel-topped tables and retro advertising design touches, breakfast is a sophisticated affair. You won't find tired standards here—the only pancakes are German potato—rather, you'll have a hard time choosing among the options. The Oscar Madison omelet combines crabmeat with asparagus and Swiss, topped with a dill hollandaise. For a real decadent start, opt for the Banana Foster: pecan-coated, cream cheese–stuffed French toast with a side of sautéed bananas in rum syrup. The offers of a ½, ¾, or full order give an indication of this item's richness. If you're especially lucky, you'll catch the sometime special of corned beef hash—this version is made from hearty pieces of the briny beef rather than the often-seen through-the-blender kind of hash. To ease the wait for a morning table, a self-serve coffee bar is available. ⊠*178 Shore Rd.* ☎*207/646–6661* ▤*D, MC, V* ⊙*Closed Christmas–Mar., and Wed. and Thurs. in spring and fall. No lunch.*

WHERE TO STAY

$$$–$$$$ ⊡**Black Boar Inn.** The original part of this inn dates to 1674, an era that
Fodor'sChoice   is reflected in the beauty of the wide-plank pine floors and the fireplaces
★   in every room. A sense of absolute luxury pervades here. The interior is exquisite, with bead board, richly colored rugs and comforters, William Morris–like wallpaper, tiled bathrooms, and many antiques. Although the manager wasn't sure where the "wild boar" name originated, evidence of the beast abounds in art and sculpture throughout. Wine and hors d'ouevres are served on weekend afternoons and can be enjoyed on the front terrace, overlooking the massive gardens and the world of Main Street beyond. Cottages are rented by the week and are notable for their exposed wood, vaulted ceilings, and full kitchens. **Pros:** Gra-

cious, historic lodging; most rooms have fireplaces; quiet retreat in the center of town. **Cons:** Most rooms accessed via steep stairs; due to home's age, rooms are on the smaller (though uncrowded) side. ✉277 *Main St., 03907* ☎*207/646–2112* ⊕*www.blackboarinn.com* ⬎*6 rooms, 3 cottages* ♿*In-room: no phone, Wi-Fi. In-hotel: no-smoking rooms, no elevator* ⊟*MC, V* ⊘*Closed Nov.–late May* ⊙*BP.*

$$$–$$$$ ⊞**Rockmere Lodge.** Midway along Ogunquit's Marginal Way, this shingle-style Victorian cottage is an ideal retreat from the hustle and bustle of Perkins Cove. All the rooms have corner locations and are large and airy, and all but one have ocean views. Rooms are fluffed to the hilt with colorful pillows, curtains, antiques, and other objects. You'll find it easy to laze the day away on the wraparound porch or in the gardens. **Pros:** Dramatic oceanfront location, easy walk to both Ogunquit and Perkins Cove, historic lodging with authentic detail. **Cons:** Many rooms accessed via steep stairs, not for those traveling with small children. ✉*150 Stearns Rd., Box 278, 03907* ☎*207/646–2985* 🖷*207/646–6947* ⊕*www.rockmere.com* ⬎*8 rooms* ♿*In-room: no a/c, no phone, VCR, DVD, refrigerator. In-hotel: no kids under 14, no-smoking rooms, no elevator* ⊟*AE, D, MC, V* ⊙*BP.*

$$–$$$$ ⊞**Ogunquit Resort Motel.** Right along U.S. 1, about 2 mi north of Ogunquit Village, sprawls this large complex that is great for families and for those who prefer larger hotels to B&Bs. Boasting the largest pool in Ogunquit, the resort also has an outdoor hot tub. Beachgoers can walk to Footbridge Beach just about a half mile away. Choose from deluxe, superior, and luxury rooms; luxury suites have fireplaces and Jacuzzi tubs. Unusual for hotels of this size is the free Continental breakfast laid out each morning. You can leave your car here and hop on the trolley to get around, saving yourself the agony (and expense) of trying to park in town or at the beach. Ask about Internet specials. **Pros:** On the Ogunquit Trolley route, good place for those traveling with kids, good-size rooms with standard large-hotel amenities. **Cons:** Not an in-town location, not for those looking for the more personalized small-lodging experience. ✉*719 Main St. (U.S. 1), 03907* ☎*877/646–8336* ⊕*www. ogunquitresort.com* ⬎*85 rooms, 8 suites* ♿*In-room: refrigerator, Wi-Fi. In-hotel: pool, gym, no-smoking rooms, no elevator* ⊟*AE, D, MC, V* ⊙*CP.*

$$–$$$ ⊞**Marginal Way House.** This may be the best location in all of Ogunquit if you want to be close to the water. The expansive lawn of the complex stretches down from the main 1880s house right to the banks of the tumbling Ogunquit River just as it breaks from the sea. One apartment sits on that edge, as does another shingled building that houses more rooms with decks atop the raging waters. Rooms have floral wallpaper, lots of wicker, and a curious assortment of attic-styled artwork—unfussy, a bit outdated, but very comfortable. Guests spend a lot of time on the back-porch area, where morning coffee is available, or out among the flowers in the yard. It's a two-minute walk to town and five minutes to the beach across the footbridge. Apartments are rented weekly in high season. **Pros:** Overlooks both ocean and tidal river, extraordinary water views from many rooms and grounds, short walk to beach. **Cons:** Rooms in main house accessed via steep stairs, some rooms are on the small side. ✉ *Wharf La., 03907* ☎*207/646–8801* ⊕*www.marginalwayhouse.com* 🛏*23 rooms, 7 suites, 1 apartment* ♿*In-room: no a/c (some), kitchen (some), refrigerator, no phone. In-hotel: some pets allowed, Wi-Fi, no-smoking rooms, no elevator* ☐*MC, V* ⊘*Closed Nov.–Apr.*

$$ 🏨**Yardarm Village Inn.** With stenciling winding up stairs and along many of its walls and tin ceilings, this inn has been lovingly cared for since its construction in the late 19th century. Set near the now-defunct trolley bed of the same era, the peaceful home is a very short walk from the activity of Perkins Cove. Standard rooms are large and suites have separate sitting rooms—a good spot to enjoy the fruits of the inn's in-house gourmet wine-and-cheese shop. Those eager to get on the water can cruise with the innkeepers on their 26-foot single sail (about $25 for two hours). A Continental breakfast is offered for an extra fee. **Pros:** Easy walk to Perkins Cove, comfortable historic lodging, in-house shop provides the means for a good picnic. **Con:** Most rooms on second and third floors. ✉*406 Shore Rd., 03907* ☎*207/646–7006 or 888/927–3276* 🖶*207/646–9034* ⊕*www.yardarmvillageinn.com* 🛏*6 rooms, 4 suites* ♿*In-room: no phone, refrigerator, Wi-Fi. In-hotel: no-smoking rooms, no elevator* ☐*No credit cards* ⊘*Closed Nov.–Apr.*

NIGHTLIFE & THE ARTS

Much of the nightlife in Ogunquit revolves around the precincts of Ogunquit Square and Perkins Cove, where people stroll, often enjoying an after-dinner ice-cream cone or espresso. Because Ogunquit is popular with gay and lesbian visitors, its club scene reflects this.

Ogunquit's summer repertory company, the **Booth Theater** (✉*13 Beach St.* ☎*207/646–8142* ⊕*www.boothproductions.com*), stages performances nightly in summer, ranging from Neil Simon and Stephen Sondheim to such popular favorites as *School House Rock!*. The season kicks off around mid-June and continues through August. **Jonathan's Restaurant** (✉*2 Bourne La.* ☎*207/646–4777*) hosts live entertainment—usually blues—during peak season, from June to mid-October. The movies are first-run at **Leavitt Fine Arts Theatre** (✉*295 Main St.* ☎*207/646–3213*), but it's also been Maine's summer theater since 1923. Look for the grand architectural elements of that earlier era before the movie starts. One of America's oldest summer theaters, the **Ogunquit Playhouse** (✉*U.S. 1* ☎*207/646–5511* ⊕*www.ogunquitplayhouse.org*) mounts plays and musicals with well-known actors of stage and screen from late June to Labor Day.

NEED A BREAK?

Whether you're looking for something hot or cold, stop in for a treat at Caffe Prego (✉44 Shore Rd. ☎207/646–7734). With more than two dozen flavors of gelato, an intriguing roster of heavenly malted frappés, granitas, and a full espresso bar, you'll find the pick-me-up you're craving. If you're hungry, there's also a good selection of brick oven–fired pizzas (their specialty), grilled panini sandwiches, salad, and pasta.

SPORTS & THE OUTDOORS

A great spot to stretch your legs and have a picnic is **Beach Plum Farm**(⊠*U.S. Route 1, 1 mi north of Ogunquit village*), a 22-acre parcel of land with several barns and a house. Maintained by the Great Works Regional Land Trust, the area is open from dawn to dusk and features ocean views and community gardens. Benches and a marked path around the perimeter welcome walkers. **Ogunquit Beach,** a 3-mi-wide stretch of sand at the mouth of the Ogunquit River, has snack bars, a boardwalk, rest rooms, and changing areas (at the Beach Street entrance). Families gravitate to the ends; gay visitors camp at the beach's middle. The less-crowded section to the north is accessible by footbridge and has portable rest rooms, all-day paid parking, and trolley service.

OUTFITTER **Liquid Dreams Surf Shop** (⊠*731 Main St.* ☎*207/641–2545*) rents surfing equipment (you will want the wet suit) and bodyboards, and also sells bathing suits and wave-riding supplies.

BOATING Anglers can sign on with **Bunny Clark Deep Sea Fishing** (⊠*Perkins Cove* ☎*207/646–2214*), which leaves the dock twice daily from early April through mid-November. The long boat ride with **Deborah Ann Whale-watching** (⊠*Perkins Cove* ☎*207/361–9501*) is worth it to witness humpback and finback whales in their natural habitat out on Jefferies Ledge. **Finestkind** (⊠*Perkins Cove* ☎*207/646–5227* ⊕*www.finestkindcruises.com*) operates cocktail cruises, lobstering trips, and cruises to Nubble Light. Pack a picnic for a billowy 1½- or 2-hour sail with *The Silverlining* (⊠*Perkins Cove* ☎*207/646–9800*), a 42-foot wooden sloop. She leaves the dock at Perkins Cove six times daily. For more deep-sea fishing adventures, climb aboard the *Ugly Anne* (⊠*Perkins Cove* ☎*207/646–7202*), for half- or full-day trips.

EN ROUTE The summer traffic isn't the only thing that may make your northern drive up U.S. 1 from Ogunquit to Wells a slow one—this stretch is an antiques lover's paradise. Individual shops with antiques spilling out into the driveways and lawns are numerous, as are the multidealer and multibuilding shops. You can find quilts, glassware, maritime items, aged books, and hundreds of other things on this route. Wells is also home to a great outdoor flea market, held on weekends and a few other days during the week; you can't miss it, it's on the right side of U.S. 1 as you drive by going north.

SHOPPING

Ogunquit Village and Perkins Cove are well stocked with shops, many carrying the ubiquitous supply of Maine lobster T-shirts and tourist-type gadgets. There are also some galleries and specialty spots, selling everything from artwork to fine linens and apparel.

More than just an art gallery, the **Barn Gallery** (⊠*Shore Rd. and Bourne La.* ☎*207/646–8400*) hosts special programs, workshops, and exhibitions by some well-known local artists. Peruse the possible treasures at the multidealer **Blacksmith's Antique Mall** (⊠*166 Main St.* ☎*207/646–9643*), where you probably won't find any bargains; but then again, you might. Stock up in case of rain at **Books Ink** (⊠ *Perkins Cove* ☎ *207/361–2602*), where you'll find an array of toys, games, and puzzles in addition to books. Besides a good collection of stained glass, the wares at **Out of the Blue** (⊠ *19 Perkins Cove Rd.* ☎ *207/646–0430*) include home and garden accoutrements, jewelry, and all things related to wine.

WELLS

5 mi north of Ogunquit on U.S. 1.

Lacking any kind of noticeable village center, Wells could be easily overlooked as nothing more than a commercial stretch on U.S. 1 between Ogunquit and the Kennebunks. But look more closely—this is a place where people come to enjoy some of the best beaches on the coast. Part of Ogunquit until 1980, this family-oriented beach community has 7 mi of densely populated shoreline, along with nature preserves where you can explore salt marshes and tidal pools, and see birds and waterfowl.

The area is also rich in history; Wells has been a thriving community in one way or another since the mid-1600s. It's actually a little more peaceful now than it was back then—the flocks of tourists that crowd the beaches and roadsides are far friendlier than the American Indians and French who engaged in near constant warfare and attacks during the 17th century.

WHAT TO SEE

The headquarters for both the Ogunquit and Wells Historical Society, the **Meetinghouse Museum and Library** hosts a series of concerts, programs, tours, and exhibits. The library is a gold mine for those interested in genealogy. ⊠ *983 U.S. 1* ☎ *207/646–4775* ⊠ *Donations accepted* ☉ *June–mid-Oct., Tues.–Thurs. 10–4; mid-Oct.–May, Wed. and Thurs. 10–4.*

The **Rachel Carson National Wildlife Refuge** (⊠ *Rte. 9* ☎ *207/646–9226*) has a mile-long-loop nature trail through a salt marsh. The trail borders the Little River and a white-pine forest where migrating birds and waterfowl of many varieties are regularly spotted.

■ NEED A BREAK?

How would you like a doughnut . . . a really superior one that the same family has been making since 1955? The doughnuts from Congdon's (⊠ *U.S. 1* ☎ *207/646–4219*) easily rival (many say there is no contest) some of those other famous places we won't mention here. Choose from about 30 different varieties, though the plain really gives you an idea of just how good these doughnuts are. There's a drive-through window so you don't have to get out of the car; or you can take a seat inside and have breakfast or lunch.

☾ A must for motor fanatics and youngsters, the **Wells Auto Museum** has more than 80 vintage cars, including a restored Model T you can ride in. ⊠ *U.S. 1* ☎ *207/646–9064* ⊠ *$5* ☉ *Memorial Day–Columbus Day, daily 10–5.*

In the **Wells Reserve at Laudholm Farm,** extensive trails lace the 1,600 acres of meadows, orchards, fields, and salt marshes, as well as two estuaries and 9 mi of seashore. Laudholm Farm, a 17th-century salt-water farm, was a thriving home to livestock for nearly four centuries, growing its own saltwater hay in the extensive marshes. Today, the site houses the visitor center, where an introductory slide show is screened and a bookstore is well stocked with publications of local and state history. Within the farmhouse are rooms with historical exhibits and information; outside in the separate ecology center are learning exhibits geared mainly for kids. In winter, cross-country skiing is permitted. ⊠ *342 Laudholm Farm Rd.* ☎ *207/646–1555* ⊕ *www.wellsreserve.org* 🎫 *$2* ⊗ *Grounds daily 8–5. Visitor center mid-Jan.–mid-Dec., weekdays 10–4 (late May–mid-Oct., weekdays 10–4, Sun. noon–4).*

Leave your car at your hotel and take the **Wells Trolley** to the beach or to the shops on U.S. 1. The seasonal trolley makes pickups at the Wells Transportation Center when the *Downeaster* (the Amtrak train with service from Boston to Portland) pulls in. If you want to continue south toward Ogunquit, the two town trolleys meet at the Wells Chamber of Commerce on U.S. 1; get a route map here. Fare is $2. ☎ *207/646–2451* ⊕ *www.wellschamber.org.*

WHERE TO EAT

$–$$$ ✕ **Billy's Chowder House.** Locals head to this simple restaurant in a salt marsh for the generous lobster rolls, haddock sandwiches, and chowders. Big windows in the bright dining rooms overlook the marsh. ⊠ *216 Mile Rd.* ☎ *207/646–7558* ⊟ *AE, D, MC, V* ⊗ *Closed mid-Dec.–mid-Jan.*

$–$$$ ✕ **Maine Diner.** It's the real thing here—one look at the nostalgic (and authentic 1953) exterior and you start craving good diner food. You'll get a little more here . . . how many greasy spoons make an award-winning lobster pie? That's the house favorite, as well as a heavenly seafood chowder. There's plenty of fried seafood in addition to the usual diner fare, and breakfast is served all day, just as it should be. Be sure to check out the adjacent gift shop, Remember the Maine. ⊠ *2265 U.S. 1.* ☎ *207/646–4441* ⊕ *www.mainediner.com* ⊟ *D, MC, V* ⊗ *Closed 1 wk in Jan.*

¢–$$ ✕ **Cafe at Merriland Farm.** There's a lot going on at this 200-year-old working farm and family affair. It's a great place for breakfast (beginning at 8 AM)—homegrown berries appear in jams, jellies, crepes, pancakes, spread over Belgian waffles, and any other place they taste good. The menu is quite creative for breakfast and lunch, going well beyond the basics with such treats as Portobello Benedict, artful crepes, grilled sandwiches, wraps, and half-pound burgers. Don't miss the desserts— luscious berries in pie, shortcake, or baked crisp. This farm is a delightful beauty. You may want to hit the on-site golf greens to fight off some of the added calories. From late July until the frost hits, you can pick blueberries to take home. ⊠ *545 Coles Hill Rd.* ☎ *207/646–5040* ⊕ *www.merrilandfarmcafe.com* ⊟ *MC, V* ⊗ *Closed mid-Dec.–Apr. No dinner Sun.–Thurs.*

WHERE TO STAY

$$–$$$**   Grey Gull Inn. This Victorian inn, built in 1893, has views of the open sea and rocks on which seals like to sun themselves. Most of the unpretentious, simply furnished rooms have ocean views. Overnight guests have access to nearby pool, golf, and tennis facilities. The restaurant ($$–$$$$) serves excellent seafood dishes such as soft-shell crabs almandine; and regional fare such as Yankee pot roast, and chicken breast rolled in walnuts. **Pros: Most rooms have great ocean views, walk to beach, many reasonable package deals available. **Cons:** Rooms accessed via steep stairs, not an in-town location. ✉ *475 Webhannet Dr., at Moody Point, 04090* 📞 *207/646–7501* 🖶 *207/646–0938* 🌐 *www.thegreygullinn.com* ➥ *5 rooms* ⚫ *In-hotel: restaurant, no-smoking rooms, public Wi-Fi, no elevator* ⊟ *AE, D, MC, V* ⍾ *CP.*

$$–$$$$ Haven by the Sea. Once the summer mission of St. Martha's Church
FodorsChoice   in Kennebunkport, this stunning, exquisite inn has retained many of the
★   original details from its former life as a seaside church. The cathedral ceilings and stained-glass windows remain, all gathering and spreading the grand surrounding light. The guest rooms are spacious, some with serene marsh views. Four common areas, including one with a fireplace, are perfect spots for afternoon refreshments. The inn is one block from the beach. **Pros:** Unusual structure with elegant appointments, nightly happy hour, walk to beach. **Cons:** Some rooms upstairs, not an in-town location. ✉ *59 Church St., 04090* 📞 *207/646–4194* 🖶 *207/646–6883* 🌐 *www.havenbythesea.com* ➥ *6 rooms, 2 suites, 1 apartment* ⚫ *In-room: Wi-Fi. In-hotel: no kids under 12, no-smoking rooms, no elevator* ⊟ *AE, MC, V* ⍾ *BP.*

$$ Beach Farm Inn. Innkeepers Nancy and Craig painstakingly renovated and decorated this 19th-century farmhouse, and its gracious appointments are a testament to their care and good taste. Craig, also a woodworker, has made a good portion of the furniture as well as sculptures throughout the home. Decorated with a multitude of antiques, four-poster beds, ample sitting areas, and artful rugs, the home is a place of real peace among the general busyness of Wells. The appealing enclosed breakfast area is the stage for Craig's monumental breakfasts served each morning; if it's nice out, eat on the deck overlooking the pool and grounds. Winter packages include wreath-making and cooking workshops. The beach is about a half-mile walk down the country road. **Pros:** Easy access to beaches and activities of Route 1, gracious historic lodging, beautiful grounds and pool. **Cons:** Some rooms share a bath, not all baths are attached, rooms located up steep stairs. ✉ *97 Eldredge Rd., 04090* 📞 *207/646–8493* 🖶 *207/646–5738* 🌐 *www.beachfarminn. com* ➥ *8 rooms, 6 with bath; 2 cottages* ⚫ *In-room: no phone (some), no TV. In-hotel: pool, no kids under 12, no-smoking rooms, no elevator* ⊟ *AE, MC, V* ⍾ *BP.*

NIGHTLIFE & THE ARTS

The **summer concert series** is held in pretty Wells Harbor Park at the gazebo (Saturday nights, July through early September). Music ranges from rock to gospel, reggae to swing; concerts begin around 6:30 and are free. Look for Harbor Road just off U.S. 1 by the fire and police stations; the park is about 1 mi down Harbor Road. **Aran Irish Pub and**

Restaurant (⊠ *52 Post Rd. [U.S. 1]* ☎*207/646–1900*) has—you guessed it—live Irish music most Thursday through Sunday nights in summer.

SPORTS & THE OUTDOORS

With its thousands of acres of marsh and preserved land, Wells is a great place to spend a lot of time outdoors. Nearly 7 mi of sand stretch along the boundaries of Wells, making beach going a prime occupation. Tidal pools sheltered by rocks are filled with all manner of creatures awaiting discovery. Parking is available for a fee (take the trolley!) at **Crescent Beach,** along Webhannet Drive; **Wells Beach** (at the end of Mile Road off U.S. 1) has public rest rooms and two parking areas. There is another lot at the far end of Wells Beach, at the end of Atlantic Avenue. Across the jetty from Wells Harbor is **Drakes Island Beach** (end of Drakes Island Road off U.S. 1), which also has parking and public rest rooms. Lifeguards are on hand at all the beaches. Rent bikes, surfboards, wet suits, boogie boards, and probably a few other things at **Wheels and Waves** (⊠ *578 U.S. 1* ☎*207/646–5774*).

FISHING Many fish are bound to be caught by anglers with **Captain Satch and Sons** (☎*207/337–0716*). It offers two trips daily, from Wells Town Dock. In addition to boat trips, a guide can take you fishing from the shore within the Rachel Carson Reserve. Go fishing along the coast or way out in the deep with *Three Ladies* (☎*207/337–8800*), leaving from Wells Harbor. There's also a two-hour scenic coastal cruise.

GOLFING The 9-hole golf course at **Merriland Farm** (⊠ *545 Cole Hills Rd.* ☎*207/646–0508* ⊕*www.merrilandfarm.com*) is pretty challenging and was built by owner-farmer Jim Morrison amid the blueberry and raspberry patches. The course is open daily (except Tuesday League Day) from April through October, with greens fees of $13. This working, 200-year-old farm also offers blueberry and raspberry picking from late July until the berries run out.

KAYAKING **World Within Sea Kayaking** (☎*207/646–0455* ⊕*www.worldwithin.com*) conducts guided kayaking tours with lessons. Departure points vary.

SHOPPING

Douglas N. Harding Rare Books (⊠ *2152 Post Rd. [U.S. 1]* ☎*207/646–8785*) has more than 100,000 old books, maps, and prints. **Goosefare Antiques** (⊠ *2232 Post Rd. [U.S. 1]* ☎*207/646–0505*) is a group shop specializing in 18th-, 19th-, and early-20th-century antiques. The **Lighthouse Depot** (⊠ *U.S. 1* ☎*207/646–0608*) calls itself the world's largest lighthouse gift store, with lighthouse-theme gifts and memorabilia. **Reed's Antiques and Collectibles** (⊠ *1773 Post Rd. [U.S. 1]* ☎*207/646–8010*) is a multidealer shop filled with all manner of antiques, from advertising to glass, tools to toys. **R. Jorgensen** (⊠ *502 Post Rd. [U.S. 1]* ☎*207/646–9444*) stocks 18th- and 19th-century formal and country antiques from the British Isles, Europe, and the United States. Thousands of 18th- and 19th-century antiques are stuffed into a 200-year-old barn at **Wells General Store** (⊠ *2023 U.S. 1* ☎*207/646–5553*).

EN
ROUTE
Drivers have a multitude of options going north from Wells to the Kennebunks. You can travel along U.S. 1, from Wells to the town of Kennebunk, stopping at every antiques shop along the way. To go directly to Kennebunkport, take Route 9A/35, which is a fairly breathtaking route as far as Colonial and Victorian architecture is concerned. Another route to take from Wells, especially if you are visiting the Rachel Carson National Wildlife Refuge, is Route 9 toward Kennebunkport, along which are beautiful views of salt marshes, farms, and plenty of impressive homes. Route 9 will connect with Route 9A/35; follow the signs to Kennebunkport.

THE KENNEBUNKS

The Kennebunks encompass Kennebunk, Kennebunk Beach, Goose Rocks Beach, Kennebunkport, Cape Porpoise, and Arundel. This cluster of seaside and inland villages provides a little bit of everything—salt marshes, sand beaches, jumbled fishing shacks, and architectural gems.

Handsome white clapboard homes with shutters give Kennebunk, an early 19th-century shipbuilding center, a quintessential New England look. The many boutiques and galleries surrounding Dock Square draw visitors to Kennebunkport. People flock to Kennebunkport mostly in summer, but some come in early December when the Christmas Prelude is celebrated on two weekends. Santa arrives by fishing boat, and the Christmas trees are lighted as carolers stroll the sidewalks.

From Kennebunk, Route 35 south leads to Kennebunk's Lower Village. Continue south on Beach Avenue for Kennebunk Beach. To reach Kennebunkport from the Lower Village, head east on Route 9/Western Avenue and cross the drawbridge into Dock Square—technically, you're not in Kennebunkport until you cross that bridge. Continue east on Route 9, or take scenic Ocean Avenue and Wildes District Road to quiet Cape Porpoise. To access Goose Rocks Beach, continue east on Route 9, which is now called the Mills Road. Arundel is between Kennebunk and Kennebunkport.

KENNEBUNK

Approximately 6 mi north of Wells via U.S. 1; 23 mi south of Portland via Maine Tpke.

Sometimes bypassed to get to its more touristed sister town of Kennebunkport, Kennebunk has its own appeal. In the 19th century the town was a major shipbuilding center; docks lined the river with hundreds of workers busily crafting the vessels that would bring immense fortune to some of the area's residents. Although the trade is long gone, the evidence that remains of this great wealth exists in Kennebunk's numerous impressive mansions. Kennebunk is a classic small New England town, with an inviting shopping district, steepled churches, and fine examples of 18th- and 19th-century brick and clapboard homes.

KENNEBUNK WALKING TOURS

To take a little walking tour of Kennebunk's most notable structures, begin from the Federal-style Brick Store Museum, on Main Street. Head south on Main Street (turn left out of the museum) to see several extraordinary 18th-century homes, including the Nathaniel Frost House at 99 Main Street (1799) and the Benjamin Brown House at 85 Main Street (1788).

When you've had your fill of historic homes, head back up toward the museum, pass the 1773 First Parish Unitarian Church (its Asher-Benjamin–style steeple contains the original Paul Revere bell) and turn right onto Summer Street. This street is an architectural showcase, revealing an array of styles from Colonial to Federal. Walking amid these grand beauties will give you a real sense of the economic prowess and glamour of the long-gone shipbuilding industry.

For a guided architectural walking tour of Summer Street, contact the Brick Store Museum at 207/985–4802.

For a dramatic walk along the rocky coastline and beneath the views of Ocean Avenue's grand mansions, head out on the **Parson's Way Shore Walk**, a paved, 4.8-mi round-trip. Begin at Dock Square and follow Ocean Avenue along the river, passing the Colony Hotel and St. Ann's Church, all the way to Walker's Point. You can simply turn back from here, or take a left onto Wildes District Road for a walk amid more luxury homes and trees.

There are also plenty of natural spaces for walking, swimming, birding, and biking.

The town of Kennebunk is divided between two villages; the upper extends around the Mousam River on Route 9 while the lower is several miles down Route 35, just shy of Kennebunkport proper. The drive down Route 35 keeps visitors agog with the splendor of the area's mansions, spread out on both sides of the road. To get to the grand and gentle beaches of Kennebunk, go straight on Beach Avenue from the intersection of Routes 9 and 35 in the lower village.

WHAT TO SEE

The cornerstone of the **Brick Store Museum,** a block-long preservation of early-19th-century commercial buildings, is **William Lord's Brick Store.** Built as a dry-goods store in 1825 in the Federal style, the building has an open-work balustrade across the roof line, granite lintels over the windows, and paired chimneys. Exhibits chronicle Kennebunk's relationship with the sea. The museum leads architectural walking tours of Kennebunk's historic Summer Street on Wednesday and Friday, from mid-June through late August. ⌧*117 Main St., Kennebunk* ☎*207/985–4802* ⊕*www.brickstoremuseum.org* ⌦*Donations accepted; walking tours $5* ⊙*Tues.–Fri. 10–4:30, Sat. 10–1.*

Built in 1773, just before the American Revolution, the stunning **First Parish Unitarian Church** is a marvel. The 1804 Asher-Benjamin–style steeple stands proudly atop the village, and the sounds of the original

Paul Revere bell can be heard for miles. It holds Sunday services, and on Tuesdays in the summer, historic tours of the sanctuary take place at 10 AM. ⊠ *Main St.*

WHERE TO EAT & STAY

\$\$\$\$ ✕ **White Barn Inn.** Formally attired waiters, meticulous service, and
★ exquisite food have earned this restaurant accolades as one of the best in New England. Regional New England fare is served in a rustic but elegant dining room. The three-course, prix fixe menu (\$90), which changes weekly, might include steamed Maine lobster nestled on fresh fettuccine with carrots, ginger, and snow peas. ⊠ *37 Beach Ave., Kennebunk* ☎ *207/967–2321* ⚄ *Reservations essential Jacket required* 🗐 *AE, MC, V* ☉ *Closed 3 wks in Jan. No lunch.*

\$\$\$–\$\$\$\$ ✕ **Windows on the Water.** Its higher perch offers glimpses of Dock Square
★ and the working harbor of Kennebunkport below, though the food within rates much higher than the views beyond. The wild shrimp and lobster ravioli is a noteworthy entrée; in summer, take advantage of the native striped bass offered. A recent addition is the popular White Porch Bistrot, offering more casual fare and some unusual wine events that have attracted much local attention. Unlike many of the other finer dining establishments in the area, this one pledges in its mission statement to keep prices moderate—something unusual in this part of town. A restaurant with a conscience, the kitchen has also long regarded the support of sustainable fisheries and locally grown meat and produce. ⊠ *12 Chase Hill Rd., Kennebunkport* ☎ *207/967–3313* ⚄ *Reservations essential* 🗐 *AE, D, DC, MC, V.*

\$\$–\$\$\$\$ ✕ **Grissini.** This popular trattoria draws high praise for its northern Italian cuisine. Dine by the stone hearth on inclement days or on the patio when the weather's fine. You can mix and match appetizers, pizzas, salads, pastas, and entrées from the menu to suit your hunger and budget. ⊠ *27 Western Ave., Kennebunk* ☎ *207/967–2211* 🗐 *AE, MC, V.*

\$–\$\$\$ ✕ **Federal Jack's.** Run by the Kennebunkport Brewing Company, the complex is housed in an old shipbuilding warehouse right on the water. Many different beers are handcrafted on-site, including such favorites as 'Taint Town Ale (so named because the brewery 'taint quite Kennebunk and taint quite Kennebunkport) and Goat Island Light—try the sampler if you can't decide. The food is American pub style with lots of seafood elements; the clam chowder is rich and satisfying. There's also Sunday brunch, and a late-night menu for those who get hungry while playing pool in the back room. Brew tours are available. You can find the restaurant and brewery just before the bridge into Kennebunkport. ⊠ *8 Western Ave., Lower Village* ☎ *207/967–4322* 🗐 *AE, MC, V.*

\$\$–\$\$\$ ✕🖃 **Kennebunk Inn.** This stately brick building has quite a presence on Main Street in downtown Kennebunk. Perpetual renovation and upgrades have been giving this inn more dignity and comfort, slowly erasing the boardinghouse feel that could come from a multitude of rooms, arranged astride long, creaky corridors. Aged wood floors have been refinished to their shining origins and rooms are simply decorated with antiques. There's nothing fussy about the place. The real pride here is in the dining room, where the husband-and-wife chef-owner team do an incredible job with their restaurant (\$\$–\$\$\$). The brasserie-

All About Lobsters

Judging from the current price of a lobster dinner, it's hard to believe that lobsters were once so plentiful that servants in rich households would have contracts stating they could be served lobster "no more than two times a week."

The going price for lobsters in the 1840s was three cents per lobster—not per pound, per lobster. Today, Maine is nearly synonymous with lobsters, the fishery being one of Maine's primary industries. Well over 60 million pounds of lobster are landed a year in the state, making Maine, by far, the biggest supplier in the nation.

Because of the size restrictions, most of the lobsters you find in restaurants weigh 1¼ to 1½ pounds. However, lobsters can actually grow much larger and live to a ripe old age. The largest lobster ever caught off the coast of Maine weighed in at nearly 45 pounds and was more than 50 years old!

For an authentic, Maine-style lobster dinner, you must go to a lobster pound. Finding one should not be difficult. Generally, these places are rustic and simple—they look more like fish-packing plants than restaurants. Hundreds of freshly caught lobsters of varying sizes are kept in pens, waiting for customers. Service is simple in the extreme. You usually sit at a wooden picnic table, and eat off a thick paper plate. A classic "Downeast" feast includes lobster—boiled or steamed—with clam chowder, steamers, potato, and corn on the cob—and, of course, a large bib tied around your neck.

—Stephen Allen

style menu is nicely varied, including such treats as black truffle French gnocchi, lobster corn croquettes, salads, and wraps. **Pros:** Great in-town location, reasonable rates for the area, comfortable and spacious rooms in historic building. **Cons:** Rooms are located on second and third floors, no water views or beachfront. ⊠*45 Main St., Kennebunk 04043* ☎*207/985–3351* 🖷*207/985–8865* ⊕*www.thekennebunkinn. com* ⤶*19 rooms, 6 suites* ⌂*In-room: no phone, kitchen (some), Wi-Fi. In-hotel: restaurant, bar, some pets allowed, no-smoking rooms, no elevator* ⊟*AE, D, MC, V* ⏐○⏐*CP.*

$$$$ ⌗**The Seaside.** This handsome seaside property has been in the hands of
ⓒ   the Severance family since 1667. The modern hotel units, all with slid-ing-glass doors that open onto private decks or patios (half with ocean views), are appropriate for families; so are the cottages with one to four bedrooms. You can't get much closer to Kennebunk Beach. **Pros:** Ideal beachfront location, lawn games available, great ocean views from upper-floor rooms. **Cons:** Rooms are hotel standard and a little out-dated (but fairly sized), not an in-town location. ⊠*80 Beach Ave., Kennebunk 04046* ☎*207/967–4461 or 866/300–6750* 🖷*207/967–1135* ⊕*www.kennebunkbeachmaine.com* ⤶*22 rooms, 11 cottages* ⌂*In-room: refrigerator, Wi-Fi. In-hotel: beachfront, laundry service, public Internet, no-smoking rooms, no elevator* ⊟*AE, MC, V* ⊘*Cottages closed Nov.–May* ⏐○⏐*CP.*

$$$$ ⌗**White Barn Inn.** For a romantic overnight stay, you need look no
★   further than the exclusive White Barn Inn, known for its attentive, pampering service. No detail has been overlooked in the meticulously appointed rooms, from plush bedding and reading lamps to robes and slippers. Rooms are in the main inn and adjacent buildings. Some have fireplaces, hot tubs, and luxurious baths with steam showers. The inn is within walking distance (10–15 minutes) of Dock Square and the beach. **Pros:** Elegant, luxurious lodging; full-service; in a historic building. **Cons:** No water views or beachfront, overly steep lodging prices, not in town. ⊠*37 Beach Ave., Box 560C, Kennebunk 04046* ☎*207/967–2321* 🖷*207/967–1100* ⊕*www.whitebarninn.com* ⤶*16 rooms, 9 suites* ⌂*In-room: VCR, DVD, Wi-Fi. In-hotel: restaurant, bar, pool, spa, bicycles, concierge, laundry service, public Internet, no kids under 12, no-smoking rooms, no elevator* ⊟*AE, MC, V* ⏐○⏐*CP.*

$$$–$$$$ ⌗**Bufflehead Cove Inn.** On the Kennebunk River at the end of a wind-ing dirt road, this gray-shingle B&B sits amid quiet country fields and apple trees. Surprisingly, however, it's only five minutes from Dock Square. Rooms in the main house are outfitted with a funky mix of antiques, Far Eastern, and eclectic art. The Hideaway Suite, with a two-sided gas fireplace, king-size bed, and large whirlpool tub, overlooks the river. The Garden Studio has a fireplace and offers the most privacy. It's a great place to bring your kayaks or canoe for paddling trips right from the dock; or simply opt to gaze upon the river from the expansive wraparound porch. The roomy cottage, set back a ways from the main house, has a large private deck with generous water views and deca-dent touches like a wood-burning fireplace and a two-person whirlpool tub; a two-night minimum stay is required. **Pros:** Beautiful and peace-ful pastoral setting, ideal riverfront location, perfect for a serene get-

1

away. **Con:** A short drive from town. ✉ *18 Bufflehead Cove Rd., Box 499, Kennebunk 04046* ☎☎ *207/967–3879* ⊕ *www.buffleheadcove. com* ◄ *2 rooms, 3 suites, 1 cottage* ☆ *In-room: no phone, refrigerator (some), Wi-Fi. In-hotel: public Internet, no kids under 12, no-smoking rooms, no elevator* ⊟ *D, MC, V* ◎ *Closed Dec.–Apr.* ⎮◎⎮*BP.*

$$ ☷ **Waldo Emerson House.** The home itself is a historical gold mine, made grand with unusual maritime architectural touches by a shipbuilder in 1784 and later home to the great-uncle of beloved poet Ralph Waldo Emerson (the writer spent many youthful summers in the house). It's believed that the house was also a stop on the famed Underground Railroad. Notice the sliding wooden panels in the windows, said to keep inhabitants safe from the soaring arrows of angry Indians. The elegance of the wide-plank pine floors remains, as does some remarkable original tile work around the many fireplaces. Rooms are spacious and filled with antiques and colorful quilts; plus all rooms have working fireplaces. Innkeepers Kathy and John Daamen provide a shuttle to area beaches and operate the Mainely Quilts gift shop next door. **Pros:** Good base for exploring both Kennebunk and Kennebunkport, authentic historic lodging, complimentary afternoon tea. **Cons:** Most rooms accessed via steep stairs, no water views or beachfront, not an in-town location. ✉ *108 Summer St. (Rte. 35), Kennebunk 04046* ☎ *207/985–4250* ⊕ *www.waldoemersoninn.com* ◄ *4 rooms* ☆ *In-room: no phone, no TV (some), Wi-Fi. In-hotel: public Internet, no kids under 6, no-smoking rooms, no elevator* ⊟ *AE, D, MC, V* ⎮◎⎮*BP.*

SPORTS & THE OUTDOORS

Kennebunk Beach has three parts: Gooch's Beach, Mother's Beach, and Kennebunk Beach. Beach Road, with its cottages and old Victorian boardinghouses, runs right behind them. Gooch's and Kennebunk attract teenagers; Mother's Beach, which has a small playground and tidal puddles for splashing, is popular with families. For parking permits (a fee is charged in summer), go to the **Kennebunk Town Office** (✉ *1 Summer St. [Rte. 35]* ☎ *207/985–2102* ◎ *Weekdays, 8:30–4:30*).

For an unusual exploring treat, visit the **Kennebunk Plains** (✉ *Rte. 99 west, a few miles out of Kennebunk* ☎ *207/729–5181*), a 1,100-acre protected grasslands habitat that is home to several rare and endangered species of vegetation and wildlife. Locally known as the blueberry plains, a good portion of the area is abloom with the hues of ripening wild blueberries in late July; after August 1 visitors are welcome to pick and eat all the berries they can find. The roads take you through vast grasslands and scrub oak woods, and by ponds. The area is maintained by the Nature Conservancy and is open daily from sunrise to sunset.

Three-mile-long **Goose Rocks**, a few minutes' drive north of town off Route 9, has plenty of shallow pools for exploring and a good long stretch of smooth sand; it's a favorite of families with small children. You can pick up a parking permit ($6 a day, $25 a week) at the **chamber of commerce** (✉ *17 Western Ave., Lower Village* ☎ *207/967–0857* ◎ *Weekdays, 10–5, weekends June—early Oct.*).

SHOPPING

The **Gallery on Chase Hill** (✉ *10 Chase Hill Rd., Kennebunk* ☎ *207/967–0049*) presents original artwork by Maine and New England artists. **Marlow's Artisans Gallery** (✉ *39 Main St., Kennebunk* ☎ *207/985–2931*) carries a large and eclectic collection of crafts. **Tom's of Maine Natural Living Store** (✉ *52 Main St., Kennebunk* ☎ *207/985–6331*) sells all-natural personal-care products.

EN ROUTE The drive from Kennebunk to Kennebunkport will take you by the **Wedding Cake House** (✉ *104 Summer St. [Rte. 35], Kennebunk*). The legend behind this confection in fancy wood fretwork is that its builder, a sea captain, was forced to set sail in the middle of his wedding; the house was his bride's consolation for the lack of a wedding cake. It is not open to the public.

KENNEBUNKPORT

Approximately 6 mi north of Wells via U.S. 1; approximately 22 mi south of Portland.

The area focused around the water and Dock Square in Kennebunkport is where you can find the most activity (and crowds) in the Kennebunks. Winding alleys reveal shops and restaurants geared to the tourist trade, right in the midst of a hardworking harbor. Kennebunkport has been a resort area since the 19th century but its most famous residents have made it even more popular—the presidential Bush family is often in residence in their immense home, which sits dramatically out on Walker's Point. The amount of wealth here is as tangible as the sharp sea breezes and the sounds of seagulls overhead. Newer mansions have sprung up alongside the old; a great way to see them is to take a slow drive out along Ocean Avenue.

Get a good overview of the sights with an **Intown Trolley** tour. The narrated 45-minute jaunts leave every hour starting at 10 AM at the designated stop on Ocean Avenue, around the corner of Dock Square. The fare is valid for the day so you can hop on and off at your leisure. ✉ *Ocean Ave., Kennebunkport* ☎ *207/967–3686* ⊕ *www.intowntrolley.com* 🎫 *$13 all-day fare* ☉ *Late May–mid-Oct., daily 10–5.*

WHAT TO SEE

The heart and pulse of this busy little area is **Dock Square,** the town center. Boutiques, T-shirt shops, art galleries, crafts stores, and restaurants encircle the square and spread out alongside streets and alleys. Many businesses close in winter, but those that stay open tend to offer nice discounts in December. Walk onto the drawbridge to admire the tidal Kennebunk River.

The **Nott House,** also known as White Columns, is an imposing Greek Revival mansion with Doric columns. The 1853 house is furnished with the belongings of four generations of the Perkins-Nott family. Maintained by the Kennebunkport Historical Society, it is open for guided tours and also serves as a gathering place for village walking tours, offered Thursday and Saturday at 11. The society also runs the

1

History Center of Kennebunkport, a mile away from the Nott House on North Street, which includes several exhibit buildings containing an old schoolhouse and jail cells; it's open year-round. ⊠ *8 Maine St., Kennebunkport* ☎ *207/967–2751* ⊕ *www.kporthistory.org* ☜ *$5 for house tours; $5 for walking tours; $9 combination ticket* ⊙ *Mid-June– mid-Oct., Wed.–Fri. 10–4, Sat. 10–1.*

★ The **Seashore Trolley Museum** displays streetcars built from 1872 to 1972
☼ and includes trolleys from major metropolitan areas and world capitals—Boston to Budapest, New York to Nagasaki, San Francisco to Sydney—all beautifully restored. Best of all, you can take a trolley ride for nearly 4 mi on the tracks of the former Atlantic Shoreline trolley line, with a stop along the way at the museum restoration shop, where trolleys are transformed from junk into gems. Both guided and self-guided tours are available. ⊠ *195 Log Cabin Rd., Kennebunkport* ☎ *207/967–2800* ⊕ *www.trolleymuseum.org* ☜ *$8.50* ⊙ *Early May– mid-Oct., daily 10–4:30; reduced hrs in spring and fall, call ahead.*

WHERE TO EAT

$$–$$$$ ✕ **Mabel's Lobster Claw.** Mabel's has long been serving lobsters, homemade pies, and lots of seafood for lunch and dinner in this tiny dwelling out on Ocean Avenue. With its paneled walls, wooden booths, autographed photos of various TV stars (plus several members of the Bush family), and paper place mats that illustrate how to eat a Maine lobster, this place is a simple little classic. The house favorite is the Lobster Savannah—split and filled with scallops, shrimp, and mushrooms in a Newburg sauce. Make sure to save room for the peanut butter ice-cream pie. Reservations are recommended. ⊠ *124 Ocean Ave., Kennebunkport* ☎ *207/967–2562* ⊟ *AE, D, MC, V* ⊙ *Closed Nov.–Apr.*

$$–$$$$ ✕ **Pier 77 Restaurant & the Ramp Bar & Grille.** The view takes center stage at this duo establishment, consisting of a fine dining portion and the more casual and boisterous Ramp. Pier 77 serves up more sophisticated fare, focusing on meats and seafood; the Ramp pays homage to a really good burger, fried seafood and other pub-style choices. The place is vibrant with live music most nights in summer and a great place for cocktails on the water. ⊠ *77 Pier Rd., Cape Porpoise* ☎ *207/967–8500* ⊟ *AE, D, DC, MC, V* ⊙ *Closed late Oct.–mid-Mar.*

WHERE TO STAY

$$$$ ▦ **Cape Arundel Inn.** This shingle-style inn commands a magnificent ocean view that takes in the Bush estate at Walker's Point. The spacious rooms are furnished with country-style furniture and antiques, and most have sitting areas with ocean views. You can relax on the front porch or by the fireplace. The Rockbound complex, a later addition (1950s), doesn't have the 19th-century charm of the main house, but the rooms are large, many have fireplaces, and all have private balconies from which to take in the views. In the candlelit dining room ($$$–$$$$), open to the public for dinner, every table has a view of the surf. The menu changes seasonally. **Pros:** Extraordinary views from most rooms, close to town and attractions. **Cons:** Most rooms accessed via stairs, not for the budget-minded. ⊠ *208 Ocean Ave., Kennebunkport 04046* ☎ *207/967–2125* ⊟ *207/967–1199* ⊕ *www.capearundelinn.com* ⇘ *19*

rooms, 1 suite ✦*In-room: no a/c, no phone, no TV (some), Wi-Fi. In-hotel: restaurant, bicycles, no-smoking rooms, no elevator* ▭*AE, D, MC, V* ⊗*Closed Jan. and Feb.* ⦿|*CP.*

$$$–$$$$ ▦ **The Colony.** You can't miss this place—it's grand, white, and incred-
Fodor'sChoice   ibly large, set majestically atop a rise overlooking the ocean. The
★   hotel was built in 1914 (after its predecessor caught fire in 1898), and much of the splendid glamour of this earlier era remains. Many of the rooms in the main hotel (there are two other outbuildings) have breezy ocean views from private or semiprivate balconies. All are outfitted with antiques and hardwood floors; the bright white bed linens nicely set off the colors of the Waverly wallpaper. The restaurant ($$–$$$$) features New England fare, with plenty of seafood, steaks, and other favorites. The Colony is also Maine's first environmentally responsible hotel. **Pros:** Lodging in the tradition of grand old hotels, many ocean views, plenty of activities and entertainment for all ages. **Cons:** Not for those looking for more intimate or peaceful lodging, rooms with ocean views come at steep prices. ✉*Ocean Ave., 04046* ☎*207/967–3331 or 800/552–2363* ⊟*207/967–8738* ⊕*www.thecolonyhotel.com/maine* ↘*124 rooms* ✦*In-room: no a/c (some), no TV (some), Wi-Fi. In-hotel: restaurant, room service, bar, pool, beachfront, bicycles, no-smoking rooms, some pets allowed* ▭*AE, MC, V* ⊗*Closed Nov.–mid-May* ⦿|*BP.*

$$$$ ▦ **Captain Lord Mansion.** Of all the mansions in Kennebunkport's his-
Fodor'sChoice   toric district that have been converted to inns, the 1812 Captain Lord
★   Mansion is the most stately and sumptuously appointed. Distinctive architecture, including a suspended elliptical staircase, gas fireplaces in all rooms, and near-museum-quality accoutrements, make for a formal but not stuffy setting. Six rooms have whirlpool tubs. The extravagant suite has two fireplaces, a double whirlpool, a hydro-massage body spa, a TV/DVD and stereo system, and a king-size canopy bed. Day-spa services are available for added luxury. **Pros:** Elegant and luxurious historic lodging, in-town location, beautiful landscaped grounds and gardens. **Cons:** Not for those on a tight budget, not a beachfront location. ✉*Pleasant and Green Sts., Box 800, Kennebunkport 04046* ☎*207/967–3141* ⊟*207/967–3172* ⊕*www.captainlord.com* ↘*15 rooms, 1 suite* ✦*In-room: no TV, Wi-Fi. In-hotel: bicycles, public Internet, no kids under 12, no-smoking rooms, no elevator* ▭*D, MC, V* ⦿|*BP.*

$$$$ ▦ **Nonantum Resort.** This sprawling resort right on the banks of the Kennebunk River combines a bit of 19th-century feel with modern amenities. Rooms in the giant main building (the Carriage House Inn), parts of which were built in the 1880s, are simply furnished with iron beds adorned with quilts. Long corridors house the numerous rooms, many of which have good views of the river. The ancient, staff-operated elevator in the main house is somewhat helpful for climbing the multiple floors to the lodging rooms, but nary a couple and their baggage would actually fit within those old doors. Rooms in the adjacent Portside Lodge are decidedly more sleek and modern, hotel-standard style, and some have private decks overlooking the water. Bustling in summer, the resort has a boat dock, a full schedule of kids' programs (and babysitting services) as well as a host of lawn games. It's also a very popular site for weddings and business conventions. Fishing, sailing, and lobster boat excursions leave right from the resort's dock; kayak rentals are also available. **Pros:** Ideal for families and business travelers, plenty of activities on the ample grounds, nice riverfront location. **Cons:** Not for those looking for a quiet retreat (think lots of kids, lots of weddings), non-water-view rooms in main inn are a little cramped and have views of the parking lot. ⊠ *95 Ocean Ave., Kennebunkport 04043* ☎*207/967–4050 or 800/552–5651* ⊕*www.nonantumresort. com* ⤏*115 rooms* ♿*In-room: kitchen (some), Wi-Fi. In-hotel: restaurant, bar, pool, beachfront, water sports, children's programs, no-smoking rooms* ▭*D, DC, MC, V* ⊗*Closed Jan.–Mar.* ⑂*BP.*

$$$ 🖳**Rhumb Line.** Although the rooms are standard motel fare, the facilities set this family-friendly motor lodge apart. It's on the trolley line, making getting around Kennebunk-area sites easy. Lobster bakes (extra charge) are held in the evening on weekends from late May through June, and daily from July through August. **Pros:** Reasonably priced lodging for area, spacious and comfortable rooms, plenty of activities on the property. **Cons:** Not a waterfront location, rooms are very standard with little character. ⊠*Ocean Ave., Box 3067, Kennebunkport 04046* ☎*207/967–5457 or 800/337–4862* 🖷*207/967–4418* ⊕*www. rhumblinemaine.com* ⤏*56 rooms, 3 suites* ♿*In-room: refrigerator, Wi-Fi. In-hotel: restaurant, pools, gym, no-smoking rooms, no elevator* ▭*AE, D, MC, V* ⑂*CP.*

THE ARTS

Lively summer theater performances are held in a 19th-century barn Tuesday through Sunday with some matinees at the **Arundel Barn Playhouse** (⊠*53 Old Post Rd., Arundel* ☎*207/985–5552*).

SPORTS & THE OUTDOORS

BIKING **Cape-Able Bike Shop** (⊠*83 Arundel Rd., Kennebunkport* ☎*207/967–4382*) rents bicycles of all types, including trailer bikes and tandems.

BOATING & To reserve a private sail for up to six people, contact Captain Jim Jan-
FISHING netti of the *Bellatrix* (⊠*Kennebunkport* ☎*207/967–8685* ⊕*www.sailingtrips.com*), a vintage racing yacht. He'll teach you the ropes if you wish. Find and catch fish with **Cast Away Fishing Charters** (✉*Box 245, Kennebunkport 04046* ☎*207/284–1740* ⊕*www.castawayfishingcharters.com*). *First Chance* (⊠*4-A Western Ave., Kennebunk* ☎*207/967–5507 or 800/767–2628*) leads whale-watching cruises and guarantees sightings in season. Daily scenic lobster cruises are also offered aboard *Kylie's Chance.* For half- or full-day fishing trips as well as discovery trips for kids, book some time with **Lady J Sportfishing Charters** (⊠*Arundel Wharf, Ocean Ave.* ☎*207/985–7304* ⊕*www.ladyjcharters.com*).

🄲 Several scenic cruises and lobster-trap hauling trips run daily aboard the *Rugosa* (⊠*Depart from Nonantum Resort, Ocean Ave.* ☎*207/967–5595*).

SHOPPING

Abacus (⊠*2 Ocean Ave., Dock Sq., Kennebunkport* ☎*207/967–0111*) sells eclectic crafts and furniture. **Kennebunkport Arts** (⊠*1 Spring St., Dock Sq., Kennebunkport* ☎*207/967–3690*) is a contemporary crafts gallery with a good selection of unusual items for the home. **Mast Cove Galleries** (⊠*Mast Cove La., Kennebunkport* ☎*207/967–3453*) sells graphics, paintings, and sculpture by 105 artists.

EN ROUTE For a rewarding drive that goes into the reaches of the coastline on the way to Old Orchard Beach, head out of Kennebunkport on Route 9. It winds through the charming resort villages of Camp Ellis and Ocean Park, so plan to do some beach walking at Goose Rocks Beach and Fortunes Rocks Beach. You could also pack a picnic and spend some time at Ferry Beach State Park. The varied landscapes in the park include forested sections, swamp, beach, and lots of dunes, all of which have miles of marked trails to hike.

Past the park, Route 9 continues to wind through wooded areas, heads through the slightly weary-looking old mill town of Biddeford, across the Saco River, and into Saco, a busy town with commerce and its accompanying traffic. Once you get past Saco, Route 9 returns to its peaceful curves and gentle scenery, leaving crowded civilization behind. It's a longer route to Old Orchard Beach but worth it for the gems to be found along the way.

OLD ORCHARD BEACH AREA

15 mi north of Kennebunkport, 18 mi south of Portland.

Back in the late 19th century, Old Orchard Beach was a classic, upscale, place-to-be-seen resort area. The railroad brought wealthy families who were looking for entertainment and the benefits of the fresh sea air. Although a good bit of this aristocratic hue has dulled in more-modern times—admittedly, the place is more than a little pleasantly tacky these days—Old Orchard Beach remains a good place for those looking for entertainment and thrills by the sea.

The center of the action is a 7-mi strip of sand beach and its accompanying amusement park, which resembles a small Coney Island. Despite the summertime crowds and fried-food odors, the atmosphere can be captivating. During the 1940s and '50s, in the heyday of the Big Band era, the pier had a dance hall where stars of the time performed. Fire claimed the end of the pier—at one time it jutted out nearly 1,800 feet into the sea—but booths with games and candy concessions still line both sides. In summer the town sponsors fireworks (on Thursday night). Places to stay run the gamut from cheap motels to cottage colonies to full-service seasonal hotels. You won't find free parking in town, but there are ample lots. Amtrak has a seasonal stop here.

WHAT TO SEE

A world away from the beach scene, **Ocean Park** (☎207/934–9068 *Ocean Park Association*) lies on the southwestern edge of town. Locals and visitors like to keep the separation distinct, touting their area as a more peaceful and wholesome family-style village. This vacation community was founded in 1881 by Free Will Baptist leaders as an inter-denominational retreat with both religious and educational purposes, following the example of Chautauqua, New York. Today the community still hosts an impressive variety of cultural happenings, including movies, concerts, recreation, workshops, and religious services. Most are presented in the Temple, which is on the National Register of Historic Places. Although the religious nature of the place is apparent in its worship schedule and some of its cultural offerings, visitors need not be a member of any denomination; all are welcome. There's even a public shuffleboard area for those not interested in the neon carnival attractions several miles up the road. Get an old-fashioned raspberry lime rickey at the Ocean Park Soda Fountain (near the library, at Furber Park); it's also a good place for breakfast or a light lunch.

☾ **Palace Playland,** open from mid-April to Labor Day, has rides, booths, and a roller coaster that drops almost 50 feet. Every week is the Fourth of July here: each Thursday night in summer, sky watchers are treated to a fireworks display. Admission to the park is free; ride passes can be purchased individually (about $1.10 per ticket, with rides requiring 2 to 4 tickets); an all-day, unlimited ride pass is about $27. ⊠*1 Old Orchard St.* ☎*207/934–2001.*

WHERE TO EAT & STAY

$$$–$$$$ ✕**Joseph's by the Sea.** Large windows frame the ocean opening up beyond the dunes at this fine restaurant, which offers outdoor dining in season. Appetizers may include goat cheese terrine and lobster potato pancake. Try the grilled Tuscan swordfish or seared sea scallops. Breakfast is also served daily in summer. ⊠*55 W. Grand Ave., Old Orchard Beach* ☎*207/934–5044* ▭*MC, V.*

$$–$$$$ ✕**The Landmark.** This restaurant almost feels as if it doesn't belong
★ here, at least not in this modern transformation of Old Orchard Beach. Tables are set either on the glassed-in porch or within high, tin-ceiling rooms. Candles and a collection of giant fringed art nouveau lamps provide a warm, gentle light. The menu has a good selection of seafood and meats, many treated with either Asian or Mediterranean flavors; the mahimahi might be seared and served with a coconut cream sauce. It's the kind of menu that encourages you to try new things and you definitely won't be disappointed. The tiramisu is divine. Reservations are recommended. ⊠*25 E. Grand Ave., Old Orchard Beach* ☎*207/934–0156* ▭*AE, D, MC, V* ☾*Closed early Jan.–late Mar.*

$–$$ ✕**DennyMike's.** In Old Orchard Beach, you can't help but notice the heavenly smells of briskets and ribs wafting down the street from this bold and authentic barbecue joint. If you've had your fill of lobster and fried seafood, bring your appetite here. Owner DennyMike is no Texan, but that's where he learned the secret of his craft. Portions are very generous; dinner feasts come with a choice of two sides—absolutely get the beans. There's also a good selection of giant burgers, specialty barbecue sandwiches, and hand-cut fries that rival any sold on the pier. It just might be the best barbecue in New England. Takeout and delivery are available. ⊠*27 W. Grand Ave., Old Orchard Beach* ☎*207/934–2207* ▤*MC, V* ⊘*Closed mid-Oct.–mid-May.*

$$–$$$$ 📷**Old Orchard Beach Inn.** Dating from 1730, this is Old Orchard Beach's oldest inn. Saved from impending demolition in the late 1990s, the entire place was completely renovated with great care and attention to historic detail. The spacious guest rooms are furnished with antiques, area rugs cover the pine floors, quilts brighten the beds, and lace curtains frame the windows. Many rooms have views over the town and of the shimmering Atlantic beyond. The location is ideal—quiet yet very close to the action in the town center. **Pros:** Authentic historic lodging (listed on the National Historic Register), set back off the busy main drag but within short distance to all the action. **Cons:** Rooms accessed via steep stairs, not a beachfront location. ⊠*6 Portland Ave., 04064* ☎*207/934–5834 or 877/700–6624* 🖷*207/934–0782* ⊕*www. oldorchardbeachinn.com* ↵*17 rooms, 1 suite* ⅋*In-room: dial-up. In-hotel: no-smoking rooms, no elevator* ▤*AE, D, MC, V* ⏣*CP.*

$$–$$$ 📷**Billow House Inn.** Right behind the dunes of the beach is this gracious B&B–motel complex. All rooms, whether in the motel-style units or within the main 1881 house, are attractively adorned with colorful quilts and ample sitting areas and have decks so guests can partake of the water views. All guests are spoiled with afternoon fresh-baked cookies in their rooms. **Pros:** Ideal beachfront location, perfect for travelers who will cook some of their own meals, set within active Ocean Park community—lots of events happening. **Cons:** Not for those who wish to be in the thick of Old Orchard Beach activity, many rooms accessed via stairs. ⊠*2 Temple Ave., Ocean Park04063* ☎*207/934–2333 or 888/767–7776* 🖷*207/934–1510* ⊕*www.billowhouse.com* ↵*13 rooms, 3 suites* ⅋*In-room: no a/c (some), kitchen (some), refrigerator. In-hotel: beachfront, public Internet, no-smoking rooms, no elevator* ▤*AE, MC, V* ⏣*CP.*

NIGHTLIFE & THE ARTS

In season, local performers play everything from country and oldies to reggae and rock in Town Square every Monday and Tuesday night at 7. Fireworks light the sky on Thursday night at 9:30 from late June through Labor Day. Concerts by classically trained musicians and choir groups are held most Sunday evenings in Ocean Park. Several bars in Old Orchard Beach feature live bands, dancing, and karaoke.

The community of **Ocean Park** (⊕*www.oceanpark.org*) has a lively and varied cultural scene. Educational lectures, musical programs and concerts, storytelling, dances, and even yoga classes are offered daily throughout summer. All are welcome; check the Web site or get a copy of their summer program for an event schedule. The home of Salvation Army Camp Meetings (the Salvation Army has been holding these religious-based meetings in this spot since the late 1800s), the **Old Orchard Beach Pavilion** (⊠*Union Ave. and 6th St., Old Orchard Beach* ☎*207/934–2024* ⊕*www.oobpavilion.org*) also hosts classical concerts including choirs, orchestras, and brass bands from throughout the New England area. Free parking is available.

SPORTS & THE OUTDOORS

Not far from Old Orchard Beach is the Maine Audubon–run **Scarborough Marsh Nature Center** (⊠ *Pine Point Rd. [Rte. 9], Scarborough* ☎ *207/883–5100* ⊕ *www.maineaudubon.org* ⊠ Free, guided tours begin at $5 ☉ *Memorial Day–Sept.*). You can rent a canoe and explore this natural haven on your own, or sign up for a guided trip. The salt marsh is Maine's largest and is an excellent place for bird-watching and peaceful paddling amid its winding ways. The Nature Center has a discovery room for kids, programs for all ages ranging from basket making to astronomy, birding and canoe tours, and a good gift shop.

THE SOUTHERN COAST ESSENTIALS

To research prices, get advice from other travelers, and book travel arrangements, visit www.fodors.com.

TRANSPORTATION

BY AIR

If traveling to the Southern Coast by air, most visitors fly into Portland International Jetport (⇨ *see Greater Portland Essentials in Chapter 2*), which is 35 mi northeast of Kennebunk. Limited air service is also available from Pease International airport in Portsmouth/Newington, New Hampshire, 25 mi south of Kennebunkport. Those flying into Boston's Logan airport can rent a car and be in the Kennebunkport area in less than two hours (traffic depending) for the 75-mi drive.

Information **Pease International airport** (⊠ *36 Airline Ave., Newington, NH 03801* ☎ *603/433–6536*).

BY BIKE

A bicycle can make it easy to get around the Kennebunks, the Yorks, and the Old Orchard Beach area, but the lack of shoulders on some roads can be intimidating. Ogunquit would seem like a good place for bikes, but traffic is hectic in the high season, making it a bit tricky. Biking around town is better, safer, and far more pleasant in the shoulder seasons (early summer or after Labor Day). Two good resources are the Bicycle Coalition of Maine and the Maine Department of Transportation (⇨ *see Maine Essentials at the back of the book).*

BY BUS

The Shuttlebus-Zoom is a localized bus service connecting the communities of Biddeford, Saco, Old Orchard Beach, Scarborough, South Portland, and Portland. Vermont Transit Lines (⇨ *see Maine Essentials at the back of the book*) has service from throughout northern New England and within Maine.

Information **Shuttlebus-Zoom** (☎ *207/282–5408* ⊕ *www.shuttlebus-zoom.com*).

CAR RENTAL

Rental-car agencies are concentrated at the Portland International Jetport in Portland. Several national rental companies are also represented at Portsmouth's Pease International (⇨ *see Car Rental in Maine Essentials at the back of the book for agency phone numbers*).

CAR TRAVEL

U.S. 1 from Kittery is the shopper's route north; other roads hug the coastline. Interstate 95 is usually a faster route for travelers headed to towns north of Ogunquit. Exits on the turnpike coincide with mileage from the border.

Route 9 goes from Kennebunkport to Cape Porpoise and Goose Rocks. Parking is tight in Kennebunkport in peak season. Possibilities include the municipal lot next to the Congregational Church ($2 an hour from May through October) and 30 North Street (free year-round).

BY TRAIN

Amtrak offers rail service from Boston to Portland, with stops in Wells and Saco and a seasonal stop in Old Orchard Beach.

Information Amtrak (☎ *800/872-7245* ⊕ *www.thedowneaster.com*).

CONTACTS & RESOURCES

EMERGENCIES

In an emergency dial 911.

Hospitals & Health Clinics Kennebunk Medical Center (⊠ *24 Portland St., Kennebunk* ☎ *207/985-3726*). **Southern Maine Medical Center** (⊠ *Rte. 111, Biddeford* ☎ *207/283-7000, 207/283-7100 emergency room*). **Wells Urgent Care** (⊠ *Rte. 109, Wells* ☎ *207/646-5211*). **York Hospital** (⊠ *15 Hospital Dr., York* ☎ *207/351-2157 or 800/283-7234*).

MEDIA

The *Biddeford Tribune* and the *Portland Press Herald*, the state's largest paper, are published daily. The *Maine Sunday Telegram* is the state's only Sunday paper. The *York County Coast Star* is published weekly.

WMEA 90.1 is the local National Public Radio affiliate. WCSH, channel 6, is the NBC affiliate. WMTW, channel 8, is the ABC affiliate. WGME, channel 13, is the CBS affiliate. WCBB, channel 10, and WMEA, channel 26, are the Maine Public Broadcasting affiliates.

VISITOR INFORMATION

Information The **Greater York Region Chamber of Commerce** (⊠ *1 Stonewall La., off U.S. 1, York 03903* ☎ *207/363-4422* ⊕ *www.gatewaytomaine.org*). **Kennebunk-Kennebunkport Chamber of Commerce** (⊠ *17 Western Ave., Kennebunk 04043* ☎ *207/967-0857* ⊕ *www.visitthekennebunks.com*). **Maine Tourism Association & Visitor Information Center** (⊠ *U.S. 1 and I-95, Kittery 03904* ☎ *207/439-1319* ⊕ *www.mainetourism.com*). **Ogunquit Chamber of Commerce** (⊠ *U.S. 1,* ☎ *207/646-2939* ⊕ *www.ogunquit.org*). **Old Orchard Beach Chamber of Commerce** (⊠ *1st St.,* ⌂ *Box 600, Old Orchard Beach 04064* ☎ *207/934-2500 or 800/365-9386* ⊕ *www.oldorchardbeachmaine.com*). **Wells Chamber of Commerce** (⌂ *Box 356, Wells 04090* ☎ *207/646-2451* ⊕ *www.wellschamber.org*).

Greater Portland

WORD OF MOUTH

"Portland is a great city with a lot to do, you should have no trouble entertaining yourself there for a couple of nights. Enjoy!"

— mamadadapaige

Updated by
John Blodgett

A CITY OF MANY NAMES throughout its history, including Casco and Falmouth, Portland has survived many dramatic transformations. Sheltered by the nearby Casco Bay Islands and blessed with a deep port, Portland was a significant settlement right from its start in the early 17th century. Settlers thrived on fishing and lumbering, repeatedly building up the area while the British, French, and American Indians continually sacked it. Many considered the region a somewhat dangerous frontier, but its potential for prosperity was so apparent that settlers came, despite the danger, to tap its rich natural resources.

Portland's first home was built on the peninsula now known as Munjoy Hill in 1632. The British burned the city in 1775, when residents refused to surrender arms, but it was rebuilt and became a major trading center. Much of Portland was destroyed again in the Great Fire on July 4, 1866, when a boy threw a celebration firecracker into a pile of wood shavings; 1,500 buildings burned to the ground. Poet Henry Wadsworth Longfellow said at the time that his city reminded him of the ruins of Pompeii. The Great Fire started not far from where people now wander the cozy streets of the Old Port.

Despite all the calamity and destruction, the city of Portland has always had a great spirit. Each time the city has fallen, its residents have rebuilt—much like a phoenix rising from the ashes.

EXPLORING PORTLAND

Maine's largest city is considered small by national standards—its population is just 64,000—but its character, spirit, and appeal make it feel much larger. In fact, it is a cultural and economic center for a metro area of 230,000 residents—one-quarter of Maine's entire population. Portland and its environs are well worth a day or two of exploration.

GETTING ORIENTED

Several distinct neighborhoods reveal the many faces of a city that embraces its history as well as its art, music, and multicultural scenes. The most visited section, the restored Old Port, features a real working waterfront where emblematic lobster boats share ports with modern cruise ships, ferries, and vintage sailing yachts. In spots along Fore, Exchange, and other streets, the asphalt has worn away to reveal the original cobblestones beneath. Stately homes built by ships' captains line the streets of the Western Promenade; artists, artisans, and other small businesses have taken over many formerly abandoned and now renovated redbrick warehouses. The nightlife is active here, with numerous clubs, taverns, and bars pouring out the sounds of live music and lively patrons. Exceptional restaurants, shops, and galleries, many featuring locally produced goods, abound here as well. Water tours of the harbor and excursions to the islands of Casco Bay depart from the piers of Commercial Street.

Downtown Portland has emerged from a years-long on-again, off-again funk, during which much retail commerce was lost to shopping malls in the outlying suburbs. Its burgeoning Arts District is connected

2

to the Old Port by a revitalized Congress Street, which runs the length of the peninsular city from alongside the Western Promenade in the southwest to the Eastern Promenade on Munjoy Hill in the northeast. Congress Street is peppered with interesting shops, eclectic restaurants, and several excellent museums. The arts really come alive here, with numerous venues for the performing arts attracting well-known names from the entertainment world. Nestled in the midst and beyond are residential areas; one of the great aspects of the city is that the business and domestic spheres constantly mingle, giving the area a friendly and approachable character.

Just beyond the Arts District is the Western Promenade, an area of extensive architectural wealth. Predominantly residential, the neighborhood is filled with stunning examples of both the city's historical and economic prominence and its emphasis on preserving this past. A handful of historic homes are open to tours.

GETTING AROUND
Portland is wonderfully walkable; an able-bodied explorer can easily take in the Old Port, the Downtown/Arts District, and the Western Promenade. Narrated trolley tours are also available (⇨ *see Take a Tour box*). However, to discover some of the other areas outlined in this chapter, such as Portland Head Light and Freeport (home of L.L. Bean), a car is necessary. To get to most any island in Casco Bay hop aboard a waterfront ferry.

WHEN TO GO
Winters are long in Maine, so when summer arrives, the city celebrates the warmer months with a full schedule of outdoor events, from movie showings and concerts to farmers' markets and festivals. The many happenings are testament to this small city's large and lively spirit.

Numbers in the margin correspond to numbers on the Portland and Around Greater Portland maps.

THE OLD PORT

FodorśChoice ★ A major international port and a working harbor since the early 17th century, the Old Port bridges the gap between the city's historical commercial activities and those of today. It is home to fishing boats docked alongside whale-watching charters, luxury yachts, cruise ships, and oil tankers from throughout the globe. Busy Commercial Street parallels the water and is lined with brick buildings and warehouses that were built following the Great Fire of 1866, and were intended to last for ages. In the 19th century, candle makers and sail stitchers plied their trades here; today, specialty shops, art galleries, and restaurants have taken up residence.

As with much of the city, it's best to park your car and explore the Old Port on foot. You can park at the city garage on Fore Street (between Exchange and Union streets) or opposite the U.S. Customs House at the corner of Fore and Pearl streets. A helpful hint: Look for the PARK & SHOP sign on garages and parking lots and get one hour of free parking for each stamp collected at participating shops. Allow a couple of hours to wander at leisure on Market, Exchange, Middle, and Fore streets. The city is very pedestrian-friendly. Maine state law requires vehicles to stop for walkers in crosswalks, and many benches allow for rest and a grand dose of people-watching.

WHAT TO SEE

❶ ☾ **Maine Narrow Gauge Railroad Co. & Museum.** Whether you're crazy about old trains or just want to see the sights from a different perspective, the railroad museum has long been delighting people with its

---

PORTLAND TOP 5

■ Sail to Peaks Island aboard a Casco Bay Lines' ferry.

■ Experience the style of Colonial Maine at the Tate House.

■ Pay homage to Winslow Homer at the Portland Museum of Art.

■ Watch ships enter Portland Harbor from the lighthouse at Portland Head Light.

■ Gear up for the outdoors at the original L.L. Bean store.

---

extensive collection of train memorabilia and specialty train tours on original narrow gauge railcars. Theme weekends include rides with Santa, a Harvest Express (pick your own pumpkin), and the July 4 fireworks ride. The museum has an extensive collection of locomotives and rail coaches; there's also a gift shop for souvenir collectors. ⊠ *58 Fore St.* ☎ *207/828–0814* ⊕ *www.mngrr.org* 🚂 *Train $10, museum $2* ☉ *Trains May 26–Oct. 14, daily on the hr 11–4; Feb. 17–May 19 and Oct. 27–Nov. 17, weekends on the hr 11–3 PM. Museum late-Oct.–May 19, weekdays 10–4; May 20–Oct. 27, daily 10–4.*

❷ **Portland Fish Exchange.** For a lively and sensory-filled (you may want to hold your nose) glimpse into the Old Port's active fish business, take a free tour of the Portland Fish Exchange. Watch as the fishing boats unload their daily haul, the catch gets weighed in, and prices are settled through an auction process. It's a great behind-the-scenes view of this dynamic market. Auctions take place Sunday at 11 AM and Monday through Thursday at noon. ⊠ *6 Portland Fish Pier* ☎ *207/773–0017* ⊕ *www.pfex.org* 🚂 *Free.*

Harbor Fish Market. A Portland favorite for more than 30 years, this freshest of the fresh seafood markets now ships lobsters and other Maine seafood delectables anywhere in the country from its waterfront location on a working wharf. A bright-red façade opens into a bustling space with bubbling lobster pens, clams, and other shellfish on ice, and employees as skilled with a fillet knife as a sushi chef. ⊠ *9 Custom House Wharf* ☎ *207/775–0251 or 800/370–1790* ⊕ *www. harborfish.com* 🚂 *Free.*

THE DOWNTOWN/ARTS DISTRICT

This district starts at the top of Exchange Street, near the upper end of the Old Port, and extends all the way up past the Portland Museum of Art. Congress Street is the district's central artery. Much of Portland's economic heart is here, including several large banking firms. It's also the area where Maine College of Art and the Portland Library make

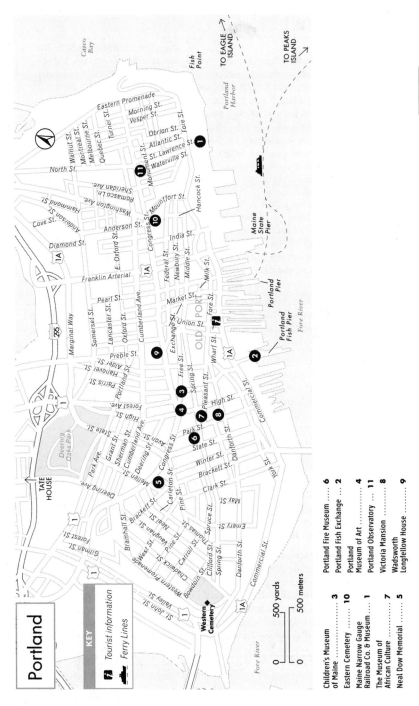

Portland

KEY

🛈 Tourist information

⛴ Ferry Lines

Children's Museum of Maine **3**	Portland Fire Museum **6**
Eastern Cemetery **10**	Portland Fish Exchange **2**
Maine Narrow Gauge Railroad Co. & Museum **1**	Portland Museum of Art **4**
The Museum of African Culture **7**	Portland Observatory ... **11**
Neal Dow Memorial **5**	Victoria Mansion **8**
	Wadsworth Longfellow House **9**

IF YOU LIKE

BOATING

Various Portland-based skippers offer whale-, puffin-, and seal-watching cruises; excursions to lighthouses and islands; and fishing trips. There are dinner-and-dancing cruises, and sunset or sunrise sails. Get aboard the mail boat to see the nearby islands, or take the ferry instead. Self-navigators can rent kayaks or canoes.

SHOPPING

Shoppers will delight in Portland—you won't find typical storefronts (unless you want to; then head straight to the Maine Mall). Specialty shops sell clothing, pottery, art, housewares, and more. Antiques

shops line the Downtown/Arts District as well as nearby U.S. 1. Freeport boasts brand-name outlet stores and the always-open L. L. Bean. Maine sales tax is 5%.

GREEN SPACE

Nearby to Portland are Fort Williams Park (home to Portland Head Light), Crescent Beach State Park, and Two Lights State Park; all offer hiking, biking, and strolling trails; picnic facilities; and water access. In Freeport is Wolfe's Neck Woods State Park, and Bradbury Mountain State Park, in Pownal, offers incredible vistas from its easily accessed summit.

their homes. Art galleries, specialty stores, and a score of restaurants line Congress Street and its larger intersecting byways of High and State streets. Parking along Congress Street is tricky; two-hour meters line the sidewalks, but there are several nearby parking garages.

WHAT TO SEE

❸ Children's Museum of Maine. Touching is okay at Portland's relatively small but fun Children's Museum, where kids can pretend they are lobster fishermen, shopkeepers, or computer experts. The majority of the museum's exhibits, many of which have a Maine theme, are best for children 10 and younger. Camera Obscura, an exhibit about optics, provides fascinating panoramic views of the city. The museum's newest addition, L. L. Bear's Discovery Woods, takes imagination to the great outdoors, with explorations below the sea, up a tree, on top of Maine's tallest mountain, and within a flowing stream. ⊠ *142 Free St.* ☎ *207/828–1234* ⊕ *www.childrensmuseumofme.org* ⊠ *Museum $6; Camera Obscura only, $3* ⊗ *Memorial Day–Labor Day, Mon.–Sat. 10–5, Sun. noon–5; day after Labor Day–day before Memorial Day, Tues.–Sat. 10–5, Sun. noon–5.*

❹ Portland Museum of Art. Maine's largest public art institution has a number of strong collections, including fine seascapes and landscapes by Winslow Homer, John Marin, Andrew Wyeth, Edward Hopper, Marsden Hartley, and other painters. Homer's *Pulling the Dory* and *Weatherbeaten,* two quintessential Maine Coast images, are here; the museum owns and displays more than 20 other works by Homer. The Joan Whitney Payson Collection of impressionist and postimpressionist art includes works by Monet, Picasso, and Renoir. Harry N. Cobb, an associate of I. M. Pei, designed the strikingly modern Charles Shipman Payson building. The nearby and entirely renovated McLellan House

GREAT ITINERARIES

Numbers in the text correspond to numbers in the margin and on the Portland map.

IF YOU HAVE 3 DAYS

Spend your first day in Portland wandering the streets and shops of the **Old Port**. Break for a harborside pub lunch along Commercial Street, before heading to the Downtown/ Arts District. Art lovers will want several hours inside the **Portland Museum of Art** ❹; families should visit the **Children's Museum of Maine** ❸. For architectural delights, take an hour or so to walk the **Western Promenade** neighborhood, followed by a baseball game at Hadlock Field (or spend the night downtown). On your second day, take a morning boat ride to **Eagle Island** or another to Casco Bay island. In the afternoon, drive to **Cape Elizabeth**, and visit Portland Head Light and Two Lights. Return to Portland for the night. On your third day, head north to **Freeport**, where you can shop at various outlets and L.L. Bean.

IF YOU HAVE 5 DAYS

Spend your first two days in Portland. Be sure to linger in the **Old Port** and stroll through the architectural splendor of the **Western Promenade**. You can leave your car at your hotel for both days and easily get around on foot. See Casco Bay's islands via a Casco Bay Lines ferry or mail boat, a whale-watch or other themed cruise, or a sportfishing adventure.

On Day 3 take a ferry to **Peaks Island** and prepare to relax. You'll have left your car in Portland; rent a bicycle on the island to explore its quiet streets; take a guided kayak trip; or sign up with a golf cart tour. Spend a peaceful night here. On Day 4, return to Portland and head out in your car for several hours of touring, including a visit to nearby **Cape Elizabeth** to see Portland Head Light. The park is a great place for a picnic lunch. Continue your scenic drive, stopping at several state parks for hiking and beachcombing, before making your way to **Prouts Neck**. Here you can stroll along the Cliff Walk and visit Winslow Homer's home and studio. Head back to the interstate and continue north to **Freeport**. Have dinner here and spend the night—but not before midnight shopping at L.L. Bean. Spend Day 5 browsing the outlets, hiking through Wolfe's Neck Woods State Park, or taking a scenic harbor cruise.

contains additional galleries housing the museum's 19th-century collection and decorative art as well as interactive educational stations. ✉ 7 *Congress Sq.* ☎ *207/775–6148* ⊕ *www.portlandmuseum.org* ⧠ *$10, free Fri. 5–9* ☉ *Memorial Day–Columbus Day, Mon.–Thurs. and weekends 10–5, Fri. 10–9; Columbus Day–Memorial Day, Tues.–Thurs. and weekends 10–5, Fri. 10–9.*

❺ **Neal Dow Memorial.** Now the headquarters of the Maine Women's Christian Temperance Union, this majestic 1829 Federal-style home is open for tours. The mansion is filled with the Civil War general's original antiques, personal effects, and papers on prohibition—the mission that gave him fame as the man responsible for Maine's adoption of the anti-alcohol bill in 1851. ✉ *714 Congress St.* ☎ *207/773–7773* ⧠ *Free* ☉ *Weekdays 11–4.*

6 **Portland Fire Museum.** Begun by the Portland Veteran's Firemen's Association in 1891, the Fire Museum is filled with a collection of fire-
related art and mementos gathered over generations. Housed in the
former fire quarters of Engine 4, the museum has a curious collection
of 19th-century firefighting equipment, an old engine, scores of documents and photographs, and even the original stalls of the horses that
once pulled the fire wagons. Watch the dramatic silent film footage
from 1912 of the horse-drawn fire cart as it heads off to a local fire. The
museum is on the National Register of Historic Places. ⊠*157 Spring
St.* ☎*207/772–2040* ⊕*www.portlandfiremuseum.com* ⊠*Free* ⊗*1st
Fri. of each month 6–9, or by appointment.*

7 **Museum of African Culture.** This is the only museum in New England
devoted exclusively to sub-Saharan African tribal arts. There are more
than 1,500 pieces in the collection ranging from large-scale, elabo-
rately carved wooden masks to smaller-scale figures, cast copper alloy
(bronze) figures, textiles, utilitarian objects, ceramic, bone, ivory, and
composite objects. The oldest mask in the collection dates back to AD
1600. ⊠*122 Spring St.* ☎*207/871–7188* ⊠*$5 suggested donation*
⊗*Tues.–Fri. 10:30–4, Sat. 10:30–4, or by special appointment.*

8 **Victoria Mansion.** This Italianate-style mansion was built between 1858
★ and 1860 and is widely regarded as the most sumptuously ornamented
dwelling of its period remaining in the country. Architect Henry Aus-
tin designed the house for hotelier Ruggles Morse and his wife, Olive.
The interior design—everything from the plasterwork to the furniture
(much of it original)—is the only surviving commission of New York
designer Gustave Herter. Inside the elegant brownstone exterior of
this National Historic Landmark are colorful frescoed walls and ceilings, ornate marble mantelpieces, gilded gas chandeliers, a magnificent 6-foot by 25-foot stained-glass ceiling window, and a freestanding
mahogany staircase; guided tours, running about 45 minutes, cover all
the details. The mansion reopens during the Christmas season, richly
ornamented and decorated to reveal the opulence and elegance of the
Victorian era. ⊠*109 Danforth St.* ☎*207/772–4841* ⊕*www.victoria-
mansion.org* ⊠*$10* ⊗*May–Oct., Mon.–Sat. 10–4, Sun. 1–5; Christ-
mas tours Nov. 24–Dec. 31.*

9 **Wadsworth Longfellow House.** The boyhood home of the poet—which
is the first brick house in Portland—is particularly interesting because
most of the furnishings are original to the house. The late-Colonial-
style structure, built in 1785, sits back from the street and has a small
portico over its entrance and four chimneys surmounting the roof.
The house is part of the Center for Maine History, which includes
the adjacent Maine History Gallery and a research library; the gift
shop has a good selection of books about Maine. ⊠*489 Congress St.*
☎*207/774–1822* ⊕*www.mainehistory.org* ⊠*$7, Center for Maine
History $4* ⊗*House and Maine History Gallery: May–Oct., Mon.–Sat.
10–5, Sun. noon–5; last tour at 4. Nov. and Dec., call for hrs. Library:
year-round, Tues.–Sat. 10–3.*

Tate House. This magnificent house fully conjures up the style—even high style—of Colonial Maine. Built astride rose granite steps and a period herb garden overlooking the Stroudwater River on the outskirts of Portland, the 1755 house was built by Captain George Tate. Tate had been commissioned by the English Crown to organize "the King's Broad Arrow"—the marking and cutting down of gigantic forest trees, which were transported overland to water and sent to England to be fashioned as masts for English fighting frigates. The house has several period rooms, including a sitting room with some fine English Restoration chairs. With its clapboard still gloriously unpainted, its impressive Palladian doorway, dogleg stairway, unusual clerestory, and gambrel roof, this house will delight all lovers of Early American decorative arts. Guided tours of the gardens are held each Wednesday from mid-June to mid-September, with tea and refreshments served afterward. House tours are offered daily in-season except Monday. Call or visit the Web site for special holiday programs during December. ✉ *1270 Westbrook St.* ☎ *207/774-6177* ⊕ *www.tatehouse.org* 💲 *$5* ⊙ *June 15–Oct. 15, Tues.–Sat. 10–4, Sun. 1–4 (1st Sun. each month).*

🔟 **Eastern Cemetery.** On Congress Street, not far from the Portland Observatory, is this historic mid-17th-century burial ground. A stroll through the cemetery reveals thousands of enchanting and artfully decorated tombstones of the centuries, carved with winged skulls, angels, and weeping willows. ✉ *Congress St. and Washington Ave.* ☎ *207/846-7753* ⊕ *www.spiritsalive.org* ⊙ *Daily, sunrise–sunset.*

⓫ **Portland Observatory.** This observatory on Munjoy Hill was built in 1807 by Captain Lemuel Moody, a retired sea captain, as a signal tower. It used lights as both aids for sea navigation and as a warning for the approach of enemy forces. It is the last remaining signal tower in the country and is held in place by 122 tons of ballast. After visiting the small museum at the base, you can climb to the Orb deck and take in views of Portland, the islands, and inland to the White Mountains. ✉ *138 Congress St.* ☎ *207/774-5561* ⊕ *www.portlandlandmarks.org* 💲 *$6* ⊙ *May 26–Columbus Day, daily 10–5.*

THE WESTERN PROMENADE

A leisurely walk through Portland's Western Promenade, beginning at the top of the Downtown/Arts District, offers a real treat to historic architecture buffs. Elaborate building began in the mid-1800s, encouraged by both a robust economy and Portland's devastating fire of 1866, which leveled nearly one-third of the city. The neighborhood, on the National Register of Historic Places, reveals an extraordinary display of architectural splendor, from High Victorian Gothic to lush Italianate, Queen Anne to Colonial Revival.

A good place to start is at the very head of the Western Promenade, which has parking, benches, and a great view. From the Old Port, take Danforth Street all the way up to Vaughn Street; take a right and then

TAKE A TOUR

Several tour operators arrange specialized group trips throughout the state as well as in and near Portland. **Maine Family Adventures** (✉ *22 Fitts St., Bath* ☎ *207/443-3310 or 800/771-7808* ⊕ *www.mainefamily-adventures.com*) offer multiday family-friendly activities packages such as kayaking and biking for groups of 12–16 people. **Ocean View Tours** (☎ *866/251-3626* ⊕ *www.mountainviewtours-online.com*) provide a handful of tours ranging from three to six hours in length, depending upon how far from Portland you'd like to tour.

BUS TOURS

The informative trolley tours of **Mainely Tours** (✉ *5½ Moulton St.* ☎ *207/774-0808* ⊕ *www.mainely-tours.com*) cover Portland's historical and architectural highlights from Memorial Day through October.

Other Mainely Tours combine a city tour with a bay cruise or a trip to four lighthouses.

WALKING TOURS

Greater Portland Landmarks (✉ *165 State St.* ☎ *207/774-5561*) conducts 1½-hour walking tours of the city from July through September; tours begin at the **Convention and Visitors Bureau** (✉ *245 Commercial St.* ☎ *207/772-5800*) and cost $7. **Working Waterfront** (☎ *207/415-0765*) walking tours are led by local Angela Clark, who shares a good deal of uncommon history about the docks and alleys of the Old Port. The hour-long tours meet in front of Union Wharf Market on Commercial Street, weekdays at 11 AM and 2 PM; Saturday at 9 AM and 11 AM. The cost is $10 per person.

an immediate left onto Western Promenade. You pass by the Western Cemetery, Portland's second official burial ground laid out in 1829 (inside is the ancestral plot of famous poet Henry Wadsworth Longfellow); just beyond that is the parking area. Once on foot, you can happily get lost on side streets, each lined with statuesque homes.

You could easily spend an hour or two wandering the back streets of the Western Promenade; longer if you bring a picnic to enjoy in the grassy park at the head of the neighborhood. If you're interested in the particular history of individual homes, pick up a pamphlet from **Greater Portland Landmarks.** A map is included as well as the stories of some of the more prominent homes. ✉ *165 State St.* ☎ *207/774–5561* ⊙ *Mon.–Fri., 9–5* ⊕ *www.portlandlandmarks.org.*

WHERE TO EAT

Despite its small size, Portland is blessed with a variety of often exceptional restaurants and cuisines rivaling that of a far larger city. Part of that quality stems from Maine's highly desirable quality of life, which attracts fine chefs that appreciate the intimacy and character of downtown and the availability of fine local ingredients.

Fresh seafood, including the famous Maine lobster, is still understandably popular and prevalent, but there are plenty more cuisines to be enjoyed. Diners can choose from waterfront seafood shacks, elaborate prix fixe French dinners, country Italian, Thai, Vietnamese, Japanese, Irish, Mexican, Mediterranean, and a fusion of many different cuisines. More and more restaurants are using local meats, seafood, and produce as much as possible, buying outside the area only when necessary; changing menus reflect what is available in the region at the moment. As sophisticated as many of these establishments have become, the atmosphere is generally quite casual; with few exceptions, you can leave your jacket and tie at home.

Smoking is banned in all restaurants, taverns, and bars in Portland.

WHAT IT COSTS					
	¢	$	$$	$$$	$$$$
AT DINNER	under $7	$7–$10	$11–$17	$18–$25	over $25

Restaurant prices are for a main course at dinner, excluding 7% tax.

$$$$
★ ✕**Hugo's.** Chef-owner Rob Evans has turned Hugo's into one of the city's best restaurants. The warmly lighted dining room is small and open, yet you can hold a conversation without raising your voice. The four-course prix fixe menu changes weekly, but a pub menu is available to mix and match downsized items for $10 to $20 a dish. These could include herb-crusted Maine wolffish, Maine diver scallops with beef tartare, and risotto steeped deep red by beets. Few other restaurants in downtown are so devoted to preparing and serving the freshest local organic foods. ⊠ *88 Middle St.* ☎ *207/774–8538* ⊟ *AE, MC, V* ✆ *Closed Sun. and Mon. No lunch.*

$$$–$$$$
✕**Cinque Terre.** The passionate and traditional art of Italian dining is celebrated at this Old Port spot, encouraging a long, relaxing eating experience that covers up to five courses and even more northern Italian flavors. Half portions are available, allowing you to savor more of the many choices. Start with an appetizer such as the pan-roasted clams, mussels, and hot salami on grilled focaccia; move on to salad, pasta, and a main entrée, which could be anything from seafood to veal, quail to venison. Save room for après-dinner cheese and dessert. Reservations are recommended. ⊠ *36 Wharf St.* ☎ *207/347–6154* ⊕ *www. cinqueterremaine.com* ⊟ *AE, MC, V* ✆ *No lunch.*

$$$–$$$$
Fodor's Choice
★ ✕**Fore Street.** Two of Maine's best chefs, Sam Hayward and Dana Street, opened this restaurant in a renovated, airy warehouse on the edge of the Old Port (heating-oil delivery trucks once were parked here—honest). The menu changes daily to reflect the freshest local ingredients available. Every copper-top table in the two-level main dining room has a view of the enormous brick oven and hearth and the open kitchen, where sous-chefs seem to dance as they create entrées such as three cuts of Maine island lamb, Atlantic monkfish fillet, and breast of Moulad duckling. Desserts include artisanal cheeses. Reservations are recommended. ⊠ *288 Fore St.* ☎ *207/775–2717* ⊕ *www.forestreet.biz* ⊟ *AE, MC, V* ✆ *No lunch.*

$$–$$$$
✕**Street and Co.** Fish and seafood are the specialties in this Old Port basement establishment. You enter through the bustling kitchen and dine

amid dried herbs and shelves of staples, at one of the copper-top tables (so your waiter can place a skillet of sizzling seafood directly in front of you). The daily specials are usually a good bet, though pasta dishes are popular (garlic and olive oil lovers rejoice; they're loaded with both). Listen to your server—chances are your plate is very, very hot indeed. ⊠*33 Wharf St.* ☎*207/775–0887* ⊟*AE, MC, V* ⊘*No lunch.*

$$–$$$$ ✕**Uffa!** Though the name means "Oh!" in Italian, this funky place is absolutely French, having imported a genuine French chef, James Tranchemontagne, from overseas. Bringing the richly textured and traditional flavors of his homeland to New England ingredients has resulted in a unique Maine dining experience. A house favorite is the seared duck breast; if you are lucky the seared trout with lobster and leek stuffing, served with herb-scented jasmine rice and a Drambuie crème sauce, will be the daily special when you visit. Sunday brunch is also a treat, served from 9 AM to 1 PM. Reservations are a good idea and can be made online. ⊠*190 State St.* ☎*207/775–3380* ⊕*www.uffarestaurant.com* ⊟*AE, MC, V* ⊘*Closed Mon. and Tues. No lunch.*

$$–$$$$ ✕**Walter's Cafe.** Capturing the 19th-century spirit of the Old Port, with its brick walls and wood floors, this casual, busy place in the heart of the Old Port's shopping area manages a good balance of local seafood and meats with Asian and more eclectic flavors. Begin with lobster bisque or deep-fried lemongrass shrimp sticks; then move on to a shrimp and andouille bake. ⊠*15 Exchange St.* ☎*207/871–9258* ⊕*www.walterscafe.com* ⊟*AE, MC, V* ⊘*No lunch Sun.*

$$–$$$ ✕**Gilbert's Chowder House.** This is the real deal, as quintessential as
  ★   Maine dining can be. Clam rakes, nautical charts, and a giant plastic marlin hang from the walls of this unpretentious waterfront diner. The flavors are from the depths of the North Atlantic, prepared and presented simply: fish, clam, and corn chowders; fried shrimp, haddock, clam strips, and extraordinary clam cakes. A chalkboard of daily specials is a must-read, and often features steamed mussels, oysters, and peel-and-eat shrimp. But don't miss out on the lobster roll—a toasted hot dog roll bursting with claw and tail meat unadulterated by mayo or other ingredients. It sits on a leaf of lettuce, but who needs more? It's classic Maine, fuss-free and presented on a paper plate. ⊠*92 Commercial St.* ☎*207/871–5636* ⊟*AE, MC, V.*

$$–$$$ ✕**Katahdin Restaurant.** Long a favorite with both locals and visitors, with its "keep it simple" philosophy, this small yet comfortable corner restaurant sits amid the Downtown/Arts District. Seafood is the pride

here, with an emphasis on the local variety, treated with extra creativity. Imagine the ubiquitous Maine lobster poached in butter with corn risotto, smoked Gouda, and watercress. The menu changes often, keeping favorite staples but reworking them. No matter what the preparation, the Prince Edward Island mussels are always worth a try, as are the Maine crab cakes. Vegetarian dishes are also represented, and a well-rounded wine list complements the menu. ⊠ *106 High St.* ☎ *207/774–1740* ⊕ *www. katahdinrestaurant.com* ⊲ *Reservations not accepted* ⊟ *AE, MC, V* ⊘ *Closed Sun. and Mon. No lunch.*

$–$$$ ✕ **Ri-Ra.** Whether you're in the mood for a pint of beer and corned beef and cabbage, or a crock of mussels and whole roasted rainbow trout, Ri-Ra delivers. Settle into a comfy couch in the downstairs pub or take a table in the upstairs dining room, where walls of windows overlook the busy ferry terminal. After dinner every Thursday, Friday, and Saturday, the lower level gets loud with live local bands playing until closing time. ⊠ *72 Commercial St.* ☎ *207/761–4446* ⊕ *www.rira.com* ⊟ *AE, MC, V.*

$–$$ ✕ **Pepperclub.** A hot spot for vegetarians and a young, casual crowd,
★ this funky little restaurant features its nightly offerings on handwritten, colorful chalkboards propped up about the place. If the portobello pie doesn't tickle your fancy, choose from selections of beef, seafood, pasta, and chicken. Don't forget dessert; a popular choice is bourbon pecan pie—yum! Breakfast is served daily, and until 1 PM on weekends. ⊠ *78 Middle St.* ☎ *207/772–0531* ⊟ *AE, MC, V* ⊘ *No lunch.*

¢–$$ ✕ **Becky's.** You won't find a more local or unfussy place—or one that is
★ more abuzz with conversation at 4 AM—than this waterfront institution, way down on the end of Commercial Street. Sitting next to you at the counter or in the neighboring booth could be rubber-booted fishermen back from sea, college students soothing a hangover, or suited business folks with cell phones. The food is cheap, generous in proportion, and has that satisfying, old-time diner quality. Breakfast is served from 4 AM to 4 PM, with lunch and dinner daily. Nightly specials add to the large menu of fried seafood platters, salads, and sandwiches. Get a pie, cake, or pudding to go. ⊠ *390 Commercial St.* ☎ *207/773–7070* ⊟ *AE, D, MC, V.*

WHAT'S ON TAP: MICROBREWERIES

Maine is home to more than 20 breweries. Within and near Portland are several larger brewing companies (Allagash Brewing, D. L. Geary Brewing, Casco Bay Brewing, and Sebago Brewing, to name a few), each open for tours and tastings, but much of the hidden treasure lies in the smaller brewpubs that make their own beer and serve it fresh from their own taps in the lively and inviting setting of a neighborhood tavern. In the Old Port alone there are several such pubs. Look for events like the Maine Brewer's Festival each November.

WHERE TO STAY

As Portland's popularity as a vacation destination has increased, so has its options for overnight visitors. Though several large hotels—geared toward high-tech, amenity-obsessed guests—have been built in the Old Port, they have in no way diminished the success of smaller, more intimate lodgings, of which there are plenty. Inns and B&Bs have taken up residence throughout the city, often giving new life to the grand mansions of Portland's 19th-century wealthy businessmen. A few chain hotels have also slipped in; most are near the interstate and the airport.

You can expect to pay from about $70 a night for a pleasant room (often with complimentary breakfast), up to more than $400 for the most luxurious of suites. In the height of the summer season, many places have minimum-stay requirements for weekends and holidays; make reservations well in advance and inquire about off-season specials.

WHAT IT COSTS				
	¢	$	$$	$$$	$$$$
FOR TWO PEOPLE	under $60	$60–$99	$100–$149	$150–$200	over $200

Hotel prices are for two people in a standard double room, excluding service charges and 7% tax.

$$$$ **Portland Harbor Hotel.** Making luxury its primary focus, the Harbor Hotel has become a favorite with business travelers seeking meetings on a more-intimate scale, and vacationing guests who want high-quality service and amenities. In season, eat on the enclosed peaceful garden patio. **Pros:** Luxurious amenities, amid the action of the Old Port and waterfront. **Con:** Not for the quaint of heart. ⊠*468 Fore St., 04101* ☏*207/775–9090 or 888/798–9090* ⊕*www.portlandharborhotel.com* ⬐*85 rooms, 12 suites* ♨*In-room: Wi-Fi. In-hotel: restaurant, laundry service, concierge, public Internet, no-smoking rooms* ▤*AE, D, DC, MC, V.*

$$$$ **Portland Regency Hotel and Spa.** One of the few major hotels in the center of the Old Port, the brick Regency building was Portland's armory in the late 19th century. Most rooms have four-poster beds, tall standing mirrors, floral curtains, and love seats. You can walk to shops, restaurants, and museums from the hotel. The Spa features a licensed massage therapist, pedicures and manicures, and even its own spa cuisine, including healthful food items such as yogurt, salads, and sandwiches. **Pros:** Convenient to town, has all the extras you'd want. **Con:** More luxurious than charming. ⊠*20 Milk St., 04101* ☏*207/774–4200 or 800/727–3436* ⊕*www.theregency.com* ⬐*87 rooms, 8 suites* ♨*In-room: Ethernet, refrigerator, Wi-Fi. In-hotel: restaurant, gym, spa, laundry service, public Wi-Fi, no-smoking rooms* ▤*AE, D, DC, MC, V.*

$$$–$$$$ **Pomegranate Inn.** The classic architecture of this handsome inn in the
Fodor's Choice   architecturally rich Western Promenade area gives no hint of the surprises
★   within. Vivid hand-painted walls, floors, and woodwork combine with contemporary artwork, and the result is both stimulating and comforting. Rooms are individually decorated, and five have fireplaces. Room 8,

in the carriage house, has a private garden terrace. **Pros:** Close to Western Promenade, private garden perfect for quiet afternoon tea. **Con:** Not within reasonable walking distance of Old Port, waterfront. ✉*49 Neal St., 04102* ☎*207/772–1006 or 800/356–0408* ⊕*www.pomegranateinn. com* ➶*8 rooms* ♿*In-room: Wi-Fi. In-hotel: no elevator, no kids under 16, no-smoking rooms* ▭*AE, D, DC, MC, V* ⦿*BP.*

$$$–$$$$ 🔛**West End Inn.** Set among the glorious aged homes of the Western Promenade, this 1871 house displays much of the era's Victorian grandeur with high ceilings and a dramatic ruby-red foyer. Spacious rooms are either brightly painted or papered with flowers, and all provide guests with down quilts, thick terry robes, and a complimentary basket of boutique toiletries. For breakfast, the inn often bakes fresh in-season fruit—blueberries, apples, pumpkin—into scones, muffins, and more. The menu also includes granola, an egg dish, and ingredients purchased at the local farmers' market. It's a short walk to the downtown area. **Pro:** Cozy library with fireplace is a great place to relax. **Con:** Minimum two-night stay during certain high-season weekends. ✉*146 Pine St., 04102* ☎*207/772–1377 or 800/338–1377* ⊕*www.westendbb. com* ➶*6 rooms* ♿*In-room: no phone. In-hotel: no elevator, public Wi-Fi, no-smoking rooms* ▭*AE, MC, V* ⦿*BP.*

$$–$$$$ 🔛**Inn on Carleton.** After a day of exploring Portland's museums and shops, you can find a quiet retreat at this elegant brick town house on the city's Western Promenade. Built in 1869, it is furnished throughout with period antiques as well as artwork by contemporary Maine artists. A trompe l'oeil painting by Maine artist Charles Schumacher, known for the technique, greets you at the entryway, and more fine examples of his work in this style are either on display or in the process of being uncovered and restored. **Pros:** European-style elegance, English garden, Western Promenade location. **Con:** It's a long walk to the Old Port. ✉*46 Carleton St., 04102* ☎*207/775–1910 or 800/639–1779* ⊕*www.innoncarleton.com* ➶*6 rooms* ♿*In-room: no phone, no TV. In-hotel: no elevator, public Wi-Fi, no kids under 9, no-smoking rooms* ▭*D, MC, V* ⦿*BP.*

$$–$$$$ 🔛**Percy Inn.** Innkeeper Dale Northrup knows how to welcome guests and keep them happy in this elegantly appointed 1830 Federal-style brick row house just on the edge of the West End. Thoughtful amenities include complimentary in-room soft drinks, 24-hour access to snacks in the well-stocked second-floor pantry, and even summer beach bags complete with blankets, towels, and minicoolers. Candles, a living room with fireplace, numerous plants, and a full library of books and movies give the inn a generous warmth. Each good-size guest room has flowered or patchwork quilts, richly painted walls, and queen beds—some of them four-posters in cherry or pine. The rooms, named for famed poets, have books of their namesakes placed about in comfortable sitting areas throughout the inn. Guests receive a complimentary pass to Bally Total Fitness. **Pro:** It's an easy walk to both the Arts District and the Old Port. **Con:** The convenient downtown location might not be peaceful for some visitors. ✉*15 Pine St., 04102* ☎*207/871–7638 or 888/417–3729* ⊕*www.percyinn.com* ➶*7 rooms* ♿*In-room: kitchen (some), refrigerator, DVD, VCR. In-hotel: parking (no fee), no elevator, no-smoking rooms* ▭*D, DC, MC, V* ⦿*CP.*

FODOR'S FIRST PERSON

John Blodgett
Writer and Maine native

No visit to Maine is complete without a trip to one of the coast's many lighthouses. My favorite is Two Lights State Park in Cape Elizabeth. I visit every time I go home.

As the park's name suggests, there are two lighthouses here. Both were built in 1828, the first twin light-houses erected on Maine's craggy, ship-busting coast. The western light was converted into a private residence in 1924; the eastern light still projects its automated cylinder of light 17 mi out to sea, and is the subject of Winslow Homer's *Light-house at Two Lights*.

Neither lighthouse is open to the public, but no matter. The rocks and the tidal pools are where it's at. My parents brought me and my siblings here as children. We would scamper about the slate-gray metamorphic rock, filling empty coffee cans with tiny snails known as periwinkles. I remember the distant clang of buoys bobbing in the waves and the smell of french fries from the Lob-ster Shack mingled with the tang of salt spray. I can still conjure up those sounds and smells.

These days I usually visit alone, and often at night to watch the piercing beam of light wrap over and beyond the dark horizon. If I'm lucky there's a bright moon, backlighting gulls as they float silently like black ghosts.

NIGHTLIFE & THE ARTS

NIGHTLIFE

Portland has a nicely varied nightlife, with a great emphasis on local, live music and pubs serving award-winning local microbrews. Big, rau-cous dance clubs are few, but darkened taverns and lively bars (smoke-free by law) pulse with the sounds of rock, blues, alternative, and folk tunes. Several hip wine bars have cropped up, serving appetizers along with a full array of specialty wines and whimsical cocktails. It's a fairly youthful scene in Portland, in some spots even rowdy and rough-around-the-edges, but there are plenty of places where you don't have to shout over the din to be heard.

Acoustic Coffee (⊠ 32 Danforth St. ☎ 207/774–0404) serves up organic coffee and vegetarian meals alongside nightly performances of folk music, open mike, or readings of poetry and prose; its walls also showcase local artwork. **Asylum Sports Bar and Grill** (⊠ 121 Center St. ☎ 207/772–8274) oozes with live entertainment and dancing on two levels, plus a sports bar; it books local and regional rock, pop, and hip-hop groups. For live blues every night of the week, try the **Big Easy Blues Club** (⊠ 55 Market St. ☎ 207/871–8817). **Brian Boru** (⊠ 57 Center St. ☎ 207/780–1506) is an Irish pub with occasional entertainment, ranging from Celtic to reggae, and an outside deck. For nightly themed brew specials, plenty of Guinness, and live entertainment, head to **Bull Feeney's** (⊠ 375 Fore St. ☎ 207/773–7210), a lively two-story Irish pub and restaurant. For laughs, try **Comedy Connection** (⊠ 6 Custom Wharf

☎207/774–5554). **Gritty McDuff's** (✉396 Fore St. ☎207/772–2739) brews fine ales and serves British pub fare and seafood dishes. **Space** (✉538 Congress St. ☎207/828–5600) sparkles as a unique and alternative arts venue, opening its doors to everything from poetry readings to live music and documentary film showings.

THE ARTS

Art galleries and studios have spread throughout the city, infusing with new life many abandoned yet beautiful old buildings and shops. Many are concentrated along the Congress Street downtown corridor; others are hidden amid the boutiques and restaurants of the Old Port and the East End. A great way to get acquainted with the city's artists is to participate in the First Friday Art Walk, a self-guided, free tour of galleries, museums, and alternative art venues happening, you guessed it, on the first Friday of each month, from May to December. Brochures and maps are available on the organization's Web site: ⊕*www.first-fridayartwalk.com.*

In summer, several organizations sponsor outdoor entertainment venues, including alfresco movies and an outdoor concert series. Portland is also home to a handful of very talented professional and community theater groups that hit the stage year-round.

Cumberland County Civic Center (✉1 Civic Center Sq. ☎207/775–3458) hosts concerts, sporting events, and family shows. **Portland City Hall's Merrill Auditorium** (✉20 Myrtle St. ☎207/842–0800) hosts numerous theatrical and musical events, including performances by the Portland Symphony Orchestra, Portland Concert Association, and Portland Opera Repertory Theater. On most Tuesdays from mid-June to September, organ recitals ($5 donation) are given on the auditorium's huge 1912 Kotzschmar Memorial Organ. **Portland's Downtown District** (☎207/772–6828 ⊕*www.portlandmaine.com*) plans a host of activities throughout the year, including Portland's beloved Old Port Festival, held the first Sunday in June, a Thursday-afternoon outdoor music series in Monument Square, movies in Congress Square, and another outdoor concert series in Post Office Park. There's also the grand Christmas tree–lighting ceremony in late November. **Portland Stage Company** (✉25-A Forest Ave. ☎207/774–0465) mounts productions year-round on its two stages.

SPORTS & THE OUTDOORS

When the weather's good, everyone in Portland heads outside. Some drive out of the city to explore, but many take to the streets and trails with their bikes, their dogs, and/or their kids to enjoy the season. Portland has quite a bit of green space in its several parks and in the heat of summer these places make for cool retreats with refreshing fountains and plenty of shade. Local sports teams are the Portland Sea Dogs (baseball) and the Portland Pirates (hockey).

THE EASTERN PROM TRAIL

To experience the city's busy shoreline and grand views of Casco Bay, walkers, cyclists, and in-line skaters head out on the Eastern Prom Trail.

Beginning at the intersection of Commercial and India streets, this paved trail follows the old railroad tracks of the Maine Narrow Gauge Railroad Co. & Museum. There are plenty of places with benches and tables for a picnic break along the way. From the trailhead, it's about 1¼ mi to the small East End Beach.

You can continue along the trail, pass underneath busy I-295, and reemerge at Portland's Back Cove to walk along a 6-mi loop; or you can return to the Old Port by either backtracking along the trail or heading up a grassy hill to the Eastern Promenade, a popular picnic spot and playground.

Take a left back toward the Old Port. Starting down the hill, a gazebo and several old cannons to your left indicate the small and unmarked Fort Allen Park. Use one of the coin-operated viewing scopes to view Ft. Gorges, a Civil War–era military garrison that was never used.

Where the Eastern Prom becomes Fore Street, either head straight back into the Old Port or take a left on India Street, which will bring you just about back to where you started.

Plan an hour to walk to East End Beach and back; add an hour or two if you continue along the Back Cove Trail.

BASEBALL

☺ The Class AA **Portland Sea Dogs** (⊠*271 Park Ave.* ☎*800/936–3647* ⊕*www.seadogs.com*), an affiliate of the Boston Red Sox, play at Hadlock Field. Tickets cost $6–$8.

BICYCLING

For state bike trail maps, club and tour listings, or hints on safety, contact the **Bicycle Coalition of Maine** (⊠*341 Water St., No. 10, Augusta* ☎*207/623–4511* ⊕*www.bikemaine.org*). Rent bikes right downtown at **Cycle Mania** (⊠*59 Federal St.* ☎*207/774–2933* ⊕*www.cyclemania1.com*). They have several models and programs to choose from. For local biking information, contact **Portland Trails** (⊠*305 Commercial St.* ☎*207/775–2411* ⊕*www.trails.org*), a group devoted to blazing (literally) new trails for cyclists and walkers. They can tell you about designated, paved routes that wind along the water, through parks, and beyond. For a map, call, stop in, or get one online. **Summer Feet** (☎*207/828–0342 or 866/857–9544* ⊕*www.summerfeet.net*) has both guided and self-guided cycling tours. Trips cover Portland history and last up to four hours. The outfit also does full-days and overnight trips in other regions of Maine.

BOAT TRIPS

For tours of the harbor, Casco Bay, and the scenic nearby islands, try **Bay View Cruises** (⊠*Fisherman's Wharf* ☎*207/761–0496*). For an extra treat, request the Lobster Bake on the Bay—a full meal of chowder, bread, mussels, lobster, and dessert. **Casco Bay Lines** (⊠*Maine State Pier, 56 Commercial St.* ☎*207/774–7871* ⊕*www.cascobaylines.com*) provides narrated cruises and transportation to Casco Bay Islands. **Eagle Island Tours** (✉*Long Wharf* ☎*207/774–6498* ⊕*www.eagleislandtours. com*) conducts daily cruises to Eagle Island as well as seal-watching cruises. **Lucky Catch Cruises** (✉*170 Commercial St.* ☎*207/761–0941* ⊕*www.luckycatch.com*) sets out to sea in a real lobster boat so passengers can get the genuine experience, which includes hauling traps and the chance to purchase the catch. Choose from several itineraries. **Old Port Mariner Fleet** (✉*Long Wharf* ☎*207/775–0727 or 800/437– 3270*) leads scenic cruises, whale-watching, and fishing trips. **Portland Schooner Co.** (✉*Maine State Pier, 40 Commercial St.* ☎*207/766–2500 or 877/724–6663* ⊕*www.portlandschooner.com*) offers daily sails aboard a vintage 1924, 72-foot racing schooner. Bring your own food and beverage and help hoist the sails of this beauty.

HOCKEY

The **Portland Pirates** (✉*94 Free St.* ☎*207/828–4665* ⊕*www.portlandpirates.com*), the American Hockey League affiliate of the Anaheim Ducks, plays its home games at the Cumberland County Civic Center. Tickets cost $8–$21.

HOT-AIR BALLOON RIDES

Hot Fun Balloon Rides (☎*207/799–0193* ⊕*www.hotfunballoons.com*) offers mainly sunrise trips and can accommodate up to three people. The price of $250 per person includes a postflight champagne toast, snacks, and shuttle to the liftoff site.

SHOPPING

Trendy Exchange Street is great for arts and crafts browsing, while Commercial Street caters to the souvenir hound—gift shops are eager to sell Maine moose, nautical items, and lobster emblems emblazoned on everything from T-shirts to shot glasses.

Several art galleries bring many alternatives to the ubiquitous New England seaside painting. Modern art, photography, sculpture, pottery, and artful woodwork now fill the shelves of many shops, revealing the sophisticated and avant-garde faces of the city's art scene.

ART & ANTIQUES

Abacus (✉*44 Exchange St.* ☎*800/206–2166* ⊕*www.abacusgallery. com*), an appealing crafts gallery, has unusual gift items in glass, wood, and textiles, plus fine modern jewelry. **F. O. Bailey Antiquarians** (✉*35 Depot Rd., Falmouth* ☎*207/781–8001* ⊕*www.fobailey.com*), carries antique and reproduction furniture and jewelry, paintings, rugs, and china. **Foundry Lane Contemporary Crafts** (✉*215 Commercial St.* ☎*207/773–2722* ⊕*www.foundrylane.com*) sells plenty of limited-edition glass, home accessories, and jewelry and is Maine's only dealer of famed Marimekko of Finland products. **Greenhut Galleries** (✉*146 Middle St.* ☎*207/772–2693 or 888/772–2693* ⊕*www.greenhutgalleries. com*) shows contemporary art and sculpture by Maine artists. The **Institute for Contemporary Art** (✉*522 Congress St.* ☎*207/775–3052*), at the Maine College of Art, showcases contemporary artwork from around the world. The **Pine Tree Shop & Bayview Gallery** (✉*75 Market St.* ☎*207/773–3007*) has original art and prints by prominent Maine painters. Representing 100 American artists, the spacious **Stein Gallery** (✉*195 Middle St.* ☎*207/772–9072*) showcases decorative and sculptural contemporary glass.

BOOKS

Carlson Turner Books and Bindery (✉*241 Congress St.* ☎*207/773–4200*) is an antiquarian-book dealer with an estimated 70,000 titles. **Cunningham Books** (✉*188 State St.* ☎*207/775–2246*) is a grand browsing (and buying) experience for book lovers. The owner knows in a moment whether your request is present amid the thousands of titles stacked high on the shelves or along the walls. **Longfellow Books** (✉*1 Monument Way* ☎*207/772–4045*) is a grand success story of the independent bookstore triumphing over the massive presence of the large chains. They're known for their good service and very thoughtful literary selection. There's also a great inventory of greeting cards; author readings are scheduled regularly.

CLOTHING

The women's clothing at **Amaryllis** (✉*41 Exchange St.* ☎*207/772–4439* ⊕*www.amaryllisclothing.com*) includes great casual wear with some unusual evening choices, not to mention shoes, jewelry, and Maine's new favorite keepsake—the souvenir embroidered pillow.

For boutique-quality women's clothing, jewelry, and other artful accessories, visit **Calypso** (✉*2 Milk St.* ☎*207/774–8800*). Family-owned **Casco Bay Wool Works** (✉*10 Moulton St.* ☎*207/879–9665 or 888/222–9665* ⊕*www.cascobaywoolworks.com*) sells beautiful, handcrafted wool capes, shawls, blankets, and scarves.

For the style-conscious man, visit **Joseph's** (✉*410 Fore St.* ☎*207/773–1274* ⊕*www.josephsofportland.com*), which features Canali, Tommy Bahama, and more. With a funky combination of good-quality consignment and new clothing for both men and women, **Material Objects** (✉*500 Congress St.* ☎*207/774–1241*) makes for an affordable and unusual shopping spree.

FURNITURE

Maine islander **Angela Adams** (✉*273 Congress St.* ☎*207/774–3523 or 800/255–9454* ⊕*www.angelaadams.com*) specializes in simple but bold geometric designs parlayed into dramatic rugs, handbags, trays, paper goods, and glassware. Her creations are sold in exclusive venues around the globe, but this small shop on Congress Street is her only studio and showroom.

Head to **Asia West** (✉*219 Commercial St.* ☎*207/775–0066*) for beautiful woodwork in benches, tables, sculpture, and more.

The handsome cherrywood pieces at **Green Design Furniture** (✉*267 Commercial St.* ☎*207/775–4234, 866/756–4730 orders* ⊕*www. greendesigns.com*) are made locally and have a classic feel. A unique system of joinery enables easy assembly after shipping.

SIDE TRIPS FROM PORTLAND

CASCO BAY ISLANDS

2

The islands of Casco Bay are also known as the Calendar Islands because an early explorer mistakenly thought there was one for each day of the year (in reality there are only 140). These islands range from ledges visible only at low tide to populous Peaks Island, a suburb of Portland. Some islands are uninhabited; others support year-round communities as well as stores and restaurants. Fort Gorges commands Hog Island Ledge, and Eagle Island is the site of Arctic explorer Admiral Peary's home. The brightly painted ferries of Casco Bay Lines are the islands' lifeline. There is frequent service to the most-populated ones, including Peaks, Long, Little Diamond, and Great Diamond. A ride on the bay is a great way to experience the dramatic shape of the Maine Coast while offering a glimpse of some of its hundreds of islands.

There is little in the way of brief overnight lodging on the islands; while the population swells during the summer months, much of the increase is due to summer-long visitors and part-time residents. Tourism is passive—there are few restaurants or organized attractions other than the natural beauty of the islands themselves. Meandering about by bike or on foot is a good way to explore the islands on a day trip; or you can spend the day viewing the areas from the ferry or mail boat's bow.

Peaks Island, nearest to Portland, is the most developed of the Calendar Islands, but it still allows you to commune with the wind and sea, explore an old fort, and ramble along the alternately rocky and sandy shore. The trip here by boat is particularly enjoyable at sunset.

A small museum with Civil War artifacts, open in summer, is maintained in the building of the **5th Maine Regiment** (⊠*45 Seashore Ave., Peaks Island* ☎*207/766–3330* ⊕*www.fifthmainemuseum.org* ◷*Memorial Day–Columbus Day, weekends 11–4; July–Aug., weekdays 12–4* PM ⊠*$5 suggested donation*). When the Civil War broke out in 1861, Maine was asked to raise only a single regiment to fight, but the state raised 10 and sent the 5th Maine Regiment into the war's first battle, at Bull Run. Guidebooks for a two-hour self-guided tour of the World War II Peaks Island Reservation are available. Ask about volunteer reenactment events staged throughout summer.

Eagle Island, owned by the state and open to the public for day trips in summer, was the home of Admiral Robert E. Peary, the American explorer of the North Pole. Peary built a stone-and-wood house on the 17-acre island as a summer retreat in 1904 but ended up making it his permanent residence. Filled with Peary's stuffed Arctic birds, the quartz he brought home and set into the fieldstone fireplace, and other objects, the house remains as it was when Peary lived in it. A boat ride here offers a classic Maine experience as you pass by a few of the hundreds of uninhabited, forested islands along the coast. Once you land on Eagle Island, there are plenty of opportunities to explore the rocky beach and myriad trails. The *Fish Hawk* departs from Long Wharf in

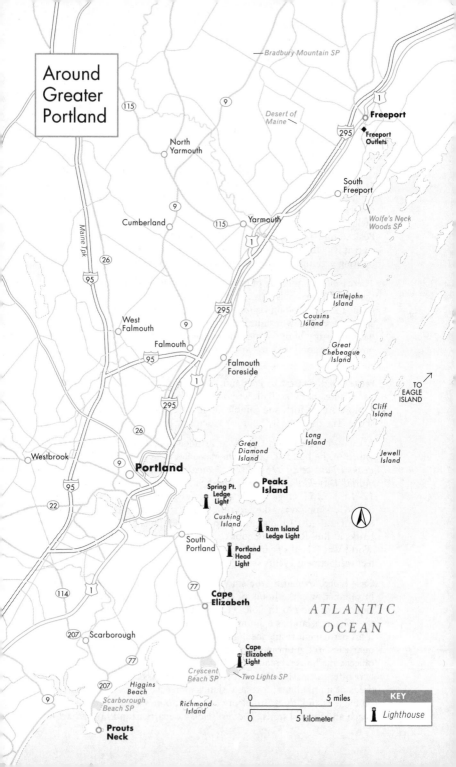

Portland and gives four-hour narrated tours; tours of Portland Head Light and seal-watching cruises are also conducted. ✉*Long Wharf* ☎*207/774–6498* ⊕*www.eagleislandtours.com* 🖅*$26* ⊙*Departures late June–mid-Sept., daily beginning 10* AM.

WHERE TO EAT & STAY

$–$$ ✕**Jones' Landing.** Order a lobster sandwich or cold beer on the outdoor deck just steps from the ferry dock. Stay for the live music on Sunday afternoons. ✉*Welch St., Peaks Island* ☎*207/766–5652* ▭*MC, V.*

$$ 🏠**Peaks Island House.** Simplicity by the sea is the motto here; the five rooms are simply decorated yet comfortable, and the views are stunning. Water and city views give one the sense of peace without feeling entirely isolated from Portland's glittering civilization beyond. The inn's restaurant serves breakfast and dinner. **Pros:** View of Mount Washington in clear weather; genuine island life experience minutes from Portland. **Cons:** Getting to and from the mainland dependent upon ferry schedule; relaxed pace of island life not for everyone. ✉*20 Island Ave., 04108* ☎*207/766–4406* ⊕*www.thepeaksislandhouse. com* 🛏*5 rooms* ♿*In-room: no a/c, no phone. In-hotel: restaurant, no elevator* ▭*AE, D, MC, V.*

SPORTS & THE OUTDOORS

Since the quieter, more independent element of ecotourism endures here, outdoor exploration is best done either by bike, foot, or kayak. If you don't have your own bike or boat, there are a couple of options for rentals and/or tours. **Maine Island Kayak Company** (✉*70 Luther St., Peaks Island* ☎*207/766–2373 or 800/796–2313* ⊕*www.maineisland-kayak.com*) provides both seasoned paddlers and curious beginners with any necessary gear, instruction, or guidance to ensure a safe and fun water exploration.

TOURS

For guided tours of Peaks Island led by longtime residents the MacIsaac family, check out **Island Tours** (✉*Peaks Island* ☎*207/766–5514* ⊕*http:// islandtours.home.att.net*). Ramble about the island in style—in an open golf cart—for a very personalized and lively experience. Tours include sunset, history, and architecture themes. The season runs from May through October; prices are $15. Reservations are recommended.

CAPE ELIZABETH TO PROUTS NECK

WHAT TO SEE

The 243-acre **Crescent Beach State Park,** about 8 mi south of Portland, has a sandy beach, picnic tables, a seasonal snack bar, and a bathhouse. Miles of nature trails head into the woods beyond the beach, ideal for bird-watching and for families with young children. ✉*Rte. 77, Cape Elizabeth* ☎*207/799–5871* 🖅*$4.50* ⊙*Memorial Day–Columbus Day, daily 9* AM*–sunset.*

Higgins Beach is a good-size and very popular sandy beach set amid a little beach-colony neighborhood. Parking costs about $4 in several privately owned lots. The beach is popular with surfers and sunbathers. ⊠*Off Rte. 77 (Spurwink Rd.), Scarborough.*

**EN
ROUTE**

Just off Route 77 (Spurwink Road) near Higgins Beach is the Higgins Beach Market (⊠*82 Spurwink Rd.* ☎*207/883–2766***), a small wooden barnlike shop filled with surprisingly sophisticated wares. Get the goods for a sunset beach picnic complete with wine or beer, freshly made sandwiches, bakery items, and even prepared cold meals, all to go. The market opens at 6 AM and closes around 6 PM, mid-May through late-October.**

Fodor'sChoice
★

Historic **Portland Head Light,** familiar to many from photographs and Edward Hopper's painting *Portland Head-Light (1927),* was commissioned by George Washington in 1790. The towering white stone lighthouse stands over the keeper's house, a white home with a blazing red roof. Besides a harbor view, its park has walking paths and picnic facilities. The keeper's house is now the Museum at Portland Head Light. The lighthouse is in Fort Williams Park, about 2 mi from the town center. *Museum* ⊠*1000 Shore Rd., Cape Elizabeth* ☎*207/799–2661* ⊕*www.portlandheadlight.com* ☜*$2* ☾*Memorial Day–mid-Oct., daily 10–4; Apr., May, Nov., and Dec., weekends 10–4.*

Scarborough Beach State Park has a large sandy beach area with ample parking, lifeguards, and lots of people-watching opportunities. There is a parking fee. ⊠*Rte. 207, Scarborough* ☾*9–7 daily.*

★

Two Lights State Park sits on just over 40 acres of Maine's quintessential rocky shoreline. Named for the two lighthouses atop the hill (one is now privately owned, the other still in use since 1828), the park has ample beach access, picnic facilities, and great views of the activities of Portland Harbor. The fee is $3. ⊠*Rte. 77, Cape Elizabeth* ☎*207/799–5871* ☾*Daily 9 AM–sunset.* ☜*$1.50.*

WHERE TO EAT & STAY

$$–$$$$

✕**Joe's Boathouse.** The two small dining rooms of this establishment are simple, clean, and finished in sea-foam green, with large windows looking out to a marina. The ocean motif extends to a lobster boat on a mantle and a bar that houses an aquarium. Dinner specials include tuna steak and lemon tarragon sea scallops; for lunch try the Red Riot, a sandwich featuring spicy sausage, capicola, and red peppers. In summer diners can enjoy the flavors and the scenery from the vantage of a patio. Altogether, it is low-key, casual, and a hit with the locals. ⊠*1 Spring Point Dr.* ☎*207/741–2780* ⊕*www.joesboathouse.com* ☐*AE, MC, V.*

$–$$

✕**Good Table.** Close to Two Lights State Park, this is a great little place to get weekend breakfast or brunch before visiting the beach. The omelets are big and moist, as is the French toast. The lunch and dinner menu is a bit reminiscent of the old diner days and includes a hot turkey dinner with mashed potatoes and gravy. You'll also find fresh fried seafood and a very tasty lobster roll. Sit under the colorful paper lanterns out on the screened-in porch and enjoy the woodsy view. ⊠*526 Ocean House Rd., Cape Elizabeth* ☎*207/799–4663* ⊕*www.thegoodtablerestaurant.net* ☐*MC, V* ☾*Closed Mon.*

¢–$$ ✕Lobster Shack. You can't beat the location—right on the water, below the lighthouse pair that gives Two Lights State Park its name—and the food's not bad either. Just as the name implies, fresh lobster is the watchword here, and you can choose your meal right from the tank. Other menu must-haves include chowder, fried clams, and fish-and-chips. It's been a classic spot since the 1920s. Eat inside or out. ✉225 Two Lights Rd. ☎207/799–1677 ⊕www.lobstershack-twolights.com ▭MC, V ☾Closed Nov.–late Mar.

$$$–$$$$ ✕⊡Inn by the Sea. Every unit in this all-suites inn includes a kitchen and a view of the Atlantic. It's a short walk down a private boardwalk to sandy Crescent Beach, a popular family spot. Dogs are welcomed with a room-service pet menu, evening turndown treats, and oversize beach towels. The Audubon dining room ($$$–$$$$), open to non-guests, serves fine seafood and regional dishes. The shingle-style design, typical of turn-of-the-20th-century New England shorefront cottages and hotels, includes a varied roofline punctuated by turretlike features and gables, balconies, a covered porch supported by columns, an open deck, and large windows. **Pros:** On Crescent Beach and a short drive to Two Lights, Portland Head, and Portland. **Con:** A bit large to be considered charming. ✉40 Bowery Beach Rd., (7 mi south of Portland) Cape Elizabeth 04107 ☎207/799–3134 or 800/888–4287 ⊕www.innbythesea.com ⇆43 suites △In-room: kitchen, refrigerator, VCR, dial-up. In-hotel: restaurant, bar, tennis court, pool, laundry service, public Internet, some pets allowed ▭AE, D, MC, V.

$$$$ ⊡Black Point Inn. Toward the tip of the peninsula that juts into the ocean at Prouts Neck stands this stylish, tastefully updated historic resort with spectacular views up and down the coast. The extensive grounds contain beaches, trails, and sports facilities—including use of the tennis courts and golf course at the nearby country club. Finer touches abound, such as nightly turndown service and in-room terry robes. The Cliff Walk, a pebbled path that wanders past Winslow Homer's former studio, runs along the Atlantic headlands that Homer often painted. The inn is 12 mi south of Portland and about 10 mi north of Old Orchard Beach. **Pros:** Stunning water views, set amid scenery that inspired Winslow Homer. **Con:** Driving required to get to area attractions ✉510 Black Point Rd., Scarborough 04074 ☎207/883–2500 ⊕www.blackpointinn.com ⇆25 rooms △In-room: DVD (some), Wi-Fi. In-hotel: restaurant, bar, pools, bicycles ▭AE, D, MC, V ▯◉MAP.

SPORTS & THE OUTDOORS

This area is home to several state parks and long stretches of beachfront that are ideal for sunbathing, strolling, and exploring. Routes 77 and 207 are ideal for cyclists who like winding roads and pastoral scenery. Walkers can choose from miles of trails within the state parks, and there are plenty of ideal spots for picnics and ocean-side barbecues. This is the region where Portland's city folk come to walk the beach and enjoy the open space.

The **Maine Audubon Society** (✉Rte. 9, Scarborough ☎207/781–2330, 207/883–5100 from mid-June to Labor Day ⊕www.maineaudubon.

org) operates guided canoe trips and rents canoes in Scarborough Marsh, the largest salt marsh in Maine. Programs at Maine Audubon's Falmouth headquarters (north of Portland) include nature walks and a discovery room for children.

FREEPORT

17 mi northeast of Portland, 10 mi southwest of Brunswick.

Those who flock straight to L. L. Bean and see nothing else of Freeport are missing out on some real New England beauty. The city's charming back streets are lined with historic buildings and old clapboard houses, and there's a pretty little harbor on the south side of the Harraseeket River. It's true, many who come to the area do so simply to shop—L. L. Bean is the store that put Freeport on the map, and plenty of outlets and some specialty stores have settled here. Still, if you choose, you can stay awhile and experience more than fabulous shopping; beyond the shops are bucolic nature preserves with miles of walking trails, well-maintained old homes, and plenty of places for leisurely ambling that don't require the overuse of your credit cards.

The **Freeport Historical Society** mounts exhibits pertaining to the town's history. You can also pick up a village walking map here. ⊠*45 Main St.* ☎*207/865–3170* ⊙*Tues., Thurs., Fri., 10–2:30; Wed. 10–7.*

☺ At the **Desert of Maine,** a 40-acre natural desert, you can tour the sand dunes in a safari coach, walk nature trails, hunt for gemstones, and watch sand artists at work. Poor agricultural practices in the late 18th century combined with massive land clearing and overgrazing uncovered this desert, which was actually formed by a glacier during the last Ice Age. ⊠*I–95, Exit 20* ☎*207/865–6962* ⊕*www.desertofmaine.com* ▭*$5.25–$8.75* ⊙*Early May–mid-Oct., 8:30–5:30 daily.*

OFF THE BEATEN PATH

Pettengill Farm. To escape Freeport's busy outlet scene, take a stroll back in time at this 19th-century farm. Operated by the Freeport Historical Society, the aged and beautiful farm is set on 140 acres of salt marsh, with open fields, exquisite gardens, and an original 1810 saltbox home. It's an excellent spot for nature watching; bring your camera and binoculars to see deer, fox, and a vast array of both migratory and native birds. You're free to wander the grounds; tours of the home can be arranged by appointment. Not too easy to find and with very little parking, the farm is a true hidden treasure. To reach the small parking area, head out of Freeport on Bow Street, pass over the Harraseeket River, and look for Pettengill Road on the right. It's a half-mile walk to the grounds. It's worth it for the sheer beauty and sense of historic solitude. ☎ *207/865-3170* ⊕ *www.freeporthistoricalsociety.org.*

WHERE TO EAT & STAY

$$–$$$$

Fodor'sChoice ★

✕**Broad Arrow Tavern.** On the main floor of the Harraseeket Inn, this dark-paneled tavern with mounted moose heads, decoys, snowshoes, and other outdoor sporty decor is known for both its casual nature and its sumptuous menu. The chefs use only organically grown food, with a nearly exclusive emphasis on Maine products, to create treats such as steaks and seafood wood-grilled in a large brick hearth. About the only non-Maine ingredient is the farm-raised South Dakota buffalo, though the burger it makes is a real favorite. For lunch, choose from the ample menu or graze on the well-stocked buffet. Lunch and dinner are served daily from 11 AM. ⊠*162 Main St.* ☎*207/865–9377* ☖*Reservations not accepted* ⊟*AE, D, DC, MC, V.*

$–$$$ ✕ **Azure Café.** This airy little café right on Main Street provides both an appealing atmosphere and an enticing menu. Local fruits, vegetables, meats, and seafood are all treated to an Italian transformation. Dinner favorites are the Tuscan pork tenderloin and the fresh Atlantic haddock with Maine crab, salmon, shrimp, and scallop stuffing. With a nod to the state of Maine, the decidedly non-Italian lunch menu offers superior clam chowder, steamed lobster, and fish-and-chips. In summer sit out on the street-side patio, listen to live jazz, savor the tiramisu, and forget about nearby outlet bargains for just a little while. Reservations are recommended. ⊠*123 Main St.* ☎*207/865–1237* ⊕*www.azure-cafe.com* ⊟*MC, V.*

$–$$$ ✕ **Harraseeket Lunch & Lobster Co.** Seafood baskets and lobster dinners are the focus at this bare-bones place beside the town landing in South Freeport. Order at the counter and find a seat inside or out, depending on the weather. ⊠*On pier, end of Main St.* ☎*207/865–4888* ☖*Reservations not accepted* ⊟*No credit cards* ♡*Closed mid-Oct.–Apr.*

$$$$ ✕▤ **Harraseeket Inn.** Despite modern appointments such as elevators
★ and whirlpool baths in some rooms, this 1850 Greek Revival home provides a pleasantly old-fashioned, country-inn experience just a few minutes' walk from L.L. Bean. Guest rooms have print fabrics and reproductions of Federal quarter-canopy beds. Ask for a second-floor, garden-facing room. The formal Maine Dining Room ($$$–$$$$) specializes in contemporary American regional (and organic) cuisine such as pan-roasted lobster and all-natural filet mignon. The casual yet excellent Broad Arrow Tavern ($$–$$$$) serves heartier fare and has a charming seasonal patio. Inn rates include a full buffet breakfast and afternoon tea. **Pros:** Excellent on-site dining, walk to shopping district. **Con:** Building updates over the years have diminished some authenticity. ⊠*162 Main St., Freeport 04032* ☎*207/865–9377 or 800/342–6423* ⊕*www.harraseeketinn.com* ➴*84 rooms* ♤*In-room: refrigerator (some), dial-up. In-hotel: 2 restaurants, pool, no-smoking rooms* ⊟*AE, D, DC, MC, V* ⑩*BP.*

$$$$ ▤ **James Place Inn.** Set on a quiet side street yet within easy walking distance of shopping paradise, this peaceful inn is tastefully decorated with brightly painted walls, colorful floral bedspreads, hooked rugs, and four-poster beds. Maine-inspired artwork and fresh flowers add to the simple elegance of the place, which serves a full, hot breakfast in a light-dappled sunroom (or on a deck when the weather is nice). Some marbled bathrooms even provide two-person Jacuzzis. For winter visits, choose the room with a working fireplace. One room has a kitchenette. **Pros:** Classic Maine Victorian-style cottage, close to shopping district. **Con:** Proximity to buzzing shopping district detracts

from country experience ⊠*11 Holbrook St. 04032* ☎*207/865–4486 or 800/964–9086* ⊕*www.jamesplaceinn.com* ➫*7 rooms* ♿*In-room: no phone, kitchen (1). In-hotel: no elevator, no kids under 8* ⊟*AE, D, MC, V* ℺*BP.*

$$$ ⊞ **Atlantic Seal Bed & Breakfast.** The nautical theme of this 1850 waterfront home complements the pleasant water views from all three of its rooms. Owner Captain Thomas Ring provides homemade quilts, antiques, and down comforters for each room; he also leads scenic boat trips from the nearby harbor (⇨ *see Atlantic Seal Cruises below*). **Pro:** Wood fireplace in one room, suite has private deck. **Con:** Window of time for breakfast shorter than usual. ⊠*25 Main St., Box 146, South Freeport 04078* ☎*207/865–6112, 877/285–7325 seasonal* ➫*2 rooms, 1 suite* ♿*In-room: VCR/DVD (1). In-hotel: bicycles, no elevator, no-smoking rooms* ⊟*AE, MC, V* ℺*BP.*

NIGHTLIFE & THE ARTS

Once a week in July and August, sit outside under the stars for the **L. L. Bean Summer Concert Series** (⊠*Morse St.* ☎*800/559–0747 Ext. 37222* ⊕*www.llbean.com*). The free concerts start at 7:30 PM in downtown Freeport at L. L. Bean's Discovery Park. The entertainment ranges from folk, jazz, and country to rock and includes some pretty big names. Bring a blanket and refreshments. Look for special Sunday concert events in late fall and in the winter holiday season. Previous summer acts have included Livingston Taylor, zydeco and bluegrass musicians, and the Don Campbell Band.

SPORTS & THE OUTDOORS

Atlantic Seal Cruises (⊠*South Freeport* ☎*207/865–6112, 877/285–7325 seasonal*) operates day trips to Eagle Island and Seguin Island lighthouse, as well as evening seal and osprey watches. Admission is $28. Reservations are recommended.

It shouldn't come as a surprise that one of the world's largest outdoor clothing and supply outfitters also provides its customers with instructional adventures to go with their products. L. L. Bean's year-round **Outdoor Discovery Schools** (⊠*Freeport* ☎*888/552–3261* ⊕*www.llbean. com/ods*) include half- and one-day classes, as well as longer trips that teach canoeing, shooting, photography, kayaking, fly-fishing, crosscountry skiing, and other sports. Classes are for all skill levels; it's best to sign up several months in advance. Check their schedule for special activities held regularly during the summer months.

STATE PARKS **Bradbury Mountain State Park** has moderate trails to the top of Bradbury Mountain. There are lovely views of the sea from the peak. A picnic area and shelter, a ball field, a playground, and 41 campsites are among the facilities. ⊠*528 Hallowell Rd., Pownal* ☎*207/688–4712* ☉*9 AM–sunset daily* ▨*$3.*

Wolfe's Neck Woods State Park has 5 mi of good hiking trails along Casco Bay, the Harraseeket River, and a fringe salt marsh. Naturalists lead walks in summer and on weekends and holidays in spring and fall; it's an excellent place to view nesting ospreys. The park has picnic tables and grills but no camping. ✉ *Wolfe's Neck Rd., follow Bow St. opposite L. L. Bean off U.S. 1* ☎ *207/865–4465* ⬛ *$3* ☉ *Apr.–Oct.*

SHOPPING

The *Freeport Visitors Guide* (☎ *207/865–1212, 800/865–1994 for a copy*) lists the more than 100 shops and factory outlet stores that can be found on Main Street, Bow Street, and elsewhere, including such big-name designers as Coach, Brooks Brothers, Polo Ralph Lauren, and Cole-Haan. Don't overlook the specialty stores and crafts galleries.

Cuddledown of Maine (✉ *237 U.S. 1* ☎ *207/865–1713*) has a selection of down comforters, pillows, and luxurious bedding. Head upstairs for discounted merchandise. Kids get their chance to shop at the educational toy store **Play and Learn** (✉ *200 Lower Main St.* ☎ *207/865–6434*). **Thos. Moser Cabinetmakers** (✉ *149 Main St.* ☎ *207/865–4519*) sells high-quality handmade furniture with clean, classic lines.

Fodor's Choice ★ Founded in 1912 as a mail-order merchandiser of products for hunters, guides, and anglers, **L. L. Bean** (✉ *95 Main St. [U.S. 1]* ☎ *800/341–4341*) attracts 3.5 million shoppers a year to its giant store (open 24 hours a day) in the heart of Freeport's shopping district. You can still find the original hunting boots, along with cotton, wool, and silk sweaters; camping and ski equipment; comforters; and hundreds of other items for the home, car, boat, and campsite. The **L. L. Bean Factory Store** (✉ *Depot St.* ☎ *800/341–4341*) has seconds and discontinued merchandise at discount prices. **L. L. Bean Kids** (✉ *8 Nathan Nye St.* ☎ *800/341–4341*) specializes in children's merchandise and has a climbing wall and other activities that appeal to kids.

GREATER PORTLAND ESSENTIALS

To research prices, get advice from other travelers, and book travel arrangements, visit www.fodors.com.

TRANSPORTATION

BY AIR

Portland International Jetport is served by Continental, Delta, Jet Blue, Northwest, United, and US Airways.

Information **Portland International Jetport** (✉ *Westbrook St. off Rte. 9, Portland* ☎ *207/774–7301* ⊕ *www.portlandjetport.org*).

BY BIKE

The craggy fingers of land that dominate this part of the coast are fun for experienced cyclists to explore, but the lack of shoulders on most roads combined with heavy tourist traffic can be intimidating. Two good resources are the Bicycle Coalition of Maine and the Maine Department of Transportation, which provide information on trails and bike shops around the state.

Information **Bicycle Coalition of Maine** (🖂 *Box 5275, Augusta 04332* ☎ *207/623–4511* ⊕ *www.bikemaine.org*). **Maine Department of Transportation Explore Maine by Bike** (⊕ *www.exploremaine.org/bike*).

BY BOAT & FERRY

Casco Bay Lines provides ferry service from Portland to the islands of Casco Bay. The CAT, a stunning, modern catamaran ferry, travels between Portland and Yarmouth, Nova Scotia.

Information **Casco Bay Lines** (☎ *207/774–7871* ⊕ *www.cascobaylines.com*). **The CAT** (☎ *877/359–3760* ⊕ *www.catferry.com*).

BY BUS

Greater Portland's Metro runs seven bus routes in Portland, South Portland, and Westbrook. The fare is $1.25; exact change is required. Buses run from 5:30 AM to 11:45 PM.

The Portland Explorer has express shuttle service to the Old Port from the Portland Jetport, the Portland Transportation Center, and other downtown locations. The shuttle runs hourly, seven days a week, from noon to 7 PM. Fare is $2.

Long-distance bus travel is available within Maine plus neighboring states. Concord Trailways offers service to Boston's Logan Airport, Boston, and points within coastal Maine. Vermont Transit Company services towns throughout Maine and northern New England. Portland's Transportation Center is close to downtown and the airport.

Bus Stations **Portland Transportation Center** (☎ *207/828–1151.*).

Bus Lines **Concord Trailways** (☎ *800/639–3317* ⊕ *www.concordtrailways.com*). **Metro Greater Portland Transit District** (☎ *207/774–0351* ⊕ *www.gpmetrobus. com*). **Portland Explorer** (☎ *207/774–9891* ⊕ *www.transportme.org*). **Vermont Transit Company** (☎ *800/642–3133* ⊕ *www.vermonttransit.com*).

BY CAR

Several car-rental options exist at the Portland Jetport; others are dispersed around the South Portland area, just outside the main city limits. *See Car Rental in Maine Essentials at the back of the book for national rental agency phone numbers.*

Congress Street leads from I–295 into the heart of Portland; the Gateway Garage on High Street, off Congress, is a convenient place to leave your car downtown. North of Portland, U.S. 1 brings you to Freeport's Main Street, which continues on to Brunswick and Bath. East of Wiscasset you can take Route 27 south to the Boothbays, where Route 96 is a good choice for further exploration. To visit the Pemaquid region, take Route 129 off U.S. 1 in Damariscotta; then pick up Route 130 and follow it down to Pemaquid Point. Return to Waldoboro and U.S. 1 on Route 32 from New Harbor.

In Portland, metered on-street parking is available at 25¢ per half hour, with a two-hour maximum. Parking lots and garages can be found downtown, in the Old Port, and on the waterfront; most charge $1 per hour or $8–$12 per day. If you're shopping or dining, remember to ask local vendors if they participate in the Park & Shop program, which provides an hour of free shopping for each vendor visited.

BY TAXI

Though sometimes bustling, Portland is still a small city, so taxis do not rush about as they do in locales that are more populous. Your best bet is to call ahead rather than wait to flag a driver down. However, the small size is an advantage in getting around, for many destinations in downtown are in close proximity. There is even a water taxi to get to and from the islands of Casco Bay. Meter rates are $1.40 for the first 1/9 mi, 25¢ for each additional 1/9 mi throughout Portland.

Taxi Companies **ABC Taxi** (☎ *207/772–8685*). **Elite Cab** (☎ *207/871–7667*). **Portland Express Water Taxi** (☎ *207/415–8493*). **South Portland Taxi** (☎ *207/767–5200*).

BY TRAIN

Amtrak runs the *Downeaster* train service from Boston to Portland, with stops (some seasonal) along the coastal route.

Information **Amtrak** (☎ *800/872–7245* ⊕ *www.amtrakdowneaster.com*).

CONTACTS & RESOURCES

DISABILITIES & ACCESSIBILITY

The Greater Portland area, especially downtown and the Old Port, have many establishments doing business out of old, historic buildings. As a result, ADA-compliance can be hit-or-miss—but it is becoming more prevalent every year. The larger, modern hotels are more likely to have elevators and fully accessible rooms than the smaller, more historic bed-and-breakfast inns. In 2006, the Convention and Visitors Bureau of Greater Portland listed 36 restaurants as being compliant.

All buses operated by the Metro Greater Portland Transit District are equipped with lifts or ramps, and Casco Bay Lines ferries are wheelchair accessible as well. Smaller vessels may be a different story, so calling in advance is a good idea.

EMERGENCIES

In an emergency dial 911.

Hospitals Maine Medical Center (✉ *22 Bramhall St., Portland* ☎ *207/662–0111*). **Mercy Hospital** (✉ *144 State St., Portland* ☎ *207/879–3000*).

MEDIA

The *Portland Press Herald* is published Monday–Saturday; the *Maine Sunday Telegram* is published on Sunday. The *Portland Phoenix*, a free weekly published each Thursday, is essential for those interested in Portland's many entertainment and arts offerings. *Portland Magazine* and the bimonthly *Port City Life*, cover Portland, while the *Maine Times* extends throughout the state.

WMEA 90.1 is the local National Public Radio affiliate; WCSH, channel 6, is the NBC affiliate; WMTW, channel 8, is the ABC affiliate; and WGME, channel 13, is the CBS affiliate. Channel 10 is the Maine Public Broadcasting affiliate.

VISITOR INFORMATION

Contacts Convention and Visitors Bureau of Greater Portland (✉ *305 Commercial St., Portland 04101* ☎ *207/772–5800 or 877/833–1374* ⊕ *www.visitportland.com*). **Freeport Merchants Association** (✉ *23 Depot St., Freeport 04032* ☎ *207/865–1212 or 800/865–1994* ⊕ *www.freeportusa.com*). **Portland Regional Chamber of Commerce** (✉ *60 Pearl St., Portland 04101* ☎ *207/772–2811* ⊕ *www.portlandregion.com*). **Portland's Downtown District** (✉ *94 Free St., Portland 04101* ☎ *207/772–6828* ⊕ *www.portlandmaine.com*).

The Mid-Coast Region

3

WORD OF MOUTH

"We love Brunswick . . . it is a quaint town with a wonderful main street, with cute stores and good choices for dining . . . it is a beautiful part of Maine!"

—Kwoo

By Sherry
Ballou Hanson

LIGHTHOUSES DOT THE HEADLANDS of Maine's Mid-Coast region, where thousands of miles of coastline wait to be explored. Defined by chiseled peninsulas stretching south from U.S. 1, this area has everything from the sandy beaches and sandbars of Popham Beach to the jutting cliffs of Monhegan Island. If you are intent on hooking a trophy-size fish or catching a glimpse of a whale, there are plenty of cruises available. If you want to explore deserted beaches and secluded coves, kayaks are your best bet. Put in at the Harpswells, or on the Cushing and Saint George peninsulas, or simply paddle among the lobster boats and other vessels that ply these waters.

Tall ships often visit Maine, sometimes sailing up the Kennebec River for a stopover at Bath's Maine Maritime Museum. Not far away, the Bath Iron Works, on the site of the old Percy and Small Shipyard, still builds the U.S. Navy's Aegis-class destroyers. In Brunswick you can visit the home (now a museum) of General Joshua L. Chamberlain, hero at the pivotal Battle of Little Round Top at Gettysburg and once a professor at Bowdoin College.

The charming towns, each unique, have their array of attractions. Brunswick has rows of historic wood and clapboard homes, while Bath is known for its maritime heritage. Wiscasset Harbor has docks where you can stroll and waterfront seafood restaurants where you can enjoy the catch of the day—Damariscotta, too, is worth a stop for its seafood restaurants. Boothbay has lots of little stores that are perfect for window-shopping, while Thomaston and environs offer scenic drives through fishing villages surrounded by water on all sides.

EXPLORING THE MID-COAST REGION

A car is helpful if you want to get away from the towns, as the remoter areas are not served by public transportation. Buses from Boston's South Station and Logan Airport serve many coastal towns, including Portland, Brunswick, and Bath. The *Downeaster* Amtrak train carries passengers to and from Portland and Boston's North Station. Visitors to the area also can take a wonderful scenic train ride between Brunswick, Bath, and Wiscasset to Rockland and back from late May to mid-October (see *www.maineeasternrailroad.com* for details).

No matter where you stay, there are plenty of places to explore within a few miles. Brunswick is only a half hour from the Harpswell Islands. Phippsburg and Georgetown are easily accessible from Bath. You can stop for lunch in Wiscasset and then continue to Boothbay Harbor for an afternoon of shopping. Take at least a day to explore the Pemaquid Peninsula, where you'll find a famous lighthouse, a museum, and art gallery perched on rocky ledges, and a tranquil beach. Farther north, Thomaston is a good place to stay if you want to explore the St. George and Cushing peninsulas, and the towns of Tenants Harbor and Port Clyde. Marshall Point Lighthouse is in Port Clyde, as is the departure point for Monhegan Island—a great place to spend a day or two hiking through woods and along spectacular cliffs.

GREAT ITINERARIES

IF YOU HAVE 3 DAYS

If you have just a few days in the area, plan to spend your nights in **Brunswick** or **Bath**. From Brunswick, drive south on Route 24 or Route 123 to explore the Harpswells. Here you'll find a small beach and the bronze Fishermen's Memorial adjacent to the Land's End Gift Shop. Stop for a haddock sandwich at one of the seafood shacks in the area. In the afternoon, take a kayaking trip along the coast. That night, have dinner in Brunswick.

On Day 2, drive south on Route 209 from Bath to Popham Beach State Park, where the Kennebec and Morse rivers meet the sea. Plan to arrive before 10 AM, as the parking lot fills fast. If you arrive at or near low tide, you can explore miles of tidal flats and walk across to Wood Island. You can hike along the beach to Fort Popham, a Civil War–era fortification that is fun to explore. Bring your lunch or pick up a clam or lobster roll near the beach.

You can't complete your time in the Mid-Coast region without an introduction to the area's shipbuilding history. Visit the Maine Maritime Museum in Bath on your third day for a tour of the old shipyard and to see the seafaring art and artifacts that fill this beautiful museum. Stroll through downtown Bath in the afternoon, stopping at Waterfront Park to watch the fishing boats, or sign up for a cruise on the Kennebec River.

IF YOU HAVE 5 DAYS

Follow the itinerary above for the first three days. On your fourth day, drive north on U.S. 1 to visit Reid State Park, where you can climb up the ledges and watch the waves pound into the rocks below. There are several lodgings in Georgetown right on the water from which you can choose. Heading north on your fifth day, leave U.S. 1 shortly after crossing the bridge at **Wiscasset** and take Route 27 to **Boothbay,** where you can browse in the antiques shops and art galleries or scan the horizon for whales on one of the many sightseeing cruises. Spend the night in Boothbay.

WHEN TO GO

In summer, temperatures typically reach the 80s and occasionally the 90s, so visitors enjoy the long stretches of sun-splashed beaches and whale-watching cruises. In autumn, the humidity is gone, the days are often sunny and warm, and the nights are crisp, dropping into the 40s and 50s. Fall foliage in the Mid-Coast region is spectacular, with brilliant reds and oranges bursting from maple trees and yellows illuminating the birch trees until late October. Fishing and hunting are popular activities, and kayaking and white-water rafting are invigorating under the brilliant blue skies.

In winter, you don't have to reserve months ahead if you want a room in your favorite country inn or bed-and-breakfast—though some close in the off-season. You can enjoy skiing and snowmobiling, or just curl up by the fire with a good book. Sea storms can be dramatic in November and December; a visit to the coastline this time of year reveals how those boulders you find atop the cliffs got there. In spring, the hotels and restaurants are not yet crowded either. Many businesses remain closed until early or mid-May, but you shouldn't have trouble finding at least a few antiques shops and art galleries that are open. April temperatures often don't reach above the 40s; the days gradually warm up in May.

ABOUT THE RESTAURANTS

Lobsters are the main draw—there are even lobster rolls on the menu at many McDonald's locations. You'll find some of the freshest crustaceans at the local lobster

---

MID COAST TOP 5

■ Savor a crustacean casserole at Cook's Lobster House.

■ Relax on a private beach at the Log Cabin Inn.

■ Take in the "Million Dollar View" at Popham Beach State Park.

■ Stroll around Wiscasset, one of Maine's prettiest villages.

■ Taste legendary walnut pie at Moody's Diner in Waldoboro.

---

pounds, which are saltwater pools where you can decide which lobster to have for dinner. The area is also famous for its haddock sandwiches, homemade chowders, crab cakes, lobster bisque, and fried clams. Of course, steak and prime rib are here too. The amount of food may be daunting to light eaters, but many restaurants also offer smaller portions. There is always a downright delicious chocolate item on the dessert menu, and Green Mountain Coffee is a local favorite. Breakfast anywhere usually features blueberry muffins.

Casual dress is perfectly fine in most restaurants along the coast. Many restaurants accept reservations in summer when business is brisk, so call ahead to check.

ABOUT THE HOTELS

The Mid-Coast offers accommodations ranging from oceanfront cabins to elegant bed-and-breakfasts to seaside resorts. Many of the most interesting lodgings are former sea captains' or shipbuilders' homes, beautifully restored and furnished with period pieces. From Memorial Day through Labor Day, rates rise, many of the pricier places require a two-night minimum stay, and reservations are advised. Most accommodations have air-conditioning and cable TV, and many now have Internet access. At the lower end of the scale, you can still find clean, comfortable rooms with basic amenities. Stunning views can crop up in any of the price ranges. Most B&Bs in Maine do not allow smoking on the property.

WHAT IT COSTS					
	¢	$	$$	$$$	$$$$
RESTAURANTS	under $7	$7–$10	$11–$17	$18–$25	over $25
HOTELS	under $60	$60–$99	$100–$149	$150–$200	over $200

Restaurant prices are for a main course at dinner, excluding sales tax of 7%. Hotel prices are for two people in a standard double room in high season, excluding service charges and 7% tax.

FROM BRUNSWICK TO WISCASSET

BRUNSWICK & THE HARPSWELLS

10 mi north of Freeport, 30 mi northeast of Portland.

Lovely brick-and-clapboard buildings are the highlight of Brunswick's Federal Street Historic District, which includes Federal Street and Park Row and the stately campus of Bowdoin College. From the intersection of Pleasant and Maine streets, in the center of town, you can walk in any direction and discover an impressive array of restaurants. Seafood? German cuisine? A Chinese buffet that beats out all the competition? It's all here. So are bookstores, gift shops, boutiques, and jewelers. From pushcart vendors on the shady town green, known as the Mall, you can sample finger foods such as hamburgers, clam rolls, and that old Maine favorite, steamed hot dogs.

From Brunswick, Routes 123 and 24 take you to the peninsulas and islands known collectively as the **Harpswells.** Small coves along Harpswell Neck shelter lobster boats, and summer cottages are tucked away amid birch and spruce trees. On your way down to Land's End at the end of Route 24, stop at Mackerel Cove to see a real fishing harbor; there are a few parking spaces where you can stop and picnic and look for beach glass, or put in your kayaks.

WHAT TO SEE

The 110-acre campus of Bowdoin College, at Maine, Bath, and College streets, off the east end of Pleasant Street, is an enclave of distinguished buildings separated by pleasant gardens and grassy quadrangles. Famous past Bowdoin graduates include Nathaniel Hawthorne, Henry Wadsworth Longfellow, and Civil War hero Joshua L. Chamberlain. Several attractions on campus are worth visiting: The **Bayview Gallery** (⊠*58 Maine St., Brunswick* ☎*207/236–4534 or 800/244–3007* ⊕*www.bayviewgallery.com* ⊗*10* AM*–5:30* PM *Mon.–Sat.*) specializes in contemporary American impressionist and realist work; it has a second location in Camden. The **Bowdoin College Museum of Art** (⊠*Bath Rd. at Upper Maine St., Brunswick* ☎*207/725–3275* ⊠*Free* ⊗*Tues., Wed., and Sat. 10–5; Thurs. 10–8; Sun. 1–5*) is set in a splendid Renaissance Revival–style building designed by Charles F. McKim in 1894. The building closed for expansion and a total upgrade, and reopened in October 2007. The museum displays interesting collections that encompass Assyrian and classical art and works by Dutch, Italian, French, and Flemish old masters; a superb gathering of Colonial and Federal paintings, notably Gilbert Stuart portraits of Madison and Jefferson; and a Winslow Homer gallery of engravings, etchings, and memorabilia (open in summer only). The museum's collection also includes 19th- and 20th-century American painting and sculpture, with works by Mary Cassatt, Andrew Wyeth, and Robert Rauschenberg. The **General Joshua L. Chamberlain Museum** (⊠*226 Maine St., Brunswick* ☎*207/725–6958* ⊠*$5* ⊗*Late May–mid-Oct., Tues.–Sat. 10–4*) displays memorabilia and documents the life of Maine's most celebrated Civil War hero. The general, who played an instrumental role in the

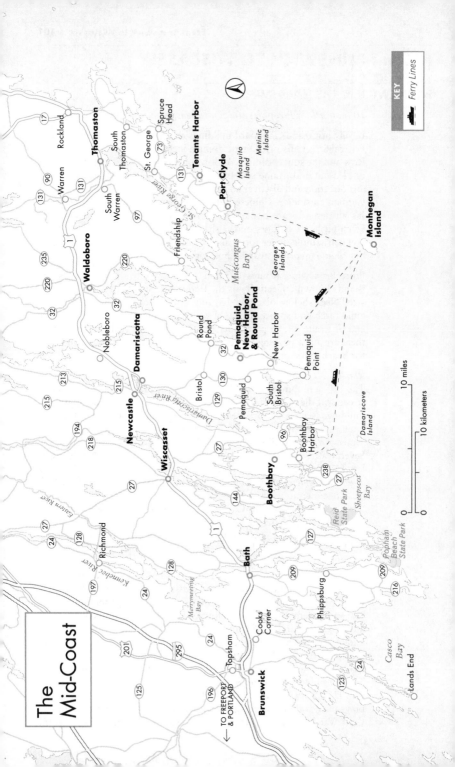

The Mid-Coast

KEY

Ferry Lines

10 miles

10 kilometers

IF YOU LIKE

BICYCLING

The best in the state, the Androscoggin River Bike Path goes between U.S. 1 and the Androscoggin River. Great blue herons prowl in the shallows, and hawks patrol above—you might even see a bald eagle surveying the landscape (the national bird, which was seldom seen in these parts a few years ago, has made a comeback, with more than 250 nesting pairs now in the state). There are also two longer bike paths in this region: The Coastal Route, a 187-mi journey, goes along the rocky coastline. The 60-mi Merrymeeting Tour travels between Bath and Wiscasset.

BEACHES

Maine has some of the country's most dramatic beaches. In the southern Mid-Coast region there are two awesome ones, both unique in their ways: Popham Beach, part of Popham Beach State Park near Phippsburg, and Mile Beach at Reid State Park. Popham stretches for miles, and when the tide is low, you can explore the sandbars and tide pools, which teem with sea creatures. On one end of the beach is Fort Popham, a fortress dating from the Civil War. At Reid State Park's Mile Beach, climb the rocky ledges and watch the surf smash into the rocks—this is the best place to watch the waves during a storm. If you are here in mid-July or later, bring insect spray for the notorious "green heads," a hardy fly that defies killing. Slap at them and they'll just go for your feet and ankles.

LIGHTHOUSES

Of the 16 lighthouses in the Mid-Coast region, about half are accessible by car. The Doubling Point Light and Kennebec River Light on the Kennebec River are accessible from Route 209 in Bath. Squirrel Point Light, south of Bath, is accessible via a three-road journey and short hike: Route 127, Steen Road, and Bald Head Road, where you leave your car and hike for about a mile. Farther north, Pemaquid Point Light stands watch over long rocky ledges. The former lighthouse keeper's cottage is now the Fishermen's Museum, featuring artifacts on the area's commercial fishing history. Marshall Point Lighthouse at Port Clyde also has been turned into a museum and small shop, with picnic tables on the grounds. On Owl's Head just south of Rockland is Owl Head Light, one of the few that still has its original Fresnel lens in place. Lighthouse cruises from Bath take in almost a dozen lights, including Seguin Light, the tallest lighthouse in Maine, while cruises from Boothbay Harbor provide a view of Ram Island Light. A Boothbay Cruise to Burnt Island Light includes two hours on the island. Visit the Rockland Lighthouse Museum on Rockland Harbor to see a dozen Fresnel lenses.

Union Army's victory at Gettysburg, was elected governor in 1867. From 1871 to 1883 he served as president of Bowdoin College. Across the street, on the edge of the Bowdoin College campus, a statue stands in his memory. Bowdoin's imposing neo-Gothic Hubbard Hall, on the campus quadrangle, is home to the **Peary–MacMillan Arctic Museum** (⊠ *Bath Rd. at Upper Maine St., Brunswick* ☎ *207/725–3416* 🖃 *Free* ⏲ *Tues.–Sat. 10–5, Sun. 2–5*), where you can find navigational instruments and other artifacts from the first successful expedition to the

North Pole. The 1909 journey was headed by two of Bowdoin's most famous alumni, Admiral Robert E. Peary and shipmaster Donald B. MacMillan. The schooner *Bowdoin,* now the flagship of the Maine Maritime Academy in Castine, was MacMillan's vessel for a later trip to the Arctic. Changing exhibits document conditions in the Arctic.

WHERE TO EAT

$$–$$$$ ✕ **Back Street Bistro.** Seafood paella and deep-sea scallops are signature
Fodor'sChoice   dishes at this rustic American-style bistro open for dinner in down-
★   town Brunswick. This two-floor establishment, next to the fire station, has two bars and an open deck upstairs. The wine list is extensive, and the service is exceptional. Try the soup of the day, especially if it's the sweet-potato bisque, which, with a dollop of cream and dash of ginger, goes down oh so smoothly. ⊠*11 Town Hall Pl., Brunswick* ☎*207/725–4060* ▤*AE, MC, V* ⊙*No lunch.*

$$–$$$$ ✕ **Cook's Lobster House.** Inhale the salt breeze as you cross the world's
Fodor'sChoice   only cribstone bridge (designed so that water flows freely through gaps
★   between the granite blocks) on your way south on Route 24 from Cook's Corner in Brunswick to this famous seafood restaurant 15 mi away, which began as a lobster shack on Bailey Island. Try the lobster casserole, or the delectable haddock sandwich. Several specialties come in smaller portions. Lobster dishes are at the $$$$ rating. Whether you choose inside or deck seating, you can watch the activity on the water: men checking lobster pots on the water and kayakers fanning across the bay. ⊠*68 Garrison Cove Rd., Bailey Island* ☎*207/833–2818* ⊕*www.cookslobster.com* ⚲*Reservations not accepted* ▤*D, MC, V* ⊙*Closed New Year's Day–mid-Feb.*

$$–$$$$ ✕ **Henry and Marty's.** Candles on the table establish the atmosphere at this intimate dinner setting in downtown Brunswick. This is the place for a quiet evening, and guests like that they're recognized by the staff when they come back to this elegant downtown restaurant. Service is courteous, the wine list is extensive, and good food is the emphasis. Organic and local are key words here, whether you order the popular beef brisket or paella valenciana. ⊠*61 Maine St., Brunswick* ☎*207/721–9141* ▤*AE, MC, V* ⊙*Closed Mon.*

$$$ ✕ **Dolphin Chowder House.** This clapboard-covered restaurant at the Dolphin Marina in Harpswell is famous for its fish chowder and lobster stew. Because it's right on the water, Dolphin is a haven for boaters. The simple but savory food makes the drive down Route 23 from Brunswick well worth it. Eat in the dining room or order takeout and eat on the dock so you can enjoy the view of Half Way Rock Lighthouse and several islands. ⊠*515 Basin Point Rd., South Harpswell* ☎*207/833–6000* ⊕*www.dolphinchowderhouse.com* ▤*AE, D, MC, V* ⊙*Closed Nov.–May.*

$–$$$ ✕ **China Rose.** There is no better or more extensive buffet in the area. Located just down Bath Road from Naval Air Station Brunswick, it serves Chinese and American dishes, including crab Rangoon, a creamy crab filling in a star-shaped light batter pinwheel. Other favorites include pork strips, king crab, and steamed mussels, with vegetables like sautéed green beans. There's also a dessert bar. The buffet is

$11.99, though you can pay more and eat off the menu if you prefer. ✉*42 Bath Rd., Brunswick* ☎*207/725–8813* ⊟*AE, D, MC, V.*

$–$$$ ✕**Richard's Restaurant.** Hankering for brats or schnitzel? Enjoy fine German cuisine or a good old American steak at this popular Brunswick establishment. Salads are scrumptious, and you can order small portions of many entrées. There's an extensive list of German draft beers and wines ✉*115 Maine St., Brunswick* ☎*207/729–9673* ⊕*www.richardsgermanamericancuisine.com* ⊟*AE, MC, V* ⊗*Closed Sun.*

$–$$$ ✕**Sea Dog Brew Pub.** Cross the Androscoggin River to reach the old Bowdoin Mill, a towering yellow brick building. Inside is the Sea Dog Brew Pub, where you can get hearty sandwiches, fresh seafood, and the specialty onion appetizer—don't miss the crispy calamari salad at the bar, and check the daily specials. Wash it down with a homemade root beer or microbrew. There's live evening entertainment Wednesday through Saturday. Eat inside or on the covered deck overlooking the river. ✉*1 Main St., Topsham* ☎*207/725–0162* ⊕*www.seadogbrewing.com* ⊟*AE, D, MC, V.*

¢–$$ ✕**Scarlet Begonias.** Personal pizzas and pasta specialties are the attractions at this busy little downtown bistro and catering establishment located across from the Bowdoin College campus. Try the sandwiches in whole or half sizes or a salad. ✉*212 Maine St., Brunswick* ☎*207/721–0403* ⊟*No credit cards* ⊗*Closed Sun.*

¢–$ ✕**Barn Door Cafe.** Stop by this convenient café on the banks of the Androscoggin River, just over the bridge from downtown Brunswick, for coffee and a delicious homemade muffin or pastry, or come for lunch. Kids can order the PB&J, but there's soup and the favorite: an Italian sandwich. It's next to the Sea Dog Brew Pub. ✉*4 Bowdoin Mill Island, Topsham* ☎*207/721–3229* ⊟*MC, V* ⊗*Closed Sun.*

¢–$ ✕**Fat Boy Drive-In.** Turn on your vehicle's lights to catch the attention of the servers at this old-fashioned drive-in restaurant. The eatery is renowned for its BLTs made with Canadian bacon. Order one with onion rings and a frappé (try the blueberry). Baskets of fried clams and shrimp are also well-liked items. ✉*111 Bath Rd., Brunswick* ☎*207/729–9431* ⊟*No credit cards* ⊗*Closed mid-Oct.–mid-Mar.*

¢–$ ✕**Wild Oats Bakery.** The scent of freshly baked scones and breads may draw you into this bakery, located inside the Tontine Mall, a downtown shopping center. Try the hot soups and chowders or made-to-order sandwiches and salads. A variety of breads are baked daily, and many entrées are baked and frozen for your take-home convenience. ✉*149 Maine St., Brunswick* ☎*207/725–6287* ⊟*D, MC, V.*

WHERE TO STAY

$$$–$$$$ ▥**Log Cabin Inn.** Each of the bright, cottage-style rooms has a view in
Fodor'sChoice this luxurious lodging on Bailey Island. Among the most popular is the
★ Mt. Washington Room, a second-story hideaway with a full kitchen and private deck with outdoor hot tub and an expansive view of the lobster boats sailing in and out of Mackerel Cove. Maine art is featured in each room, and colorful comforters drape the beds. The breakfast room has floor-to-ceiling windows with lovely views. In warm weather there are tables scattered about the patio. On the inn's decks and patio you can watch the lobster boats come and go. **Pros:** Every room has a

full view of the cove, with lobster boats coming and going. **Con:** Away from town. ⊠*5 Log Cabin La., Bailey Island 04003* ☎*207/833–5546* ⊕*www.logcabin-maine.com* ↩*9 rooms* ♿*In-room: Wi-Fi, DVD, VCR, refrigerator. In-hotel: bar, pool, beachfront, no-smoking rooms, no elevator* ⊟*AE, D, MC, V* ☉*Closed Nov.–Mar.* ⊓◯⫫*BP.*

$$–$$$$ ⬚ **Harpswell Inn Bed & Breakfast.** The smell of the salt air greets you at
★   this charming B&B on Lookout Point. The inn was originally the old cookhouse at Look Shipyard, where schooners and brigs were built around the time of the Civil War. Rooms are furnished with antiques, and many have fireplaces and balconies with a view of the sunset over Middle Bay. You can enjoy acres of oak-shaded lawns on the knoll overlooking the ocean. Ask the owners about their list of walking and hiking suggestions. The facility also rents out four cottages for $950–$1,400 a week. Pet are allowed in cottages; kids are best accommodated in suites or cottages. **Pros:** Spectacular view, a large property to explore. **Con:** Not many shops or restaurants are within walking distance. ⊠*108 Lookout Point Rd., Harpswell 04079* ☎*207/833–5509 or 800/843–5509* ⊕*www.harpswellinn.com* ↩*9 rooms, 3 suites, 4 cottages* ♿*In-room: Wi-Fi (some), no a/c (some), no phone (some). In-hotel: no-smoking rooms, no elevator* ⊟*D, MC, V* ⊓◯⫫*BP.*

$$–$$$ ⬚ **Brunswick Inn on Park Row.** Near the shops and restaurants of downtown Brunswick, this gracefully restored Greek Revival house couldn't have a more central location. Crackling fires in the main room and breakfast area keep out the winter chill. Eight bedrooms grace the main house, while the carriage house has five bedrooms and two suites. Look for thoughtful touches such as terry robes in the baths. New owners have incorporated distinctive new features such as the Cygnet wine bar and a gallery of original art. Brunswick Town Green and the Tuesday and Friday farmers' market are across the street. Two first-floor units are handicapped accessible. **Pro:** Very convenient to restaurants and shopping. **Con:** Not near the water. ⊠*165 Park Row, Brunswick 04011* ☎*207/729–4914 or 800/299–4914* ⊕*www.brunswickinnparkrow.com* ↩*13 rooms, 2 suites* ♿*In-room: Wi-Fi, no TV (some). In-hotel: no-smoking rooms, no elevator* ⊟*AE, MC, V* ⊓◯⫫*BP.*

$–$$ ⬚ **Black Lantern.** Here, comfortable and affordable lodging combines with sumptuous breakfasts in a quiet country setting—across the bridge from busy downtown Brunswick on the banks of the Androscoggin River. The inn features antique country furniture and homemade quilts, with bunting and an American flag greeting guests. Black Lantern has a walkway to its own dock on the river. Rooms are decorated country-style, with quilts on the beds and wall hangings handmade by one of the owners. There are pictures throughout, some originals, and the floors are original pine. Ask for one of the rooms with a water view. Guests can participate in the paperback book exchange, where they leave a book and take a book. **Pros:** Affordable rates, riverfront location. **Con:** A resident shih tzu. ⊠*57 Elm St., Topsham 04086* ☎*207/725–4165 or 888/306–4165* ⊕*www.blacklanternbandb.com* ↩*3 rooms* ♿*In-room: Wi-Fi. In-hotel: no kids under 10, no-smoking rooms, no elevator* ⊟*AE, D, MC, V* ⊓◯⫫*BP.*

NIGHTLIFE & THE ARTS

The **Maine State Music Theater** (⊠*Bowdoin College, Brunswick* ☎*207/725–8769* ⊕*www.msmt.org*) stages Broadway-style shows from mid-June to September. A six-week concert series at Bowdoin College, the **Bowdoin International Music Festival** (⊠*Bowdoin College, Brunswick* ☎*207/373–1400* ⊕*www.bowdoinfestival.org*) runs from late June to early August.

SPORTS & THE OUTDOORS

The 2½-mi marked and paved **Androscoggin River Bike Path** (⊠*End of Water St., Brunswick*), running along U.S. 1 and the Androscoggin River, is open from dawn to dusk for joggers, walkers, bikers, and in-line skaters. Rest rooms are available. Dogs on leashes are allowed.

The coast near Brunswick is full of hidden nooks and crannies waiting to be explored. By kayak you can seek out secluded beaches and tucked-away coves along the shore, and watch gulls and cormorants
★ diving for fish. **H2Outfitters** (⊠*Rte. 24, Orr's Island* ☎*207/833–5257 or 800/205–2925* ⊕*www.h2outfitters.com*) provides top-notch kayaking instruction and gear for people of all skill levels.

SHOPPING

Several good galleries in and around Brunswick sell everything from contemporary paintings to unusual pottery pieces. Each Tuesday and Friday, 8 AM–4 PM, from May through October, a farmers' market fills the town green between Maine Street and Park Row.

ART GALLERIES In Harpswell, **Sebascodegan Artists Cooperative** (⊠*4 Old Orr's Island Rd., Harpswell* ☎*207/833–5717*) displays work by Maine artists. In Brunswick, **Wyler Craft Gallery** (⊠*150 Maine St., Brunswick* ☎*207/729–1321*) carries decorative crafts as well as jewelry, clothing, and toys.

BOOKS & In the Cook's Corner Shopping Center, **Bookland & Café** (⊠*6 Gurnet MUSIC Rd., Brunswick* ☎*207/725–2313 or 207/725–7033*) stocks new and used books as well as magazines and newspapers. This is a great place to pick up some freshly baked scones or muffins as well as a selection of sandwiches, soups, and salads. There's a large kids' department, and on Tuesday there are senior specials. If you want a good Maine book, **Gulf of Maine Books** (⊠*134 Maine St., Brunswick* ☎*207/729–5083*) is worth a stop. Well known since 1979, it offers a superior selection of poetry, regional works, and environmental literature.

CLOTHING & Find unusual African imports, as well as jewelry and clothing at **Indrani's JEWELRY of Brunswick** (⊠*Tontine Mall, 149 Maine St., Brunswick* ☎*207/729–6448*). At the tip of Bailey Island, **Land's End Gifts** (⊠*Land's End, Bailey Island* ☎*207/833–2313* ⊙*Apr.–Nov.*) is a spacious shop overlooking the water. From April through October, it sells cards, calendars, and collectibles as well as T-shirts, sweatshirts, and hats. Browse **Whwat's Up** (⊠*Tontine Mall, 149 Maine St., Brunswick* ☎*207/725–4966*) for Pandora jewelry and fashionable women's clothing.

FOOD & WINE Look for tiny **Hawke's Lobster and Gifts** (⊠*992 Cundy's Harbor Rd., Cundy's Harbor* ☎*207/721–0472*), with its lights sparkling in the sunlight or out of the fog next to Holbrook's Wharf. It has Maine-made home-and-garden items as well as lobsters for sale. It is open May 25–Oct. 1, though it sells lobsters year-round. Turtles, brittle, and English toffee are highlights of **Island Candy Company** (✉*1795 Harpswell Islands Rd., Orr's Island* ☎*207/833–6639*), which makes its own candy and also sells Shain's ice cream made in nearby Sanford. Need a bottle of vintage wine or a wedge of imported cheese? Check out **Provisions** (✉*148 Maine St., Brunswick* ☎*207/729–9288*). **Tontine Fine Candies** (✉*Tontine Mall, 149 Maine St., Brunswick* ☎*207/729–4462*) sells locally made chocolates, fudge, and other goodies.

POTTERY See how pottery is fired at **Ash Cove Pottery** (✉*75 Ash Cove Rd., Harpswell* ☎*207/833–6004*). The cooperative gallery and its two retail shops are open all year. The main studio and showroom for **Georgetown Pottery** (✉*755 Five Islands Rd., Georgetown* ☎*207/371–2801* ⊕*www.georgetownpottery.com*) is in Georgetown, which is 15 mi from Brunswick, but there are two additional showrooms: in Brunswick (✉*11 Pleasant St., Brunswick* ☎*207/725–7500*), and in Freeport (✉*48 Main St., Freeport* ☎*207/865–0060*).

BATH

11 mi northeast of Brunswick, 38 mi northeast of Portland.

Along Front and Centre streets, in the heart of Bath's historic district are some charming 19th-century Victorian homes. Among them are the 1820 Federal-style Pryor House, at 360 Front St., the 1810 Greek Revival–style mansion at 969 Washington St., covered with gleaming white clapboards, and the Victorian gem at 1009 Washington St., painted a distinctive shade of raspberry. All three operate as inns.

Bath has been a shipbuilding center since 1607. The venerable Bath Iron Works completed its first passenger ship in 1890 and is still building ships today, turning out frigates for the U.S. Navy. It's a good idea to avoid U.S. 1 on weekdays from 3:15 to 4:30 PM, when a major shift change takes place. The massive exodus can tie up traffic for miles.

WHAT TO SEE

Follow Route 209 south 15 mi from Bath to reach the site of the short-lived Popham Colony, established in 1607. Granite-walled **Fort Popham** (✉*Rte. 209, Phippsburg* ☎*207/389–1335*) was built in 1861, for use during the Civil War. It also was employed in the Spanish-American War and World War I. Outside the walls are picnic tables.

In a cluster of buildings that once made up the Percy & Small Shipyard,
★ the **Maine Maritime Museum** examines the world of shipbuilding and is open all year. A number of impressive ships, including the 142-foot Grand Banks fishing schooner *Sherman Zwicker,* are often on display in the port. Exhibits use ship models, paintings, photographs, and historical artifacts to tell the history of the region. From May to November, hour-long tours of the shipyard show how these massive wooden ships were built. You can watch boatbuilders wield their tools in the boat shop and learn about lobstering and its impact on the local cul-

ture. In summer, boat tours sail the scenic Kennebec River. A particular favorite is the lighthouse tour that covers the area of the Kennebec from Bath down to Fort Popham at the mouth of the river. A gift shop and bookstore are on the premises, and you can grab a bite to eat in the restaurant or bring a picnic to eat on the grounds. Kids ages six and younger get in free. ⊠ *243 Washington St.* ☎ *207/442–0961* ⊕ *www. mainemaritimemuseum.org* ⌚ *$10* ⊙ *Daily 9:30–5.*

OFF THE
BEATEN
PATH

Popham Beach State Park (⊠ *Rte. 209, Phippsburg* ☎ *207/389–1335*) has bathhouses and picnic tables. There are no restaurants at this end of the beach, so pack a picnic or get takeout from Spinney's Restaurant near the Civil War–era Fort Popham or Percy's Store behind Spinney's at 6 Sea Street. Phone number is 207/389–2010. At low tide you can walk miles of tidal flats and also out to a nearby island, where you can explore tide pools or fish off the ledges. Drive past the entrance to the park and on the right you can see a vista often described as "Million Dollar View." The confluence of the Kennebec and Morse rivers creates an ever-shifting pattern of sandbars.

Fodor'sChoice
★

On Georgetown Island, **Reid State Park** (⊠ *Rte. 127* ☎ *207/371–2303*) has 1½ mi of sand split between two beaches. From the top of rocky Griffith Head, you can spot the lighthouses on Seguin Island, the Cuckolds, and Hendricks Head. In summer, parking lots fill by 11 AM on weekends and holidays. If swimming, be aware of the possibility of an undertow. During a storm, this is a great place to observe the ferocity of the waves crashing onto the shore.

WHERE TO EAT

$$$–$$$$
Fodor'sChoice
★

✕ **Robinhood Free Meetinghouse.** Though owned by acclaimed chef and owner Michael Gagné—whose 72-layer cream-cheese biscuits are shipped all over the country—this 1855 Greek Revival–style meetinghouse serves meals that are primarily made by chef de cuisine Troy Mains. The menu changes daily but always has a variety of seafood, vegetables, and dairy products purchased locally. You might begin with the lobster and crab cakes, then move on to grilled fillet of beef stuffed with crab or the confit of duck. Finish up with the signature Obsession in Three Chocolates. The wine list offers an array of choices to accompany Mains's creations. The service is excellent. The dining room evokes its meetinghouse past with cream-color walls, pine floorboards, and cherry Shaker-style chairs. Crisp linens add an elegant touch. ⊠ *210 Robinhood Rd., Georgetown* ☎ *207/371–2188* ⊕ *www. robinhood-meetinghouse.com* ▭ *AE, D, MC, V* ⊙ *No lunch.*

$$–$$$$

✕ **Anna's Water's Edge Restaurant.** This former take-out eatery serves excellent seafood dishes and has become a favorite with locals and visitors. Specialties include fresh traditional panfried fish, cooked by dipping fish fillets in a mixture of flour and egg, and then sizzling them in a skillet. Other favorites include baked stuffed fish and scallops with crabmeat stuffing topped with Parmesan cheese. Soups and chowders are all made on the premises. ⊠ *75 Black's Landing Rd., Sebasco Estates* ☎ *207/389–1803* ▭ *MC, V* ⊙ *Closed Sept.–May.*

$$–$$$$　✕**Solo Bistro.** If you like the minimalist atmosphere, try this Soho-style restaurant that opened in 2007 in downtown Bath. It features cool Scandinavian decor and trendy dishes. The potato gnocchi appetizer is a favorite, as are the lamb chops. Salads are elaborate, and the service is excellent. On Friday nights, live jazz plays in the bar downstairs. ⊠*128 Front St.* ☎*207/443–3373* ⊕*www.solobistro.com* ⊟*AE, MC, V.*

$$–$$$　✕**Kennebec Tavern & Marina.** Standing alongside the Kennebec River, Bath's only waterfront restaurant has its own marina, where you can tie up your boat and come in for a delicious lunch or dinner. Eat inside or out on the canopied deck. Specialties include the smoked cream of tomato soup and the fried calamari. Try the fried parsnip appetizer—there is nothing like it anywhere. For your entrée, there's no better choice than the pan-blackened catch-of-the-day. The dining room has wonderful views, and the walls are hung with old photos of Bath. If you prefer, you can eat in the bar, which also has a view of the boats. ⊠*119 Commercial St.* ☎*207/442–9636* ⊟*AE, D, DC, MC, V.*

$$–$$$　✕**Mae's Café & Bakery.** Some of the region's tastiest pies, pastries, and cakes are baked in this restaurant, a local favorite since 1977. Rotating selections of works by local artists hang in the two turn-of-the-20th-century houses joined together. Dine inside or on the front deck, where you can gaze down at the "City of Ships." The satisfying contemporary cuisine includes savory omelets and seafood quiche as well as seafood specials and traditional chicken, beef, and pasta dishes. Meals also can be packed to go. ⊠*160 Centre St.* ☎*207/442–8577* ⊟*D, MC, V.*

$$–$$$　✕**The Osprey.** Traditional Maine fare draws folks to this Robinhood Marina restaurant overlooking the harbor. Open only in summer, the Osprey has wonderful views of the boats as well as an osprey nest. Choice dishes include the sweet-potato encrusted haddock and grilled strawberry spinach salad. For something a little different, try the lobster corn chowder. ⊠*358 Robinhood Rd., Georgetown* ☎*207/371–2530* ⊟*AE, D, MC, V* ⊗*Closed Columbus Day–Memorial Day.*

$–$$$　✕**Beale Street Barbecue.** Ribs are the thing at this barbecue joint. For hearty eaters, ask for one of the platters piled high with pulled pork, pulled chicken, or shredded beef. If you can't decide, there's always the massive barbecue sampler. Jalapeño popovers and chili served with corn bread are terrific appetizers. Enjoy a beer at the bar while waiting for your table. ⊠*215 Water St.* ☎*207/442–9514* ⊟*MC, V.*

$–$$$　✕**Spinney's.** Looking for a really inexpensive but hearty breakfast with a great view? Omelets, pancakes, home fries, and eggs cooked to order are on the menu for early risers at this waterfront restaurant with a view of Fort Popham. For lunch or dinner there are tasty lobster rolls or rolls with clams, scallops, crab, or shrimp. Locals describe two dishes as "wicked good": the Popham Platter (every type of seafood you can imagine) and the Wood Island Wreck Platter (shrimp, scallops, and steak hot off the grill). ⊠*987 Popham Rd., Phippsburg* ☎*207/389–1122* ⊟*MC, V* ⊗*Closed late Oct.–Mother's Day.*

¢–$　✕**Café Crème.** Changing exhibitions by local artists hang on the walls of this downtown coffee shop. Its prime location, on a corner facing Front Street, lets you take a break from window-shopping. Come in for a cup of espresso, a blueberry muffin, or one of the delicious house-made

scones. Light lunches include freshly prepared salads, stuffed crois-
sants, and quiche. There's also Maine-made ice cream. ■TIP→ **If you
are in the area in fall or winter you can catch Tuesday-evening readings by
local poets and try your hand at the open mike session.** ⊠56 Front St.
☎207/443–6454 ▤MC, V.

¢ ✕**Starlight Café.** Just downhill from the corner of Lambard and Front
streets, this bright little eatery is easy to pass right by. Omelets and pancakes make for premier breakfast choices, while sandwiches and pizzas
are top lunch-menu picks. Breads are baked daily. Arrive before 2 pm,
because the café isn't open for dinner. ⊠15 Lambard St. ☎207/443–
3005 ▤No credit cards ⊙Closed weekends. No dinner.

WHERE TO STAY

$$$–$$$$ ✕⌷**Sebasco Harbor Resort.** This destination family resort, spread across
FodorśChoice 575 acres at the foot of the Phippsburg Peninsula, has an exceptional
★ range of accommodations and services, to which it continues to add.
Comfortable guest rooms in the clapboard-covered main building have
antique furnishings and new bathrooms, while rooms in a building
designed to resemble a lighthouse have wicker furniture, paintings by
local artists, and rooftop access. The Fairwinds, a luxury waterfront
spa, was added in 2007; prices for room and treatment packages range
from $369 to $399. Also added in 2007 was the Harbor Village Suites,
set into exquisitely landscaped grounds and featuring 18 spacious and
air-conditioned rooms. These units rent for $319–$459. The resort's
Pilot House restaurant ($$-$$$) is known for its innovative take on
classic dishes. Entrées include haddock stuffed with a trio of scal-
lops, shrimp, and vegetables. **Pros:** Ocean location; excellent food and
service. **Con:** Pricey. ⊠Rte. 217, ⌖Box 75, Sebasco Estates 04565
☎207/389–1161 or 800/225–3819 ⊕www.sebasco.com ⟲115
rooms, 23 cottages ⌕In-room: no a/c (some), Wi-Fi (some). In-hotel:
3 restaurants, bar, golf course, tennis courts, pool, gym, bicycles, public
Wi-Fi, airport shuttle, no-smoking rooms ▤AE, D, MC, V ⊙Closed
Nov.–mid-May ⏏MAP.

$$$$ ⌷**Kismet.** Serenity and an old-world atmosphere combine at this B&B
★ retreat within walking distance of downtown Bath, with its restau-
rants, shops, and waterfront. Adjacent to the Patten Free Library and
its famous statue, Spirit of the Sea, the inn has a spa that features mas-
sages and body exfoliation, steam showers, a Japanese soaking tub,
and organic, natural foods prepared by the owner. Guest rooms are
brightly colored and decorated with items from the owner's travels
as well as many family heirlooms. The focus here is relaxation and
rejuvenation. Dinners can be prepared for guests with advance notice.
Pros: Luxury, special services, library. **Cons:** No TV. ⊠44 Summer St.,
04530 ☎207/443–3399 ⟲5 rooms ⌕In-room: no TV, no phone. In-
hotel: public Wi-Fi, no pets, no kids allowed, no-smoking rooms, no
elevator ▤No credit cards ⏏BP.

$$$$ ⌷**Stonehouse Manor at Popham Beach.** If peace and tranquillity at the
☼ ocean are what you are looking for, this is the place. The suites and
rooms have king- or queen-size beds, original wood floors, and water
views. Sprinkled throughout are works of art. Guests are within walk-
ing distance to Popham Beach and two historic forts. At low tide you

can walk to coastal islands, and fishing can be really good where the Kennebec River meets the sea at the beach. **Pros:** Extensive grounds and gardens, always a breeze, Wi-Fi in the rooms. **Con:** Far from town. ⊠*907 Popham Rd., Phippsburg 04562* ☎*207/389–1141 or 877/389–1141* ☞*1 room, 4 suites* ♧*In-room: VCR. In-hotel: public Internet, no-smoking rooms, no elevator* ≡*No credit cards* ⦿*BP.*

$$$–$$$$　♣**Popham Beach Bed & Breakfast.** Housed in a former Coast Guard station, this casual bed-and-breakfast sits on Popham Beach not far from historic Fort Popham. Sun-filled rooms are comfortably furnished. The nicest quarters include the one aptly name Library, where two walls are lined with books, and the Bunkroom, which overlooks the ocean. Stroll along the shore before your two- or three-course breakfast in the former mess hall. Beach chairs and umbrellas, picnic tables, and barbecue grills are available for your use. A casual seafood restaurant is close by, and you can order lunch at a small market. Each room now has its own bath. **Pro:** Right on Popham Beach. **Con:** No air-conditioning. ⊠*4 Riverview Ave., Phippsburg 04562* ☎*207/389–2409* ⊕*www.pophambeachbandb.com* ☞*3 rooms, 1 suite* ♧*In-room: no a/c, no phone, no TV. In-hotel: no kids under 15, no-smoking rooms, no elevator* ≡*MC, V* ⦿*BP.*

$$$　♣**Inn at Bath.** Filled with antiques, this handsome mid-1800s Greek Revival–style lodging sits in the middle of Bath's historic district. Many downtown sights, including the local library with its distinctive shaded gazebo, and shops and restaurants are within easy walking distance. The guest rooms are tastefully decorated with works by local artists. Four have wood-burning fireplaces and two have two-person whirlpool tubs. Outside are lovely gardens and a spacious patio. **Pro:** Fresh garden fare. **Con:** Cat on premises. ⊠*969 Washington St., 04530* ☎*207/443–4294 or 800/423–0964* ⊕*www.innatbath.com* ☞*7 rooms, 1 suite* ♧*In-room: Wi-Fi, VCR. In-hotel: no kids under 5, some pets allowed, no-smoking rooms, no elevator* ≡*AE, MC, V* ⦿*BP.*

$$–$$$　♣**Coveside Bed & Breakfast.** Near the village of Five Islands, this contemporary lodging sits on five secluded acres that run along the shore. Every room has a water view and features local art. Bring your kayak, or alternatively, use the canoe or one of the several bicycles available for outings. The inn's dock is perfect for sunbathing or watching the water. Stroll along nearby nature preserves or visit Reid State Park. Gulls, herons, and osprey are frequently sighted here, and you may catch a glimpse of the occasional seal or even a moose. Amenities include complimentary beer, soda and cookies, and lots of local art on the premises. **Pro:** On the water. **Con:** 13 mi from town. ⊠*6 Gott's Cove La., Georgetown 04548* ☎*207/371–2807 or 800/232–5490* ⊕*www.covesidebandb.com* ☞*4 rooms, 1 cottage with 3 rooms* ♧*In-room: no a/c. In-hotel: bicycles, no kids under 12, no-smoking rooms, no elevator* ≡*AE, D, MC, V* ⊙*Closed mid-Oct.–late May* ⦿*BP.*

$$–$$$　♣**Kennebec Inn.** In 2006, this B&B moved uptown to the old Captain Perkins house that combines Greek Revival, Italianate, and Early American architecture into a spacious facility on 1½ acres. The two suites have private baths, four-poster beds, cable TV, and Wi-Fi, along with private entrances. Guests have the benefits of an in-town location and an outdoor lap pool measuring 40 feet by 60 feet on beautifully landscaped grounds. There is a piano available for guests who like to tickle the keys. Every morning you can enjoy a full breakfast in the formal dining room. **Pros:** Pool, convenience. **Con:** Not in a scenic location. ⊠*251 High St., 04530* ☎*207/443–5324 or 888/595–1564* ⊕*www.kennebecinn.com* ⇆*2 suites* ♿*In-room: Wi-Fi. In-hotel: no-smoking, no elevator* ⊟*D, MC, V* ⫿*BP.*

$$–$$$ ⛱**Mooring Bed & Breakfast.** Originally the home of Walter Reid, who donated the land for Reid State Park, this inn has stayed in the same family for generations. It is now owned by Reid's great-granddaughter and her family. The five guest rooms all have air-conditioning and great ocean views, and some have wood floors. Rooms with themes played out in their colors and decor include the lighthouse, violet, and rose rooms; art compliments each theme. Retreat to the Spanish Room with a good book for a quiet place, or catch the ocean breeze on a screened porch, a relaxing place to have breakfast. Well-tended gardens grace the grounds, and its location on the banks of the Kennebec River has made it a favorite for weddings, conferences, and reunions. **Pro:** On the water. **Con:** 11 mi from town. ⊠*132 Seguinland Rd., Georgetown 04548* ☎*207/371–2790 or 866/828–7343* ⊕*www.themooringb-b.com* ⇆*5 rooms* ♿*In-hotel: no-smoking rooms, no elevator* ⊟*MC, V* ⊗*Closed mid-Oct.–mid-May* ⫿*BP.*

$$–$$$ ⛱**1774 Inn.** Listed on the National Register of Historic Places, this Georgian-style mansion dating from before the Revolutionary War has handsome interior detailing and is filled with magnificent antiques. Located on a bend in the Kennebec River, the inn has spacious corner guest rooms in the main house, including two with fireplaces. One room has a deck overlooking the river. A four-bedroom cottage facing the river has its own kitchen, two baths, and four bedrooms. The breakfast menu is likely to include a smoked salmon roulade, vegetable-sausage strata, or cranberry-walnut pancakes, in addition to whole-grain cereals and home-baked breads. **Pros:** Views everywhere, pine floors, Colonial-era features. **Con:** No Wi-Fi. ⊠*44 Parker Head Rd., Phippsburg 04562* ☎*207/389–1774* ⊕*www.1774inn.com* ⇆*87 rooms, 1 cottage* ♿*In-room: no TV. In-hotel: no kids under 12, no-smoking rooms, no elevator* ⊟*MC, V* ⫿*BP.*

$$ ⛱**Pryor House Bed & Breakfast.** An elegant double staircase in the foyer welcomes you to this 1820s Federal-style home gazing down on the Kennebec River. It's in the historic district of Bath, so shops and restaurants are nearby. The Tall Chimney Room, with its own private outdoor deck, has a railroad theme, with a working model train that runs around the chimney. There's also an indoor hot tub big enough for two. Nautical themes are reflected in the Captain's Room suite, with its wide pine floorboards and windows overlooking the river, and the Elizabeth Room, decorated in Victorian style in pinks and whites. The owner is an enthusiastic cook and serves many creative dishes for breakfast, never the same thing two days in a row. Breakfast begins with a type of fruit and a muffin or tart (the apple tarts are particularly popular). Next comes the main course, which might be eggs Florentine, spinach onion quiche, or blueberry French toast with bacon or sau-

sage. **Pros:** In-town location, unusual breakfasts. **Con:** Steep driveway. ✉*360 Front St., 04530* ☎*207/443–1146* ⊕*www.pryorhouse.com* ⇥*3 rooms* ☖*In-room: no TV, Wi-Fi (some). In-hotel: no kids under 12, public Wi-Fi, no elevator* ▭*AE, D, DC, MC, V* ❦|*BP.*

SPORTS & THE OUTDOORS

GOLF An 18-hole championship golf course distinguishes the **Bath Country Club** (✉*387 Whiskeag Rd.* ☎*207/442–8411*), where you can find a tavern and the biggest pro shop in Maine. The 9-hole **Sebasco Estates Golf Course** (✉*Rte. 217, Phippsburg* ☎*207/389–1161*) sits right on the water so you can enjoy the salt breeze while you play.

HIKING The tranquil **Josephine Newman Sanctuary** (✉*Bay Point Rd., George-town* ☾*Daily*) is a 119-acre nature preserve on the Georgetown Peninsula. The walking trails are operated by the Maine Audubon Society. Protect yourself from deer ticks by wearing long pants and sleeves. **Morse Mountain Preserve** (✉*Rte. 216, Phippsburg* ☎*No phone*), a 600-acre preserve owned by Bates College, has trails through the woods that lead to Sewall Beach. There is a small parking area off the side of the road just after the junction with Route 209.

WATER SPORTS To cruise the Kennebec or other coastal rivers in the area, contact **Long Reach Cruises** (✉*75 Commercial St.* ☎*888/442–0092*), which operates excursion and sightseeing tours out of Bath's Waterfront Park; rates begin at $20. Cruises past some of the region's distinctive sights are the company's specialty; you learn all the local history from the narration given by the knowledgeable captains and crew. This outfit also heads to Merrymeeting Bay, Harpswell Sound, and Damariscotta Bay. If you want to explore on your own, **Bay Point Sports** (✉*Rte. 127, George-town* ☎*888/349–7772*) rents kayaks from April to Labor Day.

SHOPPING

ANTIQUES & COLLECTIBLES Open year-round (and evenings, for after-dinner browsing), **Brick Store Antiques** (✉*143 Front St.* ☎*207/443–2790*) displays genuine antiques—no reproductions. You'll spot an authentic tepee as you approach **Native Arts** (✉*183 U.S. 1, Woolwich* ☎*207/442–8399*), which carries fine crafts, from carvings made by Inuits in Alaska to beadwork produced in South America. Stop in and see the drums and birch-bark canoes on display, or learn how to make a native flute. The **Montsweag Flea Market** (✉*Mountain Rd. and U.S. 1, Woolwich* ☎*207/443–2809*) is a roadside attraction with treasure, trash, and everything in between. If you're looking for "Maine stuff" to take home, this might be your best bet. It's open weekends from May to October and also Fridays in summer. It's every lady for herself during the summer **Wednesday antiques market**.

CLOTHING At **Magnolia** (✉*129 Front St.* ☎*207/442–8989* ⊕*www.magnoliagift-store.com* ☾*Mon.–Sat.*), hard-to-find items, including "elegant indulgences" and cute kids' clothing, are a speciality.

HOME ACCESSORIES **Backroads by the Sea** (✉*459 Main Rd., Phippsburg* ☎*207/443–9604*) is a neat little gift shop on the way to Popham Beach. The owner is known for her colorful, restored furniture, even items like a lavender table! She also carries jewelry, quilts, handbags, and pottery, all made by Maine crafters. Maine art and a small selection of Maine books and kids' books are also available. **Now You're Cooking** (✉ *49 Front St.* ☎*207/443–1402* ⊕*www.acooksemporium.com*) carries everything you ever dreamed of for the kitchen, as well as lots of picnic supplies and nifty gadgets. The shop will ship your purchases home for you.

EN ROUTE Coastal Route 1, which runs between Bath and Wiscasset, takes you over a bridge that crosses the Kennebec River. Along the way you pass Bath Iron Works and its busy yard, where U.S. Navy destroyers are built. Between the two towns is an eclectic collection of shops. Take home a small statue for your flower garden, or a model ship for your mantel. Traffic on the highway is heavy on weekends and between 3 and 4 PM on weekdays, when the shift changes at Bath Iron Works, so plan to take your time and stop along the way.

WISCASSET

10 mi north of Bath, 46 mi northeast of Portland.

Settled in 1663, Wiscasset sits on the banks of the Sheepscot River. It bills itself "Maine's Prettiest Village," and it's easy to see why: it has graceful churches, old cemeteries, and elegant sea captains' homes (many converted into antiques shops or galleries).

Pack a picnic and take it down to the dock, where you can watch the fishing boats or grab a lobster roll from Red's Eats or the lobster shack on the dock. Wiscasset has expanded its wharf, and this is a great place to catch a breeze on a hot day. U.S. 1 becomes Main Street, and traffic often slows to a crawl. If you park in town, you can walk to most galleries, shops, restaurants, and other attractions. ▮**TIP→ Try to arrive early in the morning to find a parking space—you'll likely have success if you try to park on Water Street rather than Main.**

WHAT TO SEE

The 1807 **Castle Tucker,** a Society for the Preservation of New England Antiquities (SPNEA) property, is known for its extravagant architecture, Victorian appointments, and freestanding elliptical staircase. Standing on top of a hill overlooking the Sheepscot River, the structure was built by Judge Silas Lee when Wiscasset was the busiest port east of Boston. ✉*Lee and High Sts.* ☎*207/882–7169* ◨*$5* ⊙*June–mid-Oct., Wed.–Sun. 11–5; tours on the hr 11–4.*

★ The grand 1852 **Musical Wonder House,** formerly a sea captain's home, is now a museum with 5,000 antique music boxes from around the world, including musical porcelains, furniture, and paintings. Also see player pianos and other musical rarities. Your entry will set one of the music boxes to playing. Tours of the main floor or the entire house are available on the hour beginning at 10 AM. Kids 11 and younger are admitted free. ✉*18 High St.* ☎*207/882–7163 or 800/336–3725* ⊕*www.musicalwonderhouse.com* ◨*$10 for 45-min tour; $20 for whole-house tour* ⊙*Memorial Day–mid-Oct., daily 10–5.*

The **Wiscasset Waterville & Farmington Railway** celebrates Maine's railroad heritage with train rides and the best selection of railroad books in the state. It's run entirely by volunteers. ✉ *Rte. 218, 5 mi north of U.S. 1, Alna* ☎ *207/882–4193* ⊕ *www.wwfry.org* ✉ *Museum free; train $6* ☉ *Weekends 9–5 Memorial Day weekend–Columbus Day weekend; Saturday only remainder of year.*

WHERE TO EAT

¢–$$ ✕ **Sarah's Café.** This family-friendly restaurant is at the harbor and has lovely views to enjoy, whether you eat indoors or outside on the deck, which overlooks the water. The menu covers a lot of ground, with entrées ranging from Mexican to Italian. There is also the catch of the day and the usual seafood items at market prices. Available are variously topped hamburgers, such as the Tex Mex with salsa. Lunch and dinner are served all week, breakfast on weekends. The soups are excellent, as are the breads. ☎ *207/882–7504* ⊕ *www.sarahscafe.com* ▤ *AE, D, MC, V.*

¢   ✕ **Red's Eats.** You've probably driven right past this little red shack on the Wiscasset side of the bridge if you've visited this area and seen the long line of hungry customers. Red's is a local landmark famous for its hot dogs, burgers, crisp onion rings, lobster and crab rolls, and even its ice cream—if you spot a kid with an ice-cream cone, it probably came from Red's. Try a black raspberry and pistachio. There are a few picnic tables, or get your food to go and walk down to the dock to enjoy the view. Watch out for the seagulls; they like lobster rolls, too. ✉ *41 Water St.* ☎ *207/882–6128* ▤ *No credit cards* ☉ *Closed mid-Oct.–mid-Apr.*

WHERE TO STAY

$$–$$$ ✕▦ **Squire Tarbox Inn.** Built around 1763, this small country inn is listed on the National Register of Historic Places. The eponymous squire is buried next door in the family plot. Some of the charming guest rooms have fireplaces. Mountain bikes let you explore the surrounding woods, while a rowboat allows you to get a look at the coast. Breakfast includes European specialties like home-baked croissants, yogurt, and fresh fruit, along with traditional American pancakes or bacon and eggs. Freshly brewed coffee and a variety of teas are available. At the restaurant ($$$$), dine indoors or on the screened-in deck overlooking beautiful landscaped grounds and the organic garden that provides all of the inn's vegetables in season. Look for entrées such as rosemary-roasted rack of lamb and sea scallops in a garlic-butter sauce. Dinner is available daily in season for you as well as for the public. The hosts speak English, German, Italian, and French. The hotel accepts some credit cards, but checks are preferred. **Pros:** Organic produce, dinners available, expansive grounds. **Con:** Several miles from town. ✉ *1181 Main Rd., 04578* ☎ *207/882–7693 or 800/818–0626* ⊕ *www.squiretarbox-inn.com* ⇆ *11 rooms* ♨ *In-room: no TV. In-hotel: public Wi-Fi, bicycles, no kids under 12, no-smoking rooms, no elevator* ▤ *MC, V* ☉ *Closed Jan.–Mar.* ⏀ *BP.*

$$$–$$$$ ▦ **Cod Cove Inn.** Every room has a view of the Sheepscot River at this two-story New England–style inn perched on five acres of beautifully landscaped grounds with a heated outdoor pool and hot tub. Most

guest rooms have a private patio or balcony overlooking the river, and some have gas fireplaces. Continental breakfast includes freshly baked muffins, breads and bagels, fruits and juices, and coffee and tea. **Pros:** River views and beautiful grounds. **Con:** Not a full breakfast. ⊠*U.S. 1 and Rte. 27, Box 117, Edgecomb04556* ☎*207/882–9586 or 800/882–9586* ⊕*www.codcoveinn.com* ↩*30 rooms* ⌂*In-room: refrigerator. In-hotel: pool, no-smoking rooms, no elevator* ☰*AE, D, MC, V* ⊚*CP.*

$$–$$$ ⊞ **Snow Squall Bed & Breakfast.** Built in the early 1850s, this carefully renovated inn is convenient to the harbor and Wiscasset Village, with its art galleries, antiques shops, and some of the region's finest sea captains' homes. Each of the four guest rooms is named for a clipper ship built in Maine: the White Falcon, the Golden Horn, the Flying Eagle, and the Red Jacket. Two rooms have fireplaces. There are also a pair of two-bedroom suites, located in the carriage house, with private entrances. Children are welcome here. The public area offers wireless access and a TV. Special offerings include complimentary bottled water and Molton Brown personal items.**Pros:** Owners Paul and Melanie's specialties are, respectively, cooking, and massage and yoga. **Con:** On busy Route 1. ⊠*5 Bradford Rd., 04578* ☎*207/882–6892* ⊕*www. snowsquallinn.com* ↩*4 rooms, 2 suites* ⌂*In-room: no TV (some). In-hotel: no-smoking rooms, no elevator, public Wi-Fi* ☰*MC, V* ⊘*Closed Nov.–May, except by reservation* ⊚*BP.*

$$ ⊞ **Marston House.** Two light and airy upstairs rooms with private baths in a carriage house provide a quiet retreat from the hustle and bustle of Main Street, yet they are just a stone's throw from the galleries and shops. Both have private entrances and fireplaces and are furnished simply, with Shaker- and Colonial-style pieces. The rooms can be joined to make a suite perfect for families. The inn, serving guests since 1987, has retained its 19th-century character. A hearty Continental breakfast is delivered to your room, or to the garden upon request. The owner's antiques business is adjacent to the property in case you want to browse. **Pro:** Antiques galore. **Cons:** Property is small, no Web access. ⊠*101 Main St., Box 517, 04578* ☎*207/882–6010 or 800/852–4137* 🖷*207/882–6965* ↩*2 rooms* ⌂*In-room: no a/c, no TV. In-hotel: no elevator* ☰*AE, MC, V* ⊘*Closed Nov.–Apr.* ⊚*CP.*

$ ⊞ **Highnote Bed & Breakfast.** You may hear the owner singing operatic arias when you arrive at this delightful B&B, which will give you a clue as to its unusual name. Antiques fill this one-of-a-kind Victorian abode dating from 1876. You're within walking distance of the harbor plus many antiques shops and art studios. Each room is a gallery in itself, hung with works by local artists. Reserve the master bedroom and enjoy a claw-foot tub that has been sunk into the floor. Breakfast is traditionally European, with whole-grain cereals, yogurt, and fresh fruit, as well as something just out of the oven. A resident horse delights kids in summer. **Pros:** Beautiful antiques and a delightful eccentricity—and the seasonal horse outside. **Con:** Cats on the premises. ⊠*26 Lee St., 04578* ☎*207/882–9628* ⊕*wiscasset.net/highnote* ↩*3 rooms* ⌂*In-room: no a/c, no TV. In-hotel: public Wi-Fi, no elevator* ☰*No credit cards* ⊚*BP.*

SHOPPING

ANTIQUES & HOME FURNISHINGS   The Wiscasset area rivals Searsport as a destination for antiquing. Shops line Wiscasset's main streets and extend over the bridge into Edgecomb. The **Butterstamp Workshop** (⊠*55 Middle St.* ☎*207/882–7825*) carries handcrafted folk-art pieces made from antique molds. **Jenkins and Ingram Gallery** (⊠*75 Main St.* ☎*207/882–7790*) carries antiques as well as Oriental rugs and contemporary art. **Marston House American Antiques** (⊠*101 Main St.* ☎*207/882–6010*) specializes in 18th- and 19th-century painted furniture, homespun textiles, and antique garden accessories and tools. If you have a garden, don't miss the roadside spread at **North of the Border** (⊠*605 Bath Rd.* ☎*207/882–5432* ☉*Mid-Apr.–late Nov.*), which includes an array of stone and terra-cotta lawn and garden ornaments imported from Mexico.

ART & CRAFTS   **Blooms of Wiscasset** (⊠*65 Main St.* ☎*207/882–9901* ⊕*www.bloomsofwiscasset.com*) displays lots of metalware for sale, in addition to plants, flowers, and homemade chocolates. Not to be missed is **Edgecomb Potters** (⊠*727 Boothbay Rd., Edgecomb* ☎*207/882–9493* ⊕*www.edgecombpotters.com*), which specializes in pricey exquisitely glazed porcelain. Open year-round, the shop has one of the best selections in the area and also carries jewelry. There are plenty of studios and galleries with eclectic collections in this part of Maine, and the **Maine Art Gallery** (⊠*315 Warren St.* ☎*207/882–7511*) is no exception. Presenting works by local artists, the bright and colorful gallery sports a variety of new and exciting pieces. **Rock, Paper, Sissors** (⊠*78 Main St.* ☎*207/882–9930*) is a stationery store with lots of items for children's activities also. **Sheepscot River Pottery** (⊠*34 U.S. 1, Edgecomb* ☎*207/882–9410* ⊕*www.sheepscot.com*) boasts beautifully glazed kitchen tiles as well as kitchenware and home accessories. A second store is located in Damariscotta. The **Wiscasset Bay Gallery** (⊠*67 Main St.* ☎*207/882–7682* ⊕*www.wiscassetbaygallery.com*) displays a fine collection of works by 19th- and 20th-century artists.

▌ **NEED A BREAK?**   Treats (⊠*80 Main St.* ☎*207/882–6192*) stocks wonderful cheeses, wines, and fresh-baked breads, as well as decadent sandwiches that are perfect for an impromptu picnic at Waterfront Park.

BOOTHBAY & PEMAQUID PENINSULAS

If you head north from Wiscasset on U.S. 1, you'll reach Route 27 just after crossing the Wiscasset Bridge into Edgecomb. Route 27 brings you into the heart of Boothbay Harbor, a seaside community with myriad shops and restaurants. Whale-watching, lighthouse trips, puffin-spotting, and sightseeing cruises are popular pastimes. Farther south along Route 27 is Southport Island, where you can enjoy the ocean scenery and peek into a gallery or two. Route 96 takes you from Boothbay Harbor to East Boothbay, where you can see Ocean Point's rocky ledges and a handful of lobster shacks.

If you bypass Route 27 and continue north on U.S. 1 from Wiscasset, you'll come to Route 130, which leads to the Pemaquid Peninsula. Art galleries, antiques shops, and lobster shacks are found here and there along the country roads that meander through the countryside. At the tip of the point, you can find a much-photographed lighthouse perched on an unforgiving rock ledge. Exploring here reaps many rewards, including views of salt ponds and boat-filled harbors. The twin towns of Damariscotta and Newcastle anchor the region, but small fishing villages such as Pemaquid, New Harbor, and Round Pond give the peninsula its pure Maine flavor.

BOOTHBAY

13 mi southeast of Wiscasset via U.S. 1 to ME–27.

When Portlanders want a break from city life, many come north to the Boothbay region, which is made up of Boothbay proper, East Boothbay, and Boothbay Harbor. This part of the shoreline is a craggy stretch of inlets where pleasure craft anchor alongside trawlers and lobster boats. Commercial Street, Wharf Street, Townsend Avenue, and the By-Way are lined with shops and ice-cream parlors. You can browse for hours in the trinket shops, crafts galleries, clothing stores, and boutiques around the harbor. Excursion boats leave from the piers off Commercial Street. Boats to Monhegan Island are also available. Drive out to Ocean Point in East Boothbay for some incredible scenery.

WHAT TO SEE

At the **Boothbay Railway Village,** about 1 mi north of Boothbay, you'll find more than 50 antique automobiles and a gift shop, and you can ride 1½ mi on a coal-fired, narrow-gauge steam train that goes through a model of a century-old New England village. ⊠ *Rte. 27* ☏ *207/633–4727* ⊕ *www.railwayvillage.org* 💲*$8* ⊘ *Memorial Day–Columbus Day, daily 9:30–5.*

Lighthouses are always fun to see, and two of them stand at attention near Boothbay Harbor. **Burnt Island Light,** built in 1821, can best be seen on harbor cruises that allow two hours on the island; however, it also can be viewed from the mainland on the west side of the harbor near the northern end of Southport Island. To catch a glimpse of it, follow Route 27 south from Boothbay Harbor. **Cuckolds Light,** which lies less than a mile off the southern tip of Southport Island, can easily be seen unless it is fogged in. The fog signal was built in 1892, and the light was added in 1907 to prevent heavy shipping traffic entering the harbor from running aground.

The **Department of Marine Resources Aquarium** has a petting pool where you can pet a baby shark, tide pools where you can see marine creatures up close, and tanks with rare blue lobsters. Bring a picnic lunch and enjoy the views of Boothbay Harbor. ⊠ *194 McKown Point Rd., Boothbay Harbor* ☏ *207/633–9559* ⊕ *www.maine.gov/dmr* 💲*$5* ⊘ *Memorial Day–Sept. 30, daily 10–5.*

WHERE TO EAT

$$–$$$$ ✕ **McSeagull's.** A mouthwatering, rich lobster bisque and the fresh fish of the day are specialties at this casual eatery on Pier 1 overlooking the harbor, where you can eat inside or out on the deck. The service is great. If you are hankering after a lobster roll, this one is packed to bursting, honest, and is accompanied by the salad of the day or fries. There's also a wide selection of soups, chowders, salads, and sandwiches. Reservations are recommended for dinner, but not accepted for the outdoor deck perched above the water. There's live entertainment daily. ⊠ *14 Wharf St., Boothbay Harbor* ☎ *207/633–5900* ▤ *MC, V* ⊙ *Closed Columbus Day–Memorial Day.*

> ### GOTTA LOTTA MOXIE?
>
> It's difficult to get very far in Maine without running into Moxie—the nation's oldest soft drink, invented by Dr. Augustin Thompson of Union, Maine, in 1884. You'll recognize it by its bright orange label. It comes in bottles and cans and is sold in just about every supermarket and convenience store in Maine. A word of warning, however; you gotta get past that first taste!

$–$$$ ✕ **Lobster Dock.** Dine inside or out at this waterfront restaurant, built on the site of the Reed Shipyard, which operated here from the late 1800s to the early 1900s. There's nothing like twin lobsters and a pitcher of cold beer out on the deck. Specialties of the house include the area's only hot lobster roll. Daily specials might feature lobster spring rolls, seafood risotto, or lobster gnocchi. If you want a landlubber meal, they serve a rack of lamb and a filet mignon Oscar. No meal is complete without a slice of the homemade pie. Rover can come, too, if you eat on the outside deck. ⊠ *49 Atlantic Ave., Boothbay Harbor* ☎ *207/633–7120* ⊕ *www.thelobsterdock.com* ▤ *MC, V* ⊙ *Closed Oct.–May.*

$–$$ ✕ **Boothbay Lobster Wharf.** Crustacean lovers will find something to satisfy their craving at this dockside working lobster pound. It's nothing fancy, but needless to say, you won't find fresher lobster anywhere else and the steamed mussels and clams are mouthwatering. Eat in the dining room or outside, where you can watch the lobstermen at work. Pick up fresh fish from the fish market. The restaurant is on the pier near the Fisherman's Memorial across the harbor. ⊠ *97 Atlantic Ave., Boothbay Harbor* ☎ *207/633–4900* ⊕ *www.boothbaylobsterwharf. com* ▤ *D, MC, V* ⊙ *Closed mid-Oct.–mid-May.*

¢–$$ ✕ **Ebb Tide.** Open all year, this friendly seaside restaurant is easy to spot because of its red-and-white awnings. Many original wooden booths in the dining room have views of the harbor. The establishment is known for its fish sandwiches, shrimp baskets, and lobster dinners. It also serves a good grilled cheese sandwich. Everything on the menu can be packed for takeout. Many people stop by in the afternoon for a cup of coffee and a piece of downright delicious homemade pie; the walnut is especially scrumptious. If you're here off-season, this is a great place to meet friends for a cup of coffee. ⊠ *46 Commercial St., Boothbay Harbor* ☎ *207/633–5692* ▤ *No credit cards.*

WHERE TO STAY

$$$–$$$$ 🏨 **Spruce Point Inn.** Escape the hubbub of Boothbay H;
★   sprawling resort with 92 lodgings spread over 57 beautifully ι₄..
acres. Lodgings consist of ocean house condominiums, oceanfront suites,
and deluxe family cottages, all with private decks and baths, mini-refrig-
erators, and cable TV. There are plenty of sporting activities here. Guest
rooms in the main inn are comfortable, and most have fireplaces, whirl-
pool baths, and a view of the ocean. A full-service spa offers massages
and other treatments. Evening entertainment takes place in the formal
dining room ($$–$$$), which serves dishes such as fillet of sole stuffed
with crabmeat, shallots, and Asiago and chèvre cheese. Or eat in Bogie's
Hideaway, a casual pub-style bistro. A nearby foghorn blows in inclem-
ent weather. **Pros:** Spacious grounds on hill overlooking ocean, lots of
activities, children's programs. **Cons:** Big place, lots of people. ⊠*88
Grandview Ave., Box 237, Boothbay Harbor 04538* ☎*207/633–4152
or 800/553–0289* ⊕*www.sprucepointinn.com* ⇆*21 rooms, 41 suites,
7 cottages* ⌂*In-room: no a/c (some). In-hotel: 2 restaurants, bar, tennis
courts, pool, spa, no-smoking rooms* ⊟*AE, D, DC, MC, V* ⊗*Closed
late Oct.–mid-May.*

$$$–$$$$ 🏨 **Admiral's Quarters Inn Bed & Breakfast.** Open all year, this renovated
1830 sea captain's house is ideally situated for exploring Boothbay
Harbor. Many shops, galleries, and restaurants are within walking dis-
tance. Fresh-baked goods greet you upon your return. All rooms have
fireplaces, and some have private decks overlooking the water. On rainy
days you can relax by the cozy woodstove in the sunroom. **Pros:** The
water view, convenience. **Con:** No handicapped access. ⊠*71 Commer-
cial St., Boothbay Harbor 04538* ☎*207/633–2474 or 800/644–1878*
⊕*www.admiralsquartersinn.com* ⇆*2 rooms, 5 suites* ⌂*In-room: Wi-
Fi. In-hotel: public Internet, no kids under 12, no-smoking rooms, no
elevator* ⊟*AE, D, MC, V* ⏀*BP.*

$$$–$$$$ 🏨 **Blue Heron Seaside Inn.** Experience the charm of a bygone era in this
romantic B&B bedecked with flowers and plantings on the waterfront
in Boothbay Harbor but still enjoy all the comforts. Large, elegant
air-conditioned rooms have four-poster beds throughout, water views,
sitting areas, high-definition TV, and phones. Period antiques dress the
lobbies and rooms. Each floor has a different theme: Victorian, Colo-
nial, and nautical. Bring your own kayaks or borrow the owners' here
and launch off their property. **Pros:** Convenience, comfort, compli-
mentary beverages. **Con:** No elevator. ⊠*65 Townsend Ave., 04538*
☎*207/633–7020 or 866/216–2300* ⊕*www.blueheronseasideinn.com*
⇆*5 rooms, 1 suite* ⌂*In-room: Wi-Fi, refrigerator. In-hotel: water
sports, no-smoking rooms, no elevator* ⊟ *V, MC* ⊗*Closed Jan. and
Feb.* ⏀*BP.*

$$$–$$$$ 🏨 **Five Gables Inn.** You can see this beautifully restored Victorian inn
★   from the water. It is the last of the turn-of-the-20th-century hotels that
once welcomed guests in the Boothbays. The gabled roof and beautiful
gardens give this hillside lodging a distinctive look. The guest rooms
tucked underneath the eves have the most charm, though not ideal for
tall people. All rooms have period furnishings, including four-poster
beds. Some have fireplaces, and all but one have views of the islands

scattered around Linekin Bay, so bring your kayaks and access the water directly off this property. The broad veranda overlooking the bay has plenty of comfy chairs from which you can enjoy the view along with your breakfast or afternoon tea and cookies. **Pros:** Water access, quiet. **Con:** Low ceilings. ⊠ *107 Murray Hill Rd., East Boothbay 04544* ☎ *207/633–4551 or 800/451–5048* ⊕ *www.fivegablesinn. com* 🖙 *16 rooms* ♿ *In-room: Wi-Fi, no a/c, no TV. In-hotel: no kids under 12, no-smoking rooms* ⊟ *MC, V* ⊗ *Closed mid-Oct.–Memorial Day* ⦿ *BP.*

$$$–$$$$ 🏨 **Greenleaf Inn.** Built in 1849, this tastefully restored B&B is filled with antiques and wicker furniture. There are great ocean views from many of the rooms. Guests congregate in the sunroom, on the wrap-around porch, or in the hot tub that overlooks the harbor. After breakfast you can take your coffee out on the deck and watch the cruise boats set off in search of whales. **Pros:** View and convenience. **Con:** No handicapped access. ⊠ *65 Commercial St., Boothbay Harbor 04538* ☎ *207/633–7346 or 888/950–7724* ⊕ *www.greenleafinn.com* 🖙 *7 rooms* ♿ *In-room: VCR, Wi-Fi. In-hotel: no pets, no kids under 12, bicycles, no-smoking rooms, no elevator* ⊟ *AE, D, MC, V* ⦿ *BP.*

$$–$$$$ 🏨 **Ocean Point Inn.** Less than 7 mi from Boothbay Harbor, this lodging at the end of Ocean Point lets you enjoy some spectacular scenery. Choose a rustic cottage or a room in the main building or in the old farmstead. Some are warmed by gas fireplaces. The inn has one of the area's largest outdoor heated pools and a hot tub and direct access to the bay, making it perfect for rowing and kayaking. You can stroll along the shore and watch lobstermen bringing in their catch.**Pro:** Location on the point. **Con:** Away from town. ⊠ *Shore Rd.* ⦿ *P.O. Box 409, East Boothbay 04544* ☎ *207/633–4200 or 800/552–5554* ⊕ *www.oceanpointinn.com* 🖙 *61 rooms, 7 cottages* ♿ *In-room: refrigerator. In-hotel: restaurant, pool, public Wi-Fi, no-smoking rooms, no elevator* ⊟ *AE, D, MC, V* ⊗ *Closed mid-Oct.–Memorial Day.*

$$–$$$$ 🏨 **Welch House.** This 1889 shipbuilder's house sits high on a hill near Boothbay Harbor. Antiques, artworks, and bric-a-brac from the owner's travels around the world adorn the rooms. From the shared third-floor deck, you can take in the 180-degree views of the water. Breakfast on the lower deck usually includes one of the chef's specialties, which might mean caramel-apple and pecan-crusted French toast. The location puts you a few minutes' walk from the center of town. **Pros:** The view, convenience. **Cons:** No elevator, no handicapped access. ⊠ *36 McKown St., Boothbay Harbor 04538* ☎ *207/633–3431 or 800/279–7313* ⊕ *www.welchhouseinn.com* 🖙 *14 rooms* ♿ *In-room: Wi-Fi, VCR. In-hotel: public Wi-Fi, some pets allowed, no-smoking rooms, no elevator* ⊟ *AE, MC, V* ⊗ *Closed Dec.–Mar.* ⦿ *BP.*

$$$ 🏨 **Anchor Watch Bed & Breakfast.** The bright and spacious rooms at this hillside B&B are named for the boats that delivered mail to Monhegan Island in the early 20th century. Comfortable beds are piled high with colorful quilts, and each room has a balcony with a view of the ocean. Drive to the end of Commercial Street where you'll find Eames Road. The inn is only a few minutes from the harbor, yet it feels completely out of the way. Breakfasts may include the owners' spe-

cialty, baked cheese omelets. Other favorites are blueberry blintzes with raspberry sauce and baked French toast topped with orange-honey butter. **Pro:** Out of the way but convenient. **Con:** No handicapped access. ✉*9 Eames Rd., Boothbay Harbor 04538* ☎*207/633–7565 or 800/718–7565* ⊕*www.anchorwatch.com* ➫*45 rooms* ♿*In-*

room: Wi-Fi, no a/c (some). In-hotel: no kids under 8, no-smoking rooms ☰*MC, V* ⊗*Closed Dec.–Feb.* ⋈*BP.*

$$–$$$ ⬚**Linekin Bay Bed & Breakfast.** If you are looking for a quiet retreat, consider this charming B&B. The bright sunroom and outdoor patio are ringed by lovely gardens, where guests tend to gather after their daily adventures to enjoy the view of the bay and boats moored below from chairs on the lawn. Enjoy a full breakfast in the morning in the sunroom; return for delicious desserts in the afternoon. The sunroom has guest refrigerators and a microwave, as well as an area to prepare snacks. All rooms have hardwood floors, handsome fireplaces, and water views. Bathrooms are stocked with products such as Tom's of Maine toothpastes. **Pros:** Immaculate rooms, peaceful. **Con:** Quiet. ✉*531 Ocean Point Rd., East Boothbay 04544* ☎*207/633–9900 or 800/596–7420* ⊕*www.linekinbaybb.com* ➫*4 rooms* ♿*In-room: Wi-Fi, VCR. In-hotel: no kids under 12, no-smoking rooms, no elevator* ☰*MC, V* ⋈*BP.*

$$–$$$ ⬚**Topside.** If you want a glimpse of the harbor, this 19th-century sea captain's house perched on a hillside has views from every room. The front lawn is a great place to watch the activities on the harbor below. From here you can walk to dozens of antiques shops, art galleries, and restaurants. Rooms are divided between the main house and two annexes called the Windward House and the Leeward House. The rooms in the main house are decorated in a comfortable beach-house style. The guest houses are styled a bit more simply. **Pros:** Always a breeze, the view. **Con:** No elevator. ✉*60 McKown St., Boothbay Harbor 04538* ☎*207/633–5404 or 877/486–7466* ⊕*www.topsideinn. com* ➫*21 rooms* ♿*In-room: Wi-Fi (some), no a/c. In-hotel: public Wi-Fi, no kids under 6, some pets allowed (summer only), no-smoking rooms, no elevator* ☰*D, MC* ⊗*Closed late Oct.–mid-Apr.* ⋈*BP.*

$–$$$ ⬚**Harbor House Inn.** Built in the 1880's by Captain Mitchell Reed, this inn sits atop McKown Hill above Boothbay Harbor and offers a full breakfast in the dining room or on the veranda. Enjoy the perennial breeze and the water views, all within a two-minute walk from shops and restaurants and the waterfront. Two rooms have Jacuzzi baths and two have wireless access; one has air-conditioning, but you don't really need it up here on the hill. Kids are welcome here, but not pets. Guests have the use of a refrigerator and there are snacks and complimentary bottled water daily. One owner speaks German. **Pros:** An old-world feel, convenient to everything. **Cons:** Shih Tzu on-site, no elevator. ✉*80 McKown St., 04358* ☎*207/633–2941 or 800/856–1164*

⊕*www.harborhouse-me.com* ⌁*7 rooms* &*In-room: Wi-Fi (some), no a/c (some). In-hotel: public Wi-Fi, no-smoking rooms, no elevator* ▤*MC, V* ⊗*Closed Columbus Day–Memorial Day weekend* ⍧|*BP.*

$$ ⚏**Linekin Bay Resort.** All your meals are included when you stay at this
⚙ all-inclusive resort, with 37 cabins and 5 lodges that will accommodate 150 guests. The only thing you have to worry about is whether you'll spend the day hiking in the 15 acres of wooded land or fishing at the edge of the harbor, or learning to sail one of the resort's 20 Rhodes sailboats. You can fish from the dock, swim in the outdoor heated saltwater pool, or challenge a friend to a game of tennis, basketball, or Ping-Pong. Kayaks, canoes, and rowboats are available for guests. Open only to guests, the dining room has lobster bakes twice a week. **Pros:** Informal camp atmosphere, lots to do, kids under 3 are free. **Con:** No-frills rooms. ⊠*92 Wall Point Rd., Boothbay Harbor 04538* ☎*207/633–2494 or 866/847–2103* ⊕*www.linekinbayresort. com* ⌁*37 cabins* &*In-room: Wi-Fi, no a/c, no phone, no TV. In-hotel: restaurant, tennis court, pool,no-smoking rooms, no elevator* ▤*MC, V* ⊗*Closed late Sept.–mid-June* ⍧|*AI.*

SPORTS & THE OUTDOORS

When you are ready to escape the hustle and bustle of Boothbay Harbor, rent a kayak and explore the harbor to your heart's content. To get a bit farther away, sign up for one of the sightseeing or whale-watching cruises from the piers on Commercial Street. You can also catch a ride on a lobster boat and help haul the traps. Don't miss the new Coastal Maine Botanical Gardens, the largest in the United States.

BOATING On Pier 8, **Balmy Day Cruises** (⊠*62 Commercial St., Boothbay Harbor* ☎*207/633–2284 or 800/298–2284* ⊕*www.balmydaycruises.com*) offers day trips to Monhegan Island, cruising or sailing tours of the harbor, and mackerel fishing. A guided tour of the Burnt Island Lighthouse is available, with two hours on the island. Cruises run from mid-April to mid-October. Setting sail from Pier 6, **Boothbay Whale Watch** (⊠*Pier 6, Boothbay Harbor* ☎*207/633–3500 or 888/WHALE–ME [800/942–5363]* ⊕*www.whaleme.com*) conducts whale-watching tours and sunset cruises on the *Harbor Princess* from June to mid-October.

On Pier 1, **Cap'n Fish's Boat Trips** (⊠*Pier 1, Boothbay Harbor* ☎*207/633–3244 or 800/636–3244* ⊕*www.capnfishsboats.com*) runs regional sightseeing cruises, including puffin-watching adventures, or can take you on lobster-hauling and whale-watching rides, trips to Damariscove Harbor and Pemaquid Point, and Kennebec River to Bath excursions. Cruises run from late May to late October.

HIKING Explore more than 30 mi of groomed trails crisscrossing more than 1,700 acres of natural habitat at the **Boothbay Region Land Trust** (⊠*1 Oak St.* ☎*207/633–4818*); hikes range from easy to difficult. Located about a mile from Boothbay Center, the **Coastal Maine Botanical Garden** (⊠*Barters Island Rd.* ⌂*P.O. Box 234, 04537* ☎*207/633–4333* ⊕*www.mainegardens.org*) celebrated its grand opening in 2007 and has 248 acres, including magnificent ornamental gardens, sculpture, tidal frontage, and wooded areas, all open to visitors. This is the biggest botanical garden in the United States and the only one a U.S. shore.

KAYAKING **Tidal Transit Ocean Kayak Co.** (✉*18 Granary Way, Boothbay Harbor* ☎*207/633–7140* ⊕*www.kayakboothbay.com*) has equipment to rent and offers guided tours of the coastline. The company also rents bicycles. It's open from Memorial Day to late September.

SHOPPING

CRAFTS & GIFTS The **Custom House** (✉*8 Wharf St.* ☎*207/633–3525* ⊕*www.thecustomhouse.biz* ☉*Feb.–Dec.*) carries marine-related items, fine pottery, glassware, and handmade jewelry. **McKown Square Quilts** (✉*14-B Boothbay House Hill Rd., Boothbay Harbor* ☎*207/633–2007* ☉*Mon.–Sat.*) displays handmade quilts and fiber art in seven rooms. Find Maine- and other American-made pottery and wood carvings, jewelry, collectibles, and fruit preserves at **Mung Bean** (✉*37 Townsend Ave., Boothbay Harbor* ☎*207/633–5512* ☉*Daily*); it's open until 9:30 PM in summer, so it's perfect for after-dinner browsing. For antiques and crafts, visit the **Palabra Shop** (✉*53 Commercial St., Boothbay Harbor* ☎*207/633–4225* ⊕*www.palabrashop.com* ☉*Daily, Mar.–Dec.; weekends in Feb by appt.*). **Sadie Green's Curiosity Shop** (✉*48 Commercial St.* ☎*207/633–0573* ⊕*www.sadiegreens.com* ☉*Closed winter*) is one of six Sadie Green's shops in New England. This one in an old waterfront warehouse carries an amazing array of gifts, jewelry, clothing, nautical items, and art.

CLOTHING & ACCESSORIES The **Cannery** (✉*3 By-Way* ☎*207/633–6503 or 888/633–6503* ☉*May– mid-Dec.*) is a bright, colorful shop on the water, offering pretty jewelry, colorful and fashionable summer clothing, and cute things for kids. The upscale **House of Logan** (✉*20 Townsend Ave., Boothbay Harbor* ☎*207/633–2293*) stocks casual and formal attire for men and women. **A Silver Lining** (✉*17 Townsend Ave.* ☎*207/633–4103*) has a large selection of original jewelry, as well as older pieces from estates. It's open all year. Beautiful housewares and attractive clothing for the kids can be found at the **Village Store & Children's Shop** (✉*20 Townsend Ave., Boothbay Harbor* ☎*207/633–2293*).

FOOD No trip to Boothbay Harbor is complete without a stop at **Orne's Candy Store** (✉*11 Commercial St., Boothbay Harbor* ☎*207/633–2695* ⊕*www.ornescandystore.com*), a must for anyone with a sweet tooth. All the candy is made in Maine. Try the turtles and fudge.

NEWCASTLE

18 mi north of Boothbay Harbor via Rte. 27 and U.S. 1.

The town of Newcastle, between the Sheepscot and the Damariscotta rivers, was settled in the early 1600s. The earliest inhabitants planted apple trees, but the town later became an industrial center, home to several shipyards and a couple of mills. The oldest Catholic church in New England, St. Patrick's, is here, and the church still rings its original Paul Revere bell to call parishioners to worship. Newcastle's B&Bs put you close to everything on the Boothbay and Pemaquid peninsulas.

WHERE TO EAT & STAY

$$$–$$$$ ✕🏠 **Newcastle Inn.** A riverside location and an excellent dining room make this country inn a classic. All the guest rooms are filled with antiques and decorated with sumptuous fabrics; some rooms have fireplaces and whirlpool baths. On pleasant mornings, breakfast is served on the back deck overlooking the river. The dining room ($$$$), which is open to the public by reservation, serves six-course meals and is open Tuesday through Saturday in season. The emphasis is on local seafood. **Pros:** Innkeepers' reception evenings with cocktails and hors d'oeuvres. **Con:** Away from town. ⊠ *60 River Rd., 04553* ☎ *207/563–5685 or 800/832–8669* ⊕ *www.newcastleinn.com* ⤏ *14 rooms, 3 suites* ⚷ *In-room: no phone, no TV (some). In-hotel: restaurant, bar, no kids under 12, no-smoking rooms, no elevator* ▤ *AE, MC, V* ⊙ *BP.*

$$–$$$ 🏠 **Flying Cloud.** Each room here is named for a legendary port of call made by the *Flying Cloud*, a clipper ship that was christened in 1851. The main house elegantly combines the original 1790 Cape Cod–style house with an 1840 Greek Revival–style addition. There are water views of the Damariscotta River from every room and from the outdoor deck. The sumptuous full breakfast is a great way to start the day. You can enjoy it indoors or on a screen porch looking out on the owners' lovely gardens. Many area attractions are close by, including hiking trails at the Great Salt Bay Preserve. Wi-Fi access is available in the library. **Pros:** Peaceful. **Cons:** no elevator. ⊠ *45 River Rd., 04553* ☎ *207/563–2484* ⊕ *www.theflyingcloud.com* ⤏ *4 rooms, 1 suite* ⚷ *In-room: no a/c, no TV. In-hotel: public Wi-Fi, no-smoking rooms* ▤ *AE, MC, V* ⊙ *BP.*

$$–$$$ 🏠 **Tipsy Butler Bed & Breakfast.** The view from the porch of this 1845 ★   hillside home is of the twin villages of Damariscotta and Newcastle. The large guest rooms have separate sitting areas and are tastefully decorated with period furnishings. Distinctive features include ceramic friezes on some walls and authentic ceiling medallions. The out-of-the-way location assures privacy, but you are only a five-minute walk from many shops and restaurants. The new innkeeper goes far out of her way where service is concerned, offering guests bottled water, bathrobes, totebags, towels for the beach, umbrellas, and rain gear. Bathrooms have baskets of amenities replenished daily. And when was the last time you stayed at a B&B that did daily bed turndowns? There is wireless Internet and satellite TV for those who are seeking these services. **Pros:** Coming for Christmas? You'll find a tree in your room! **Cons:** No elevator. ⊠ *11 High St., 04553* ☎ *207/563–3394* ⊕ *www. thetipsybutler.com* ⤏ *4 rooms* ⚷ *In-room: VCR, DVD. In-hotel: public Wi-Fi, no-smoking rooms* ▤ *MC, V* ⊙ *BP.*

DAMARISCOTTA

6 mi east of Newcastle via U.S. 1.

The Damariscotta region comprises several communities along the rocky coast. The town of Damariscotta, which sits on the water, is filled with attractive shops and several good restaurants. Bremen, which encompasses more than a dozen islands and countless rocky outcrops, offers numerous sporting activities. Nobleboro was settled in the 1720s by Colonel David Dunbar, sent by the British to build the fort at Pemaquid. Neighboring Waldoboro is situated on the Medomak River and was settled largely by Germans in the early 1770s. You can still visit the old German Meeting House, built in 1772. The peninsula stretches south to include Bristol, Round Pond, South Bristol, New Harbor, and Pemaquid.

WHAT TO SEE

One of the oldest houses in Damariscotta, the **Chapman-Hall House** was completed in 1754 by Nathaniel Chapman. Unlike nearby houses that have been remodeled, it closely resembles the original design. Tours are given in July and August. ⊠ *Main St. at Church St.* ☎ *No phone* 💲 *Free* ⊙ *Mid-June–mid-Sept., Tues.–Sun. 1–5.*

On U.S. 1, the **Glidden Oyster Shell Middens** includes a hiking trail with views of the Damariscotta River. ⊠ *U.S. 1* ☎ *207/563–1393* ⊕ *www. draclt.org* 💲 *Free* ⊙ *Daily.*

WHERE TO EAT & STAY

$$–$$$ ✕**Damariscotta River Grill.** Whether you eat in the dining room or outside on the deck, you'll have a lovely view of the water at this convenient downtown restaurant. Lobster risotto and Thai fish stew are popular entrées, and so are the Pemaquid oysters, the scallops, and the Italian seafood stew. You can also get a good steak here anytime, and Friday is prime rib night. There are full bars upstairs and down for your enjoyment. Sunday brunch is delicious year-round. ⊠ *155 Main St.* ☎ *207/563–2992* ⚐ *Reservations essential* ⊟ *MC, V.*

$$–$$$ ✕**King Eider's Pub & Restaurant.** The classic pub bills itself as having the
★ finest crab cakes in New England. Other specialties of the house include lobster Courvoisier and house-made raviolis that vary day to day. A crabmeat-stuffed ravioli was out of this world, as was the penne pasta in a creamy dill sauce with a mound of sea scallops. With exposed brick walls and low wooden beams, it's a cozy place to enjoy your favorite ale. There is also seating on the deck. Stop by in the evening for live entertainment. ⊠ *2 Elm St.* ☎ *207/563–6008* ⊕ *www.kingeiderspub. com* ⚐ *Reservations essential* ⊟ *D, MC, V.*

$–$$$ ✕**Salt Bay Café.** Seafood devotees as well as those who hanker for meat or vegetarian fare will all like this downtown restaurant. On the menu you can find sandwiches and burgers or such delicious dishes as fettuccine Florentine, seafood Alfredo, and filet mignon cooked to perfection. Not to be missed are the scallops Mediterranean and pecan-crusted salmon. Want meat? Roasted rack of lamb is available and a Gaelic steak might be to your liking. Everything on the menu is made from scratch, from the soups to the desserts. A fireplace keeps the place toasty on winter nights. ⊠ *88 Main St.* ☎ *207/563–3302* ⚐ *Reservations essential* ⊟ *MC, V.*

$$–$$$ 🗋**Oak Gables.** Nestled on 11 pristine acres and surrounded by natural beauty, this facility is a little bit of heaven, but a short walk to town. There are four rooms in the main house, as well as two immaculate apartments and a separate cottage with a full kitchen, all available for weekly rentals only. The in-ground pool is heated, and you can sit on the boathouse right above the water to watch gulls and ducks winging in over the bay. **Pro:** Walking distance to town. **Con:** Weekly rentals only. ⊠*36 Pleasant St., 04543* ☎*207/563–1476 or 800/335–7748* ⊕*www.oakgablesbb.com* ↪*3 rooms, 2 apartments, 1 cottage* ♿*In-room: no a/c, kitchen (some). In-hotel: pool, no-smoking rooms, no elevator* ⊟*MC, V* ⦿*BP for rooms, not for cottage and apartments.*

NIGHTLIFE & THE ARTS

Musicals and plays are staged regularly at the downtown **Lincoln County Community Theater** (⊠2 *Theater St.* ☎*207/563–3424* ⊕*www.lcct.org*). It also hosts concerts and screens movies throughout the year.

SPORTS & THE OUTDOORS

To rent a sea kayak, or to sign up for lessons, visit **Midcoast Kayak** (⊠47 *Main St.* ☎*207/563–5732* ⊕*www.midcoastkayak.com*). Great local excursions include Muscongus Bay and the Damariscotta River.

In the Sheepscot River valley, **Sheepscot Links** (⊠824 *Townhouse Rd., Whitefield 04353* ☎*207/549–7060*) is a 9-hole course with greens fees of $15 for 9 holes, and $22 for 18 holes. It's in Whitefield, about 16 mi northwest of Damariscotta. From U.S. 1 take Route 215 west to Route 194 north to Townhouse Road. In Walpole, **Wawenock Country Club** (⊠685 *Rte. 129, Walpole 04573* ☎*207/563–3938*) is just minutes from Damariscotta. Take Route 129 south from U.S. Route 1 at Damariscotta. Open in late May to November, the country club includes a public-access course, driving range, and pro shop. Greens fees are $15 for 9 holes, $20 for 18 holes.

SHOPPING

Create your own necklace or bracelet from a large selection of new and vintage beads at **Aboca Beads** (⊠157 *Main St.* ☎*207/563–1766*), in the Damariscotta Center. If plants are your passion, **Bramble's** (⊠157 *Main St.* ☎*207/563–2800*) carries gardening tools, topiaries, and pots. **Delphiniums Glassworks** (⊠112 *Main St.* ☎*207/563–6333*) carries gifts and more; it specializes in glass engraving. You can browse to your heart's content through the shelves at **Maine Coast Book Shop & Café** (⊠158 *Main St.* ☎*207/563–3207*). Enjoy a cup of coffee and a blueberry muffin at the adjoining café. If you're looking for a fine wine or special beer, you'll find them at **Quacks** (⊠50 *Main St.* ☎*207/563–8259*). It also carries cheeses from Artisanal shops in New York and Salumeria Biellese deli meats. You never know what you'll find at **Reny's** (⊠121 *Main St.* ☎*207/563–5757*). Sometimes there's merchandise from L.L. Bean or a coat from a famous designer. This bargain chain has outlets in many Maine towns, but this is its flagship store. **River Gallery, L.L.C.** (⊠79 *Main St.* ☎*207/563–6330 or 207/529–5558* ⊕*www.rivergalleryfineart.com*) carries fine European and American paintings for the discriminating buyer. The barnlike **Stable Gallery** (⊠26 *Water St.* ☎*207/563–1991*) stocks paintings and prints by the more than 100 Water Street artists in a big open space that sets off each item at its best. Jewelry, metals, textiles, ceramics, and furniture make this a must-see for art aficionados. Color everywhere, fun stuff, and unique clothing is what customers keep coming back for at **Two Fish Boutique** (⊠133 *Main St.* ☎*207/563–2220*), which carries special gifts and children's items.

PEMAQUID, NEW HARBOR & ROUND POND

17 mi south of Damariscotta via U.S. 1 to Rte. 129 to Rte. 130.

Route 130 brings you to Pemaquid Point, home of the famous lighthouse and its attendant fog bell and tiny museum. If you are going to New Harbor or Round Pond, take a left onto Route 32 where it intersects Route 130 just before Pemaquid Point. New Harbor is about 4 mi away, and Round Pond about 6 mi beyond that. Just north of New Harbor on Route 32 is the Rachel Carson Salt Pond Preserve.

WHAT TO SEE

At the **Colonial Pemaquid Restoration,** set on a small peninsula jutting into the Pemaquid River, English mariners established a fishing and trading settlement in the early 17th century. The excavations at Fort William Henry, begun in the mid-1960s, have turned up thousands of artifacts from the settlement, including the remains of an old customs house, a tavern, a jail, a forge, and several homes. Some older items are from earlier American Indian settlements. The state operates a museum that displays many of these artifacts. The Colonial Pemaquid Tavern is on-site, as are a picnic area and rest rooms. ⊠ *Rte. 130, New Harbor* 🕾 *207/677–2423* 🖃 *$2* ⊙ *Memorial Day–Labor Day, daily 9:30–7.*

☽ Route 130 terminates at the **Pemaquid Point Light,** which looks as though
★ it sprouted from the ragged, tilted chunk of granite that it commands. The former lighthouse keeper's cottage is now the Fishermen's Museum, which displays historic photographs, scale models, and artifacts that explore commercial fishing in Maine. Also here is the original fog bell and bell house built in 1897 for the two original Shipman engines. Pemaquid Art Gallery, on-site, mounts exhibitions by area artists in July and August, and admission to the gallery, once you have paid your fee to be on the lighthouse property, is free. Rest rooms, picnic tables, and barbecue grills are all available on this site. Next door to this property is the Sea Gull Shop, with a dining room, gift shop, and ice-cream parlor. *The museum on-site is adjacent to the lighthouse.* ⊠ *Rte. 130 (Bristol Rd.), Pemaquid* 🕾 *207/677–2494* 🖃 *$1* ⊙ *Memorial Day– Columbus Day, Mon.–Sat. 10–5, Sun. 11–5* 🖃 *$5.*

Author Rachel Carson gathered most of the material for her book *The Edge of the Sea* from the quarter-acre tide pool now known as **Rachel Carson Salt Pond Preserve,** just north of New Harbor. The land, donated to the Nature Conservancy in 1966, is home to many of the creatures who live in a tidal zone. ⊠ *Rte. 32, New Harbor* 🕾 *207/677–2423.*

WHERE TO EAT

$$–$$$$ ✕**Anchor Inn Restaurant.** You can't get any closer to the water than this restaurant that overlooks beautiful Round Pond harbor on Anchor Inn Road. Scallop Peepers are a popular appetizer. Sample their lobster stew, maybe with a small house salad. Fresh fish, pasta specials, lobster . . . it's all here and the atmosphere is casual and comfortable, the scenery peaceful. Desserts always feature home-baked pies as well as cheesecakes and cakes. ⊠*Anchor Inn Rd. off Rte. 32, Round Pond* ☎*207/529–5584* ▭*D, MC, V* .

$–$$ ✕**Round Pond Lobster Company.** Lobster doesn't get any fresher or any
★ cheaper than what's served at this no-frills dockside takeout. The best deal in town is the nightly dinner special: a 1-pound lobster, steamers, corn-on-the-cob, and a bag of chips. Regulars often bring their own beer, wine, bread, and salads. Settle in at a picnic table and take in the view over dreamy Round Pond Harbor. ⊠*Town Landing Rd., Round Pond* ☎*207/529–5725* ▭*MC, V* ⊗*Closed Labor Day–Memorial Day.*

WHERE TO STAY

$$$–$$$$ 🛏 **Bradley Inn.** Picture a country inn and you've got the Bradley. Within walking distance of Pemaquid Point Light, this former rooming house was originally built as a private residence for sea captain John Bradley. It has guest rooms that are comfortable and uncluttered; some have fireplaces, and those on the third floor have ocean views. Nautical knickknacks and works by local artists decorate the rooms in the main inn, the carriage house, and the garden cottage. The Bradley Inn has one of the region's best dining rooms ($$$–$$$$). The menu changes nightly but always emphasizes fresh, local foods. You can eat in the dining room or outside on the deck. The pub has piano music on weekends in summer. **Pros:** Spa, with yoga, massage, and Pilates available. **Con:** Far from town. ⊠*3063 Bristol Rd., New Harbor 04554* ☎*207/677–2105 or 800/942–5560* 🖷*207/677–3367* ⊕*www.bradley-inn.com* ⇱*12 rooms, 4 suites* ⓖ*In-room: no a/c, no TV (some). In-hotel: restaurant, bar, bicycles, spa, public Wi-Fi, no-smoking rooms, no elevator* ▭*AE, MC, V* ⓘ❙*BP.*

$$–$$$$ 🛏**Hotel Pemaquid.** As they say, location is everything. Step back in time
  ⓒ at this beautifully restored 1888 inn located less than 500 feet from the lighthouse at Pemaquid Point. The main building is Victorian in style; cottages and bungalow units have a more contemporary feel. The carriage-house suite is ideal for honeymooners or others seeking a romantic retreat. Relax on the big wraparound porch or enjoy sitting in front of a fire in the stone fireplace. Antiques decorate the comfortable rooms. The grounds are good for kids because they are open and large, and it is a short walk to the Pemaquid Point lighthouse site. **Pros:** Quiet, reasonably priced. **Cons:** No frills, no food. ⊠*3098 Bristol Rd., New Harbor 04554* ☎*207/677–2312* ⊕*www.hotelpemaquid.com* ⇱*28 rooms, 6 suites, 2 cottages, 1 apartment* ⓖ*In-room: no a/c, no phone. In-hotel: no breakfast, no-smoking rooms, no elevator* ▭*No credit cards* ⊗*Closed mid-Oct.–mid-May.*

$$–$$$ 🛏**Inn at Round Pond.** Once a stagecoach stop, this 1830s mansard-roofed Colonial sits on the eastern shore of Pemaquid Peninsula and has a picture-postcard view straight from the front lawn where you can sit in the colorful Adirondack chairs all lined up and waiting. At this restful retreat you won't be bothered by ringing telephones or blaring televisions. Instead, enjoy the gardens and private pond. Kayaking, golf, fishing, and boat cruises are all nearby. The trio of tastefully appointed suites—the Foster Suite, the Prentice Suite, and the Monhegan Suite—have separate sitting areas decorated with original artwork. All have harbor views. A full country breakfast is served each morning. **Pros:** Scenery and tranquillity. **Con:** No Internet access. ⊠ *1442 Rte. 32, Round Pond 04564* ☎ *207/529–2004* ⊕ *www.theinnatroundpond. com* ⟿ *3 suites* ᝮ *In-room: no phone, no TV. In-hotel: no kids under 12, no-smoking rooms, no elevator* ☰ *AE, D, MC, V* ⊙ *Closed Columbus Day–Memorial Day* ⦙○⦙*BP.*

$$\ $$

$$
FodorśChoice
★
▥ **Unique Yankee Bed & Breakfast.** Spectacular views of the Gulf of Maine, John's Bay, and Monhegan Island and the sound of crashing surf greet you at this hilltop B&B. The facility is at Christmas Cove, named when explorer Captain John Smith anchored here one Christmas Eve in the early 1600s. Since that time the cove has been a snug harbor for watercraft of all kinds. If you are looking for an oasis away from the crowds, you will enjoy the 11 gorgeous perennial gardens and the fact that this 2.3-acre property is surrounded by a 2-acre greenbelt. The owners' artwork from all over the world adorns the walls. Extensive libraries of books, videos, and DVDs wind around the staircases going up to the cupola towers, and you will even find a couple of pieces of exercise equipment tucked in a corner on the way. The hosts offer afternoon snacks and a selection of wines every evening. If you are looking for the experience of a lifetime, take that glass of wine up two or three floors to the tower, inside or on the outdoor decks. You can see all the way to Monhegan Island. Each of the guest rooms has a four-season electric fireplace, microwave, coffee pot, and two-person jetted bath (plus separate shower). The inn accepts kids and pets—in fact, pets have their own outdoor courtyard. **Pros:** Amenities, view, grounds, hosts. **Con:** Dogs on premises. ⊠ *53 Coveside Rd., South Bristol 04568* ☎ *207/644–1502 or 866/644–1502* ⊕ *www.uniqueyankeeofmaine. com* ⟿ *4 rooms* ᝮ *In-room: Wi-Fi, refrigerator, DVD. In-hotel: no-smoking rooms, no elevator, some pets allowed* ☰ *MC, V* ⦙○⦙*BP.*

SPORTS & THE OUTDOORS

CRUISES You can take a cruise to Monhegan with **Hardy Boat Cruises** (⊠ *Shaw's Wharf, New Harbor* ☎ *207/677–6026*). On the sightseeing cruises you can spot seals and puffins. At **Salt Water Charters** (⊠ *Round Pond Harbor, Round Pond* ☎ *207/677–6229* ⊕ *www.saltwater-charters. com*), the fishing vessel *Paige Elizabeth* takes passengers on sightseeing cruises.

PARK **Pemaquid Beach Park** (⊠ *Rte. 130, New Harbor* ☎ *207/677–2754*) has a
☺ sandy beach that's popular with families. There's a snack bar, changing facilities, and picnic tables overlooking John's Bay.

SHOPPING

Of the villages on Pemaquid Peninsula, Damariscotta has the most boutiques and galleries. New Harbor and Round Pond have crafts stores and antiques shops as well as artisans' studios. Antiques shops also dot the main thoroughfares through the region. The **Granite Hall Store** (⊠ *9 Back Shore Rd., Round Pond* ☎ *207/529–5864*) has penny candy, wicker baskets, and cards on the first floor and antiques and books on the second. Order ice-cream cones through a window on the side. It's open May to mid-October.

ART GALLERIES   Sculpture and art can both be found at **Kathleen Mack Studio** (⊠ *1360 Rte. 32, Walpole* ☎ *207/529–5633* ⊕ *www.kathleenmack.com* ◔ *Daily, but call first in winter*) in the village of Round Pond. At the **Library Art Studio** (⊠ *1467 Rte. 32, at Munro Brook, Round Pond* ☎ *207/529–4210* ◔ *Year-round, but call ahead during off-season*), artist-writer-editor Sally DeLorme Pedric produces oils, woodcuts, and fiber art based on Acadian traditions and Bauhaus principles. The work of more than 50 Maine artisans is displayed in the 15 rooms of the **Pemaquid Craft Co-op** (⊠ *2545 Bristol Rd., New Harbor* ☎ *207/677–2077* ◔ *May–Sept,, daily,; Oct.–Dec. 24, Tues.–Sat.*). **Susan Bartlett Rice Studio** (⊠ *36 Split Rock Rd., Walpole* ☎ *207/563–6023* ⊕ *www.susanbartlettrice.com*), loff Route 129 on the way south toward Pemaquid, is worth a stop if you like oil paintings that show real life in Maine.

CUSHING & ST. GEORGE PENINSULAS

These two peninsulas bring to life the state's seafaring traditions. The town of Waldoboro has a beautiful downtown filled with houses that combine several architectural styles. Sea captains were intrigued by what they saw during their travels and came back with ideas for their own homes. Thomaston, another seaside town, is known for the clapboard houses lining its streets.

On a rocky part of the coast, Tenants Harbor has a lobstering tradition that is still strong today. The harbor is full of boats that go out once or twice daily to retrieve crustaceans from the ocean floor. You can grow familiar with their distinctive chug-chug as they enter and leave the harbor. Artists favor this area, and you can browse in many of their studios. Port Clyde is the jumping-off point to Monhegan Island, but has some sights of its own. Marshall Point Lighthouse is within walking distance of the town landing, and there is a small museum, shop, and picnic area on the site.

WALDOBORO

10 mi northeast of Damariscotta.

Veer off U.S. 1 onto Main Street or down Route 220 or 32, and you can discover a seafaring town with a proud shipbuilding past. Waldoboro's Main Street is lined with houses representing numerous architectural styles: Cape Cod, Queen Anne, Stick, Greek Revival, and Italianate.

WHAT TO SEE

☯ **Fawcett's Toy Museum** comes up fast on Route 1, but the flags and banners are flying, so look for them on your left as you head north. Adults and children alike will be delighted with collectible toys, from Betty Boop and Popeye to Charlie Brown and Mickey Mouse. There's also original comic art. ⊠*3506 U.S. 1* ☎*207/832–7398* ☞*$5* ☉*Memorial Day–Columbus Day, Thurs.–Mon. 10–4; Columbus Day–Christmas Eve, weekends noon–4.*

Friendship is the birthplace of the distinctive *Friendship Sloop,* and you can visit the **Friendship Museum** to see exhibits on this popular sailing ship, as well as local historical artifacts. Dating from 1857, the building first served as a one-room schoolhouse. ⊠*Hatchet Cove Rd. and Rte. 220, Friendship* ☎*207/832–4826* ☞*Free* ☉*July–Labor Day, Mon.– Sat. 1–4, Labor Day–Columbus Day 1–4, Sat.1–4, Sun. 2–4.*

One of the oldest churches in Maine, the **Old German Church** was built in 1772. It originally sat on the eastern side of the Medomak River, then was moved across the ice to its present site in 1794. Inside you can find box pews and a 9-foot-tall chalice pulpit. ⊠*Rte. 32* ☎*No phone* ☉*July and Aug., daily 1–3.*

Between 1893 and 1968, Andrew Wyeth painted his famous Christina pictures in the **Olson House.** Reproductions of many of these enigmatic portraits are hung throughout this historic house, now part of the Farnsworth Museum. ⊠*384 Hathorn Point Rd., Cushing* ☎*207/354–0102* ⊕ *www.farnsworthmuseum.org* ☞*$4* ☉*Memorial Day–Columbus Day, daily 11–4.*

Several buildings make up the **Waldoborough Historical Society Museum,** including the one-room Boggs Schoolhouse, built in 1857; the Town Pound, built in 1819; and a barn filled with artifacts, from hooked rugs, housewares, and tools to clothing and antique toys. ⊠*Main St. and Rte. 220* ☎*No phone* ☞*Free* ☉*July–Labor Day, daily 1–4:30.*

WHERE TO EAT & STAY

¢–$ ✕**Moody's Diner.** Settle into one of the well-worn wooden booths or snag a counter stool at this old-style diner known for its home cooking. It's right on Route 1, so you can't miss it. Breakfast is served all day (except no oatmeal or omelets after 11 AM) at this local landmark where coffee is only 85¢. Don't miss the legendary walnut pie. ⊠*1885 U.S. 1* ☎*207/832–7785* ▭*D, MC, V.*

$$ ▦ **Blue Skye Farm.** Guests often choose this historic 18th-century country house for superior bird-watching opportunities. Waterfowl, eagles, and ospreys can be seen regularly, and the light over the marshes is ideal for the many watercolor painters who stay here. There are lots of interesting nooks and crannies, old beams, and wide views of the marshes. Hundreds of acres await your visit outside the back door. Guests have use of the kitchen in the evenings. The rooms are furnished in period antiques and vary in size; one has bunks and is good for kids. Extra cots and cribs available. **Pros:** Peaceful, lots of land to explore, all rooms have a view. **Cons:** No Internet, no TVs. ⊠*1708 Friendship*

Rd., 04572 ☎*207/832–0030* ⌂*5 rooms, 4 with bath* ♿*In-room: no a/c. In-hotel: no-smoking rooms* ▤*MC, V* ¶©*BP.*

$ ⊞**Outsiders' Inn Bed & Breakfast.** If you are looking for a quiet retreat that is convenient to the sights, consider this inn at the corner of Routes 97 and 220. The original homestead was built by Zenas Cook in 1830, and the current owners have preserved much of the charm with period furnishings and decorations. Rooms, some with private baths, are comfortably furnished. A full breakfast with home-baked specialties is served every morning. The owners also operate Wild Bill's Outfitting and Guide Service and will rent you kayaks and equipment to paddle to your heart's content, or take you on a guided tour. At the end of your day, take a stroll to the harbor. **Pros:** Water access, low price. **Cons:** No air-conditioning, no TVs. ✉*4 Main St., Friendship 04547* ☎*207/832–5197* ⌂*3 rooms, 2 of them share a bath, 1 cottage with private bath* ♿*In-room: no a/c, no TV. In-hotel: no-smoking rooms, no elevator* ▤*MC, V* ¶©*BP.*

SHOPPING

The **Waldoboro 5 & 10** (✉*17 Friendship St.* ☎*207/832–4624*) is the oldest continually operated five-and-ten store in the country. It offers deli-type sandwiches, soups, and ice cream, plus it sells a nice selection of toys. There's also a penny-candy counter popular with kids.

THOMASTON

10 mi northeast of Waldoboro, 72 mi northeast of Portland.

Thomaston is a delightful town, full of beautiful sea captains' homes and dotted with antiques and specialty shops. A National Historic District encompasses parts of High, Main, and Knox streets. The town is the gateway to the two peninsulas, so you will be looking at water on both sides as you arrive.

WHAT TO SEE

Check out more than 100 boats at the **Maine Watercraft Museum.** This is an in-the-water display of classic crafts that are indigenous to the area. You can learn about shipbuilding and even ride in one of these beauties. ✉*4 Knox St.* ☎*207/354–0444* ☉ *May–Sept., daily.*

Built in 1930, **Montpelier** is a replica of the late-18th-century mansion of Major General Henry Knox, a commander in the Revolutionary War and secretary of war in George Washington's cabinet. Antiques, including many Knox family possessions, fill the interior. Architectural appointments include an oval room and a double staircase. Groups should call ahead to reserve space on the half-hourly tours. ✉*U.S. 1 at Rte. 131* ☎*207/354–8062* ⊕*www.generalknoxmuseum.org* ▤*$6* ☉*Memorial Day–Columbus Day, Tues.–Sat. 10–4.*

WHERE TO EAT & STAY

$$–$$$$ ✕**Harbor View Restaurant.** The location couldn't be more perfect for this convenient waterfront restaurant in Thomaston. Seafood is the specialty here, and it comes in all forms. The menu features everything from steak and Gorgonzola pie to scallops au gratin, and, of course, delicious crab

and lobster rolls, steamed clams, and boiled or baked stuffed lobsters. This is the kind of place where you can order everything from escargot to fish-and-chips. Like lobster but don't want the mess? Try the "lazy" variety, with the lobster meat already pulled out for you! Eat in the dining room or outside on the porch overlooking the water. ☒*Public Landing* ☎*207/354–8173* ⊕*www.harborviewrestaurant.com* ⌔*Reservations essential* ⊟*MC, V.*

$$–$$$$ ✕**Waterman's Beach Lobster.** You can eat lunch and dinner inside or out at this casual seaside restaurant in South Thomaston, or take your meal with you. Steamed clams and lobster and clam rolls are among the many favorites that draw people to this popular spot. Freshly baked pies from old family recipes are always on the menu, and in 2008 Maine-made ice cream will be available. There's a private beach where you can stroll while you wait for your dinner, so bring your binoculars to get a closer look at the lobster boats. ☒*359 Waterman Beach Rd., off Rte. 73, South Thomaston 04858* ☎*207/596–7819 or 207/594–7518* ⊟*No credit cards* ☉*Closed Labor Day–Father's Day.*

$$–$$$ ✕**Thomaston Café & Bakery.** A changing selection of works by local artists adorns the walls of this small café, and you are next door to an independent bookstore. You might actually run into a writer or an artist or two here, since this is a popular meeting place for locals. Entrées, prepared with locally grown ingredients, include seared fresh tuna on soba noodles, lobster ravioli with lobster sauce, and filet mignon with béarnaise sauce. Soups and sandwiches are delicious. ☒*154 Main St.* ☎*207/354–8589* ⊟*MC, V* ☉*No dinner Sun.–Thurs.*

$$ 🛏**Weskeag Inn.** Built in the 1830s, this charming B&B is near the reversing falls in the village of South Thomaston. Anglers line the banks in search of stripers in spring, and sun worshippers swim or float on inner tubes in summer. Bring your kayaks because you can launch right here. Watch herons, egrets, and osprey; sometimes even eagles come here to catch their dinner. Guest rooms are bright and tastefully decorated with period antiques; make sure to ask for one with a view of the water. **Pro:** A staircase leads to the water. **Con:** No Internet. ☒*14 Elm St. (Rte. 73), South Thomaston 04858* ☎*207/596–6676* ⊕*www.weskeag.com* ⌔*7 rooms, 1 suite, all with private baths* ⌔*In-room: no TV (some). In-hotel: public Internet, no-smoking rooms, no elevator* ⊟*MC, V* ⍥*BP.*

SHOPPING

The **Maine State Prison Showroom Outlet** (☒*Main St.* ☎*207/354–2535*), on the right as you come into the village, carries furniture, bowls, cutting boards, decorative boxes, and other wooden items including children's toys, fashioned by prisoners. Browse the comprehensive selection of books and original art and cards, and you might drop in at the moment when a local poet is reading at the **Personal Book Shop** (☒*144 Main St.* ☎*207/354–8058* ⊟*AE, D, MC, V*).

TENANTS HARBOR

13 mi south of Thomaston.

Tenants Harbor is a quintessential coastal town—its harbor is dominated by lobster boats, its shores are rocky and slippery, and its downtown streets are lined with clapboard houses, a church, and a general store. It's a favorite with artists, and galleries and studios welcome browsers.

WHERE TO EAT & STAY

$–$$$

Fodor'sChoice
★

×⊞ **Craignair Inn.** From Route 1 just east of Thomaston, take Route 131 south 6 mi, then turn left on Route 73 for one mile, right at Clark Island Road 1½ miles, all the way to the end of the road to find this lodging dating from 1928. Sitting on four acres right on the water, it was originally built to house granite workers from nearby quarries. The annex was the chapel where the stonecutters and their families worshipped. Rooms are comfortably furnished with antique furniture, and the beds are piled high with colorful quilts. Most rooms have views of the water, and the semi-suite rents for $200 a night. A recent addition here is an apartment with kitchen, gas fireplace, washer and dryer, ceiling fans, cable TV and phone, as well as a private deck, water access, and two kayaks for use by apartment guests. The apartment rents for $200 a night. Chef extraordinaire Chris Seiler, most recently from the Samoset Resort, wins awards for his creative cuisine served in the inn's dining room ($$$). You might want to start with the Caribbean jerk grilled shrimp brochettes, or steamed great eastern mussels, and move on to pecan-crusted salmon, bacon-wrapped tenderloin, or baked stuffed haddock. The dessert menu might feature pastry chef Meg Joseph's lemon pudding cake, Key lime square, or a mini créme bruleé. **Pros:** The stellar food, some air-conditioned rooms. **Con:** Pets allowed in some rooms. ⊠ *5 3rd St., Spruce Head 04859* ☎ *207/594–7644 or 800/320–9997* ⊕ *www.craignair.com* ⌐*21 rooms, 13 with bath* ♿ *In-room: no a/c. In-hotel: public Wi-Fi, no elevator, some pets allowed, no-smoking rooms* ⊟*D, MC, V* †◯*IBP.*

PORT CLYDE

2 mi south of Tenants Harbor via Rte. 131.

The fishing village of Port Clyde sits at the end of the St. George Peninsula. The road leading to Port Clyde meanders along the St. George River, passing meadows and farmhouses. Shipbuilding was the first commercial enterprise here, and later the catching and canning of seafood. You can still buy Port Clyde sardines. Port Clyde's boat landing is home to the *Elizabeth Ann* and the *Laura B,* the mail boats that serve nearby Monhegan Island. Several artists make their homes in Port Clyde, so check to see if their studios are open while you are visiting.

WHAT TO SEE

The 1895 keeper's house at the **Marshall Point Lighthouse** has been turned into a museum containing memorabilia from the town of St. George (a few miles north of Tenants Harbor) with a small shop in the facility. The setting has inspired Jamie Wyeth and other noted artists. You can stroll the grounds, have a picnic, and watch boats sail in and out of Port Clyde. The lighthouse is about 1 mi from the Port Clyde boat landing, and the original 1898 fog bell is also here. Grounds are open all year. ✉*Marshall Point Rd.* ☎*207/372–6450* ✇*Free* ☉*Memorial Day–Columbus Day., weekdays 1–5, Sat. 10–5; May and Oct., weekends 1–5.*

Ocean House Gallery (✉ *870 Port Clyde Rd., 04855* ☎*207/372–6930* ⊕*www.oceanhousehotel.com*) This is a new gallery above the apartment adjacent to the Ocean House hotel in Port Clyde. It displays the work of many artists, including Jamie Wyeth, Jerry Cable, Susan Cooney, and Susan Murdock.

At Owls Head Light State Park, the beautifully maintained **Owls Head Light** (✉*Rte. 73, Owls Head* ☎*207/941–4014*) has shown the way since 1825. On West Penobscot Bay, the local landmark indicates the entrance to Rockland Harbor. The grounds are open to the public, but the lighthouse and keeper's house are not. This lighthouse still has its original Fresnel lens in place, in use since it was installed in 1856.

WHERE TO EAT & STAY

$-$$$ ✕ **Miller's Lobster Company.** Enjoy a lobster at this family-owned restaurant overlooking beautiful Wheeler's Bay. People come here for its friendly vibe and great food. Lobster rolls, crabmeat rolls, and shrimp are on the menu, as are steamed clams and mussels, and lobsters fresh from the fishermen who bring them in daily. If you've got room, order a twin lobster special and top it off with a slice of homemade pie. Miller's also serves a good steamed hot dog. Eat in the dining room or outside on the deck. ✉*38 Fuller Rd., Spruce Head* ☎*207/594–7406* ▭*No credit cards* ☉*Closed Labor Day–late June.*

¢–$ ✕ **Dip Net Diner.** On a summer day you can grab a crab or lobster roll or a slice of pizza or sandwich here before taking a boat to Monhegan Island or hiking to Marshall Point Lighthouse. Lobster doesn't get any fresher than those cooked right beside the sea where they are caught. Dine inside or eat out on the deck at tables with umbrellas for your comfort. You can also order takeout. Beer and wine are available here. ✉*1 Cold Storage Rd.* ☎*207/372–6307* ▭*No credit cards* ☉*Closed Labor Day–Memorial Day.*

$-$$ ⊡ **Ocean House.** Little has changed at the Ocean Hotel since it first opened for business in the 1820s, but it now has wireless access in the common room and a new apartment next door with the Ocean House Gallery upstairs. The cottage has two bedrooms and two baths. Most of the furniture in the main building is original, including some of the wrought-iron beds. From the rooms and the apartment there are excellent views of the harbor. On the walls hang several Jamie Wyeth paintings, and the hotel often hosts the artist himself. Breakfast is available for guests of the inn and their visitors, and a specialty of the house is blueberry pancakes. The hotel is within walking distance of the boat dock, Dip Net Diner, the general store, the post office, and the lighthouse. **Pros:** View, original art and artists. **Con:** No handicap access. ✉*At Monhegan Island boat landing, Box 66, 04855* ☎*207/372–6691*

Lighting the Way

Ever wonder what makes Maine's more than five dozen lighthouses so bright? It has to do with the lens; you need the right kind of lens to magnify the light. Resembling giant beehives, the original Fresnel lenses used in these lighthouses were made of prisms that redirected light from a lamp into a concentrated beam.

The first Fresnel lens was made in France in 1822 by French physicist Augustine Fresnel. Most lenses that were placed in lighthouses along the coasts of Europe and North America were handmade and shipped unassembled from France. The largest of these lenses, called a first-order lens, could be as much as 12 feet tall. Rings of glass prisms arranged above and below the center drum were intended to bend the light beam. Later designs incorporated a bull's eye into the center of the lens, which acted like a magnifying glass to make the beam even more powerful. A Fresnel lens captured all but 17% of the available light, whereas an open flame, even with reflectors behind it, lost 83% of its light.

You can see some of the smaller original lenses in museums in Maine, but you can also see a first-order lens in the Mid-Coast area in the lighthouse on Seguin Island, 10 mi from shore. You can go by boat from the Maine Maritime Museum. The Seguin Light is the only first-order lens in Maine, and one of only two remaining lenses still in use north of Virginia. The lens shines with 282 prisms.

The Seguin Island Light was commissioned by George Washington in 1795, and is one of the oldest lighthouses in the United States. Most of the original lenses used in lighthouses in this part of the country were mounted on mercury bases that were designed to rotate; these lenses were later replaced because of the danger of mercury poisoning. The lens at Seguin is a fixed light, meaning that it does not rotate. It used no mercury, so it could be kept in place. Ships can see this beacon 20 mi out to sea. Today the lens reflects the light of a 1,000-watt bulb. Before electricity, incandescent oil vapor was used.

Early Fresnel lenses were fairly standard in size and shape, but that posed problems as more and more lighthouses were built along the coasts. The captain of a ship could not tell one light from another in the dark and stormy night, so he didn't know what headland or ledge he was approaching. The lenses eventually were designed to have different personalities that made them easily identifiable. Many lights became known for their distinctive flash patterns. Seguin Island Light is a fixed white light, whereas the Pemaquid Point Light is a white light that flashes every 6 seconds. Monhegan Island Light, visible from Port Clyde, has a white light that flashes for 2.8 seconds every 30 seconds. In Phippsburg, Pond Island Light shines a white beam with 6-second intervals of white and dark.

or 800/269–6691 ⊕www.oceanhousehotel.com ↩10 rooms, 8 with bath ⚂ In-room: no a/c, no TV. In-hotel: no-smoking rooms, no elevator, public Wi-Fi ▭ No credit cards ⊘ Closed Nov.–Apr. �⦿*|BP.*

SHOPPING

If you need to stock up on anything before heading out to Monhegan Island,drive to the end of Route 131 to the dock-side **Port Clyde General Store** (⊠ *Cold Storage Rd., ✆ P.O. Box 276* ☎ *207/372–6543*), under new ownership. Open throughout the year, it now has a full service deli, expanded meat counter and produce section, 20 boat moorings and marine fuel, as well as gas for cars. There are daily lunch specials that people literally line up for, and coffee is always available.

MONHEGAN ISLAND

East of Pemaquid Peninsula, 10 mi south of Port Clyde. Remote Monhegan Island, with its high cliffs fronting the sea, was known to Basque, Portuguese, and Breton fishermen well before Columbus discovered America. About a century ago, Monhegan was discovered again by some of America's finest painters, including Rockwell Kent, Robert Henri, A. J. Hammond, and Edward Hopper, who sailed out to paint its open meadows, savage cliffs, wild ocean views, and fishermen's shacks. Tourists followed, and today three excursion boats dock here *(⇨ By Boat in Mid-Coast Essentials at the end of this chapter)*. The village bustles with activity in summer, when many artists open their studios. You can escape the crowds on the island's 17 mi of hiking trails, which lead to the lighthouse and to the cliffs.

Enjoy the silence and serenity of Cathedral Woods on your way to or from the high cliffs at White Head, Black Head, and Burnt Head. Bring drinking water or plan to purchase same, as there is no potable drinking water except in restaurants, inns, and private cottages. You might consider bringing a picnic if you're visiting during the day, or eat at one of the island's restaurants, though they are busy at lunch. If you are planning on hiking, bring sunblock and insect repellant, as well as a hat, and a jacket for the boat trip, which will be an hour or longer, depending on where your boat originates. Plan to pack out whatever trash you generate while you are out and about, as there are few trash receptacles in public places. All trash on Monhegan Island has to be taken off the island by boat. Use the toilet on your boat before you come ashore; the only public toilets on the island are located behind the old Monhegan House, and these are privately maintained and the owners appreciate a small donation. All that being said, if you love the rocky cliffs, this is your place. And if you happen to be an artist you might never leave. Studios and galleries are all over the island and all schedule certain days to be open. Several shops are available for browsers. Bring your camera!

The **Monhegan Museum,** housed in an 1824 lighthouse and the adjacent assistant keeper's house, has wonderful views of Manana Island. Inside, informative displays depict island life and local flora and fauna. Outside is one of the original dory boats used by the first Monhegan fishermen.

✉White Head Rd. ☎No phone 🎫Donations accepted ⏲July–mid-Sept., daily 11:30–3:30.

> **WORD OF MOUTH**
>
> We stayed at the Island Inn. Staying overnight gives you the chance to hike the whole island. It's also kind of neat when the daytrippers leave. It's a very small community. The hotel is pleasant and old-fashioned and maybe a little expensive for what it is. Spectacular view.
>
> —Pausanias

WHERE TO STAY

$$–$$$$ **Island Inn.** This three-story inn, which dates from 1907, has a commanding presence on Monhegan Island's harbor. Design has remained authentic and there is original art everywhere, reflecting the presence of many studios and galleries on this island known for decades for its artist colony. The waterfront rooms are the nicest, with views of the sunset over stark Manana Island. The suites are priced higher, at $250–$315. Facilities now include the adjacent Pierce Cottage with two suites with private baths. The property includes a small café on the pier and a dining room that serves breakfast, lunch, and dinner. Note that the property takes credit cards but prefers cash or check. **Pros:** Great food and view. **Con:** Pricey. ✉*1 Ocean Ave., 04852* ☎*207/596–0371* 🌐*www.islandinnmonhegan.com* *28 rooms, 20 with bath; 4 suites* *In-room: no a/c, no phone, no TV. In-hotel: restaurant, public Internet, no-smoking rooms, no elevator* 💳*MC, V* ⏲*Closed Columbus Day–Memorial Day* *BP.*

$$–$$$$ **Shining Sails Bed & Breakfast.** Near the ocean, this B&B has the finest accommodations on Monhegan Island and is just up the street from the pier where your boat will land. Rooms are light and airy, and are kept cheery with fresh flowers. Most have private decks with ocean views. A common room in the B&B facility with a wood-burning stove is filled with games. This facility has nine efficiency apartments, four of them acquired in 2007, and also rents out 30 cottages, all with private baths and electricity. **Pro:** Close to pier and restaurants. **Con:** Not handicapped accessible. ✉*Monhegan Island, 04852* ☎*207/596–0041* 🌐*www.shiningsails.com* *2 rooms, 9 efficiency apartments, 30 cottages* *In-room: no a/c, no phone, kitchen (some), no TV. In-hotel: public Wi-Fi, no-smoking rooms, no elevator* 💳*D, MC, V* *CP.*

$ **Trailing Yew.** Step back in time in any of the four houses at Trailing Yew. This is a good opportunity for a single traveler, as rates are per person. Rooms are furnished simply but attractively in an early-1900s style reflecting the island's heritage. Your luggage will be picked up by one of the island trucks, as you'll have to walk over from the pier when your boat lands. Guests enjoy a communal dining atmosphere. **Pro:** Nice price, especially for the solo traveler. **Con:** Many rooms have no electricity. ✉*Lobster Cove Rd., 04852* ☎*207/596–0440* *4 houses without bath* *In-hotel: no-smoking rooms* 💳*No credit cards* ⏲*Closed Columbus Day–mid-May* *MAP.*

THE MID-COAST ESSENTIALS

To research prices, get advice from other travelers, and book travel arrangements, visit www.fodors.com.

TRANSPORTATION

BY AIR

The Portland Jetport is convenient to the Mid-Coast region, being half an hour from Brunswick via the Maine Turnpike or Interstate 295. Manchester International Airport, in New Hampshire, is two hours from the Mid-Coast region. Bangor International Airport is also about two hours away, but be aware that there are frequent cancellations at this small airport.

BY BIKE

There are two major bike routes in the Mid-Coast region. The Coastal Route tour goes all the way from Brunswick to Ellsworth, a distance of 187 mi, along the rocky coastline. Some stretches are along heavily traveled roads. You can do a mostly level 5-mi round-trip ride along this route in Brunswick. You begin on Water Street at the west end of the Androscoggin River Bike Path. There are rest rooms along the way and shady spots to rest along the river. The 60-mi Merrymeeting Tour, traversing small hills and one major climb, originates in Bath and travels round-trip to Wiscasset. Along the way you can see the Kennebec River and Merrymeeting Bay, famous for its variety of birds, including several types of ducks.

BY BOAT

Port Clyde is the point of departure for the *Laura B.*, the mail boat that runs to Monhegan Island. It's operated by the Monhegan Boat Line. In summer the *Balmy Days* sails daily between Boothbay Harbor and Monhegan Island. Boats operated by Hardy Boat Cruises leave daily from Shaw's Wharf in New Harbor.

Boat Lines *Balmy Days* (☎800/298–2284). **Hardy Boat Cruises** (☎207/677–2026 or 800/278–3346). **Monhegan Boat Line** (☎207/372–8848).

BY BUS

Vermont Transit Lines services the Brunswick area from Portland.

Bus Lines **Vermont Transit Lines** (☎207/729–5301).

BY CAR

Travelers visiting the Mid-Coast region in summer and early fall may encounter fog, especially on the peninsulas and points of land. It's best to leave headlights on. Fog may stay around all day, or it may burn off by late morning. Winter driving in Maine can be challenging when snow and ice coat the roads. "Black ice" is a special hazard along the coast, as the road may appear clear but is actually covered by a nearly invisible coating of ice. Four-wheel-drive vehicles are recommended for driving in winter. Always carry warm clothing and blankets, as well as food and drinking water in case of an emergency.

BY TRAIN

Portland is the closest city with train service (⇨ *see* Greater Portland Essentials in Chapter 2 for train details).

CONTACTS & RESOURCES

EMERGENCIES

In an emergency, dial 911.

Hospitals Mid-Coast Hospital (✉ *123 Medical Center Dr., Brunswick* ☎ *207/729–0181*). **St. Andrews Hospital** (✉ *6 St. Andrews La., Boothbay Harbor* ☎ *207/633–2121*).

MEDIA

The *Times Record,* which covers the Bath-Brunswick region, publishes weekdays, with a weekend entertainment section on Thursday. A number of weekly newspapers provide local coverage and entertainment listings, including the *Coastal Journal* (Brunswick to Waldoboro), the *Wiscasset Newspaper,* the *Boothbay Register,* and the *Lincoln County News.* WMEA 90.1 is the local National Public Radio affiliate. WCSH, channel 6, is the NBC affiliate; WMTW, channel 8, is the ABC affiliate; and WGME, channel 13, is the CBS affiliate. Channel 11 is the Maine Public Broadcasting affiliate.

VISITOR INFORMATION

Contacts Boothbay Harbor Region Chamber of Commerce (✉ *Box 356, 04538* ☎ *207/633–2353* ⊕ *www.boothbayharbor.com*). **Convention and Visitors Bureau of Greater Portland** (✉ *245 Commercial St., Portland 04101* ☎ *207/772–5800* ⊕ *www.visitportland.com*). **Damariscotta Region Chamber of Commerce** (✉ *Box 13, Damariscotta 04543* ☎ *207/563–8340* ⊕ *www.damariscottaregion.com*). **Freeport Merchants Association** (✉ *23 Depot St., Freeport 04032* ☎ *207/865–1212 or 877/865–1212* ⊕ *www.freeportusa.com*). **Greater Portland Chamber of Commerce** (✉ *60 Pearl St., Portland 04101* ☎ *207/772–2811* ⊕ *www.portlandregion. com*). **Maine Tourism Association** (✉ *1100 U.S. 1 [I–95, Exit 17], Yarmouth 04347* ☎ *207/846–0833 or 888/624–6345* ⊕ *www.mainetourism.com*). **Southern Midcoast Maine Chamber** (✉ *Border Trust Business Center, 2 Main St., Topsham 04086* ☎ *877/725–8797* ⊕ *www.midcoastmaine.com*).

Penobscot Bay

WORD OF MOUTH

"In Rockland, there's a great art museum (the Farnsworth) plus nearby Owl's Head Lighthouse. Camden is a not-to-miss place for shops and a beautiful harbor. Dine at off-times or picnic at the top of Mt. Battie. We also like staying in Searsport, which is far enough up to make Acadia National Park a doable one-day trip."

—dfrostnh

By Stephen and Neva Allen

FEW COULD DENY THAT PENOBSCOT BAY is one of Maine's most dramatically beautiful regions. Its 1,000-mi-long coastline is made up of rocky granite boulders, wild and often undeveloped shore, a sprinkling of colorful towns, and views of the sea and shore that are a photographer's dream.

The second-largest estuary in New England, Penobscot Bay stretches 37 mi from Port Clyde in the south to Stonington, the little fishing village at the tip of Deer Isle, in the north. The bay begins where the Penobscot River ends, near Stockton Springs, and terminates in the Gulf of Maine, where it is 47 mi wide. It covers an estimated 1,070 square mi and is home to hundreds of islands.

Initially, shipbuilding was the primary moneymaker here. In the 1800s, during the days of the great tall ships, or Down Easters as they were often called, more wooden ships were built along Penobscot Bay than in any other place in America. This golden age of billowing sails and wooden sailing ships did not last long, however. It came to an end with the development of the steam engine. Ships propelled by steam-fed pistons were faster, safer, more reliable, and could hold more cargo. By 1900, sailing ships were no longer a viable commercial venture in Maine. However, as you will see when traveling the coast, the tall ships have not disappeared—they have simply been revived as recreational boats, known as windjammers. Today, once again, there are more tall ships along Penobscot Bay than anywhere else in the country.

EXPLORING PENOBSCOT BAY

The only route for exploring this region is the historic two-lane U.S. 1, which winds all the way along Penobscot Bay, from Rockland to Bucksport and farther. Although the distance from Rockland to Bucksport is only 45 mi, the going is slow; U.S. 1 is an old highway, and the summer months bring heavily congested traffic. There are some impressive coastal views along the drive, but don't expect to see the ocean continuously. The water is blocked for a good part of the way by woods, which are beautiful in their own right. Driving the entire distance without stopping should take about two hours, but you'll probably want to stop along the way and spend a day or two in some of the more colorful towns. If you're driving at night, be wary of moose crossing the road.

There is no train service or public transportation in the Penobscot Bay area, but there is a luxury bus service, Concord Trailways, which runs from Bangor to Logan Airport in Boston (⇨ *See by Bus in Penobscot Bay Essentials at the end of this chapter*). Exploring the Penobscot Bay coast by water is also a possibility. Ferries travel back and forth to islands such as Islesboro and Vinalhaven, and romantic windjammer cruises sail from Camden and Rockland to various islands or town destinations (⇨ *See by Boat in Penobscot Bay Essentials*).

WHEN TO GO

High season starts in the middle of May and goes until mid-October. Crowds are a little thinner just after the public schools open in early September and just before they close in mid-June. Though many residents enjoy the long cold winters, most visitors avoid them. The Camden Snow Bowl, with its 11 downhill ski trails, is one of the few attractions to entice visitors in the wintery months. Many of the motels, bed-and-breakfasts, restaurants, and other businesses along U.S. 1 close for winter.

ABOUT THE RESTAURANTS

Seafood is the name of the game along Penobscot Bay. "Lobstah" is, of course, a staple on most menus, and it comes cooked in myriad ways: whole lobster dinners (boiled or steamed in the shell), broiled lobster tails, fried lobster, lobster stew, and lobster rolls, which are even sold at McDonald's.

Dining establishments are generally informal, and casual dress is almost always acceptable. Most restaurants are open for lunch and dinner, and some are open for breakfast. From June through August, reservations are always a good idea, particularly at the more popular or smaller restaurants.

For a truly authentic Maine experience, try one of the lobster pounds in Lincolnville or Belfast. For something a little more upscale, there are a few outstanding gems to be tried, notably Primo, in Rockland; Marcel's, at the Samoset Resort in Rockport; and the Rhumb Line, in Searsport.

ABOUT THE HOTELS

Large luxury hotels are few and far between in this region; motels, B&Bs, and campgrounds are more the norm. Accommodations are generally modest, but many of them sit right on the edge of the ocean. A good share of the B&Bs are in historic Federal or Colonial-style homes that date back to the 1850s and are filled with period antiques. Please note that while many of the smaller accommodations and B&Bs—as well as some of the restaurants and many of the museums—are not air-conditioned, ocean breezes usually keep things amply cool. ■ TIP➡ **If you are handicapped, call ahead to see if a property can accommodate you. Many B&Bs along the Maine Coast do not have ramps.**

■ TIP➡ **If you're planning to come between mid-May and mid-October, reservations are recommended at least a month in advance.**

WHAT IT COSTS				
	¢	$	$$	$$$	$$$$
RESTAURANTS	under $7	$7–$10	$11–$17	$18–$25	over $25
HOTELS	under $60	$60–$99	$100–$149	$150–$200	over $200

Restaurant prices are for a main course at dinner, excluding sales tax of 7%. Hotel prices are for two people in a standard double room in high season, excluding service charges and 7% tax.

ROCKLAND AREA

The name "Rockland" defines this area's history. If you set fishing aside, rock cutting—specifically granite and limestone—was once the area's principal occupation. In fact, numerous government buildings across the United States were built using granite blocks from Rockland and other nearby quarries. Just outside the town of Rockland, a large cement factory on U.S. 1 serves as a reminder of this rocky past.

ROCKLAND

4 mi northeast of Thomaston, 14 mi northeast of Tenants Harbor.

In September 2007, *National Geographic Adventure* magazine named Rockland "one of the top 50 adventure towns in the United States." The town is considered the gateway to Penobscot Bay and is the first stop on U.S. 1 offering a glimpse of the often sparkling and island-dotted blue bay. Though once merely a place to pass through on the way to tonier ports like Camden, Rockland now attracts attention on its own, thanks to this trio of attractions: the renowned Farnsworth Museum, the increasingly popular summer Lobster Festival, and the lively North Atlantic Blues Festival.

Rockland's Main Street Historic District, with its Italianate, Mansard, Greek Revival, and Colonial Revival buildings, is on the National Register of Historic Places. Specialty shops and galleries line the main street, and at least one of the restaurants, Primo, has become nationally famous. The town has a growing popularity as a summer destination, but it is still a large fishing port and the commercial hub of this coastal area. You can find plenty of working boats moored alongside the yachts.

Rockland Harbor is the berth of more windjammer ships than any other port in the United States. The best place in Rockland to view these beautiful vessels as they sail in and out of the harbor is the mile-long granite breakwater, which bisects the outer portion of Rockland Harbor. To get there, go north on U.S. 1, turn right on Waldo Avenue, and right again on Samoset Road; go to the end of this short road.

WHAT TO SEE

Fodor's Choice ★ The **Farnsworth Art Museum** is one of the most important small museums in the country. The **Wyeth Center** is devoted to Maine-related works of the famous Wyeth family: N. C. Wyeth, an accomplished illustrator whose works were featured in many turn-of-the-20th-century books; his son Andrew, one of America's best-known painters; and Andrew's son James, also an accomplished painter who lives nearby on an island. Some works from the personal collection of Andrew and Betsy Wyeth include *The Patriot, Adrift, Maiden Hair, Dr. Syn, The Clearing,* and *Watch Cap.* Also on display are works by Fitz Hugh Lane, George Bellows, Frank W. Benson, Edward Hopper (his paintings of old Rockland are a highlight), Louise Nevelson, and Fairfield Porter. Works by living Maine artists are shown in the **Jamien Morehouse Wing.** The **Farnsworth Homestead,** a handsome circa-1852 Greek Revival dwell-

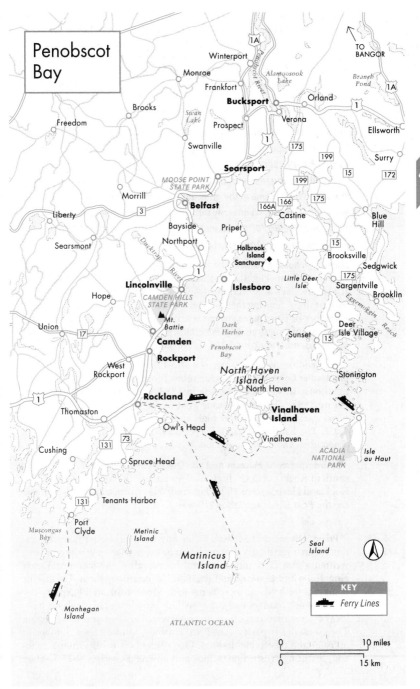

Penobscot Bay

TO BANGOR

Winterport

Monroe

Frankfort

Brooks

Bucksport

Orland

Alamoosook Lake

Branch Pond

1A

Freedom

Swan Lake

Prospect

Verona

Ellsworth

Swanville

175

Surry

Searsport

199

15

172

MOOSE POINT STATE PARK

199

Morrill

166A 166 175

Belfast

Castine

Blue Hill

Liberty

Bayside

Pripet

3

Searsmont

Northport

Holbrook Island Sanctuary

15

Brooksville

Sedgwick

Lincolnville

Little Deer Isle

175

Sargentville

Brooklin

Hope

CAMDEN HILLS STATE PARK

Islesboro

Eggemoggin Reach

Duckrap River

1

Union

17

Mt. Battie

Dark Harbor

Sunset

Deer Isle Village

15

Camden

Rockport

Penobscot Bay

West Rockport

Rockland

North Haven Island

North Haven

Stonington

1

Thomaston

Vinalhaven Island

Owl's Head

Vinalhaven

ACADIA NATIONAL PARK

Isle au Haut

Cushing

131

73

Spruce Head

Tenants Harbor

131

Port Clyde

Muscongus Bay

Metinic Island

Seal Island

Matinicus Island

KEY

Ferry Lines

Monhegan Island

ATLANTIC OCEAN

0 — 10 miles

0 — 15 km

4

ing that is part of the museum, retains its original lavish Victorian furnishings. There is a museum store next to the Morehouse Wing (⇨ *See Shopping*). In Cushing, a tiny town a few miles south of Thomaston, on the St. George River, the museum also operates the **Olsen House** (⊠*Hathorn Point Rd., Cushing*), which is depicted in Andrew Wyeth's famous painting *Christina's World.* ⊠*16 Museum St., Rockland 04841* ☎*207/596–6457* ⊕*www.farnsworthmuseum.org* ⊠*$10 for museum and Olsen House; $4 for Olsen House only* ⊙*Daily 10–5.*

OFF THE BEATEN PATH

Maine Eastern Railroad. You can't really say this attraction is "off the beaten track" since it operates *on* tracks. If your kids have never been on a train, this might be their opportunity. Composed of restored vintage railroad cars, this train will take you from Rockland to Wiscasset ("the most beautiful village in Maine") to Bath (home of the great shipyard) to the end of the line in Brunswick. The train runs Wednesday through Sunday, four times a day. ⊠*4 Union St.* ☎*207/596–6770* ⊕*www.maineeasternrailroad.com* ⊠*$40 round-trip* ⊙*Closed Nov. thru Apr. except for some holiday trains in Dec.*

Maine Lighthouse Museum. The museum displays the largest collection of the famed Fresnel lighthouse lenses to be found anywhere in the world. It also displays a collection of lighthouse artifacts and Coast Guard memorabilia. Sharing the same building is the Penobscot Bay Regional Chamber of Commerce, where tourists and visitors can pick up maps and area information. ⊠*1 Park Dr.* ☎*207/594–3301* ⊕*www.maine-lighthousemuseum.com* ⊠*$5* ⊙*Weekdays 9–5, weekends 10–4.*

At the end of the breakwater is a late-19th-century light, the **Rockland Breakwater Lighthouse,** a popular subject for photographers. A wooden lighthouse was first erected here in 1888, but it was moved four times before 1895. The current stone light tower, which is at the end of the breakwater, is only 18 feet high and was erected between 1900 and 1902. The lighthouse had a keeper until 1963 but is now automated. ⊕*www.rocklandlighthouse.com.*

The **Transportation Museum** and the **Owls Head Lighthouse** are only 3 mi south of Rockland in Owls Head. This landmark has shown the way to Rockland Harbor since 1825. *For complete information on these sights see the Port Clyde section in chapter 3.*

WHERE TO EAT

$$$–$$$$
Fodor'sChoice
★

✕**Primo.** Owner-chef Melissa Kelley and her world-class gourmet restaurant in a restored Victorian home has won many awards and been written about favorably in several high-quality publications, *Vanity Fair, Town and Country,* and *Food and Wine* among them. The cuisine combines fresh Maine ingredients with Mediterranean influences. The menu, which changes daily, may include wood-roasted black sea bass, local crab-stuffed turbot, or diver-harvested-scallop and basil ravioli. The co-owner is pastry chef Price Kushner, who offers a number of unusual and delectable desserts. One of the best is his Cannoli Siciliana, featuring crushed pistachios and amarena cherries. ⊠*2 S. Main*

GREAT ITINERARIES

IF YOU HAVE 3 DAYS

On the morning of your first day, visit the Farnsworth Museum in **Rockland** with its wonderful collection of paintings by the Wyeth family. Then drive up to **Camden,** one of the most charming towns along the coast, and take a two-hour excursion on a windjammer high-masted sailing ship. Consider staying at the Lord Camden Inn, in the heart of the downtown, or at one of the many delightful B&Bs.

On Day 2, drive up to **Belfast,** where you can wander around the downtown area, walk down to the harbor, and have a seafood lunch at the Weathervane restaurant at the harbor. In the afternoon, drive north on U.S. 1 to **Searsport** to browse its antiques shops and flea markets. Plan on spending the night at a B&B, such as the Captain A.V. Nickels Inn, on U.S. 1. A good choice for dinner would be Anglers, a favorite of the locals.

On Day 3, continue north on U.S. 1 to **Bucksport** to explore historic Fort Knox and go from there to the highest bridge observatory tower in America, atop the Penobscot Narrows Bridge. Spend the night in Bucksport, and have dinner at McLeod's restaurant.

IF YOU HAVE 5 DAYS

Begin your itinerary in **Rockland.** Start with a morning visit to the Farnsworth Museum. Then head to Rockland's Maine State Ferry Terminal. Take the ferry (with your car) to **Vinalhaven Island** and spend the day exploring and watching the lobster boats and fishermen down by the harbor. Stay overnight at the Tidewater Motel (make advance reservations).

On Day 2 take the ferry back to Rockland and drive north to **Camden,** where you can explore the shops and galleries, try the excellent restaurants, and stay the night in a charming B&B. Spend your third day and night aboard a windjammer (arrange this ahead of time).

On your fourth day, drive to **Belfast,** where you can walk down the colorful main street, shop, and explore the harbor. For an authentic Maine dinner, take U.S. 1 across the bridge on the way to Searsport and turn right on Mitchell Avenue to reach Young's Lobster Pound. Stay overnight at the Belfast Harbor Inn nearby. On your last day, drive to **Searsport** and spend the morning exploring the Penobscot Marine Museum with its wonderful exhibits on the history of Penobscot Bay.

St., Rockland ☎*207/596–0770* ⊕*www.primorestaurant.com* ▭*AE, D, DC, MC, V* ⊗*Closed mid-Jan.–mid-Apr.*

\$\$–\$\$\$ ✕**Amalfi.** A well-chosen and affordable wine list and excellent service
★ have made this storefront bistro a hit with locals and visitors alike. Chef-owner David Cooke serves delicious Mediterranean cuisine, influenced by the culinary traditions of France, Spain, Italy, Greece, and Morocco. The menu changes seasonally but may include the house paella with chorizo or the duck risotto. The seafood is always fresh. ✉*421 Main St.* ☎*207/596–0012* ▭*AE, MC, V* ⊗*Closed Mon. No lunch.*

\$\$–\$\$\$ ✕**Café Miranda.** The huge menu at this friendly, casual restaurant changes daily to include fresh seasonal ingredients. Chef-owner Kerry

Alterio is someone who apparently likes to play with his food, since the menu listings are whimsical and tongue-in-cheek, with ethnic selections from countries such as Italy, Thailand, Mexico, and Armenia. Here's a sample from the original menu: "Sorta Kefta. Lamb patties with parsley and garlic, yogurt and tomato, lemon and sesame." ⊠ *15 Oak St.* ☎ *207/594–2034* ⊕ *www. cafemiranda.com* ⚓ *Reservations essential* ⊟ *MC, V.*

> ## PENOBSCOT BAY TOP 5
>
> ■ Take a trip on a windjammer.
>
> ■ Ascend Bucksport's 420-foot Penobscot Narrows Bridge Observatory, the highest in the world.
>
> ■ Visit the mysterious Fort Knox (not the one with all the gold). It was built in 1844 to protect the Penobscot River from a British invasion (which never came).
>
> ■ Dig into an authentic Maine dinner at an area lobster pound.
>
> ■ Learn all you ever wanted to know about Maine's maritime history at Searsport's Penobscot Marine Museum.

$–$$$ ✕ **Landings Restaurant & Marina.** If you'd like a traditional Maine lobster dinner with a view, try the Landings. It's right on the dock, next to the marina. The restaurant serves lobster prepared in a variety of ways, plus other seafood dinners, steak, poultry, and pasta. If the restaurant is crowded, you can order food at the bar. ⊠ *1 Commercial St.* ☎ *207/596–6563* ⊟ *AE, DC, MC, V* ⊙ *Closed Nov.–Apr.*

$–$$$

Fodor'sChoice

★

✕ **Rockland Cafe.** It may not look like much from the outside, but the Rockland Café is probably the most popular eating establishment in town, especially among locals. It's famous for the size of its breakfasts and is also open for lunch and dinner. The restaurant is a real bargain if you go for the all-you-can-eat seafood special. At dinner, the seafood combo of shrimps, scallops, clams, and fish is excellent, or there's the classic liver and onions. ⊠ *441 S. Main St., Rockland* ☎ *207/596–7556* ⊕ *www.rocklandcafe.com* ⊟ *AE, DC, MC, V.*

$–$$$ ✕ **Rustica.** Chef and owner John Stowe's Italian restaurant (formerly the Market on Main) opened in 2005 and has been popular from the start. The food is traditional Italian, and the entire menu is available for takeout. An unusual special is the salmon fettuccine with prosciutto. ⊠ *315 Main St.* ☎ *207/594–0015* ⊟ *MC, V.*

WHERE TO STAY

$–$$$ ⌂ **Navigator Motor Inn.** Across the street from the Maine State Ferry terminal, the Navigator is extremely convenient if you'll be heading out on an island ferry to Vinalhaven, North Vinalhaven, or Mantinicus. All rooms have bay views. Smokers will feel welcome in a number of rooms; 14 are pet-friendly. All areas are handicapped accessible; one guest room has a handicapped-accessible bathroom. The inn's Oceanside Seafood & Steakhouse ($–$$$) is open for breakfast, lunch, and dinner. **Pro:** Convenience to ferry. **Con:** Location on U.S. 1 means lots of traffic in summer. ⊠ *520 Main St (U.S. 1).,* 04841 ☎ *207/594–2131 or 800/545–8026* ⊕ *www.navigatorinn.com* ⇌ *80 rooms, 5 suites* ⌂ *In-room: refrigerator. In-hotel: restaurant, bar, no-smoking rooms* ⊟ *AE, DC, MC, V* �ODCP.*

$–$$ **Trade Winds Motor Inn.** Rockland's largest accommodation by far, Trade Winds sits on the edge of the harbor and across from the Lighthouse Museum. Many rooms have balconies overlooking the harbor and marina. The restaurant ($–$$$) seats up to 150 and features dishes such as steamed mussels, pecan-encrusted halibut, and Maine shrimp in a garlic cream sauce over pasta. Some smoking rooms are available. **Pros:** Great location, convenient to nearly everything. **Con:** Can be noisy in summer. ⊠ *2 Park Dr., 04841* ☎ *207/596–6661 or 800/834–3130* ⊕ *www.tradewindsmaine.com* ⇆ *138 rooms, 4 suites* ⚿ *In-room: Some pets allowed, no-smoking rooms. In-hotel: restaurant, pool, gym, no-smoking rooms* ⊟ *AE, DC, MC, V* ⏐⌾⏐*CP.*

$$$–$$$$ **Berry Manor Inn.** Originally the residence of prominent Rockland ★ merchant Charles H. Berry this 1898 inn is in a historic residential neighborhood. The large guest rooms are elegantly furnished with antiques and reproduction pieces. All rooms have fireplaces; TVs are available upon request, and some rooms have whirlpools. A guest pantry is stocked with sweets. **Pros:** In a nice, quiet neighborhood, within walking distance of downtown and the harbor. **Con:** Not handicapped accessible. ⊠ *81 Talbot Ave., 04841* ☎ *207/596–7696 or 800/774–5692* ⊕ *www.berrymanorinn.com* ⇆ *12 rooms* ⚿ *In-room: no TV, Wi-Fi. In-hotel: Wi-Fi, no-smoking rooms* ⊟ *AE, MC, V* ⏐⌾⏐*BP.*

$$–$$$$ **Captain Lindsey House.** Originally owned by a sea captain, this charming inn is filled with artifacts and treasures from all over the world, much as a sea captain's home would have been in the early 1800s. It is now owned by co–sea captains, Ken and Ellen Barnes, who for many years captained the historic windjammer *Stephen Tabor.* The spacious rooms are furnished with antiques. All of the beds have European-style down comforters. One room is handicapped accessible, and small pets are allowed. **Pro:** The common rooms are a veritable treasure of seafaring memorabilia and antiques. **Cons:** If you're expecting a typical B&B, this is not as quaint as you may like; the walls are a trifle thin. ⊠ *5 Lindsey St., 04841* ☎ *207/596–7950 or 800/523–2145* ⊕ *www.lindseyhouse.com* ⇆ *9 rooms* ⚿ *In-hotel: no-smoking rooms, some pets allowed.* ⊟ *AE, DC, MC, V* ⏐⌾⏐*BP.*

$$–$$$$ **Limerock Inn.** This inn is in the center of town, so you can easily walk ★ to the Farnsworth Museum or any of the other downtown attractions and restaurants. The house is built in the Queen Anne–Victorian style, and among the meticulously decorated rooms is one called Island Cottage, which features a whirlpool tub and doors that open onto a private deck overlooking a garden. The Grand Manan room has a fireplace, a whirlpool tub, and a four-poster king-size bed. Room TVs are available upon request. **Pro:** Free Wi-Fi. **Con:** No dinner options within walking distance. ⊠ *96 Limerock St., 04841* ☎ *207/594–2257 or 800/546–3762* ⊕ *www.limerockinn.com* ⇆ *8 rooms* ⚿ *In-room: no phone, no TV, Wi-Fi. In-hotel: no-smoking rooms* ⊟ *AE, DC, MC, V* ⏐⌾⏐*BP.*

NIGHTLIFE & THE ARTS

Although there is not much in the way of nightlife in Rockland, the **Black Bull Tavern** (⊠ *420 Main St.* ☎ *207/593–9060*), in the center of town, offers live entertainment throughout summer. The tavern has large picture windows offering a view of downtown Rockland; weather permitting, patrons can drink and dine alfresco. Tin ceilings and pleasant mustard and mahogany furnishings give the Bull an authentic pub feel. The menu includes specials such as chicken, broccoli, and sun-dried tomato penne, and Jack Daniels–marinated sirloin tips. The **Time Out Pub** (✉ *275 Main St.* ☎ *207/593–9336*) is known as the home of the blues even though it has live music only on Monday nights.

CHAMELEON COAST
Residents who live along the coast will tell you that the bay presents a different face and color nearly every day. Some days, it's as blue and placidly flat as a mirror. Other days, especially in winter before a storm, it's black, angry, and crashing, with 5-foot waves and cresting whitecaps.

FESTIVALS More than a dozen well-known
☾ artists gather for the **North Atlantic Blues Festival** (☎ *207/593–1189*
★ ⊕ *www.northatlanticbluesfestival.com*), a two-night affair each July. The show officially takes place at Harbor Park, but it also includes a Blues Club Crawl through downtown Rockland, which gives this staid old Maine town the atmosphere of New Orleans. Admission is $25. Rockland's annual **Maine Lobster Festival** (☎ *207/596–0376 or 800/562–2529* ⊕ *www.mainelobsterfestival.com*), in early August, is more than 60 years old and has become the biggest local event of the year. People come from all over the country to sample lobster in every possible form: steamed, fried, chowder, lobster rolls—you name it. During the few days of the festival, tons of lobsters (about 10 tons, to be exact) are steamed in the world's largest lobster cooker—you have to see it to believe it. In addition, there's shrimp in its many forms, steamed clams, and Maine mussels. The festival, held in Harbor Park, includes a parade, entertainment, craft and marine exhibits, food booths—and, of course, the crowning of the Maine Sea Goddess. In mid-September, the **Rockland Harborfest Jazz and Art Festival** (☎ *207/596–3076*), a traditional end-of-summer one-night musical event, takes place at Buoy Park, which is at the Public Landing, off S. Main St. There are tours of windjammer ships, kids' activities, arts and crafts, food, and entertainment, including the event's highlight: the annual Bay Chamber Concert Jazz Gala.

SPORTS & THE OUTDOORS

AERIAL TOURS **Maine Atlantic Aviation/Downeast Air** (☎ *207/596–5557 or 800/780–*
☾ *6071* ⊕ *www.maineatlanticaviation.com*) offers lighthouse or island tours—or name your own destination—by plane, helicopter, or glider.

BOATING **Bay Island Yacht Charters** (✉ *117A Tillison Ave.* ☎ *207/596–7550 or 800/421–2492*) has a sailing school and day rentals.

☾ **Maine Windjammer Association** (☎ *800/807–9463* ⊕ *www.sailmaine-coast.com*) can set you up with a sailing excursion that very well may end up the highlight of your vacation. Windjammer ships docked in Rockland include *Wendameen* (one-night cruises), *American Eagle, Heritage, Isaac Evans, J&E Riggin, Nathaniel Bowditch*, and *Simplicity*. Other windjammers can be found in the nearby towns of Rockport and Camden. Prices are about $180 for an overnighter, and $395 to $875 for a three- to six-day cruise, with all meals included.

SHOPPING

The **Farnsworth Art Museum Store** (⊠ *356 Main St.* ☎ *207/596–5789*) sells jewelry, books, and prints of the museum's paintings. The motto at **Planet Inc.** (⊠ *318 Main St.* ☎ *207/596–5976*), Maine's largest toy store, is "You're never too old to play." Planet Inc. also has a store in Camden. **Rock City Books & Coffee** (⊠ *328 Main St.* ☎ *207/594–4123* ⊕ *www. rockcitybooksandcoffee.com*) is a wonderful place for book lovers. There's a huge selection, the staff is friendly, and you can enjoy coffee and a homemade pastry while browsing. The **Wine Seller** (⊠ *15 Tillison Ave.* ☎ *207/594–2621* ⊕ *www.fruitothevine.com*) has domestic and imported wines and can prepare gift baskets. It's closed on Sundays.

ART GALLERIES There are more art galleries in this little working-class town than you would expect. Most are on Main Street—note that Main Street was originally called Elm Street, and some of the older businesses still use Elm Street in their address. The **Caldbeck Gallery** (⊠ *12 Elm St.* ☎ *207/594–5935* ⊕ *www.caldbeck.com*) displays contemporary Maine works. **Elan Fine Arts** (⊠ *8 Elm St.* ☎ *207/596–9933* ⊕ *www. elanfinearts.com*) displays works by contemporary American artists. The **Gallery at 357 Main** (⊠ *357 Main St.* ☎ *207/596–0084*) specializes in marine paintings. **Harbor Square Gallery** (⊠ *374 Main St.* ☎ *207/594– 8700*) has roomfuls of Maine-related arts and crafts.

VINALHAVEN

★ *East of Rockland via Maine State Ferry on U.S. 1.*

The largest inhabited island in Maine, Vinalhaven has 1,200 residents. It's nearly 8 mi long by 5 mi wide and is mostly wooded. At one time the granite industry was booming here, but the quarries are now mostly used for swimming and fishing. Many islanders work in the lobster-harvesting business. They even have a special season when they can gather lobsters while those on the mainland cannot (to compensate them for living on an island).

Most of Penobscot Bay's islands have infrequent ferry service, or are totally uninhabited. Vinalhaven, however, is relatively accessible—*relatively* being the key word here. There are six ferry trips per day to and from Vinalhaven in summer. The Maine State Ferry Terminal is right in the center of Rockland, on U.S. 1, across from the Navigator Motor Inn. The ferry runs throughout the year (except on major holidays), but the times change somewhat from the end of October through December, so it's best to call first. Ferry service to North Haven and to Mantinicus, a small island 23 mi from Rockland, is also available.

■ TIP→ These old ferries are very minimal in their amenities. You won't find a restaurant, snack bar, lounge, or even a vending machine.

The village of Vinalhaven is small and easy to explore. There is a designated walking path on the north side of Main Street that runs from

Windjammer Excursions

Nothing defines the Maine coastal experience more than a sailing trip on a windjammer. Windjammers were built throughout the East Coast in the 19th and early 20th centuries. Designed to carry cargo primarily, these iron- or steel-hulled beauties have a rich past—the *Nathaniel Bowditch* served in World War II, for example, while others plied the waters in the lumbering and oystering trades. They vary in size, but could be as small as 40 feet and hold 6 passengers (plus a couple of crew members), or more than 130 feet and hold 40 passengers and 10 crew members. During a windjammer excursion, not only do passengers have the opportunity to ride on a historical vessel, but in most cases they are able to participate in the navigation, be it hoisting a sail or playing captain at the wheel.

The majority of windjammers are berthed in Rockland, Rockport, or Camden. You can get information on the fleets by contacting one of two windjammer organizations: The Maine Windjammer Association (☎800/807–9463 ⊕www.sailmaine

coast.com) or Maine Windjammer Cruises (☎207/236–2938 or 888/692–7245 ⊕www.mainewindjam mercruises.com). Cruises can be anywhere from one day or one overnight to up to eight days. The price, ranging from nearly $200 to $900, depending on length of trip, includes all meals. Trips leave from Camden, Rockland, and Rockport.

Here is a selection of some of the best windjammer cruises in the area.

CAMDEN-ROCKPORT *Angelique,* Yankee Packet Co., 207/236–8873. *Appledore,* which can take you out for just a day sail, 207/236–8353. *Mary Day,* Coastal Cruises, 207/236–2750. *Olad,* Downeast Windjammer Packet Co., 207/236–2323. *Yacht Heron,* 207/236–8605 or 800/599–8605.

ROCKLAND *American Eagle* and *Schooner Heritage,* North End Shipyard, 207/594–8007. *Nathanial Bowditch,* 207/273–4062. *Summertime,* 800/562–8290. *Victory Chimes,* 207/265–5651. *Wendameen,* 207/594–1751.

the ferry terminal to the center of town. Within a 1-mi radius of the ferry dock you will find two town parks and a nature conservancy area. There is only one road on the island, so it's pretty easy to find your way around. Biking the island can be fun, though there are no designated bike paths and the road can be a little rough outside the village. There is no public transportation on the island.

OFF THE BEATEN PATH

Mantinicus Island is one of Maine's most-remote inhabited islands. It's 23 mi from the mainland, more than two hours by ferry (from the Maine State Ferry Terminal in Rockland). During the off-season, the ferry runs only once a month; in June, July, and August, it runs once a week. **Tuckanuck Lodge** (☎ *207/366–3830*) is the only place to stay on the island ($–$$).

CATCH THE FERRY

Be aware of the ferry schedule. If you miss the last ferry back, or if there simply is not enough room for your car on the last ferry, you will have to spend the night on the island, and chances are you'll be sleeping in your car since there is not a lot in the way of accommodations on Vinalhaven.

■**TIP**➔ A good way not to get caught overnight on the island is not to take your vehicle—merely board as a walk-on passenger. The fare is about a third of what it is if you take your vehicle, and Vinalhaven can be easily explored on foot.

North Haven Island is appropriately just north of Vinalhaven across a small stretch of sea, 12 mi from the mainland. This is the smaller of the two islands, but it's home to some large summer residences of the rich if not famous. There is one general store, a small restaurant, and a small B&B on the island. The year-round population is only about 330. The Maine State Ferry runs between North Haven and Rockland three times a day throughout the year (except for major holidays).

WHERE TO EAT & STAY

$–$$$ ✕**Harbor Gawker.** Decorated with old wooden lobster traps and fishing gear, this mariner-theme restaurant has been in business for 30 years. The fare, seafood of course, is abundant and tasty. Try a lobster dinner or the ever-popular lobster roll. ⊠*Main St., Vinalhaven* ☎*207/863–9365* ▤*MC, V* ✆*Closed Sun. and mid-Nov.–mid-Apr.*

$$–$$$$ ⊡**Tidewater Motel.** This little motel is the only place to stay that's on the waterfront and near the ferry dock. It was built on a bridge overlooking the harbor, and all rooms have wonderful views. If you want a real treat, get up early enough to watch the lobster boats leave around 5 AM. They usually come back sometime between 3 and 5 PM the same day. The property has one car available for rent by guests. **Pro:** Location on the harbor and in the center of town. **Con:** Not that easy to get a room here during high season. ⬭*Box 546* ⊠*Carver's Harbor, Vinalhaven 04863* ☎*207/863–4618* ⬚*www.tidewatermotel.com* ⬯*19 rooms* ⬧*In-room: no a/c, kitchen (some). In-hotel: bicycles, water sports, no-smoking rooms* ▤*AE, DC, MC, V* ⭘*CP.*

$–$$ ⊡**Our Place Inn.** On North Haven Island, this is a classic 19th-century farmhouse with five rooms in the main house and three separate but self-contained cottages. The inn is 2 mi from town but only a short walk from Pulpit Harbor. Three of the rooms in the main house have private baths. The cottages are small but all have private baths and kitchenettes. For something different, request to stay in the lighthouse room. **Pro:** Taking one of the inn's bicycles for a ride on this island can be a lot of fun. **Con:** It's a bit of a walk to town. 🖉 *Box 704* ✉ *Crabtree Point Rd., North Haven,04853* ☎ *207/867–4998* ⊕ *www. ourplaceinn.com* 🛏 *5 rooms, 3 with bath; 3 cottages* ⚒ *In-room: no a/c. In-hotel: bicycles, no-smoking rooms* ▤ *MC, V* ⦿ *CP.*

ROCKPORT, CAMDEN & LINCOLNVILLE

ROCKPORT

4 mi north of Rockland on U.S. 1.

Heading north on U.S. 1, you come to Rockport before you reach the tourist mecca of Camden. The most interesting part of Rockport—the harbor—is not right on U.S. 1, so many people drive by without realizing it's here. Much of the movie *In the Bedroom* with Sissy Spacek was filmed at this colorful harbor. You can get there by following the first ROCKPORT sign you see off U.S. 1 at Pascal Road.

Rockport, originally called Goose River, was part of Camden until 1891. The cutting and burning of limestone was once a major industry in this area. The stone was cut in nearby quarries and then burned in hot kilns. The resulting lime powder was used to create mortar. Some of the massive kilns are still here.

One of the most famous sights in Rockport is the **Rockport Arch,** which crosses Union Street at the town line. It was first constructed of wood and mortar in 1926, was demolished in 1984, then rebuilt by popular demand in 1985. The arch has been displayed in a number of movies, including *Peyton Place* and *In the Bedroom.*

WHAT TO SEE

The **Center for Maine Contemporary Art** has exhibited work by some of Maine's best—and newest—artists for more than 50 years. The exhibits, in four galleries, range from traditional art and photography to various forms of artistic expression. Exhibits change on a rotating basis. ✉ *162 Russell Ave., Rockport 04856* ☎ *207/236–2875* ⊕ *www.arts-maine.org* 🎟 *$5* ⊙ *Tues.–Sat. 10–5, Sun. 1–5.*

WHERE TO EAT

$$$–$$$$
Fodor's Choice
★

✕ **Marcel's.** If you're a serious gourmet and only have time to sample one dining experience in the Rockport-Rockland-Camden area, this lavish restaurant in the big Samoset Resort ought to be the one. Marcel's offers a fine array of Continental cuisine. Enjoy table-side preparation of a classic rack of lamb, châteaubriand, or Steak Diane while admiring the bay view. The menu includes a variety of Maine seafood and a fine wine list. The Sunday brunch buffet, with some of the finest seafood along the coast, is famous and draws a crowd. ✉ *220 Warrenton St.,*

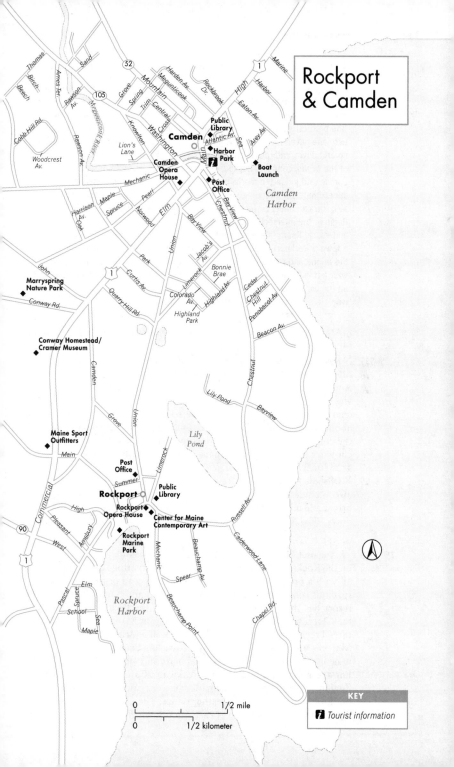

THE PRETTIEST WALK IN THE WORLD

A few years ago, *Yankee*, the quintessential magazine of New England, did a cover story on what it called "the prettiest walk in the world." The two-lane paved road, which winds up and down, with occasional views of the ocean, connects Rockport to Camden. To judge the merits of this approximately 2-mi journey for yourself, you can travel by foot or by car. Begin at the intersection of U.S. 1 and Pascal Road. Take a right off U.S. 1 toward Rockport harbor, then cross the bridge and go up the hill. On your left is Russell Avenue. Take that all the way to Camden. Lining the way are some of the most beautiful homes in Maine, surrounded by an abundance of flora and fauna. Keep an eye out for a farm with Belted Galloway cows, as well as views of the sparkling ocean—for those who may not know, these rare white cows get their name from the foot-wide black "belt" around their middles. The walk or drive is beautiful at any time of the year, but in fall it's breathtaking. Like the rest of New England, the coast of Maine gets a large number of fall foliage "leaf peepers," and the reds and golds of the chestnut, birch, and elm trees along this winding route are especially beautiful.

off U.S. 1 ☎ *207/594–2511* ⚑ *Reservations essential Jacket required* ▭ *AE, D, DC, MC, V* ☻ *No lunch.*

$–$$$ ✗ **Helm Restaurant.** In addition to the expected seafood, the Helm offers French and American cuisine, accompanied by excellent views. Among the specialties on the French side are bouillabaisse, coq au vin, and coquille St. Jacques. On the American side, there's seafood, charbroiled steaks, and homemade soups and chowders. Locals rave about the huge salad bar. Specials include baked stuffed haddock, and the complete Maine Shore Dinner, which comes with lobster, stew or chowder, steamed or fried clams, corn on the cob, and dessert. ⊠ *U.S. 1* ☎ *207/236–4337* ▭ *MC, V* ☻ *Closed Tues.*

$–$$ ✗ **Offshore Restaurant.** Seafood is the specialty here, but the large menu also includes steak, prime rib, liver, and chicken. The restaurant is bright and airy, and there is a lovely view of the bay from the large windows. ⊠ *U.S. 1* ☎ *207/596–6804* ▭ *AE, DC, MC, V* ☻ *Closed Mon.*

WHERE TO STAY

$$–$$$$
FodorsChoice
★
    Samoset Resort. This 230-acre, all-encompassing, ocean-side resort on the Rockland-Rockport town line offers luxurious rooms and suites, all with a private balcony or patio, and an ocean or garden view. The spacious rooms are decorated in deep green and burgundy tones. The resort has three dining options: Marcel's, the Breakwater Cafe, and the Clubhouse Grille. The flagship restaurant Marcel's ($$–$$$$) features French and American cuisine, as well as seafood specials (⇨ *see* Marcel's under Where to Eat). It also has an extensive and impressive wine list. Reservations are essential here, and men must wear a jacket. For a less-formal affair, try the Breakwater Cafe, featuring basic New England fare, such as homemade chowder and lobster rolls; there's outdoor seating when the weather is nice. The Clubhouse Grille, catering to the golf crowd, serves casual food, which you can enjoy inside

or on the porch. *Golf Digest* called the resort's 18-hole championship golf course the "Top Ranked Resort Course in New England," and the "Seventh Most Beautiful Course in America." **Pro:** This is a resort property that seems to meet every need. **Con:** Not within walking distance of Rockland or Camden shops. ⊠ *220 Warrenton St., Rockport 04856* ☎ *207/594–2511 or 800/341–1650* ⊕ *www.samoset.com* ⇨ *156 rooms, 22 suites* ⟨⟩ *In-room: dial-up, Wi-Fi. In-hotel: 3 restaurants, bar, golf course, tennis courts, pools, gym, concierge, children's programs (ages 3–12), laundry service, public Internet, airport shuttle, no-smoking rooms* ⊟ *AE, D, DC, MC, V* ⟨⟩*CP.*

$$–$$$$ 📷**Country Inn at Camden-Rockport.** This inn has 36 country-style rooms in the main building and 11 private cottage suites. All rooms have private decks; some also include fireplaces and Jacuzzis. Five of the rooms are pet-friendly, and smoking is allowed in one of the rooms. Two of the rooms are handicapped accessible, including the bathroom. **Pro:** It's well situated between Rockport and Camden. **Con:** You have to drive to dinner. ⊠ *40 Commercial St. (U.S. 1), 04856* ☎ *207/236–2725* ⊕ *www.countryinnmaine.com* ⇨ *36 rooms, 11 cottage suites* ⟨⟩ *In-room: refrigerator. In-hotel: public Internet, public Wi-Fi, pool, gym, laundry service, no-smoking rooms* ⊟ *AE, DC, MC, V* ⟨⟩*CP.*

$–$$ 📷**Claddagh Motel & Suites.** You may be in Maine, but you'll get "Irish hospitality" from hosts Alex and Sioban Gilmore. (They joke that Irish hospitality means they're "friendlier than the British.") The main building resembles a New England–style clapboard house with white paint and green awnings. Rooms are in a small wing in the back. Potted flowers and plants add extra charm to this small motel. All rooms are handicapped accessible (but have no special fixtures in the bathrooms). **Pros:** The rooms are more spacious than you would expect, and the rates are lower than you would expect. **Con:** U.S. 1 can get a little noisy at night. ⊠ *1038 Commercial St. (U.S. 1), Box 988, 04856* ☎ *207/594–8479 or 800/871–5454* ⊕ *www.claddaghmotel.com* ⇨ *13 rooms, 6 suites* ⟨⟩ *In-room: VCR, Wi-Fi. In-hotel: pool, no-smoking rooms* ⊟ *AE, DC, MC, V* ⟨⟩*Closed mid-Nov.–mid-Apr.* ⟨⟩*CP.*

$–$$ 📷**White Gates Inn.** This family-run inn is nestled in a quiet rural setting, surrounded by huge oak trees and spacious lawns and gardens. The rooms, many of which are rustic in nature with knotty-pine paneling, are all on the ground level (however they are not considered handicapped accessible). Adorning each room is an old-fashioned Maine quilt. (A big cottage industry in the state, Maine quilts are all hand-stitched.) The proprietors, Charlie and Ann Emerson, live on the property. **Pro:** All rooms are on the ground floor, so there are no stairs to climb. Also, you can park right in front of your room. **Con:** You need to drive to dinner or shopping. ⊠ *700 Commercial St. (U.S. 1), 04856* ☎ *207/594–4625* ⊕ *www.whitegatesinn.com* ⇨ *15 rooms* ⟨⟩ *In-hotel: Wi-Fi, some pets allowed* ⊟ *AE, MC, V* ⟨⟩*CP.*

¢–$ ⚠ 📷**Megunticook Campground by the Sea.** You can't have a better location for an RV park and campground than this: it is easy to find since the entrance is right on U.S. 1 just north of Rockland, and many of the sites in the campground face the sea. In addition to RV spots and tent-camping sites, cabin rentals are available. Rates during the high season are $35 a night for basic campsites, $45 a night for full-hookup sites, and $72 a night for cabins. **Pro:** A great location for easy access to Rockland or Camden. **Con:** It can get crowded and noisy with children during the peak season. ✉ *620 Commercial St. (U.S. 1), 04856* ☎ *207/594–2428 or 800/ 884–2428* ⊕ *www.campgroundbythesea.com* ⇱ *82 tent/RV sites, 10 cabins* ⌂ *Full hookup, basic hookup* ▤ *MC, V* ☯ *Closed mid-Oct. until mid-May.*

NIGHTLIFE & THE ARTS

The **Bay Chamber Concerts** (☝ *58 Bay View St., Camden 04843* ☎ *207/236–2823 or 888/707–2770* ⊕ *www.baychamberconcerts.org*) feature major artists performing classical, jazz, dance, and more. Past performers have included the St. Lawrence String Quartet, Joseph Silverstein, Regina Carter, and Dave Brubeck and his sons. Concerts are held Wednesday and Thursday nights in July and August; Wednesday at the Strand Theater (345 Main St., Rockland) and Thursday at the historic Rockport Opera House (6 Central St., Rockport). Additional concerts take place at other times during the year.

SPORTS & THE OUTDOORS

OUTFITTER **Maine Sport Outfitters** (✉ *115 Commercial St. [U.S. 1]* ☎ *207/236–7120 or 888/236–8797* ⊕ *www.mainesport.com*) offers a big selection of sports clothing and gear in its huge, two-story building. It also rents bikes, camping equipment, canoes, kayaks, cross-country skis (for skiing at popular Camden Snow Bowl), ice skates, and snowshoes.

CAMDEN

8 mi north of Rockland, 5 mi south of Lincolnville.

★ More than any other town along Penobscot Bay, Camden is the perfect picture-postcard of a Maine coastal village. It is one of the most popular destinations on the Maine Coast, so June through September the town is crowded with visitors—but don't let that scare you away; Camden is worth it. Just come prepared for busy traffic on the town's Main Street (U.S. 1), and make lodging reservations well in advance. You'll also want to make restaurant reservations whenever possible.

"The Jewel of the Maine Coast" is the publicity slogan for Camden-Rockport-Lincolnville, and it is an apt description. Camden is famous not only for its geography but also for its large fleet of windjammers—relics and replicas from the age of sailing—with their romantic histories and great billowing sails. At just about any hour during the warm months, you're likely to see at least one windjammer tied up in the harbor. The excursions, whether for an afternoon or a week, are best from June through September.

WORD OF MOUTH

"You will LOVE Camden, Maine. The town itself is as pretty as any town in Vermont, and it's on the water as well."

—natcam

The town's compact size makes it perfect for exploring on foot: shops, restaurants, and galleries line Main Street (U.S. 1), as well as side streets and alleys around the harbor. Especially worth inclusion on your walking tour is Camden's residential area. It is quite charming and filled with many fascinating old period houses from the time when Federal, Greek Revival, and Victorian architecture were the rage among the wealthy. Many of them now are B&Bs. The chamber of commerce, at the Public Landing, can provide you with a walking map.

★ One of the biggest and most colorful events of the year in Camden is **Windjammer Weekend,** which usually takes place at the beginning of September and includes the single largest gathering of windjammer ships in the world, plus lots of good eats. ☎207/374–2993 or 800/807–9463.

4

NEED A BREAK? Down by the harbor, a number of independent fast-food stands offer clam chowder, fried fish, and lobster rolls. For something sweet, try **Boynton-McKay** (⊠ *30 Main St.* ☎ *207/236–2465*), an 1890s ice-cream parlor serving ice cream made the old-fashioned way, as well as modern-day smoothies.

WHERE TO EAT

$$$$ ✕ **Hartstone Inn.** At this elegant restaurant, the specialty is a five-course
★ prix fixe menu that changes daily. Items prepared by acclaimed chef Michael Salmon may include grilled salmon nicoise, with rosemary roasted potatoes; haddock "Oscar," with Maine crabmeat; and, of course, Maine lobster. Breakfast is exclusively for inn guests (⇨ *see review under Where to Stay*). Cooking classes are offered. ⊠*41 Elm St. (U.S. 1)* ☎*207/236–4259 or 800/788–4823* ⊕*www.hartstoneinn. com.* ⊟*MC, V* ⊗*No lunch.*

$$$–$$$$ ✕ **Atlantica.** Right on the water's edge, the Atlantica is in a historic clapboard building. Its lower deck is cantilevered over the water, offering a romantic setting with great views. The interior decor is a mix of red walls and contemporary paintings. Fresh seafood with French and Asian accents is the specialty here. Favorites include pan-roasted split lobster tails with lemon butter, lobster stuffed with scallops, and pan-roasted king salmon. ⊠*Bayview Landing* ☎*207/236–6011 or 888/507–8514* ⊕*www.atlanticarestaurant.com* ⌕*Reservations essential* ⊟*AE, MC, V* ⊗*No lunch.*

$$–$$$$ ✕ **Ephemere Cafe.** If you want to be a success in the difficult restaurant business, here's what you do: start small but build a BIG reputation. That's what Patrick and Heidi Cazemajou have done with Ephemere. The small restaurant, done in a minimalist design with simple tables and bare walls, has only been around for a relatively short time, but its word-of-mouth reputation is growing fast. Menu items include coconut shrimp, mussels marinière, and, of course, lobster. ⊠*51 Bayview St., a little south of downtown* ☎*207/236–4451* ⊟*DC, MC, V* ⊗*Closed Sun. No lunch.*

$$–$$$ ✕ **Francine Bistro.** A small place in a little old house, Francine's doesn't
★ look like much from the outside, but, boy, what a following Francine has! Actually, the restaurant is the brainchild of chef/owner Brian Hill, who uses the freshest of local produce, meats, and seafood. The menu changes daily depending on Brian's whims. ⊠*55 Chestnut St., in south*

end of town ☎*207/230–0083* ⊕*www.francinebistro.com* ⌖*Reservations essential* ☰*MC, V* ☾*Closed Sun. and Mon. No lunch.*

$$–$$$ ✕**Natalie's.** This restaurant is now conveniently a part of the Camden Harbour Inn (⇨ *see review under Where to Stay*). Fine dining with a French-American menu is the name of the game here. There's also a prix fixe meal and a Grand Lobster dish. The lounge is a perfect place for a cocktail in front of the big fireplace. ⌂*83 Bay View St.* ☎*207/236–7008* ☰*AE, DC, MC, V.*

$–$$$ ✕**Cappy's Chowder House.** Cappy's has been around for so long (more
★ than two decades) it's become somewhat of a Camden institution. As you would expect from the name, Cappy's "chowdah" is the thing to order here—it's been written up in the *New York Times* and in *Bon Appétit* magazine—but there are plenty of other seafood specials on the menu, too. Don't be afraid to bring the kids—this place has many bargain meals. ⌂*1 Main St.* ☎*207/236–2254* ⊕*www.cappyschowder. com* ⌖*Reservations not accepted* ☰*MC, V.*

$–$$$ ✕**Waterfront Restaurant.** Come here for a ringside seat on Camden Harbor. The best view, when the weather cooperates, is from the deck. The fare is primarily seafood, but also on the menu are beef and chicken entrées, and salads. Lobster and crabmeat rolls are highlights at lunch. ⌂*40 Bay View St.* ☎*207/236–3747* ⊕*www.waterfrontcamden.com* ⌖*Reservations not accepted* ☰*AE, MC, V.*

$–$$ ✕**CMF.** This odd name for a restaurant stands for "Camden Maine Foods." It has been attracting a following since it opened in 2007 (replacing the former Italian restaurant Sonny G's). The specialties are seafood and steaks—just what tourists seem to want—with a Southern flair; also on the menu is a nice array of chowders and wraps. Japanese cuisine is served on the second floor. ⌂*31 Elm St. (U.S. 1)* ☎*207/236–4477* ☰*MC, V* ☾*Closed Sun.–Wed.*

WHERE TO STAY

$$–$$$$ ▦**Hartstone Inn.** This downtown 1835 mansard-roofed Victorian home
★ has been turned into an elegant and sophisticated retreat and a fine culinary destination. No detail has been overlooked, from soft robes, down comforters, and chocolate truffles in the guest rooms to china, crystal, and silver in the elegantly decorated dining room (⇨ *see review under Where to Eat*). The inn hosts seasonal food festivals. **Pro:** The on-site restaurant is excellent. **Con:** Not handicapped accessible. ⌂*41 Elm St. (U.S. 1), 04843* ☎*207/236–4259 or 800/788–4823* ⊕*www. hartstoneinn.com* ⌸*6 rooms, 6 suites* ⌖*In-room: dial-up. In-hotel: restaurant, no-smoking rooms.* ☰*MC, V* ⦿*BP.*

$$–$$$ ▦**Whitehall Inn.** One of Camden's best-known inns, the Whitehall is
★ an 1834 white clapboard sea captain's home just north of town. The Millay Room, off the lobby, preserves memorabilia of the poet Edna St. Vincent Millay, who grew up in the area and read her poetry here. The inn is a delightful blend of the old and the new. The telephones are antiques, but the electronics are brand new. The rooms, remodeled in 2007, have dark-wood bedsteads, white bedspreads, and claw-foot tubs. The dining room serves traditional and creative American cuisine as well as many seafood specialties, and the popular prix fixe dinner is $36 a person. One room is handicapped accessible. **Pro:** Edna St. Vin-

A CHILD OF PENOBSCOT BAY

It was a warm August night in 1912 when the young Rockland poet Edna St. Vincent Millay appeared at the Whitehall Inn. She was there to read her poem "Renascence," to an audience of inn guests and employees.

All I could see from where I stood Was three long mountains and a wood; I turned and looked another way, And saw three islands in a bay.

(Edna St. Vincent Millay, "Renascence")

The woman who was to become one of America's most famous poets was born in 1892 in the unlikely city of Rockland, a working town of seamen and stonecutters. Like many artists before her, she became famous almost by accident. At the age of 20, she entered a poem, "Renascence," in a poetry contest. The poem only took

fourth place, but it was enough to bring her attention from academics, and she was awarded a scholarship to the prestigious Vassar College.

She continued writing and winning awards, and eventually she was awarded a Pulitzer Prize for her poetry. She was renowned for her beauty and spent most of her adult life leading a rather wild existence in Greenwich Village, in New York City.

Eventually, she married a man much older than herself, Eugen Boissevain, who became her manager and supporter. A heavy smoker, she died in 1950 at the age of 58. She had written in one of her most famous poems that she was a person who had burned her candle at both ends, and she lamented that it "would not last the night."

cent Millay—wow! **Con:** No a/c, but usually it's fine without it. ✉️ *52 High St., 04843* ☎️ *207/236–3391 or 800/789–6565* ⊕ *www.white-hall-inn.com* ⬦ *50 rooms, 45 with bath* ♿ *In-room: no a/c, no phone (some), Wi-Fi. In-hotel: restaurant, tennis court, public Internet, no-smoking rooms* ☰ *AE, MC, V* ☺ *Closed mid-Oct.–mid-May* 🍴BP.

$$$$ 🏨 **Camden Harbour Inn.** This inn, which has been in existence since 1874, is well named since it has a panoramic view of Camden's colorful harbor. All of the rooms include hand-picked flowers or a basket of fruit. While retaining some of its 19th-century characteristics, the inn also blends in the modern. Its new owners from the Netherlands renovated it in 2007 with new furnishings, a gourmet restaurant, and a cozy bar. Some rooms have decks or balconies, some have fireplaces, and many have claw-foot bathtubs. King-size feather beds and flat-screen TVs (with DVD player) are in all rooms. **Pro:** The inn's Natalie's restaurant is one of the best in the Camden area and features outstanding American-French cuisine. **Con:** A bit pricey. ✉️ *83 Bay View St., a little south of downtown, 04843* ☎️ *207/236–4200 or 800/236–4266* ⊕ *www.camdenharbourinn.com* ⬦ *17 rooms, 1 suite* ♿ *In-room: Wi-Fi. In-hotel: no-smoking rooms, no elevator* ☰ *AE, DC, MC, V* ☺ *Closed Nov.–Apr.* 🍴BP.

$$$$ 🏨 **Inn at Sunrise Point.** Guests are offered a spectacular setting in this
★   luxury inn. (The Irish manager prides himself on having the highest rates of any Camden inn.) The main house and cottages are right on the ocean, resulting in beautiful ocean views from nearly all rooms.

Amenities such as plush robes and oversize tubs and showers are standard; some rooms include romantic wood-burning fireplaces and Jacuzzis. One of the cottages is handicapped accessible. All rooms have flat-screen TVs with DVD players. **Pros:** Spectacular views, a delightful Irish manager. **Cons:** Pricey, no restaurants nearby. ⊠ *U.S. 1, Box 1344, 04843* ☎ *207/236–7716* ⊕ *www.sunrisepoint.com* ◄ *3 rooms, 4 cottages, 2 suites* & *In-room: no a/c, Wi-Fi. In-hotel: no-smoking rooms, no elevator* ⊟ *MC, V* ⦾ *BP.*

$$$–$$$$
★
Lord Camden Inn. The Lord Camden Inn is an excellent location if you want to be in the very center of town near the harbor. The exterior of the building is red brick with bright blue-and-white awnings. The colorful interior is furnished with restored antiques and paintings by local artists. Despite being downtown, the inn offers plenty of ocean views from the upstairs rooms, and some of the rooms have lovely old-fashioned, four-poster beds. There's no on-site restaurant but you can find plenty of dining options within walking distance. Two of the rooms are handicapped accessible, including the bathrooms. All of the rooms are no-smoking, but the hotel is pet-friendly. An elevator goes to the upper floors. **Pro:** The most centrally located accommodation in Camden. **Con:** In the front rooms, the U.S. 1 traffic may keep you awake. ⊠ *24 Main St. (U.S. 1), 04843* ☎ *207/236–4325 or 800/336–4325* ⊕ *www. lordcamdeninn.com* ◄ *37 rooms* & *In-room: refrigerator (some), dial-up. In-hotel: no-smoking rooms* ⊟ *AE, MC, V* ⦾ *BP.*

$$$–$$$$
Fodor'sChoice
★
Norumbega. The Norumbega is probably the most unusual-looking B&B you'll ever see. When you see this ivy-coated, gray stone castle, from the outside you may think, *Wow, Count Dracula would feel right at home here.* But inside it's cheerier, and elegant, with many of the antiques-filled rooms offering fireplaces and private balconies overlooking the bay. The inn was built in 1886 by local businessman and inventor (of duplex telegraphy) Joseph Stearns. Before erecting his home, he spent a year visiting the castles of Europe and adapting the best ideas he found. He named the castle after the original 17th-century name for what is now Maine, "Norumbega." The home was converted into a B&B in 1984 and has been named by the *Maine Times* as the most-photographed piece of real estate in the state. There are no ground-floor guest rooms, and no elevator. Pets are not allowed. **Pro:** You will never again stay in a place this dramatic looking. **Con:** While this is an unusually beautiful property, guests with handicaps or who have difficulty in climbing stairs will not find it comfortable. ⊠ *63 High St., (U.S. 1), just a little north of downtown Camden, 04843* ☎ *207/236–4646 or 877/363–4646* ⊕ *www.norumbegainn.com* ◄ *13 rooms* & *In-room: no a/c, dial-up, Wi-Fi. In-hotel: no-smoking rooms, no elevator* ⊟ *AE, DC, MC, V* ⦾ *BP.*

$$–$$$$
Beloin's on the Maine Coast. Beloin's sits on a natural sea ledge on the edge of the ocean, so it offers spectacular views and easy shore access. There are nine rooms in the motel, five one-bedroom shore cottages, and two two-bedroom shore cottages. The property includes a private beach, and there are picnic tables and grills. Camden Hills State Park is nearby. Smoking is allowed throughout. **Pros:** Wonderful views of the sea or, alternatively, very inexpensive rooms on the nonwater side; one

room is handicap accessible. **Con:** Some rooms have been smoked in. ⊠*254 Belfast Rd. (U.S. 1), 04843* ☎*207/236–3262* ⊕*www.beloins. com* ⋑*9 rooms, 7 cottages* ⌂*In-room: no a/c (some), kitchen (some), some pets allowed. In-hotel: no-smoking rooms* ⊟*DC, MC, V.*

$–$$$ ⛺ **High Tide Inn.** If you look one way from this inn, you will see the bay across the lawn. Look in the other direction, and you see Mt. Battie. The inn has been under the ownership of Jo Freilich for nearly two decades now. **Pro:** A home-baked breakfast in a room overlooking the sea is one of the perks. **Con:** No dinner spots within walking distance. ⊠*505 Belfast Rd (U.S. 1), 04843* ☎*207/236–3724 or 800/778–7068* ⊕*www.hightideinn.com* ⋑*30 rooms, 1 deckhouse* ⌂*In-room: refrig (some). In hotel: beachfront, some pets allowed, no-smoking rooms, no elevator* ⊟*AE, DC, MC, V* ⊗*Closed mid-Oct.–mid-May* ⅋*CP.*

$–$$ ⛺ **Towne Motel.** In high-price Camden, this is one of the few affordable places to stay within easy reach of the colorful harbor. You won't find many frills here, but you will find simple, clean rooms with private baths and air-conditioning. One room is handicapped accessible, and one room is an efficiency with a full kitchen. All rooms are no-smoking. **Pros:** Closest motel to Camden Harbor, comparatively inexpensive. **Con:** Rooms are pretty spare-looking. ⊠*68 Elm St. (U.S. 1), 04843* ☎*207/236–3377 or 800/656–4999* ⊕*www.camdenmotel.com* ⋑*18 rooms* ⌂*In-room: Wi-Fi, a/c. In-hotel: no-smoking rooms, no elevator* ⊟*AE, DC, MC, V* ⅋*CP.*

$–$$ ⛺ **Camden Hills State Park Camping.** The 107-site camping area, open from mid-May to mid-October, operates on a first-come, first-served basis. The entrance is 2 mi north of Camden off U.S. 1. **Pro:** RVs allowed. **Con:** Seasonal. ☎*207/236–3109* ⌂*Flush toilets, water, electric, sewer, cable, dumping, recreation hall, store, laundry, Internet access, swimming, pets allowed.*

NIGHTLIFE

Offering live music, dancing, pub food, and local brews, **Gilbert's Public House** (⊠*12 Bay View St., underneath Peter Ott's pub* ☎*207/236–4320*) is the favorite drinking place of the windjammer crowd.

SPORTS & THE OUTDOORS

☺ Although their height may not be much more than 1,000 feet, the hills ★ in **Camden Hills State Park** (⊠*U.S. 1 just north of Camden* ☎*207/236–3109*) are lovely landmarks for miles along the low, rolling reaches of the Maine Coast. The 5,500-acre park contains 25 mi of hiking trails, including the easy nature trail up Mt. Battie. Hike or drive to the top for a magnificent view over Camden and island-studded Penobscot Bay. There also is a campground here. **Merryspring Nature Park** (⊠*Conway Rd. off U.S. 1* ☎*207/236–2239* ⊕*www.merryspring.org* ⎘*Free* ⊗*Daily dawn–dusk*) is a 66-acre retreat with herb, rose, rhododendron, hosta, and children's gardens as well as 4 mi of walking trails.

SAILING For the voyage of a lifetime, you and your family should think seri-
☺ ously about a **windjammer trip**—which can be as little as a couple of
★ hours or as much as a week. The following day-sailer windjammers leave from Camden Harbor; most are of the schooner type: *Lazy Jack* (☎*207/230–0602* ⊕*www.schoonerlazyjack.com*); *Olad* (☎*207/236–*

2323 *www.maineschooners.com*); *Shantih II* (☎207/236–8605 or 800/599–8605 *www.woodenboatco.com*); and *Windjammer Surprise* (☎207/236–4687 *www.camdenmainesailing.com*). Prices range from \$395 to \$875, with all meals included—and often that means a lobster bake on a deserted island beach.

OUTFITTER **Maine Sport Outdoor Adventures** (✉*Bay View Landing* ☎207/236–8797 or 800/722–0826) offers harbor tours. Its store in nearby Rockport, Maine Sport Outfitters, rents bicycles, canoes, and kayaks.

SKI AREAS The Maine Coast isn't known for skiing, but the **Camden Snow Bowl**
☺ (✉*Hosmer Pond Rd.* ☎207/236–3438, 207/236–4418 *snow phone*
★ *www.camdensnowbowl.com*) has a 950-foot-vertical mountain with 11 trails accessed by one double chair and two T-bars. The complex also includes a small lodge with a cafeteria, and ski and toboggan rentals. Activities include skiing, night skiing, snowboarding, tubing, tobogganing, and ice-skating—plus magnificent views over Penobscot Bay. The North American Tobogganing Championships, a tongue-in-cheek event open to anyone, is held annually in early February. At **Camden Hills State Park** (✉*U.S. 1 just north of downtown Camden* ☎207/236–0849), there are 10 mi of cross-country skiing trails.

SHOPPING

Camden has some of the best shopping in the region. The downtown area is a shopper's paradise with lots of interesting places to spend money. Most of the shops and galleries are along Camden's main drag, U.S. 1, so you can easily complete a shopping tour on foot. Start at the Camden Harbor, turn right on Bay View, and walk to Main/High Street. ■TIP➔ **U.S. 1 has three different names within the town limits—it starts as Elm Street, changes to Main Street, then becomes High Street. So don't let the addresses listed below throw you off.**

ABCD Books (✉*23 Bay View St.* ☎207/236–3903 or 888/236–3903) has a discriminating selection of quality antiquarian and rare books. **Lily, Lupine & Fern** (✉*43 Main St.* ☎207/236–9600) sells an appealing selection of beer and fine wines, plus gourmet foods and cheese. It also dishes up New York deli–style sandwiches. **Maine Gold** (✉*12 Bay View St.* ☎702/236–2717) sells authentic Maine maple syrup. **Planet Toys** (✉*10 Main St.* ☎207/236–4410) has unusual gifts—including books, toys, and clothing—from Maine and other parts of the world.

GALLERIES **Bayview Gallery** (✉*33 Bay View St.* ☎207/236–4534 *www.bayview-gallery.com*) specializes in original art, prints, and posters, most with Maine themes. **Small Wonder Gallery** (✉*Public Landing* ☎207/236–6005 *www.smallwondergallery.com*) has watercolors, wood engravings, metal sculptures, tiles, porcelain, and prints.

LINCOLNVILLE

6 mi north of Camden via U.S. 1.

Looking at a map, you may notice there are two parts to Lincolnville: Lincolnville Beach on U.S. 1 and the town of Lincolnville Center a little

inland on Route 73. The area of most interest—where you can find the restaurants and the ferry to Islesboro—is Lincolnville Beach. This is a tiny area; you could be through it in less than a minute. Still, it has a history going back to the Revolution, and you can see a few small cannons on the beach that were intended to repel the British in the War of 1812 (they were never used). Lincolnville is close to Camden, so it's a great place to stay if rooms in Camden are full—or if you just want someplace a little quieter.

WHERE TO EAT & STAY

$$–$$$ ✕**Chez Michel.** This little restaurant on U.S. 1 offers nice views of the bay. The menu consists of French and American cuisine, with an emphasis on steak and seafood. Owner-chef Michel Hetuin's bouillabaisse is the specialty. The potpourri of ingredients are all local and fresh, just like they are in Marseille, France, the birthplace of bouillabaisse. A bargain for the traveler is the less-expensive early-bird menu, served 4 PM–5:30 PM. ⊠*2532 Atlantic Hwy. (U.S. 1), Lincolnville Beach* ☎*207/789–5600* ⊟*AE, DC, MC, V* ⊘*No lunch weekdays.*

$–$$$ ✕**Lobster Pound Restaurant.** If you're looking for an authentic place to
Fodor's Choice   have your Maine lobster dinner, this is it. This simple restaurant looks
★   more like a cannery than a restaurant, with rustic wooden picnic tables and hundreds of live lobsters swimming in tanks—you can pick out (if you want) your own lobster. It'll be served to you with clam chowder and corn. Forget about ordering a predinner cocktail or wine with dinner; have an ice tea instead. On U.S. 1, right on the edge of the sea, the Lobster Pound provides beautiful views from both its indoor and outdoor seating. On the menu here you will see the classic "Shore Dinner," which consists of lobster stew or fish chowder, steamed or fried clams, 1½-pound lobster, potato, and dessert. Lobster and seafood are, of course, the reason to come here, though turkey and steak are also available. This restaurant has seating for nearly 300, so even if it's a busy time, you won't have to wait long. There's also a 70-seat picnic area if you want to take your food to go. ⊠*2521 Atlantic Hwy. (U.S. 1)* ☎*207/789–5550* ⊕*www.lobsterpoundmaine.com* ⊟*AE, DC, MC, V* ⊘*Closed Nov.–Apr.*

$–$$$ ✕**Whale's Tooth Pub & Restaurant.** The Revolutionary patriots could have
★   met in a pub that looked like this. It's in a historic old brick building with an interior that is reminiscent of an old English pub: dark heavy woods, dark atmosphere, a wood-burning fireplace, copper kettles. The restaurant and the pub are basically one, and among the things on the menu, you will find steamed lobsters and mussels, fried calamari, broiled scallops, and other seafood, as well as prime rib, charbroiled steaks, and pasta dishes—the most popular dish is the British style fish-and-chips. There is a deck for nice weather days. ⊠*2531 Atlantic Hwy. (U.S. 1)* ☎*207/789–5200* ⊕*www.whalestoothpub.com* ⊟*MC, DC, V* ⊘*Closed Tues.*

$$$ ✕▥**Youngtown Inn and Restaurant.** Inside this white Federal-style farm-
Fodor's Choice   house you'll find a French-inspired country retreat. The inn's bucolic
★   location, which is only five minutes by car from busy Camden, guarantees quiet, and it is a short walk from beautiful Lake Megunticook. Simple, airy rooms open to decks with views of the rolling countryside.

LOBSTER TRIVIA

How old is this lobster on my plate? It is probably around seven years old. It takes them that long to reach a size where you would want to eat them (about 1½ pounds).

What's that yucky-looking green stuff on its belly? That's the lobster's liver. It won't kill you; some people like it, most don't.

Why do lobsters start out being green and then turn red when they're cooked? Like fall leaves, the red was there all the time as background. The other colors disappear when the lobster is cooked.

Do lobsters feel pain when they are cooked? There is some con-

troversy about this. According to the state's Lobster Institute, the lobsters feel no pain because they don't have complex brains like you and I do but rather a cortex of ganglia that reacts to stimuli, sort of like an involuntary muscle reaction. A recent Norwegian study also concluded that lobsters' nervous systems don't register pain. People for the Ethical Treatment of Animals (PETA) and some scientists disagree.

For more on lobsters, check out the book *The Secret Life of Lobsters: How Fishermen and Scientists Are Unraveling the Mysteries of Our Favorite Crustacean* by Trevor Corson.

Four have fireplaces. The restaurant ($$–$$$), open to the public for dinner, serves entrées such as rack of lamb and breast of pheasant with foie gras mousse. All rooms are nonsmoking. **Pros:** This is a nationally renowned establishment, with one of the best restaurants in Maine. **Con:** If you want to do some shopping in Camden, you'll have to drive. ✉ *581 Youngtown Rd., Rte. 52 off U.S. 1 to Youngtown Rd., Lincolnville, ME 04849* ☎ *207/763–4290 or 800/291–8438* ⊕ *www.youngtowninn.com* ➾ *6 rooms* ⌂ *In-hotel: restaurant, no-smoking rooms, no elevator* ⊟ *AE, MC, V* ⊺⊙⏐*BP.*

$$$$
Fodor's Choice
★ **Inn at Ocean's Edge.** This beautiful white inn on 22 acres has one of the loveliest settings in the area, with heavy forest on one side and the ocean on the other. The inn looks as if it has been here for decades, but the original building was only built in 1999, with the upper building following in 2001. The rooms are styled simply but with old-fashioned New England elegance: a lot of quilts and throws and Colonial-style furniture. Every room has a king-size bed, an ocean view, a fireplace, and a whirlpool for two. One room is handicapped accessible; and there is an elevator for the upper floors. The elevator is small and unobtrusive, not affecting the basic look of the hotel. The inn also includes a fine restaurant, the Edge, with oceanfront dining. **Pro:** It would be tough to find an accommodation in a more beautiful setting than this. **Cons:** Abundant shopping and dining options not within walking distance; lodging is pricey. ✉ *20 Stone Coast Rd. (U.S. 1), Lincolnville* ⌖ *04843* ☎ *207/236–0945* ⊕ *www.innatoceansedge.com* ➾ *29 rooms, 3 suites* ⌂ *In-room: VCR, DVD, Wi-Fi, dial-up. In-hotel: bar, gym, pool, restaurant, no-smoking rooms* ⊟ *AE, DC, MC, V* ⊺⊙⏐*BP.*

$$$–$$$$
★ **Victorian by the Sea.** With a quiet waterside location well off U.S. 1, the Victorian feels as if it's a world away from all the hustle and bustle

of town. Most rooms and the wraparound porch have magnificent views over island-studded Penobscot Bay. Romantic touches include canopied brass beds, braided rugs, white wicker furniture, and floral wallpapers. Six guest rooms have fireplaces; four more fireplaces are in common rooms, including the glass-enclosed breakfast room. The inn is not handicapped accessible, and no pets are allowed. **Pro:** It has the romantic touch. **Con:** You'll have to drive to dinner. ⊠*33 Sea View Dr., Lincolnville* ✆*Box 1385, Camden 04843* ☎*207/236–3785 or 800/382–9817* ⊕*www.victorianbythesea.com* ⋑*5 rooms, 2 suites* ⌂*In-room: Wi-Fi, no TV. In-hotel: no-smoking rooms, no elevator* ▤*AE, MC, V* ⫿⦿*BP.*

SHOPPING

Maine Artisans Collective (⊠*2528 Atlantic Hwy. [U.S. 1]* ☎*207/789– 5376* ⊗*May–Oct.*) is a large artisans craft gallery right across from Lincolnville Beach. The **Windsor Chairmakers** (⊠*2526 Atlantic Hwy. [U.S. 1]* ☎*207/789–5188 or 800/789–5188*) sells custom-made hand-crafted beds, chests, china cabinets, dining tables, highboys, Shaker furniture, and chairs. You can even go to the back of the shop and watch the furniture being made. It's open seven days a week, from 9 to 5.

ISLESBORO

★ *3 mi east of Lincolnville via Islesboro Ferry (terminal on U.S. 1).*

If you would like to visit one of Maine's area islands but don't have much time, Islesboro is the best choice. The island is only a 20-minute ferry ride off the mainland. You can take your car with you. The drive from one end of the island to the other (on the island's only road) is lovely. It takes you through Warren State Park, a nice place to stop for a picnic and the only public camping area on the island. There are two stores on the island where you can buy supplies for your picnic: the Island Market is a short distance from the ferry terminal on the main road; and Durkee's General Store is 5 mi farther north at 863 Main Road. Next to the island's ferry terminal are the Sailor's Memorial Museum and the Grindle Point Lighthouse, both worth a brief look.

The permanent year-round population of Islesboro is about 625, but it swells to around 3,000 in summer. Most of the people who live on the island full time earn their living in one way or another from the sea. Some of them work at the three boatyards on the island, others are fishermen, and still others run small businesses. Seasonal residents may include some familiar faces: John Travolta and his wife, Kelly Preston, have a home here, as does Kirstie Alley.

The **Islesboro Ferry,** operated by the Maine State Ferry Service, departs from Lincolnville Harbor, a few hundred feet from the Lobster Pound Restaurant. Try to head out on one of the early ferries so you have enough time to drive around and get back. If you miss the last ferry, you'll have to stay on the island overnight. The ferry runs back and forth nine times a day from April through October and seven times a day from November through March. There are fewer runs on Sunday.

The round-trip cost for a vehicle and one passenger is $22.25, slightly more with additional passengers, less if you leave the vehicle behind. Call for schedules. ☎*207/789–5611.*

WHERE TO EAT & STAY

$$　✕🖼 **Village Bed & Breakfast.** If you want to stay over on Islesboro, this is pretty much it. This New England style B&B is 4 mi from the ferry. It has four rooms, all upstairs, but they're cozy and comfortable. It also has just about the only eatery on the island, a small café ($–$$) with three entrées. ✉*119 Derby Rd., 04848* ☎*207/734–9772* ⊕*www. thevillagebedandbreakfast.com* ⇆*4* ♿*In-hotel: restaurant, no elevator* ☰*MC, V* ⓄⓁ*BP.*

EN ROUTE A brief detour off U.S. 1, a few miles south of Belfast on your way up from Lincolnville, will take you through **Bayside,** a delightful little Victorian resort village by the sea. In the past, it was a summer Methodist community. Small old houses are clustered in a truly beautiful setting.

BELFAST TO BANGOR

The farther you get up the coast and away from Camden, the less touristy the area becomes and the more you see of the real Maine. Traffic jams and crowded restaurants give way to a more-relaxed and casual atmosphere, and locals start to treat you like a potential neighbor.

As you drive north on U.S. 1, you pass through the charming coastal towns of Belfast, Searsport, and Bucksport. Bangor is 20 mi inland. If you're driving up U.S. 1 on a "coastal trip," you can probably leave Bangor off your itinerary. If you want to fly in, however, Bangor International Airport is the quickest point of access to northern Penobscot Bay, Bar Harbor, Mount Desert Island, and Acadia National Park.

BELFAST

10 mi north of Lincolnville, 46 mi northeast of Augusta.

A number of Maine coastal towns, such as Wiscasset and Damariscotta, like to think of themselves as the prettiest little town in Maine, but Belfast may be the true winner of this title. It has a full variety of charms: a beautiful waterfront; an old and interesting main street climbing up from the harbor; a delightful array of B&Bs, restaurants, and shops; and a friendly population. The downtown even has old-fashioned street lamps, which set the streets aglow at night. If you like looking at old houses, many of which go all the way back to the Revolution and are in the Federal and Colonial style, just drive up and down some of the side streets. The only thing Belfast does not have is traffic jams. In 2007, Belfast was called "one of the top 10 culturally cool towns in the country" by *USA Today.*

The economy of Belfast (which was originally to be named Londonderry) has seen many changes over the years. In the 1800s, Belfast was a shipbuilding center and home to many ship captains. Starting in the early 1900s, a shoe factory, a chicken-processing plant, and a sardine-packing factory were the primary employers. The first two disappeared about 30 years ago, and the sardine-packing plant packed up in 2002. The biggest employer in Belfast now is Bank of America (which took over the facilities formerly owned by MBNA), the credit card giant, although tourism is also becoming an important industry.

WHAT TO SEE

In the mid-1800s, Belfast was home to a number of wealthy business magnates. Their mansions still stand along High Street, offering some excellent examples of Greek Revival and Federal architecture. The Belfast Chamber of Commerce Visitor Center (⊠ *17 Main St., at harbor* ☎ *207/338–5900*) can provide you with a free walking tour brochure that describes the various historic homes and buildings, as well as the old business section in the harbor area.

■ TIP → As you walk around Belfast, you will see a number of cream-color signs labeled the MUSEUM IN THE STREETS. Be sure to read them. They will tell you in easy-to-access fashion everything that you'd want to know about the history of Belfast. They are written in both English and French, for the benefit of Maine's neighbors to the north.

■ NEED A BREAK?

If you're looking for a quick and easy place to have lunch, **Alexia's** (P 207/338–9676), at the main corner of Main and High streets, serves the best pizza in town plus sandwiches and Italian food.

WHERE TO EAT

$$–$$$ ✕**Papa J's.** A subtitle to the name of this restaurant is "The Lobster Bar." "Papa J's" is not a terribly impressive name for a restaurant, but the food, service, and prices are all very attractive. Some of the specials are lobster stew, feta lobster pasta, baked haddock, and lobster pizza. ⊠ *193 Searsport Ave. (U.S. 1), between Belfast and Searsport* ☎ *207/338–6464* ▤ *AE, MC, V* ⊙ *Closed Mon. Nov.–Mar.*

$–$$$ ✕**Maine Chowder House.** An excellent place for seafood, this large, popular restaurant has been standing watch over the bay for a long time. Ask for a table by a window—the view, particularly at sunset, is spectacular. Lobster, prepared any way you like it, is a specialty, as is the chowder. Favorites include the Lazy Man's Lobster (they crack the shells for you), and the Chowder House Mariner's Platter. It also offers steaks for those who may not like seafood. If it's just a cocktail you want, you also will find the Scallywag Tavern here. This restaurant is only a short distance from the two biggest motels in the area, the Belfast Harbor Inn and the Comfort Inn. ⊠ *139 Searsport Ave. (U.S. 1), between Belfast and Searsport* ☎ *207/338–5225* ▤ *AE, DC, MC, V.*

$–$$$ ✕**Weathervane Seafood Restaurant.** Part of a New England seafood chain, this restaurant is large—so you shouldn't have to wait long for a table—and has usually good food and service, although things can get a little rushed in summer. The restaurant sits right on the edge of Belfast Harbor, overlooking the bay, and tugboats are parked outside. In summer, you can sit on the outside deck. The large menu features seafood, pasta, and steaks. A popular special is the Maine Lobster Clambake, which is boiled lobster, steamed clams, and corn on the cob.

Fresh seafood is also available to go. ✉*1 Main St., Public Landing, at base of Main St.* ☎*207/338–1777* ⊕*www.weathervaneseafoods.com* ⊟*AE, DC, MC, V.*

$–$$$ ✕**Young's Lobster Pound.** The place looks more like a corrugated steel
Fodor's Choice fish cannery than a restaurant, but this is one of the places to have an
★ authentic Maine lobster dinner. Young's sits right on the edge of the water, across the river from Belfast Harbor (cross Veterans Bridge to get here and turn right on Mitchell Avenue). When you first walk in, you'll see tanks and tanks and tanks of live lobsters of varying size. The traditional meal here is the Shore Dinner: fish or clam chowder; steamed clams or mussels; a 1½-pound boiled lobster; corn on the cob; and rolls and butter. Order your dinner at the counter then find a table inside or on the deck. ■ TIP➔ **If you are enjoying your lobster at one of the outside tables, don't leave the table with no one to man it. Seagulls are notorious thieves—and they LOVE lobster.** ✉*2 Fairview St.* ☎*207/338–1160* ⊟*AE, DC, MC, V* ⊘*Closed Labor Day–Easter.*

$–$$ ✕**Darby's Restaurant and Pub.** Darby's, a charming old-fashioned res-
★ taurant and bar, is probably the most popular restaurant in town with the locals. The building, with pressed-tin ceilings, was constructed in 1865 and has been a bar or a restaurant ever since. The antique bar is an original and has been there since 1865. The first Darby is long gone, but his name remains. Artwork on the walls is by local artists and may be purchased. A lot of the regular items on the menu, such as the pad thai and the Seafood à la Greque, are quite unusual for a small-town restaurant. It also has hearty homemade soups and sandwiches, as well as dishes with an international flavor. ✉*155 High St.* ☎*207/338–2339* ⊟*AE, DC, MC, V.*

$–$$ ✕**Dockside Family Restaurant.** On Main Street, less than a block from the
☾ harbor, Dockside has convenience strongly in its favor. It also has really good seafood—it's famous for the lobster stew. The decor is plain and simple, and the emphasis is on family dining, meaning that kids are always welcome, and the menu has special portions for them. When the weather is nice, you can sit out on the back deck and watch the boats in the harbor. ✉*30 Main St.* ☎*207/338–6889* ⊟*AE, DC, MC, V* ⊘*Closed Mon.*

$–$$ ✕**Dos Amigos.** This great Mexican restaurant is much larger than it looks from the outside. Its multiple rooms are nearly always filled with people enjoying good food and drinks at reasonable prices. The smoked-duck quesadilla is excellent, as are the burritos and margaritas. It has both indoor and outdoor dining. ✉*125 Bayside Rd. (U.S. 1), Northport, 3 mi south of Belfast* ☎*207/338–5775* ⊟*AE, DC, MC, V* ⊘*Closed mid-Dec.–mid-Mar.*

¢–$$ ✕**Belfast Co-op.** The Co-op is a very special place in Belfast, and it's
★ not unusual to hear the expression: "I'll meet you at the Co-op." The French Club meets here, and the Writers Club sometimes meets here. Everyone in town seems to meet here at one time or another. As the name would imply, this is a members cooperative store that sells organic locally produced vegetables and other food provisions. But you don't have to be a member to buy things. It operates a popular café serving coffees, teas, sandwiches, and homemade pastries. A local wag

once said: "Belfast is a retired hippie heaven." That is not really true, but if you just visited the Co-op, you might think it was. ⊠ *123 High St., 1 block from town center* ☎ *207/338–3522* ⊕ *www.belfast.coop. com* ▭ *AE, DC, MC, V.*

¢–$$ × **Ming's Restaurant.** On U.S. 1 between Belfast and Searsport, Ming's is a relatively new addition to the local dining scene, and it's an odd little place. The building that houses it is big and white, while the restaurant is small with virtually no ambience and only a couple of tables. Despite that, its been voted the area's best Chinese restaurant in a 2007 poll conducted by the *Republican Journal* newspaper. Most of the business seems to be from takeout. If you're staying in one of the nearby motels (Comfort Inn or Belfast Harbor Inn), and you have a hankering for Chinese food, call Ming's. We recommend ordering the Hunan Triple Delight. Its sister restaurant, Ming's Garden, is in Bucksport. ⊠ *185 Searsport Ave. (U.S. 1)* ☎ *207/338–2216* ▭ *DC, MC, V.*

¢–$$ × **Three Tides.** Owners and managers David and Sarah Carlson have cre-
★ ated a labor of love here, and if you like the idea of dinner on a deck overlooking the bay, this is the place. Some of the popular-with-locals favorites are the varied tapas, the crab quesadilla, and the steamed mussels and oysters. They also make their own home-brewed beer and ale. ⊠ *26 Marshall Wharf, near Belfast Landing* ☎ *207/338–1707* ▭ *DC, MC, V* ☉ *Closed Mon.*

$ × **Bay Wrap.** This is a good place if you're just looking for a quick and refreshing bite. The small but popular establishment offers an unusual and original variety of wraps. The Wraptor, roast turkey with tarragon-garlic aioli on a bed of greens, tomatoes, and onions, is delicious. The restaurant is downtown, one block off the main street. ⊠ *20 Beaver St.* ☎ *207/338–9757* ▭ *MC, V.*

WHERE TO STAY

$$–$$$ × ▦ **Comfort Inn.** This is the largest accommodation facility in the Belfast-Searsport area, and truly does have a lot of amenities. For one thing, every one of its 83 rooms and its two cottages overlook beautiful Penobscot Bay. The second-and third-floor rooms have private balconies, and the ground-floor rooms have patios. Some rooms are handicapped accessible, and some are designated for smokers. Small pets are welcome. Thanks to the Ocean's Edge ($$–$$$), you don't have to leave the property for dinner. You can get your boiled lobster right here. An elevator goes to the upper floors. **Pros:** This facility does seem to have everything, including an excellent restaurant. **Con:** You will have to drive if you want to visit the Belfast downtown. ⊠ *159 Searsport Ave. (U.S. 1), between Belfast and Searsport, 04915* ☎ *207/338–2090 or 800/303–5098* ⊕ *www.comfortinnbelfast.com* ⇆ *83 rooms, 2 cottages, 1 house.* ♿ *In-hotel: restaurant, pool public Internet, public Wi-Fi, some pets allowed, no-smoking rooms* ▭ *AE, DC, MC, V* ⦿ *CP.*

$–$$$ × ▦ **Penobscot Bay Inn.** Formerly the Belfast Bay Meadows Inn, this lovely
Fodor's Choice accommodation is on five meadowed acres overlooking Penobscot Bay
★ and is owned and managed by Kristina and Valentinas Kurapka. The rooms are bright and airy and decorated in pastel shades, with old-fashioned New England quilts on the beds. Some of the rooms even have their own fireplaces. The inn's Continental gourmet restaurant

($$–$$$$) is one of the best in the area. No smoking and no pets are allowed, but one room is handicapped accessible, as is the restaurant. **Pro:** You don't have to go out for dinner. **Con:** If you want to explore Belfast's colorful downtown, you will have to drive. ✉ *192 Northport Ave., 04915* ☎*207/338–5715 or 800/335–2370* ⊕*www.penobscot-bayinn.com* ⇨*19 rooms* ⌂*In-hotel: restaurant, no-smoking rooms, no elevator* ⊟*AE, DC, MC, V* ⦿*BP.*

$$–$$$ ⬚**Jeweled Turret Inn.** Turrets, columns, gables, and magnificent wood-
★ work embellish this inn, originally built in 1898 as the home of a local attorney. The inn is named for the jewel-like stained-glass windows in the stairway turret. The gem theme continues in the den, where the ornate rock fireplace is said to include rocks from every one of the contiguous 48 states. Elegant Victorian pieces furnish the rooms: the Opal Room has a marble bath with whirlpool tub, in addition to a French armoire and a four-poster bed. No smoking is allowed in the rooms, but there is a wraparound veranda where you can smoke. No pets are allowed. **Pros:** This is truly a beautiful place and within easy walking distance to the downtown, with its shops and restaurants. **Con:** No handicapped-accessible rooms. ✉*40 Pearl St., 04915* ☎*207/338–2304 or 800/696–2304* ⊕*www.jeweledturret.com* ⇨*7 rooms* ⌂*In-room: no a/c (some), no phone, no TV. In-hotel: no-smoking rooms, no elevator* ⊟*AE, DC, MC, V* ⦿*BP.*

$$–$$$ ⬚**White House.** This 1840 landmark by Maine architect Calvin Ryder is considered to be one of the most-sophisticated examples of Greek Revival architecture in New England. An eight-sided cupola tops the house; inside are ornate plaster ceiling medallions, Italian marble fireplaces, an elliptical flying staircase, and intricate moldings. Crystal chandeliers, Oriental rugs, antiques, and reproduction pieces elegantly decorate the spacious rooms. You can relax in the English garden, in the gazebo, or under the enormous copper beech tree. **Pro:** If you like staying in a place with a lot of early American history, this would be it. **Con:** The house is a rather long walk to Belfast shopping and restaurants. ✉*1 Church St., 04915* ☎*207/338–1901 or 888/290–1901* ⊕*www.mainebb.com* ⇨*4 rooms, 2 suites* ⌂*In-room: VCR (some). In-hotel: no-smoking rooms, no elevator* ⊟*D, MC, V* ⦿*BP.*

$–$$$ ⬚**Seascape Motel & Cottages.** An attractive and well-kept little place, Seascape has a long history, since it has been around for more than four decades. All rooms are no smoking, and the motel is not handicapped accessible, but small well-behaved pets are allowed. **Pros:** Reasonable prices, plus senior and club discounts. **Cons:** You will need to drive for dinner, and U.S. 1 can be a little noisy in summer. ✉*202 Searsport Ave. (U.S. 1), 04915* ☎*207/338–2130 or 800/477–0786* ⊕*www.seascapemotel.com* ⇨*7 rooms, 8 cottages* ⌂*In-room: refrigerator. In-hotel: pool, some pets allowed, no-smoking rooms, no elevator* ⊟*MC, V* ⊘*Closed mid-Oct.–mid-May* ⦿*CP.*

$–$$ ⬚**Belfast Harbor Inn.** Facing U.S. 1 in one direction and Penobscot Bay in the other, the Harbor Inn is the second-largest accommodation in the area. Half of the rooms have beautiful views of the sea across the spacious lawn; the other half overlook the pool. The upstairs rooms have private balconies; the lower ones have patios. There is also a nice bridal suite with a king-size bed. The rooms have been remodeled, and the complimentary Continental breakfast is more generous than most, with a lot of fresh fruit and homemade pastries. A good place for dinner is Foxy's Steakhouse, right next door. One room is handicapped accessible, and five rooms are available for smokers. Small dogs are welcome but cats aren't. **Pros:** Abundant, complimentary breakfast; Foxy's is next door, so you can walk to dinner. **Con:** You have to drive for downtown shopping. ⊠*91 Searsport Ave. (U.S. 1), 04915* ☎*207/338–2740 or 800/545–8576* ⊕*www.belfastharborinn.com* ↩*61 rooms* ⚬*In-hotel: pool, some pets allowed, no-smoking rooms, no elevator* ⊟*AE, DC, MC, V* ⦿*CP.* ·

$–$$ 🏨 **Londonderry Inn.** The name is appropriate since "Londonderry" was the first name proposed for the town of Belfast. This charming old farmhouse was originally built in 1803. The 6-acre property includes gardens, fruit trees, and bird feeders. The formal living room has a fireplace and cozy leather furniture. In the library, you can find more than 200 videos for your evening's diversion. Complimentary beverages and dessert are served in the early evening. There are no handicapped-accessible rooms. No pets are allowed, however there are two resident cats, so a warning to those who are allergic. Every room has a VCR, with a selection of movies found in the inn library. All rooms are nonsmoking. **Pro:** In a lovely and quiet setting. **Con:** You will have to drive for dinner. ⊠*133 Belmont Ave. (Rte. 3), 2 mi from downtown Belfast, 04915* ☎*207/338–2763 or 877/529–9566* ⊕*www.londonderry-inn. com* ↩*5 rooms* ⚬*In-room: refrigerator, VCR. In-hotel: no-smoking rooms, no elevator* ⊟*AE, DC, MC, V* ⦿*BP.*

NIGHTLIFE & THE ARTS

NIGHTLIFE The **Lookout Pub** (⊠*37 Front St.* ☎*207/338–8999*) offers a 40-foot "Lobster Bar," pub food, gourmet lobster rolls, some of the best burgers in town, and 17 draft beers on tap. It also has pool tables and dancing with live music on weekends.

★ **Rollie's Bar & Grill** (⊠*37 Main St.* ☎*207/338-4502* ⊟*MC, V*) looks like it's been here 100 years, but actually it's been here only since 1972. The tavern is right in the heart of Main Street, and at first glance it might look like a bikers bar. It is that—and a lot more. If you recognize the interior, it's because it was used as a setting in the Stephen King film *Thinner.* The vintage bar is from an 1800s sailing ship. Rollie's is the most popular watering spot in town with the locals, and it just may serve the best cheeseburger in the state of Maine.

THE ARTS The **Colonial Theater** (⊠*163 High St.* ☎*207/338–1930*) is a wonderful old-fashioned movie palace with an elephant on the roof. If you ask: Why is there a statue of an elephant on the roof? Belfast Mayor Mike Hurley, who owns the place, would simply respond: "Why not?" **Belfast Maskers** (⊠*43 Front St.* ☎*207/338–9668* ⊕*www.belfastmaskers. org*) is a small award-winning theater company with its own theater down by the waterfront. Two recent spokespersons there were Swedish actress Liv Ullman and Canadian actress Margot Kidder.

FESTIVALS &	**Arts in the Park** (⊕*www.belfastmaine.org/artsinthepark* ✉*Free*) takes
EVENTS	place in mid-July down by the harbor and features the works of more
than 70 Maine-area artists. **Belfast Summer Nights** (☎*207/338–8448*)
features a variety of interesting live music events every Thursday evening, from 5:30 to 7:30, for 11 weeks in summer. It takes place at the
Belfast Commons Park near the harbor and is free of charge.

SPORTS & THE OUTDOORS

AERIAL TOURS	**Coastal Helicopters.** Now here's what we call a fun trip. Take the kids
☺	up for a spectacular view of the Maine Coast from a helicopter. See
★	lighthouses, schooners, islands, and maybe even wildlife. Prices start at
$225 for ½-hour rides. ⊠*26 Airport Rd., Belfast Airport* ☎*207/338–*
3755 ⊕*www.950B.com* ☉*Tours are not on any schedule, they are
offered year-round on an as-called basis* ▭*MC, V.*

BOATING	**Belfast Bay Cruises** (⊠*Thompson Wharf, near Belfast Landing*
☺	☎*207/338–1063 or 207/322–5530* ⊕*www.belfastbaycruises.com*
★	✉*$13–$25* ☉*Mid-June–mid-Oct.*) sets passengers asea on the *Good
Return*, which seats about 45 people and takes trips to the beautiful little town of Castine and back. During the layover in Castine,
you might want to have lunch at Dennett's, which sits right over the
water. The *Good Return* also offers harbor cruises, lobstering cruises,
and an ice-cream cruise. Owner Melissa Terry is your captain. It is
handicapped accessible, and well-behaved leashed pets are welcome.
If you just wanted to go on a short and inexpensive sailing trip on
Penobscot Bay, the **Friendship Sloop Amity** (⊠*Belfast Landing, 1 Main
St.* ☎*207/469–0849 or 207/323–1443* ⊕*www.friendshipsloopamity*
✉*Morning sail $20 a person, afternoon sail and sunset sail $30 a person* ☉*Late May–early Oct.*) may be the one for you. The sloop was
built in 1901 but is still in fine shape. You can even help to raise the
sails or take a turn at the helm if you want. Morning sails are 1½ hours,
afternoon sails are 2½ hours, and there are also two-hour sunset sails.
Wanderbird Expedition Cruises (⊠*Belfast Landing, 1 Main St.* ☐*Box
272, 04915* ☎*207/338–3088 or 866/732–2473* ⊕*www.wanderbird-
cruises.com* ☉*May–Oct.*) is a fairly new arrival to the Belfast Harbor.
The boat is large and looks like it was once a blue-collar working boat.
As a result of the size, they are able to take trips to distant points, as
far away as northern Labrador. Look at the Web site for a complete list
of the many cruises. Owners and captains are Rick and Karen Miles.
There is a big difference in the prices of the trips based on the distance
of the destination. A 3-day "Spring on the Bay" trip cost $750, while
a 12-day trip to Newfoundland and Labrador cost $3,000 (prices are
per person). The Miles' shop at 33 Main Street near the harbor also
takes reservations and sells many nautical items.

CURLING	**Belfast Curling Club** (⊠*211 Belmont Ave. [Rte. 3], 3 mi west of Belfast*
☎*207/338–9851*) is just about the only place in this area of Maine
where you can see the strange sport of curling, and they love visitors.
Activities take place throughout the week, November through March.
Call for times.

HIKING **Secret Trail.** We're going to tell you about a great little hiking trail that hardly anyone knows about—not even many of the people who live in the area. It's called the **Belfast Reservoir Trail,** and here's how you find it. Go south on U.S. 1 from Belfast a short distance. You will see the Little River Church on your right. Just past that—look closely—you will see a sign for the Belfast Water District. Pull in there and park at the sign that says HIKERS. The beautiful woodland trail, which winds along the Little River, is 2.8 mi each way.

KAYAKING **Water Walker Sea Kayak** (⌂ *152 Lincolnville Ave.* ☎ *207/338–6424* ⊕ *www.touringkayaks.com* ▭ *AE, DC, MC, V*) provides guided sea kayak trips among the islands of Penobscot Bay. Paddlers of all levels are welcome. Instructions, rentals, and sales also are available.

4

NEED A BREAK?

What could be better for you and the kids than an ice-cream break? You will find a wonderful array of all things ice cream, including crepes, at Scoops (⌂ *35 Main St.* ☎ *207/338–3350*), right in the heart of downtown.

🕙 **SHOPPING**

Belfast is an easy town in which to shop: nearly all of the interesting little stores are centered around the intersection of Main and High streets. **All About Games** (⌂ *78 Main St.* ☎ *207/338–9984*) sells any kind of game you could want, including a "Maine" version of Monopoly. The name and the storefront window of the **Chocolate Drop Candy Shop** (⌂ *60 Main St.*) are a little deceiving since they imply simple old-fashioned candies, but the reality is that on the inside, it's a gourmet candy shop with handmade luxury chocolates. Try the white Russian Kahlua truffle. We're not sure why a clown would be selling fine wines and luxury gourmet gifts, but the **Clown** (⌂ *74 Main St.* ☎ *207/338–4344* ⊕ *www.the-clown.com*) is a good shop for browsing and for sampling wine at its frequent wine tastings. **Colburn Shoe Store** (⌂ *79 Main St.* ☎ *207/338–1934 or 877/338–1934*) is worth a visit simply because it's the oldest shoe store in America. At one time, the making of shoes was a major industry in Belfast. The **Fertile Mind Book Shop** (⌂ *105 Main St.* ☎ *207/338–2498*) has all kinds of reading matter, much of it about Maine. The **Green Store** (⌂ *71 Main St.* ☎ *207/338–4045*) sells environmentally friendly products from lightbulbs to clothing. The **Purple Baboon** (⌂ *31 Front St., just off Main near the harbor* ☎ *207/338–6505*) is an unusual shop that sells gifts, collectibles, and souvenirs. The **Shamrock, Thistle & Rose** (⌂ *39 Main St.* ☎ *207/338–1864* ⊕ *www.shamrockthistlerose.com*) sells clothing, jewelry, art, and music from Ireland, Scotland, and England.

GALLERIES At the **Parent Gallery** (⌂ *92 Main St.* ☎ *207/338–1553* ⊕ *www.neal-parent.com*), a talented father and daughter have their painting and photographic works displayed. The **Phoenix Gallery** (⌂ *157 High St.* ☎ *207/338–0087* ⊕ *www.phoenixloftgallery.com*) has an interesting collection of regional and local artists.

SHOP EN
ROUTE

One of the first places you come to after you cross the U.S. 1 bridge, heading north toward Searsport, is the legendary **Perry's Nuthouse** (✉ *17 Searsport Ave. [U.S. 1]* ☎ *207/338–1630*). Perry's has been here since 1927, and the building dates back to 1850. The delicious treats for sale include nuts from around the world, homemade fudge, local honeys, and Maine maple syrup. American Indian handicrafts are also available. **Mainely Pottery** (✉ *181 Searsport Ave. [U.S. 1]* ☎ *207/338–1108* ⊕ *www.mainelypottery.com*) offers outstanding pottery from 30 Maine potters. **Yankee Trader Gift Shop** (✉ *169 Searsport Ave. [U.S. 1]* ☎ *207/338–2475*) offers a wide variety of gifts, many of them made in Maine.

SEARSPORT

6 mi northeast of Belfast, 57 mi northeast of Augusta.

Searsport is well known as the antique and flea market capital of Maine, and with good reason: the Antique Mall alone, on U.S. 1 just north of town, contains the offerings of 70 dealers, and flea markets during the visitor season line both sides of U.S. 1.

But antiques are not the town's only point of interest; Searsport also has a rich history of shipbuilding and seafaring. In the early to mid-1800s, there were 10 shipbuilding facilities in Searsport. The population of the town was about 1,000 people more than it is today because of the ready availability of jobs. By the mid-1800s, Searsport was home to more than 200 sailing ship captains, more than any other town in America, according to the Penobscot Marine Museum. It was commonly said then that when a captain took a cargo to Hong Kong, if he walked down the main street, he was more likely to meet someone from Searsport than from China.

Except for a few rotting pilings down at the waterfront, signs of the shipbuilding industry are gone now. It all disappeared after the invention of the steam engine and the growth of the steamship business. Steamships were larger, could carry more cargo, and were more efficient and safer. But thanks to those old shipyards, Searsport still has the second-deepest port on the coast of Maine, after Portland. If you read the Tom Clancy novel *The Hunt for Red October*, or saw the movie, you may recall that the men on the stolen submarine were looking on a sea chart for a little-used deepwater port on the Atlantic Coast where they could hide out submerged and undetected. They found it at Searsport. For further info, check the Searsport Web site: ⊕*www.searsportme.net.*

NEED A
BREAK?

For a delicious selection of homemade pastries and coffee, stop in at **Coastal Coffee** (✉ *25 Main St.* ☎ *207/548–2400*) right in the heart of downtown. It's open 6 AM–2 PM, Monday through Saturday.

The seafaring history of Searsport can best be observed at Maine's largest maritime museum, the Penobscot Marine Museum. It's also evident in the many former sea captains' homes along U.S. 1, many of which have been converted to bed-and-breakfasts. Searsport's downtown area is only a block long and can easily be explored in less than an hour.

WHAT TO SEE

Fodor'sChoice The **Penobscot Marine Museum** is dedicated to the history of Penobscot
★ Bay and the maritime history of Maine. The exhibits, artifacts, souve-
☺ nirs, and paintings are displayed in a unique setting of seven historic buildings, including two sea captains' houses, and five other buildings in an original seaside village. The various exhibits provide fascinating documentation of the region's seafaring way of life. The museum's outstanding collection of marine art includes the largest gathering in the country of works by Thomas and James Buttersworth. Also of note are photos of local sea captains; a collection of China-trade merchandise; artifacts of life at sea (including lots of scrimshaw); navigational instruments; tools from the area's history of logging, granite cutting, fishing, and ice cutting; treasures collected by seafarers from around the globe; and models of famous ships. The museum also has a rotating exhibit every year on a different theme. Two recent themes have been "Pirates!" and "Lobstahs!" Next to the museum, you can find the Penobscot Marine Museum Store, where you can buy anything nautical. ⌧ *5 E. Main St. (US. 1)* ☎*207/548–2529* ⊕*www.penobscotmarinemuseum.org* ⌧*$8* ☾*Memorial Day–mid-Oct., Mon.–Sat. 10–5, Sun. noon–5.*

OFF THE
BEATEN
PATH

Sears Island. This is the largest uninhabited island off the coast of Maine, measuring some 940 acres. The forested island is about a mile long and a half mile wide and is home to a variety of wildlife, plants, and birds. Although you cannot drive on the island—you have to walk across a causeway to get here—a paved road bisects the island, making it an excellent place for a bike ride, hike, or picnic. The 9-mi shoreline perimeter also makes an excellent hike at low tide (check the daily paper). You might even see seals sunning themselves on the rocks. Camping is not allowed. ⌧ *Take U.S. 1 north from Searsport and turn right on Sears Island Rd.* ⌧*Free.*

WHERE TO EAT

$$$–$$$$ ✕**Rhumb Line.** Yes, there is such a word as "rhumb." For those who
Fodor'sChoice are not sailors, a rhumb line is one of the points of a mariner's com-
★ pass. But more important than that, this is a dining experience which many people come a long distance to sample. The restaurant, in an 18th-century sea captain's home, delivers fine dining and is operated by owners/chefs Charles and Diana Evans. Specials include pan-seared peppered swordfish with Vidalia onion piccalilli, horseradish-crusted salmon with rémoulade sauce, and grilled rack of lamb with fig-infused balsamic mint sauce. ⌧*200 E. Main St. (U.S. 1)* ☎*207/548–2600* ⊕*www.therhumblinerestaurant.com* ▤*MC, V* ☾*Closed Mon. and Tues. No lunch.*

$–$$$ ✕**Old Mill Stream Eatery.** In the facilities of the former Chocolate Grille, this relatively new eatery—the largest in the Searsport area—is right beside a stream that was once used by an old mill. Due to its size, you will not have to wait for a table. The fare is basic seafood and steaks,

A Vanished Industry

In the mid-1800s, there was a major industry in Maine that gave work to thousands of men each winter. The product of this industry was so valuable that it was shipped around the world in the great tall-masted schooners. The industry no longer exists, although the product does. Can you guess what this profitable product and industry was? Believe it or not, it was ice.

During Maine's freezing cold winter months, loggers and farmers who couldn't do their normal work would go out to Maine's freshwater rivers and lakes and cut ice from the frozen waters. Using string lines, the men would section the ice off into 2-by-4-foot rectangles. Then they would use one-handled saws to cut the ice into blocks, weighing about 200 pounds each. The blocks of ice would be loaded onto horse-drawn sleds and taken to an icehouse. Finally, the ice would be loaded aboard a schooner for transport. They packed the ice in straw and sawdust to help insulate it, but they still lost about 20% to melt. The other 80% could be sold for a generous profit all over the world. On the way back, they could even sell the dried-out straw. There are pictures and examples of tools left from the ice industry on display at the Penobscot Marine Museum, in Searsport.

but the chef is especially known for his stuffed baked haddock. The large bar is a popular spot where locals meet up with friends for watching sporting events. It is handicapped accessible. ⊠*1 E. Main St. (U.S. 1)* ☎*207/548–0365* ▤*AE, D, DC, MC, V.*

$–$$ ✕**Abbracci.** If an Italian restaurant is good, it does not take long for it to gain a following, and that has been the story with Abbracci. Fairly new on the scene, it started out as a little bakery and espresso bar, and then it got into simple Italian food, such as pizza, calzones, and sandwiches. Now, its popular signature dish is the eggplant Parmesan, just like they make it in southern Italy. Fans say Abbracci's makes the best pizza in Maine. ⊠*225 W. Main St. (U.S. 1)* ☎*207/548–2010* ⊕*www. abbraccime.com* ▤*DC, MC, V* ☉*Closed Mon.*

$–$$ ✕**Anglers.** This little restaurant has been around for a long time and has a large local following. It can be a little hard to get into on a busy night, but it's worth the wait. The seafood is good, the prices are reasonable, and the service is friendly—this is the kind of place where the waitresses call you "Hon." ⊠*U.S. 1, 1 mi north of downtown* ☎*207/548–2405* ▤*DC, MC, V.*

$–$$ ✕**The Mariner.** This cozy spot in the heart of downtown has a simple, pub-like atmosphere, with good drinks and good, inexpensive food. In summer, lobster and crabmeat rolls are on the menu, along with the year-round selections of burgers, sandwiches, and, of course, lobster stew. Dinner entrées include fried jumbo shrimp and fried haddock. ⊠*23 E. Main St. (U.S. 1)* ☎*207/548–6600* ▤*MC, V.*

WHERE TO STAY

$$–$$$ 🏠 **Captain A. V. Nickels Inn.** For many years, this huge old ship captain's
Fodor'sChoice home on U.S. 1 stood like a skeleton of what it had once been. It was
★ empty and unused. But then Daniel and Sherri Hanson came along,

bought the property, and with some imaginative design and a lot of paint turned it into what is now the most beautiful house in Searsport. Even if you are not staying there, you will want to stop and have a look. You can't miss it since it's right on U.S. 1. The house was built originally in 1874 by sea captain A. V. Nickels and has been placed on the National Registry of Historic Homes. The Hansons have wisely opened the property up to many functions. In addition to a B&B inn, it is also available for weddings, receptions, and various gatherings. All rooms are no smoking and there is no handicapped access. **Pros:** You will go a long way to find anything as beautiful as this, and the rates are not bad. **Con:** It's a little bit of walk to downtown shopping and dining. ⊠ *127 Main St. (U.S. 1), 04974* ☎ *207/548–0055* ⊕ *www. captainavnickelsinn.com* ⮑ *6 rooms, 1 suite* ♿ *In-room: Wi-Fi. In-hotel: no-smoking rooms, no elevator* ▭ *AE, MC, V* ⓇCP.

$$–$$$ ★ 🏨 **1794 Watchtide . . . By the Sea.** This inn, on the National Register of Historic Places, was built, as the name implies, in 1794. It has been a favorite of many visitors, among them Eleanor Roosevelt, who stayed here many times on her way up to Campobello Island. The first owner of the property was Henry Knox, George Washington's Secretary of War. Today's owners are Patricia and Frank Kulla, former publishing mavens who created Lyceum Books. All of the rooms are furnished in New England style, and two of them have great views of Penobscot Bay. Breakfast out on the glassed-in porch overlooking the sea is a three-course affair. Watchtide is not handicapped accessible. **Pro:** You can sleep in the room where Eleanor Roosevelt slept! **Cons:** You will need to drive to dinner or shopping; also, right on U.S. 1, some of the rooms can be a little noisy when you are trying to sleep. ⊠ *190 W. Main St. (U.S. 1), 04974* ☎ *207/548–6575 or 800/698–6575* ⊕ *www. watchtide.com* ⮑ *4 rooms, 1 suite* ♿ *In-room: refrigerator, no phone, no TV. In-hotel: no-smoking rooms, no elevator* ▭ *AE, DC, MC, V* ☽ *Closed Nov.–Apr.* ⓇBP.

$–$$ 🏨 **Carriage House Inn.** Ernest Hemingway liked this place. How's that for an endorsement? This stately Victorian mansion is listed on the National Register of Historic Places. The home was built in 1874 by one of Searsport's many clipper-ship captains, John McGilvery. Later, it became the home of the impressionist painter Waldo Pierce. Pierce was a close friend of Ernest Hemingway's, whom he met in the ambulance corps, and Hemingway came here a number of times. One can only imagine what their conversations in the library must have been like. The house is filled with heirlooms from the 19th-century era of the great clipper ships, and there is a solid stone fireplace in the downstairs den. **Pro:** You could stay in the room where Hemingway slept! **Con:** Not really near any restaurants; you will need to drive for dinner. ⊠ *120 E. Main St. (U.S. 1), 04974* ☎ *207/548–2167 or 800/578–2167* ⊕ *www.carriagehouseinmaine.com* ⮑ *3 rooms* ♿ *In-room: no a/c, no phone, no TV. In-hotel: no-smoking rooms, no elevator* ▭ *AE, DC, MC, V* ⓇBP.

$–$$ 🏨 **Yardarm Motel.** Originally built in 1953, the Yardarm has been renovated and expanded and offers attractive, moderately priced rooms. **Pros:** Inexpensive rooms, large free Continental breakfast, a laundry facility across the street. Con: U.S. 1 can be a bit noisy in summer. ✉ *172 E. Main St. (U.S. 1), 04974* ☎ *207/548–2404* ⤶ *15 rooms* ☖ *In-room: Wi-Fi. In-hotel: no-smoking rooms* ☰ *AE, DC, MC, V* ☾ *Closed Nov.–Apr.*

¢–$ 🏠 **Bait's Motel.** If you ever saw the Alfred Hitchcock movie *Psycho,* then you probably stopped taking showers if you're a woman, and you may think you should avoid a place called the "Bates Motel." Well, with tongue-in-cheek, the new name of this old motel is "Bait's." The owners justify the name by being right next door to an excellent seafood restaurant, Anglers . . . so, if someone named Norman checks in, it's okay, really. The rooms in this small, single-story motel are small and simple but also clean and inexpensive. **Pros:** Lowest rates in the area and right next to a good restaurant. **Cons:** The rooms and their decor are simplicity in the extreme; no lobby. ✉ *215 E. Main St. (U.S. 1), 04974* ☎ *207/548–7299* ⤶ *14 rooms* ☖ *In-hotel: no-smoking rooms* ☰ *D, MC, V.*

¢–$ 🏕 **Searsport Shores Ocean Camping.** This campsite sits right on the edge
★   of the ocean, and offers spectacular views from most of its sites. It has 120 sites on 40 acres for RVs and tents. Also offered are attractive gardens, nature trails, art classes, and activities for the kids. **Pro:** It's rare to find a camping site with a view, but this one has spectacular views of the bay. **Cons:** Searsport Shores is nationally famous, and as a result it fills up quickly during peak season; there are no sit-down restaurants within walking distance. ✉ *216 W. Main St. (U.S. 1), 04974* ☎ *207/548–6059* ⊕ *www.campocean.com* ☖ *Beachfront, flush toilets, partial hookup, drinking water, guest laundry, showers, fire pits, picnic tables, public telephone, play area* ☰ *D, MC, V* ☾ *Closed Nov.–Apr.*

DID YOU KNOW?   The word "penobscot" is believed to be a derivative of the original Algonquin Indian word meaning "waters of descending ledges." Descending rock ledges can, in fact, be seen along the Penobscot River.

NIGHTLIFE & THE ARTS

FESTIVALS &   **Fourth of July Fireworks.** People come from miles around to watch Sears-
EVENTS   port's free annual Fourth of July fireworks display, which is set off from Mosman Park, at the edge of the sea. The fireworks start at 9 PM, and the best place to view them is from the nearby public pier at the end of
★   Steamboat Avenue. The **Lobster Boat Races** are an annual series of events that take place in the major fishing communities (eight of them) up and down Penobscot Bay. The original intention of the races was to give lobstermen a way to blow off a little steam and to show off their boats and abilities. Thanks to the American spirit of obsessive competition, however, some boatmen in recent years have had high-powered lobster boats constructed specifically for these races. They'll burn up an expensive engine and swamp other nearby boats just to win the competition and a $50 trophy. "Bragging rights," it's called. But hey, it's all in the spirit of fun, and for observers and participants, it *is* a lot of fun. The Searsport race takes place in the middle of July at the town pier at the end of Steamboat Avenue. Call the town office at 207/548–6372 for the exact date. There's no charge to watch the race, and everyone—especially the boatmen—turns it into a big party.

SPORTS & THE OUTDOORS

The Searsport Town Landing, at the end of Steamboat Avenue, provides several floats where you can fish for mackerel or, occasionally, stripers. Kids like to do a little crabbing with bait at the end of a line here as well. Shore fishing can be done at the Sears Island Causeway, at the end of Sears Island Road, off U.S. 1.

GOLF The **Searsport Pines Golf Course** (✉ *240 Mt. Ephraim Rd.* ☎ *207/548–2854*) is a 9-hole, 36-par public course just west of town. It also has a pro for golf lessons. Greens fees are $20 ($30 with cart). Mt. Ephraim Road starts in the very heart of the two-block downtown.

NEED A BREAK? If you're looking for a quick, easy, and inexpensive place to make a stop on U.S. 1 for breakfast or lunch, the most popular eating place in the Stockton Springs area is Just Barb's (✉ *24 W. Main St. (U.S. 1)* ☎ *207/567–3886*), which has simple food and friendly waitresses.

SHOPPING

ANTIQUES In Searsport, shopping usually implies antiques or flea markets. Both stretch along both sides of U.S. 1 a mile or so north of downtown. **All Small Antiques** (✉ *357 W. Main St.* ☎ *207/338–1613*) has just what the name implies. In the very heart of town, **Captain Tinkham's Emporium** (✉ *34 E. Main St.* ☎ *207/548–6465*) offers antiques, collectibles, old books, magazines, records, paintings, and prints. Hundreds of teddy bears and antiques can be found at **Cranberry Hollow** (✉ *157 W. Main St.* ☎ *207/548–2647*). The owner even makes custom bears from old fur coats. **Pumpkin Patch Antiques** (✉ *15 W. Main St.* ☎ *207/548–6047*) displays such items as quilts, nautical memorabilia, and painted and wood furniture from about 20 dealers. It's open April through Thanksgiving or by appointment. The biggest collection of antiques is in the **Searsport Antique Mall** (✉ *149 E. Main St. [U.S. 1]* ☎ *207/548–2640*), which has more than 70 dealers.

BOOKS & ART **Cronin & Murphy Fine Art** (✉ *36 E. Main St.* ☎ *207/548–0073*) features 20th-century paintings, art, pottery, and items from the Modernist movement. **Left Bank Books** (✉ *21 E. Main St.* ☎ *207/548–6400*) is a labor of love by three book-loving ladies. The shop is in a historic old brick building that was the home of Searsport's first bank in 1840. It displays 6,000 books in the categories of fiction, nonfiction, biography, history, travel, and children's. **Penobscot Books & Gallery** (✉ *164 W. Main St.* ☎ *207/548–6490*) carries nearly 40,000 books, specializing in books about fine art and architecture. From U.S. 1 you can't miss this place—it's huge and yellow. The store is closed Monday.

GIFTS & MORE The **Grasshopper Shop** (✉ *37 E. Main St.* ☎ *207/548–2244*) is devoted to clothing, jewelry, and Maine-made gifts. More than 70 craft dealers show their wares at **Silkweeds Country and Victorian Gifts** (✉ *191 E. Main St. [U.S. 1]* ☎ *207/548–6501*), which is part of a chain. The store is large and specializes in Christmas goodies, among other things, including many varieties of homemade fudge. If you're looking for live lobsters to cook on your own and a nice wine to go with them, you can't go wrong at Searsport's large and varied market, **Tozier's** (✉ *220*

E. Main St. ☎*207/548–6220).* It has lobsters in the tank, sandwiches made to order, excellent pizza, and a fine variety of wines.

MARINE-
RELATED **Bluejacket Shipcrafters** (✉*160 E. Main St., just a little north of downtown* ☎*207/548–9970* ⊕*www.bluejacketinc.com*) is the largest model-ship company in the United States. The **Penobscot Marine Museum Store** (✉*40 E. Main St.* ☎*207/548–0334* ⊕*www.penobscotmarinemuseum.org*) is right next to the museum and has a large collection of pottery, paintings, books, and ship paraphernalia. The store is closed November through April.

EN
ROUTE As you head north on U.S. 1 from Searsport, a detour at the little town of Stockton Springs will take you to the **Fort Point State Park & Lighthouse** (✉*Cape Jellison* ☎*207/567–3356).* This lovely park sits on a peaceful peninsula jutting into the bay. This is a delightful place for a picnic and there are many nice walks through the woods. The 1837 lighthouse is open by appointment only.

Maine is famous for its blueberries, one of the most important crops in the state. In August and September, you can pick your own blueberries at **Staples Homestead** (✉*1194 Cape Jellison Rd., Stockton Springs* ☎*207/567–3393).* This farm has been in the same family since 1838. Call first for directions.

A little north of Stockton Springs, U.S. 1 separates into U.S. 1 and U.S. 1A. U.S. 1 goes to Bucksport and Bar Harbor, while U.S. 1A goes to Bangor. If you take 1, you will go through Bucksport and Ellsworth before you get to Mount Desert Island. If you take 1A, you will go through Frankfort, Winterport, and Hampden before you get to Bangor. The Old Winterport Commercial House (E. 114 Main St. [U.S. 1], Winterport ☎207/223–5854 ⊕www.antiquesandreusables.com), on the road from Searsport to Bucksport, is worth a stop. It has 3,200 square feet of American and European furniture, antiques, and curios. If you're heading up U.S. 1A to Bangor, an interesting and inexpensive place you can stop for lunch is **Rosie's Homestyle Diner** (✉*136 Main St. (U.S. 1A), Winterport* ☎*207/223—5003).* Inside, it feels like you've entered a *Twilight Zone* set of the 1950s.

BUCKSPORT

9 mi north of Searsport via U.S. 1.

The new Penobscot Narrows Bridge, spanning the Penobscot River, welcomes visitors to Bucksport, a town founded in 1763 by Jonathan Buck. A Puritan, Buck hated witchcraft and sentenced to death a local woman thought to be a witch. Legend has it that before she was hanged, she cast a curse upon him, saying that he would never escape her presence, even in his grave.

Buck died in 1795 and was buried in a cemetery east of Bucksport. A monument to honor the founder of the town was erected at the gravesite in 1852. As the monument weathered, an image in the shape of a woman's leg began to form under his name. You can see her leg on his stone to this day.

WHAT TO SEE

☉ **Fort Knox State Park.** Since Fort Knox and the Penobscot Narrows Bridge Observatory are two of the top sights along Maine's Mid-Coast region, you can visit both of them at the same time, since they are side by side. Your $5 ticket to the observatory will include free admission to Fort Knox. The largest fort in Maine, Fort Knox was built between 1844 and 1869 when the British were

> **BIG FOOT IN MAINE?**
>
> Guess what they found when they blasted the rocks in the huge cliff near the Penobscot Narrows Bridge. A nearly 20-foot-high footprint, complete with five toes, imprinted on the rock. You can see it if you stop at the observation area on U.S. 1 just before the bridge, walk up toward the bridge and look up to your left. What's the explanation for it? Nobody knows, but it's fun trying to guess.

disputing the borderline between Maine and New Brunswick. The fort was intended to protect the Penobscot River valley from a British naval attack. The fort never saw any actual fighting, but it was used for troop training and a garrison during the Civil War and the Spanish-American War. Visitors are welcome to explore the fort's passageways and many rooms, but few areas of it are accessible to those in wheelchairs. Guided tours are available during the summer season. ⊠ *Rt. 174, right next to Penobscot Narrows Bridge* ☎ *207/469–6553* ⊕ *www.fortknox.maine-guide.com* ⊠ *$3* ⊗ *May–Oct., daily 8:30–dusk.*

☉ **Penobscot Narrows Bridge & Observatory Tower.** This new, 2,120-foot-long

Fodor's Choice bridge, opened at the end of 2006, has been declared an engineering

★ marvel. It is certainly beautiful to look at or to drive over (no toll). Spanning the Penobscot River at Bucksport, the bridge replaced the old Waldo-Hancock bridge, built in 1931. The best part of it is the three-story observation tower at the top of the western pilon. This was the first bridge observation tower built in America and, at 420 feet above the river, it's the highest bridge observation tower in the world. An elevator shoots you to the top. The cost is $5. Don't miss it—the view, which encompasses the river, the bay, and the sea beyond, is breathtaking. ⊠ *711 Ft. Knox Rd., at U.S. 1, 04416.*

WHERE TO EAT & STAY

$$ ✕ **MacLeod's Restaurant.** There are not many places to eat in Bucksport, so MacLeod's, right across the street from the Best Western motel, is probably your best option. The menu is impressive for a small-town place, and includes dishes such as raspberry roasted duck and a seafood dinner called the Captain's Boat. ⊠ *51 Main St.* ☎ *207/469–3963* ⊟ *DC, MC, V* ⊗ *No lunch.*

$ ⊞ **Spring Fountain Motel.** A large place (for Bucksport), Spring Fountain is easy to find right on U.S 1. The rooms are simple and modestly priced. **Pros:** Smokers welcome in some rooms, pet-friendly, some kitchen units. **Con:** No handicapped-accessible rooms. ⊠ *196 Main St. (U.S. 1), 04416* ☎ *207/469–3139* ⊕ *www.springfountainmotel.com* ⇆ *42 rooms* ⊘ *In-hotel: some pets allowed, no-smoking rooms, no elevator* ⊟ *AE, DC, MC, V.*

EN
ROUTE

★

Halfway between Bucksport and Ellsworth, an abandoned chicken-process-ing facility has been converted into the **Big Chicken Barn Books & Antiques** (✉ *1768 Bucksport Rd. [U.S. 1]* ☎ *207/667–7308* ⊕ *www.bigchickenbarn. com*). Have a love for books? Especially old books? Here's the place for you. Antiques, collectibles, and thousands of books cover 21,000 square feet of retail space. It's worth a stop.

BANGOR

133 mi northeast of Portland, 20 mi northwest of Bucksport, 46 mi west of Bar Harbor.

The second-largest city in the state (Portland being the first), Bangor is about 20 mi from the coast and is the unofficial capital of northern Maine. Back in the 19th century its most important product and export in the "Queen City" was lumber from the state's vast North Woods. Bangor's location on the Penobscot River helped make it the world's largest lumber port. A 31-foot-tall statue of legendary lumberman Paul Bunyan stands in front of the Bangor Auditorium.

Lumber is no longer at the heart of its economy, but Bangor has thrived in other ways. Because of its airport, Bangor has become a gateway to Mount Desert Island, Bar Harbor, and Acadia National Park.

Bangor International is also the first American airport where troops returning from Iraq touch down. There is always a welcoming party of locals waiting for them, no matter what hour of the day or night. Free cell-phone use, gifts, and eats are available to any soldier.

The city is also home to author Stephen King, who lives in an old Vic-torian house on West Broadway notable for its bat-winged iron gate. King and his wife, Tabitha, are active members of the community and contribute to local charities, the arts, and education.

WHAT TO SEE

The **Cole Land Transportation Museum** chronicles the history of transporta-tion in Maine through historical photographs and 200 vehicles. This is also the home of a World War II Memorial, a Vietnam Veterans Memo-rial, and a Purple Heart Memorial. ✉ *405 Perry Rd.* ☎ *207/990–3600* ⊕ *www.colemuseum.org* 🎫 *$5* ☉ *May–mid-Nov., daily 9–5.*

☙ The **Maine Discovery Museum** is the largest children's museum north of Boston. It has three floors with more than 60 interactive exhibits. Kids can explore Maine's ecosystem in Nature Trails, travel to foreign countries in Passport to the World, and walk through Maine's literary classics in Booktown. ✉ *74 Main St.* ☎ *207/262–7200* ⊕ *www.maine-discoverymuseum.org* 🎫 *$5.50* ☉ *Tues.–Thurs. and Sat. 9:30–5, Fri. 9:30–8, Sun. 11–5.*

WHERE TO EAT

$$–$$$
★

✕ **Opus Restaurant.** Opus, which is an odd name for a restaurant, is a relatively new addition to the Bangor scene. It is the love child of chef Roger Gelis and manager Virginia Yonek. The menu is large, varied, and unusual. You can have your duck three different ways, including one with a soy glaze. For a new twist on the way you enjoy lobster, try it fried. If you call 24 hours in advance, you can get the eight-course chef's tasting menu ($65 a person), which we highly recommend. ✉*193 Broad St.* ☎*207/945–5100* ▭*AE, MC, V* ☽*Closed Sun. and Mon.*

$$–$$$ ✕**Thistle's.** Paintings by local artists adorn the walls in this bright store-front restaurant. The diverse menu includes entrées such as Argentinian steak with chimichurri sauce, pickled ginger salmon piccata, and roast duckling. Musicians often perform during dinner. ✉*175 Exchange St.* ☎*207/945–5480* ▭*MC, V* ☽*Closed Sun.*

$–$$ ✕**Baldacci's.** It was Momma Baldacci, grandmother of the current governor of Maine John Baldacci, who started this restaurant way back in 1933, and she called it "Momma Baldacci's." Now it is just "Baldacci's," but it is still run by the family. Because of the restaurant's relationship to the governor, it often has charity dinners, at which one of the servers may be a Bangor writer named Stephen King. Ever heard of him? The full range of Italian food is offered, including pizzas. ✉*12 Alden St.* ☎*207/945–5813* ▭*AE, DC, MC, V* ☽*Closed Sun.*

$–$$ ✕**Nicky's Cruisin' Diner.** If you just want something that is fast, easy,
★ inexpensive, and most of all, *fun,* drive up to Nicky's. And we do mean drive up, because you can eat in your car or go inside. Just like a scene out of the movie *Grease,* on weekends you'll usually find a bunch of cars from the 1950s in the parking lot. Fare includes burgers, fries, and shakes. ✉*957 Union St.* ☎*207/942–3430* ▭*AE, DC, MC, V.*

WHERE TO STAY

$–$$$ ✕▤**Lucerne Inn.** This is one of the most famous and respected inns in
Fodor'sChoice New England. Nestled in the mountains, the Lucerne overlooks beauti-
★ ful Phillips Lake. The inn was established in 1814, and in keeping with that history, every room is furnished with antiques. The rooms all have a view of the lake, gas-burning fireplaces, and a whirlpool tub; some have wet bars, refrigerators, and balconies as well. There's a golf course directly across the street. The inn's restaurant ($$–$$$$) is nearly as famous as the inn and draws many of the local people for its lavish Sunday brunch buffet. The traditional dinner among guests is the boiled Maine lobster. The inn is about 15 mi from Bangor. Several rooms are available for smokers; two rooms are handicapped accessible. No pets are allowed. **Pros:** Some of the rooms have lovely views of Phillips Lake (you can request one), and the Sunday brunch is famous—but be sure to make a reservation for it. **Con:** The inn, while famous, has been around for awhile, and some of the rooms are a little on the shabby side. ✉*2517 Main St. (Rte. 1A), Dedham 04429* ☎*207/843–5123 or 800/325–5123* ⊕*www.lucerneinn.com* ⬅*31 rooms, 4 suites* ⌂*In-room: Wi-Fi. In-hotel: restaurant, bar, pool, no-smoking rooms* ▭*AE, DC, MC, V* ⦿*CP.*

$–$$ ▤**Best Western Black Bear Inn.** This hotel is close to Bangor Mall and the University of Maine at Orono. The rooms are large and airy with king-size beds. Some of the rooms have balconies. Some pets are allowed. **Pro:** This is a good choice if you're planning to visit the nearby University of Maine. **Con:** The breakfast buffet seems a little skimpy. ✉*4 Godfrey Dr., Exit 51 off I–95 going north, 04473* ☎*207/866–7120* ⊕*www.black-*

bearinnorono.com   ⇌*68 rooms* ☂*In-room: Wi-Fi. In-hotel: gym, executive floor, some pets allowed, no-smoking rooms* ⊟*AE, DC, MC, V* ⊚|*CP.*

NIGHTLIFE & THE ARTS

The **Bangor Symphony Orchestra** (⊠*51A Main St., Maine Center for the Arts, Orono* ☎*207/942–5555 or 800/639–3221*) performs in nearby Orono (home of the University of Maine) at the Maine Center for the Arts. The **Penobscot Theatre Company** (⊠*131 Main St.* ☎*207/942–3333* ⊕*www.ptc.maineguide.com*) stages live classic and contemporary plays from October to May. From mid-July to mid-August, the company hosts the **Maine Shakespeare Festival** on the riverfront. Admission to the festival is $17.

BANGOR'S CHAINS

Large chain hotels with standard rooms and amenities in Bangor are the **Holiday Inn** (☎*207/947–0101* ⊕*www.holiday-inn.com*), **Motel 6** (☎*207/947–6921* ⊕*www.atmotel6.com*), and **Ramada Inn** (☎*207/947–6961* ⊕*www.bangorramada.com*). Chain hotels near Bangor's airport include the **Sheraton Four Points** (☎*207/947–6721* ⊕*www.fourpoints.com*), which is connected to Bangor International Airport via a skywalk; the **Fairfield Inn by Marriott** (☎*207/990–0001* ⊕*www.fairfieldinn.com*); and the **Days Inn** (☎*207/942–8272* ⊕*www.daysinn.com*).

Fodor's Choice ★   The **American Folk Festival** (☎*207/992–2630 or 800/916–6673* ⊕*www.americanfolkfestival.com*), is the biggest event of summer, attracting thousands of people. The three-day, multistage event takes place on the waterfront and includes traditional folk performers from around the country and around the world. Events include a rich array of music and dance performances, workshops, storytelling, parades, craft exhibits, and tons of food. Music may include blues, gospel, jazz, bluegrass, country-western, Cajun, mariachi, honky-tonk, and zydeco. Some of the craft exhibits include pottery, blacksmithing, quilting, musical instrument making, boatbuilding, and wood carving, as well as a variety of crafts from the American Indian groups in Maine. The festival is held at the end of August, and admission is free.

SPORTS & OUTDOORS

GOLFING   The **Bangor Municipal Golf Course** (⊠*35 Webster Ave.* ☎*207/941–0232*), a public club, has both an 18-hole course and a 9-hole course. Both courses are fairly flat and easy to walk. Greens fees are $27 for 18 holes, $13 for 9. Golf carts are available for an additional fee. The **Penobscot Valley Country Club** (⊠*366 Main St., take I-95 north from Bangor and then follow signs to Orono, Orono* ☎*207/866–2060* ⊕*www.penobscotvalleycc.com* ☉*Mid-Apr.–mid-Oct.*) has an 18-hole, par-36 golf course designed by Donald Ross. Facilities include a dining room, grill room, snack bar, and pro shop. Guests are allowed to play the course, with or without a sponsor, up to four times per calendar year. Guest fees are $60 without a golf cart, $75 with.

CRUISES   **Bangor Harbor Cruises** (⊠*1 Bar Harbor Pier* (⊓*Box 28, Cherryfield* ☉ *04622* ☎*207/941–0952 or 207/546–2927* ⊕*www.bangorharbor-*

cruises.com) takes passengers on scenic cruises of the Penobscot River aboard a 72-foot replica of a 19th-century steam ferry, *The Patience*. You can choose a 1-hour harbor cruise, a 1½-hour sunset cruise, or a 2-hour dinner cruise; boats depart from Bangor Landing thrice daily, Thursday through Sunday, mid-June through mid-October. Prices begin at $20. The company also operates the *Margaret Todd* windjammer trips in Bar Harbor. The relatively new **American Cruise Lines** (✉ *64 Front St., Bangor Landing* ☎ *203/453–6800 or 800/814–6880* ⊕ *www.americancruiselines.com*) offers seven-night itineraries aboard the "American Star" to a variety of Maine Coast destinations. Cruises depart from Portland or Bangor, and make calls at Bar Harbor, Rockland, Belfast, Camden, Bucksport, and Bath. The luxury cruise, with service, food, and prices to match, is aboard a 215-foot-long ship with capacity for 100 passengers. The well-equipped staterooms are spacious, and the lounges are cozy. The ships run from mid-June until late-September. Prices range from $2,740 per person for one-week cruise to $6,380 for a two-week cruise.

SHOPPING

The **Bangor Mall** (✉ *Hogan Rd., Exits 48A and 49 off I–95* ☎ *207/947–7333* ⊕ *www.bangormall.com*) has the best shopping in the area. Anchor stores include Macy's, JC Penney, Sears, and Dick's Sporting Equipment. Ruby Tuesdays is a good lunch spot in the mall.

PENOBSCOT BAY ESSENTIALS

To research prices, get advice from other travelers, and book travel arrangements, visit www.fodors.com.

TRANSPORTATION

BY AIR

Bangor International, off I–95, is the major airport in the Penobscot Bay area. Delta, Northwest, and US Airways service Bangor International to and from the key cities of Boston, New York, Newark, Philadelphia, Cincinnati, Atlanta, Detroit, and Minneapolis–St. Paul. From the airport you can access local and regional bus service, taxis, and rental cars.

Airport Bangor International Airport (✉ *287 Godfrey Blvd., Bangor* ☎ *207/992–4600* ⊕ *www.flybangor.com*).

BY BIKE

The most popular bike route on Maine's Penobscot Bay is historic U.S. 1. But note that for most of it, this is a two-lane highway, and tourists naturally are gawking at the sights. Most of the highway does have a designated bike lane—but you still need to be very careful.

BY BOAT

Ferry service runs from Rockland to several islands.

Contact Maine State Ferry Service at Rockland Harbor. ✆ *Box 645, Rockland 04841* ☎ *207/596–2202 or 800/491–4883.* .

BY BUS

Bangor has a very good bus system, the BAT Community Connector (☎207/992–4670 ⊕ *www.bgrme.org*), going in a number of directions and as far away as Hampden to the south. Within the region, Concord Trailways, a luxury bus service (with snacks, drinks, and movies) runs two buses a day from the University of Maine, at Orono, through Bangor and then down the coast all the way to Boston's Logan International Airport. It stops at all major towns along the way. There is also a bus terminal in Bangor for Greyhound and Vermont Transit Lines, both of which have three buses a day heading south to destinations such as Portland, Boston, and New York City.

Bus Lines **Concord Trailways** (⊠ *1039 Union St.* ☎ *207/945-4000*). **Greyhound Bus Lines** (E. *158 Main St.* ☎ *207/945-3000*). **Vermont Transit Lines** (⊠ *158 Main St.* ☎ *207/945-3000*).

BY CAR

Major roads going near or through the Penobscot Bay region are U.S. 1 and, for faster travel, I–95. Historic U.S. 1 is a two-lane highway. Despite its narrowness, it is a fairly good road. If you are coming up I–95 and want to get off to begin your coastal tour in the Penobscot Bay area, take the Augusta exit and follow the signs to Rt. 3 and U.S. 1. ■TIP➔ **U.S. 1 is old and only two lanes. Look at the scenery if you wish, but also keep your eyes on the road. At night, watch out for the possibility of a moose running out on the road. Moose can weigh up to 800 pounds, so hitting one will not be good for you, or the moose.**

In winter, the Maine Department of Transportation keeps most major roads plowed and graveled. However, you should always drive with caution in snowy conditions and carry a survivor kit, which includes water, extra food, warm blankets, a flashlight, and a cell phone.

BY TRAIN

Amtrak's *Downeaster* train goes from Boston to Portland and back (⇨ *see Greater Portland Essentials in Chapter 2*).

CONTACTS & RESOURCES

DISABILITIES & ACCESSIBILITY

For those who suffer from disabilities and may be in a wheelchair, life has gotten better in recent years—especially in comparison to much of the rest of the world. Most accommodations and restaurants in America where the owners are able to make their property handicapped accessible have done so. And we say "able" because in the case of some B&Bs, owners don't want to negatively affect the architectural integrity of the old home by installing a ramp—or the guest rooms in fact may all be on the second floor. Also, accommodations and restaurants are finally realizing that "handicapped accessible" means the bathroom is accessible as well. It's best to call first and find out for sure.

EMERGENCIES

In an emergency, dial 911.

24-Hour Medical Care **Eastern Maine Medical Center** (⊠ *489 State St., Bangor* ☎ *207/973-7000*). **Penobscot Bay Medical Center** (⊠ *6 Glen Cover Dr. [off U.S. 1],* between Camden and Rockland, Rockport ☎ 207/596–8000). **St. Joseph Hospital** (✉ 360 Broadway, Bangor ☎ 207/262–1000). **Waldo County General Hospital** (✉ 130 Northport Ave., Belfast ☎ 207/338–2500 or 800/649–2536).

MEDIA

NEWSPAPERS & MAGAZINES The major daily newspaper in the Penobscot Bay area is the *Bangor Daily News,* but you also will be able to find at most convenience stores and service stations, the *Boston Globe, Portland Telegram, New York Times, and USA Today.* Each major town along Penobscot Bay also has its own traditional weekly newspaper (Courier Publications in Rockland owns many of them).

TELEVISION & RADIO You can access all of the major networks, such as NBC (WLBZ channel 2), CBS (WABI channel 6), and ABC (WMTW channel 8) along the coast, and most hotels and motels are equipped with cable. You can access National Public Radio (90.9 FM), and Voice of Maine (103.9 FM). If you like music from the Big Band era, try 105.5 on your FM dial. For classical, tune to 106.9 or 107.7 FM.

VISITOR INFORMATION

Information **Bangor Region Chamber of Commerce** (✉ 519 Main St., Bangor 04402 ☎ 207/947–0307 ⊕ www.bangorregion.com) **Belfast Area Chamber of Commerce** (✉ 10 Main St., Belfast 04915 ☎ 207/338–5900 ⊕ www.belfastmaine. org). **Camden-Rockport-Lincolnville Chamber of Commerce** (✉ 2 Public Landing, Camden 04843 ☎ 207/236–4404 ⊕ www.visitcamden.com). **Greater Bangor Convention & Visitors Bureau** (✉ 40 Harlow St., Bangor 04401 ☎ 207/947–5205 or 800/91-MOOSE [916–6673] ⊕ www.bangorcvb.org). **Penobscot Regional Chamber of Commerce** (✉ 1 Park Dr., Rockland 04841 ☎ 207/596–0376 or 800/562–2529 ⊕ www.therealmaine.com). **Searsport Chamber of Commerce** (✉ 1 Union St., Searsport 04974 ☎ 207/548–0173 ⊕ www.searsportme.com).

The Blue Hill Peninsula

WORD OF MOUTH

"While along the northern Maine Coast, check out the area around Blue Hill/Castine/Stonington..it is spectacular that time of year (mid-October) and often overlooked for the more famous Vermont drives. To my mind, the combination of seacoast and fall color beats the mountains of Vermont/NH and it's great fun to explore the areas around Wiscassett and further along the Maine Coast. "

—LJ

By Lelah Cole

Updated
by George
Semler

IF YOU WANT TO SEE unspoiled Down East Maine land- and sea-scapes, explore art galleries, savor exquisite meals, or simply enjoy life at a relaxed and unhurried pace, you should be quite content on the Blue Hill Peninsula. The area is not at all like its coastal neighbors, as very little of it has been developed. There aren't any must-see attractions, so you are left to investigate the area on your own terms, seeking out the villages, hikes, artists, restaurants, or views that interest you most. Blue Hill and Castine are the area's primary business hubs.

The peninsula, approximately 16 mi wide and 20 mi long, juts out into Penobscot Bay. Not far from the mainland are the islands of Deer Isle, Little Deer Isle, and the picturesque fishing town of Stonington. It lacks the mountains, lakes, ponds, and vast network of trails of neighboring Mount Desert Island. Instead, a twisting labyrinth of roads rolls over fields and around coves, linking the towns of Blue Hill, Brooksville, Sedgwick, and Brooklin. This is a place to meander for views of open fields reaching to the water's edge or, around the next bend, a tree-shaded farmhouse with an old stone wall marking the property line.

Painters, photographers, sculptors, and other artists are drawn to the area. You can find more than 20 galleries on Deer Isle and Stonington, and at least half as many on the mainland. And with its small inns, charming bed-and-breakfasts, and outstanding restaurants scattered across the area, the Blue Hill Peninsula may just persuade you to leave the rest of the coastline to the tourists.

EXPLORING THE BLUE HILL PENINSULA

To explore the Blue Hill Peninsula thoroughly, you should have a car, a good map, and a relaxed schedule. Be prepared to get lost, and don't worry if you do. The roads can be confusing to those unfamiliar with the area, as they crisscross, overlap, branch off in odd directions, and sometimes seem to run parallel to themselves. If you are traveling north through the state on U.S. 1 and Route 3, you can reach the peninsula from Route 175, just east of Bucksport. If you're traveling south, your best bet is to follow Route 172 where it branches off near Ellsworth. Acadia National Park (⇨ see Chapter 6) is an easy day trip.

Deer Isle, Little Deer Island, and Stonington are accessible by bridge. Route 15 leads you on to Little Deer Isle and Deer Isle. When you reach the village of Deer Isle the road splits, with Route 15 following a more or less direct route to Stonington, while Route 15A reaches the same destination but meanders along the island's western edge. Neither route has great views. For those wishing to travel on to Isle au Haut in Acadia National Park, ferry service is the only way to get there.

Exploring the area on bicycle or boat will give you a more complete picture than if you stick to the car. In fact, an ideal (if extremely strenuous) way to explore the peninsula is by sea kayak. Because the mainland is so undeveloped and there are so many islands to explore, traveling by kayak allows you to take in spectacular scenery at every turn, observe marine mammals and birds, and get away from civilization for a while.

GREAT ITINERARIES

IF YOU HAVE 1 DAY

For a comprehensive one-day tour of the Blue Hill Peninsula, without spending all of it in an automobile, start with a stroll around **Blue Hill** and hike up Blue Hill Mountain, for 360-degree views. Then drive 45 minutes to **Stonington** via panoramic Caterpillar Hill and Deer Isle bridge for lunch in one of the restaurants over the harbor, followed by a walk around town. In the afternoon, drive back to the mainland, taking scenic Route 175 through Sargentville, Sedgwick, and Brooklin before crossing the Blue Hill Falls bridge and driving west on Route 172 to Route 177 and South Penobscot. Continue on to **Castine** for an exploratory tour through town.

IF YOU HAVE 3 DAYS

If you have three days on the peninsula, stay in **Blue Hill**. Visit the town's shops and galleries your first morning, then take the afternoon tour to neighboring **Brooklin**, home to the world-famous Wooden Boat School, and **Brooksville**, where you can find the Sow's Ear Winery. On Day 2, climb Blue Hill Mountain for 360-degree views of the peninsula, then head to **Castine** and take the town walking tour—be sure to see historic homes like the Ives House and landmarks like the Abbott School and the Unitarian Church. On Day 3, explore **Deer Isle** and **Stonington** to learn about the region's rocky past at the Deer Isle Granite Museum and Settlement Quarry.

Beyond the peninsula, an archipelago of uninhabited islands known as Merchant's Row is a favorite with kayakers.

WHEN TO GO

Because it is relatively undiscovered, the Blue Hill Peninsula does not have what you would call a high season. The best time to visit is from late May or early June to mid-October (the Blue Hill Peninsula Chamber of Commerce does not open until Memorial Day weekend, and the Deer Isle–Stonington Chamber of Commerce begins its season in mid-June; *see Essentials at the end of the chapter for contact information*). There are few lodging options, so it's a good idea to reserve rooms well in advance. Outside of these months you will find that many restaurants and hotels have closed for the season. During the summer months, galleries open their doors, concerts enliven the evenings, and a handful of festivals draw locals and visitors alike. Check with the local chambers of commerce for schedules of events.

ABOUT THE RESTAURANTS

Dining options on the Blue Hill Peninsula tend to fall into one of two categories: expensive restaurants where you can expect expertly prepared cuisine, or more casual places where you can grab a sandwich, burger, or crab roll. The fine-dining establishments tend to offer more organic foods than you might expect to find elsewhere. You can always count on finding freshly caught seafood, but many restaurants on the peninsula proudly promote their locally grown produce and locally raised meats. This emphasis is not just about eating healthier foods; it's also a deliberate effort to support local farmers and fishermen.

ABOUT THE HOTELS

You won't find grand hotels on the Blue Hill Peninsula. Instead, the countryside is dotted with inns, bed-and-breakfasts, and small but distinguished hotels. Be prepared to find that your room lacks a TV or even a phone. Without these amenities, you can more easily slip away from your day-to-day life. Many accommodations also do without air-conditioning. Although occasional summer days in August can still get quite warm, ocean breezes will cool your room off at night, providing what locals call "free air-conditioning."

WHAT IT COSTS					
	¢	$	$$	$$$	$$$$
RESTAURANTS	under $7	$7–$10	$11–$17	$18–$25	over $25
HOTELS	under $60	$60–$99	$100–$149	$150–$200	over $200

Restaurant prices are for a main course at dinner, excluding sales tax of 7%. Hotel prices are for two people in a standard double room in high season, excluding service charges and 7% tax.

BLUE HILL & ENVIRONS

Blue Hill and Castine are the most visited towns on the peninsula, but they manage to retain an off-the-beaten-path charm. For villages with an even more secluded feel, visit Brooklin, Brooksville, and Sedgwick.

CASTINE

30 mi southeast of Searsport.

A summer destination for more than 100 years, Castine is a well-preserved seaside village rich in history. Although a few different American Indian tribes inhabited the area before the 1600s, French explorer Samuel de Champlain was the first European to record its location on a map. The French established a trading post here in 1613, naming the area Pentagoet. A year later, Captain John Smith claimed the area for the British. The French regained control of the peninsula with the 1667 Breda Treaty, and Jean Vincent d'Abbadie de St. Castin obtained a land grant in the Pentagoet area, which would later have his name. Castine's strategic position on Penobscot Bay and its importance as a trading post meant there were many battles for control until 1815. The Dutch claimed the area in 1674 and 1676, and England made it a stronghold during the Revolutionary War. In the 19th century, Castine was an important port for trading ships and fishing vessels. The Civil War and the advent of train travel brought its prominence as a port to an end, but by the late 1800s, some of the nation's wealthier citizens discovered Castine as a pleasant summer retreat.

WHAT TO SEE

Federal- and Greek Revival–style architecture, spectacular views of Penobscot Bay, and a peaceful setting make Castine an ideal spot to spend a day or two. Well worth exploring are its lively harbor front,

IF YOU LIKE

FLOWER FESTIVAL

In June the fields and roadsides of the Blue Hill Peninsula are decorated with the blues, pinks, and purples of one of Maine's most popular flowers, the lupine. Although the flower thrives throughout coastal Maine, nowhere is it more celebrated than here. The Deer Isle–Stonington Lupine Festival, the third Saturday in June, showcases everything you can do with the buds. Festival events include a bean cook-off, a rummage sale and bazaar, and an art show. There's also food and live music. A map indicating prime viewing spots is available from area businesses.

FOLIAGE FOOD & WINE FESTIVAL

The Annual Foliage Food and Wine Festival (⊕ www.bluehillpeninsula. org/foodandwine) in mid-October brings the area's restaurants, chefs, and food producers together for a wine dinner, a champagne luncheon, and tasting events, all at the height of the autumnal riot of hardwood reds, yellows, and ochers (not to mention the magentas of the blue-berry barrens). The second edition of the festival held in October 2007 was a major success, starring local chefs Mickey Jowders from Wescott Forge, and Arborvine's John Hikade, along with an ample cast of cheese makers, chocolatiers, vegetable growers, and cider brewers.

GALLERY HOPPING

If you're visiting the Blue Hill Peninsula area to collect antiques or find new artwork, you might want to pick up a copy of the annual Arts Guide, which showcases shops and galleries on Deer Isle–Stonington and the Blue Hill Peninsula. Make sure to see the Haystack Mountain School of Crafts, which has tours every Wednesday at 1 PM, as well as interesting evening lectures. You can find galleries in and around downtown Deer Isle that exhibit oil and watercolor paintings, photography, and sculpture. Stonington has a few galleries, as does the village of Blue Hill. As you drive along the peninsula's winding roads, you can find studios selling everything from pottery to handmade paper.

two small museums, and the ruins of a British fort. For a nice stroll, park your car at the landing and walk up Main Street toward the white Trinitarian Federated Church. Among the white clapboard buildings ringing the town common are the Ives House (once the summer home of poet Robert Lowell), the Abbott School, and the Unitarian Church, capped by a whimsical belfry. Historical markers are posted throughout town, making it ideal for a self-guided walking tour.

The **Castine Historical Society Museum** has changing exhibits that portray Castine's tumultuous history, highlighting the American Indian tribes that lived here and its rise as a trading port. Look for the town's Bicentennial Quilt, created in 1996 to celebrate the town's 200th birthday. ⊠ Court St., Town Common, Box 238, 04421 ☎ 207/326–4118 ☐ Free ☉ July 1–Labor Day, Tues.–Sat. 10–4, Sun. 1–4.

The **Wilson Museum** is made up of four historic structures. The main building houses anthropologist-geologist John Howard Wilson's collection of prehistoric artifacts from around the world, including rocks, minerals, and other intriguing objects. The **John Perkins House** is a restored Colonial-era house originally built on what is now Court Street, in 1763, and enlarged in 1774 and 1783. The house fell into disrepair until the 1960s, when the Castine Scientific Society had the house taken down piece by piece and reassembled it here on the grounds of the Wilson Museum. Inside you can find Perkins family heirlooms and 18th- and early-19th-century furnishings. The kitchen and four front rooms appear as they did in 1783. The **Blacksmith Shop** holds demonstrations showing all the tricks of this old-time trade. Inside the **Hearse House** you can see the summer and winter hearses that serviced Castine more than a century ago. ⊠*107 Perkins St.* ☎*207/326–9247* ⊕*www.wilsonmuseum.org* ⊠*Museum, Blacksmith Shop, and Hearse House free; John Perkins House $5* ⊗*Museum late May–late Sept., Tues.–Sun. 2–5; John Perkins House, Blacksmith Shop, Hearse House July and Aug., Sun. and Wed. 2–5.*

> ### BLUE HILL TOP 5
>
> ■ Go to sleep with an ocean view at the Castine Inn.
>
> ■ Listen to a chamber music concert at Kneisel Hall in Blue Hill.
>
> ■ Watch the boats from a lighthouse tower at First Light Bed & Breakfast.
>
> ■ Count blue herons and bald eagles at the Holbrook Island Sanctuary.
>
> ■ Learn blacksmithing at Haystack Mountain School of Crafts.

WHERE TO EAT & STAY

$–$$$ ✕**Dennett's Wharf.** Originally built as a sail rigging loft in the early 1800s, this longtime favorite is a good place for fresh seafood. The waterfront restaurant also serves burgers, sandwiches, and other light fare. There are several microbrews on tap, including the tasty Dennett's Wharf Rat Ale. Eat in the dining room or outside on the deck. ⊠*15 Sea St.* ☎*207/326–9045* ▤*MC, V* ⊗*Closed Columbus Day–May.*

$$–$$$$ ✕▦**Manor Inn.** Bordering a 95-acre forest with trails that lead all the way to the bay, this 1895 inn resembles an English manor house. Rooms are individually decorated—four have fireplaces and one has a private porch. Some bathrooms have marble tubs and walk-in showers. The dining room ($$–$$$), overlooking the lawn and gardens, offers eclectic international cuisine emphasizing local ingredients and accommodates up to 200 people. The pub serves lighter fare. Yoga classes are held in a fully equipped studio three times a week. **Pros:** Great breakfast buffet, lovely walking opportunities. **Con:** Somewhat removed from the waterfront. ⊠*15 Manor Dr., off Battle Ave., 04421* ☎*207/326–4861* ⊕*www.manor-inn.com* ↪*14 rooms* ᗒ*In-room: no a/c (some), no TV (some). In-hotel: restaurant, bar, no-smoking rooms, some pets allowed, no elevator* ▤*AE, D, DC, MC, V* ⦿*BP.*

$$–$$$$ ✕▦**Pentagoet Inn.** With period lithographs in the common rooms, claw-foot tubs in the bathrooms, and a cozy pub, the owners of this inn strive to create an air of romance. Guest rooms are in the Queen Anne–style main building with a three-story turret and numerous gables, or in a nearby 18th-century sea captain's home. The most memorable is Room 3, which has a balcony covered with flowers and views of town. With

The Blue Hill Peninsula

Penobscot

West Brooksville

Blue Hill

Castine

Dyce Head Light

Smith Cove

Harborside

South Brooksville

Brooksville

Blue Hill Falls

Cape Rosier

Bucks Harbor

Walker Pond

Caterpillar Hill

Sedgwick

North Brooklin

Head of the Cape

Eggemoggin Reach

Sargentville

Blue Hill Bay

Little Deer Isle

Long Island

East Penobscot Bay

Brooklin

Flye Point

Deer Isle

Naskeag Point

Deer Isle Village

Jericho Bay

North Haven Island

Swans Island

KEY
Ferry Lines
Lighthouse

Stonington

TO ISLE AU HAUT

0   5 miles

0   5 kilometer

tables in the dining room or on a porch, the restaurant ($$$) specializes in fresh fish. You might try the Stonington crab cake appetizer, followed by the seared duck on a Belgian endive salad. The perfect finale is profiteroles with vanilla ice cream and chocolate ganache sauce. Enjoy a full breakfast in a room adjacent to the garden, and freshly baked cookies each afternoon. **Pros:** At the center of Castine's bustling town life, superb breakfast buffet. **Con:** Rooms somewhat cluttered and creaky. ⊠ *26 Main St., 04421* ☎ *207/326–8616 or 800/845–1701* ⊕ *www.pentagoet.com* ⌨ *Reservations essential* ⏎ *16 rooms* ⌂ *In-room: no a/c, no phone, no TV. In-hotel: restaurant, bar, no-smoking rooms, no elevator* ⊟ *MC, V* ⊙ *Closed late Oct.–May* ⏍*BP.*

$$–$$$$ **Castine Inn.** Originally built in 1898, the Castine Inn is a delightful place to stay. Most of the guest rooms are rather simple, but they are bright and airy, and have views of the ocean. A seascape mural covers the walls of the dining room, now used exclusively for breakfast. After dinner in town, you can relax outside in the garden or unwind in the English-style pub. **Pro:** At the hub of Castine's buzzing day and nightlife. **Cons:** A bit urban and occasionally noisy. ⊠ *33 Main St., 04421* ☎ *207/326–4365* ⊕ *www.castineinn.com* ⌨ *Reservations essential* ⏎ *15 rooms, 4 suites* ⌂ *In-room: no a/c, no phone, no TV. In-hotel: restaurant, bar, no kids under 8, no-smoking rooms, no elevator* ⊟ *MC, V* ⊙ *Closed Nov.–late Apr.* ⏍*BP.*

SPORTS & THE OUTDOORS

At Dennett's Wharf, **Castine Kayak Adventures** (⊠*15 Sea St.* ☎*207/326–9045*) operates tours with a registered Maine guide. Walk through the restaurant to the deck, where you can sign up for a half day of kayaking along the shore, or a full day of kayaking by shipwrecks, reversing falls, and islands in Penobscot Bay. The steam launch *Laurie Ellen* (⊠*Dennett's Wharf* ☎*207/326–9045 or 207/266–2841*) is the only wood-fired, steam-powered passenger steam launch in the country. Climb aboard for a trip around Castine Harbor and up the Bagaduce River.

SHOPPING

Compass Rose Bookstore & Café (⊠*3 Main St.* ☎*207/326–9366*) carries books, music, and games. The coffee shop has cookies and a self-serve lunch. **Four Flags** (⊠*19 Water St.* ☎*207/326–8526*) has nautical charts, prints of old maps, and other souvenirs. **Leila Day Antiques** (⊠*53 Main St.* ☎*207/326–8786*) specializes in interesting antiques, colorful quilts, and nautical accessories. **M&E Gummel Chairworks** (⊠*600 The Shore Rd.* ☎*207/326–8122* ⊕*www.gummelchairworks.com*) crafts authentic handmade Windsor chairs. The **McGrath-Dunham Gallery** (⊠*9 Main St.* ☎*207/326–9175* ⊕*www.mcgrathdunhamgallery.com*) sells paintings, sculpture, and pottery.

EN ROUTE As you approach the village of Castine, you'll notice a large sign on the right side of the road that reads: BRITISH CANAL 1779. Just before the sign, turn right and follow the road to the **Back Shore**. This large pebble beach is a favorite local hangout. It's the perfect place to enjoy a picnic by the ocean.

BLUE HILL

19 mi east of Castine.

Snuggled between 943-foot Blue Hill Mountain and Blue Hill Bay, the village of Blue Hill is perched dramatically over the harbor. Originally known for its granite quarries, copper mines, and shipbuilding, today the town charms with its pottery, and a plethora of galleries, shops, and studios line its streets. Blue Hill is also a good spot for shopping, as there are numerous bookstores and antiques shops. The Blue Hill Fair (⊕*www.bluehillfair.com*), held Labor Day weekend, is a tradition in these parts, with agricultural exhibits, food, rides, and entertainment.

WHAT TO SEE

Now housing the Blue Hill Historical Society, the **Holt House** was built in 1815 by Jeremiah Thorndike Holt, grandson of one of the first European settlers to the area. Today, the property is in the process of being furnished with period antiques while society members collect and maintain documents and other memorabilia important to the town. Visitors will find reproductions of the home's original stenciled decorations and a kitchen with a restored fireplace and the original iron pot hooks. ⊠*3 Water St.* ☎*207/374–9933* ⊙*July and Aug., Tues. and Fri. 1–4, Sat. 10–1* ⊠*$3 donation suggested.*

Focusing on how pollution affects marine mammals, the **Marine Environmental Research Institute** has programs for all ages, including guided walks along the beach. A weekly story hour for kids includes crafts projects, usually directed by a local artist. Children can hold small sea creatures from a "touch tank," including green crabs, sea stars, whelks, and periwinkles. Two viewing tanks house lobsters, rock crabs, anemones, and other small sea creatures. ⊠*55 Main St.* ☎*207/374–2135* ⊕*www.meriresearch.org* ☜*Free* ⊙*Mon.–Fri., 9–5.*

With 50 different types of bread, each made by hand, Pain de Famille (⊠7 Main St. ☎207/374-3839) is a good place to stop if you're packing a picnic or putting together a midday snack. The shop also sells a selection of vegetarian sandwiches and pizza—made with homemade crust, of course.

Jonathan Fisher was the first permanent minister of Blue Hill. The **Parson Fisher House,** which he built from 1814 to 1820, provides a fascinating look at his many accomplishments and talents, which included writing and illustrating books, painting, farming, and building furniture. Also on view is a wooden clock he crafted while a student at Harvard; the face holds messages about time written in English, Greek, Latin, Hebrew, and French. The site is on the National Register of Historic Places. ⊠*Rte. 15/176, west of intersection with Rte. 172* ☎*No phone* ☜*$5* ⊙*July–mid-Sept., Mon.–Sat. 1–4.*

WHERE TO EAT & STAY

$$$–$$$$
Fodor'sChoice
★
✕**Arborvine.** Glowing (albeit ersatz) fireplaces, period antiques, exposed beams, and hardwood floors covered with Oriental rugs create an elegant and comforting atmosphere in each of the four candlelit dining rooms in this renovated Cape Cod–style house. You might begin with a salad of mixed greens, sliced beets, and pears with blue cheese crumbled on top. For your entrée, choose from among dishes such as medallions of beef and goat cheese with shoelace potatoes, or pork tenderloin with sweet cherries in a port-wine reduction. The specials and fresh fish dishes are superb, as are the crab cakes. Be sure to save room for a dessert, such as lemon mousse or wonderfully creamy cheesecake. A take-out lunch menu is available at the adjacent Moveable Feasts deli, where the Vinery serves drinks and tapas in the evening. ⊠*33 Tenney Hill, 04614* ☎*207/374–2119* ⊟*AE, DC, MC, V* ⊙*Closed Mon. and Tues. Sept.–June. No lunch.*

¢–$$
✕**Marlintini's Grill.** Locals go to Marlintini's for specialties like the fried haddock sandwich, which is perfectly crispy. The restaurant also has a selection of other sandwiches and seafood. The brightly painted walls are adorned with colorful paintings and athletic paraphernalia, reflecting the sports bar vocation of this quintessential town watering hole. ⊠*Rte. 15* ☎*207/374–2500* ⊟*AE, DC, MC, V.*

$$–$$$
✕⬚**Barncastle.** Opened in June 2007 as a hotel, restaurant, and wood-oven pizza specialist, this establishment has had solid success, especially as a restaurant offering top value. Its location is in an unusual building, resembling, as its name suggests, an architectural hybrid between a barn and a castle. Designed in 1890 by architect George Clough, Boston's first city architect, the wooden conical towers and turrets around

the open drive-through carport create a whimsical Loire-meets-Maine effect. The pizzas ($–$$$) are excellent, as is the selection of salads and sandwiches. Rooms are quirky and rambling but charming. **Pro:** Views over woodlands to Mount Desert. **Cons:** Landlocked and facing Blue Hill's fastest and least-appealing thoroughfare. ☒*125 South St. (Rte. 175) 04614* ☎*207/374–2300* ⊕*www.barncastlehotel.com* ⌂*3 suites, 2 rooms* ⌂*In-room: no a/c, no phone, no TV. In-hotel: no-smoking rooms, no elevator* ☐*AE, DC, MC, V* ⦿*BP.*

$$$–$$$$ ★ ▦**Blue Hill Inn.** This rambling inn dating from 1830 is a comfortable place to relax after climbing Blue Hill Mountain or exploring nearby shops and galleries. Original pumpkin pine and painted floors set the tone for the mix of Empire and early-Victorian pieces that fill the two parlors and guest rooms, several of which have working fireplaces. One of the nicest rooms is No. 8, which has exposures on three sides and views of the flower gardens and apple trees. Two rooms have antique claw-foot tubs perfect for soaking. The spacious Cape House Suite (available after the rest of the inn has closed for the season) has a bed as well as two pullout sofas, a full kitchen, and a private deck. The inn has a bar offering an ample selection of wines and whiskies. Here you can enjoy appetizers before you head out to dinner or try specialty coffees and liqueurs when you return. **Pros:** The bedroom fireplaces and the antique floorboards make you want to stay here forever. **Cons:** Rooms are on the small side, and the walls are thin. ☒*40 Union St., 04614* ☎*207/374–2844 or 800/826–7415* ⊕*www.bluehillinn.com* ⌂*11 rooms, 1 suite* ⌂*In-room: no phone, no TV. In-hotel: bar, public Internet, no-smoking rooms, no elevator* ☐*AE, MC, V* ⦿*BP.*

$$–$$$ ▦**First Light Bed & Breakfast.** In the quiet village of East Blue Hill, this bed-and-breakfast sits right on the water's edge. The tower of a lighthouse is open to guests and has chairs and a telescope for viewing passing boats by day and stars by night. Rooms are individually decorated to reflect their names. The Seaside Garden Room, which has views of McHeard's Cove and Blue Hill Bay, shares a bath with the Maine Room, overlooking McHeard's stream and its estuary, a sizable salt pond where occasional dolphins have been known to frolic. The Lighthouse Suite, on the main floor of the tower, has a great view of Blue Hill Bay and Mount Desert Island across the water. When the tide is low, you can walk down to the shore; when it's high, enjoy the views from a seaside seating area. The inn is at the east end of the green metal bridge that connects East Blue Hill with Blue Hill. **Pros:** Lovely views and proximity to the charming village of East Blue Hill. **Con:** Tight quarters. ☒*821 E. Blue Hill Rd., East Blue Hill 04629* ☎*207/374–5879* ⊕*www.firstlightbandb.com* ⌂*2 rooms without bath, 1 suite* ⌂*In-room: no a/c, no phone, refrigerator, no TV. In-hotel: no elevator* ☐*No credit cards* ⦿*BP.*

$–$$$ ▦**Captain Isaac Merrill Inn.** This Federal-style mansion, built during the 1800s for sea captain Isaac Merrill, one of Blue Hill's founding fathers, is presently run by Captain Merrill's great-granddaughter Florence Jane, an expert on local history—feel free to discuss it with her over breakfast. The inn has charming guest rooms that overlook Main Street. Many have hardwood floors and windows that let in lots of light. **Pros:**

Walking distance from everything in town, views from the front steps down over the inner harbor. **Cons:** Rooms a bit cramped, heavy traffic through town in summer. ⊠*5 Union St., 04614* ☎*207/374–2555* ⊕*www.captainmerrillinn.com* ↪*6 rooms, 1 suite* ⅋*In-room: no a/c (some), no phone (some), no TV (some). In-hotel: no-smoking rooms, no elevator* ⊟*AE, D, MC, V* ⊺⊙⊺*BP.*

NIGHTLIFE & THE ARTS

The **Kneisel Hall Chamber Music Festival** (⊠*137 Pleasant St.* ☎*207/374–2203*) has concerts on Sunday afternoons and Friday evenings in summer. The first Saturday of each month, a **Contra Dance** is held at the **Blue Hill Town Hall** (⊠*18 Union St.*). Similar to square dancing, contra dancing involves two couples dancing specific patterns.

SPORTS & THE OUTDOORS

Maps of hiking trails in the area are available at **Blue Hill Heritage Trust** (⊠*101 Union St., Blue Hill* ☎*207/374–5118* ⊕*www.bluehillheritage-trust.org*). The Osgood Trail provides hikers with breathtaking 360-degree views of the Blue Hill Peninsula as it leads up **Blue Hill Mountain** (⊠*Mountain Rd., Blue Hill*). The dirt path meanders through the woods, over rocky ledges, and up stone steps. A second trail is accessible to hikers as well as all-terrain vehicles.

You can rent sea kayaks, canoes, and bicycles at the **Activity Shop** (⊠*61 Ellsworth Rd., Blue Hill* ☎*207/374–3600*). Pick them up at the shop, or have them delivered. **Rocky Coast Outfitters** (⊠*5 Webster Rd., Blue Hill* ☎*207/374–8866*) has sea kayaks, canoes, and bicycles by the day or by the week. Delivery is available.

SHOPPING

ANTIQUES **Blue Hill Antiques** (⊠*8 Water St.* ☎*207/374–8825*) collects and sells books, furniture, and carefully selected objects of all kinds collected on André Strong's annual buying trips to Europe.

HANDCRAFTED ITEMS **Andean Downeast** (⊠*27 Water St.* ☎*207/374–2313*) has a surprising collection of alpaca wool products, pottery, and Mapuche textiles from the Andes. **Bella Colore** (⊠*27 Water St.* ☎*207/374–5343*) stocks handcrafted gifts and jewelry, much of it by gifted store owner Ginger Manna. **Handworks Gallery** (⊠*48 Main St.* ☎*207/374–5613*) carries unusual crafts made by local artists such as bookshelves fashioned from bark-peeled tree branches, wooden boxes, jewelry, dishes, and other items. **North Country Textiles** (⊠*38 Main St.* ☎*207/374–2715* ⊕*www.northcountrytextiles.com*) specializes in fine woven shawls, throws, baby blankets, place mats, and pillows in subtle patterns and color schemes. **Pashminas of Blue Hill** (⊠*54 Main St.* ☎*207/374–2015*) specializes in shawls of woven Himalayan goat wool from Nepal and Kashmir. **String Theory** (⊠*132 Beech Hill Rd.* ☎*207/374–9990*) makes and markets hand-dyed yarn and fine arts from local artists.

ART GALLERIES **Blue Hill Bay Gallery** (⊠*11 Tenny Hill* ☎*207/374–5773* ⊕*www.blue-hillbaygallery.com* ⊙ *Memorial Day–Labor Day, daily; mid-May–Memorial Day and Labor Day–mid-October, weekends*) sells oil and watercolor paintings of the local landscape. Bird carvings and other items are also available. **Jud Hartmann Gallery** (✉ *Main and Pleasant Sts.* ☎*207/359–2544* ⊕*www.judhartmanngallery.com*) displays bronze sculptures of Iriquois and Abenaki American Indians. Some sculptures are busts, while others depict a scene. Oil and watercolor paintings by other artists are also on display. **Leighton Gallery** (✉*24 Parker Point Rd.* ☎*207/374–5001* ⊕*www.leightongallery.com*) shows oil paintings, lithographs, watercolors, and other contemporary art. Many pieces are abstract. Outside, granite, bronze, and wood sculptures are displayed in a gardenlike setting under apple trees and white pines. **Liros Gallery** (✉*14 Parker Point Rd.* ☎*207/374–5370* ⊕*www.lirosgallery. com*) exhibits oil and watercolor paintings, hand-colored engravings, and woodcuts of birds and flowers.

HOUSEHOLD GOODS
New Cargoes (✉*49 Main St.* ☎*207/374–3733*) sells cookware, glassware, tea towels, clothing, quilts, and other products, many of them made in Maine. **Rackliffe Pottery** (✉*126 Ellsworth Rd., Blue Hill* ☎*207/374–2297*) sells colorful pottery made with lead-free glazes. You can choose among water pitchers, tea-and-coffee sets, and sets of canisters. **Rowantrees Pottery** (✉*9 Union St.* ☎*207/374–5535*) has an extensive selection of dinnerware, tea sets, vases, and decorative items. The shop makes many of the same pieces it did 60 years ago, so if you break a favorite item, you can find a replacement.

WINE
In what was once a barn out behind one of Blue Hill's earliest houses, the **Blue Hill Wine Shop** (✉*138 Main St.,* ✛*halfway between intersection of Rtes. 172 and 176 and Rte. 15 in center of town* ☎*207/374–2161*) carries more than 1,000 carefully selected wines. Wine tastings are held on the last Saturday of every month.

EN ROUTE
Offering kayakers surfable currents when the tide is running full force, **Blue Hill Falls**, is a reversing falls on Route 175 between Blue Hill and Brooklin. Water flowing in and out of the salt pond from Blue Hill Bay roars in and out under the Stevens Bridge. See it by foot or by kayak, but use extreme caution, especially with children, on the bridge itself as the hydraulic roar drowns out the sound of oncoming motorists. (✉*Rte. 175 south of Blue Hill).*

SEDGWICK, BROOKLIN, & BROOKSVILLE

Winding through the hills, the roads leading to the villages of Sedgwick, Brooklin, and Brooksville take you past rambling farmhouses, beautiful ocean coves, and blueberry fields with the occasional mass of granite. It's a perfect leisurely drive, ideal for a Sunday afternoon.

Incorporated in 1798, **Sedgwick** runs along much of Eggemoggin Reach, the body of water that separates the mainland from Deer Isle, Little Deer Island, and Stonington. The village of **Brooklin,** originally part of Sedgwick, established itself as an independent town in 1849. Today, it is home to the world-famous Wooden Boat School, a 64-acre oceanfront campus offering courses in woodworking, boatbuilding, and seamanship. The town of **Brooksville,** incorporated in 1817, is almost completely surrounded by water, with Eggemoggin Reach, Walker Pond, and the Bagaduce River marking its boundaries.

WHAT TO SEE

Gardens filled with brightly colored poppies, as well as lovely perennials, are the attraction at the **Blue Poppy Garden** (⌂*1000 Reach Rd., Sedgwick* ☎*207/359–8392* ⊕*www.bluepoppygarden.com* ⌘*Free*). A nature trail winds through the woods past native plants identified by small signs. There's a dining room that serves lunch and afternoon tea in July and August. At the gift shop you can purchase blue poppy plants and seeds. The gardens are open mid-May to mid-October.

A few miles south of Brooklin, Naskeag Point Road leads to a broken-shell beach called **Naskeag Point.** From here you can take in views of the small islands in Jericho Bay as you picnic under the apple trees. A bench remembers "all the fishermen who brave the sea." This area, famous for being the site of the 1778 Battle of Naskeag, has a long history. An ancient Nordic coin was discovered on the beach. To find Naskeag Point Road, turn at the Brooklin General Store.

To taste locally produced fruit wines, visit the **Sow's Ear Winery** (⌂*303 Coastal Rd., Brooksville* ☎*207/326–4649* ☉*Daily*). Owner Tom Hoey grows apples and rhubarb for his cider and rhubarb wine, and he uses locally grown blueberries and cranberries for his berry wines.

WHERE TO EAT & STAY

$$–$$$
Fodor'sChoice
★

✕ **Buck's.** Popular among cruisers mooring in Buck's Harbor, this fine dining gem is behind **Buck's Harbor Market,** itself a key food destination for its wines, cheeses, olive oils, and sandwiches. Jonathan Chase, formerly of the Pilgrim's Inn in Deer Isle Village, has put together a superlative and constantly changing market-based menu strong in local ingredients, starring fresh fish, scallops, duck, and lamb. The seared duck breast with cranberries, beer, and maple barbecue sauce is a favorite, as are the sautéed sea scallops. The restaurant has a reasonably priced, carefully selected wine list and a deck for outdoor dining in summer. ⌂*6 Cornfield Hill Rd., at Rte. 176, South Brooksville* ☎*207/326–8683* ⊟*MC, V* ☉*Closed Sun.–Tues. Sept.–June.*

$$–$$$$
★

✕⊡ **Oakland House Seaside Resort.** Set between Eggemoggin Reach and a private pond, this relaxing retreat sits on more than 50 acres of shorefront property. Open since 1889, the resort has accommodations ranging from comfortable guest rooms furnished in Arts and Crafts style to more rustic cottages with fireplaces. Ask for Room 7, which has a sitting area and ocean views on three sides. The resort's well-known restaurant ($$$–$$$$) offers a five-course menu that changes daily. Dinner might begin with seared tuna with wasabi vinaigrette followed by lobster bisque and prime rib. Every Thursday you can join a lobster picnic. The resort has hiking trails leading through the woods, including one that ends at a peak overlooking Pumpkin Island Lighthouse and beyond. A dock is available for boaters. Weeklong artist workshops are held throughout the season, including painting and photography. **Pros:** Panoramic seascapes and cozy fireplaces for northeasterly storms. **Con:** Frequent weddings here may add more excitement than you bargained for. ⊠*435 Herrick Rd., Brooksville 04617* ☎*207/359–8521 or 800/359–7352* ⊕*www.oaklandhouse.com* ➳*10 rooms, 7 with bath; 15 cottages* ⚬*In-room: no a/c, no phone, kitchen, no TV. In-hotel: restaurant, beachfront, no-smoking rooms, no elevator* ▤*MC, V* ⊘*Closed mid-Oct.–late May* ♟*BP, MAP.*

$-$$ ✕🏠 **Brooklin Inn.** A comfortable yet elegant atmosphere distinguishes this
★ B&B in downtown Brooklin. There are plenty of homey touches like hardwood floors and an upstairs deck. The sunny rooms have attractive bureaus and beds piled with cozy quilts. The restaurant ($$–$$$$) specializes in fresh fish and locally raised beef, poultry, and lamb. It also has fine soups, salads, and desserts worth saving room for. In summer you can dine on the enclosed porch. An Irish pub downstairs showcases local musicians most Saturday nights. **Pros:** Relaxing, on-site dining. **Cons:** Rooms are small, walls are paper thin. ⊠*Rte. 175, Brooklin 04616* ☎*207/359–2777* ⊕*www.brooklininn.com* ➳*5 rooms, 3 with bath* ⚬*In-room: no a/c, no phone, no TV. In-hotel: restaurant, no-smoking rooms, no elevator* ▤*AE, D, DC, MC, V* ♟*BP.*

$-$$$ 🏠 **Hiram Blake Camp.** Established in 1916, this camp sits on Cape Rosier. The waterside cottages, with one to three bedrooms, have exposed wood beams, separate sitting areas, full kitchens, and screened porches. There are miles of hiking trails, a pebble beach, and plenty of open areas where children can play. You can hop in one of the camp's kayaks and head to nearby Spectacle Island. The restaurant serves a set menu each night, but you can always call ahead to order lobster. The dining room is lined with bookshelves and has long wooden tables to encourage family-style dining. **Pros:** Cozy, rustic cabins; pristine simplicity. **Con:** Not for those seeking luxury. ⊠*220 Weir Cove Rd., Harborside 04642* ☎*207/326–4951* ⊕*www.hiramblake.com* ➳*15 cabins* ⚬*In-room: no a/c, no phone, no TV. In-hotel: restaurant, beachfront, no-smoking rooms, no elevator* ▤*No credit cards* ⊘*Closed late Sept.–June* ♟*MAP.*

NIGHTLIFE & THE ARTS

A popular way to spend Monday evenings is to attend a street dance sponsored by a steel-drum band called **Flash! In the Pans** (☎*207/374–5247* ⊕*www.peninsulapan.org*). The energetic group performs every other week from late June to early September at the Buck's Harbor Market in South Brooksville. There are also performances in Castine, Blue Hill, and Sedgwick. Proceeds from the dances benefit area schools, fire departments, and ambulance crews.

SPORTS & THE OUTDOORS

The 1,230-acre **Holbrook Island Sanctuary** (⊠*172 Indian Bar Rd., Brooksville* ☎*207/326–4012*) protects the region's fragile ecosystem. You have a good chance of spotting a blue heron, osprey, or bald eagle. Open from 9 AM to sunset, the park has nine hiking trails, a gravel beach with splendid views, and a picnic area. You can get a trail map at the parking areas.At Buck's Harbor Marina, the 44-foot cruising ketch ***Perelandra*** (⊠*Coastal Rd., South Brooksville* ☎*207/326–4279*) sails from Buck's Harbor Marina daily. A maximum of six people can

5

cruise around Penobscot Bay and the nearby islands. Prices start at $40 for two hours.

SHOPPING

The **Gallery at Caterpillar Hill** (⊠*328 Caterpillar Hill Rd.* ☎*207/359–4600*) is a spectacular refuge for looking at landscape paintings and other artifacts competing, sometimes successfully, with the Penobscot Bay panorama out the window. On Rte. 15 just north of Caterpillar hill, **Old Cove Antiques** (⊠*106 Caterpillar Hill Rd.* ☎*207/359–8585*) specializes in antique furniture, quilts, wood carvings, and more.

EN ROUTE As you travel south toward Deer Isle, scenic Route 15 passes through Sedgwick before taking you over the graceful green suspension bridge that crosses Eggemoggin Reach. The picnic area at **Caterpillar Hill,** on the mainland about 1 mi south of the junction of Routes 15 and 175, has a fabulous view of Penobscot Bay dotted with hundreds of deep-green islands. You can even see across the bay to the Camden Hills, southwest of the Blue Hill Peninsula. With good reason, this spot is known as **Million Dollar View.**

DEER ISLE & STONINGTON

Separated from the Blue Hill Peninsula by Eggemoggin Reach, Deer Isle and Stonington are significantly off the beaten path. The area was settled by farmers in 1755 but today is primarily devoted to fishing. That's why the annual Fishermen's Day, in late July, is so popular. Coast Guard demonstrations, rowboat races, and a codfish relay race mark the celebration. A Stonington Independence Day festival includes a "fish and fritter fry" and fireworks.

DEER ISLE VILLAGE

16 mi south of Blue Hill.

Around Deer Isle Village, thick woods give way to tidal coves. Stacks of lobster traps populate the backyards of shingled houses, and dirt roads lead to secluded summer cottages. This region is prized by artists, and studios and galleries are plentiful. (*See Sports & the Outdoors for park and preserve listings.*)

Exhibiting works by area artists in summer, the gallery of the **Deer Isle Artists Association** is open daily. ⊠*6 Dow St., off Rte. 15, Deer Isle* ☎*207/348–2330* ☉*Late June–Aug., daily 1–5.*

Haystack Mountain School of Crafts offers two- and three-week-long courses for people of all skill levels in such crafts as blacksmithing, basketry, printmaking, and weaving. Artisans from around the world present evening lectures throughout summer (*see Blue Heron Gallery in Shopping to learn about buying their work*). You can take a free tour of the facility at 1 PM on Wednesday, June through September. In autumn, shorter courses are available to New England residents. The school is

6 mi from Deer Isle Village, off Route 15. ⊠*89 Haystack School Dr., Deer Isle* ☎*207/348–2306* ⊕*www.haystack-mtn.org.*

WHERE TO EAT & STAY

$$$–$$$$ ✕⊡ **Goose Cove Lodge.** A country lane leads to this spectacular ocean-front property, where cottages and suites are scattered through the woods and along a sandy beach. Most of the guest rooms have fire-places to keep out the chill. At low tide you can walk across a sandbar to the beautiful Barred Island Preserve. Reservations are essential at the superb restaurant ($$–$$$). The expertly prepared contemporary American fare includes at least one vegetarian entrée. On Monday nights in July and August you can join a lobster feast on the beach. **Pros:** Lovely sea views and sense of isolation and escape. **Con:** Cold and dreary in bad weather. ⊠*300 Goose Cove Rd., Box 40, Sunset 04683* ☎*207/348–2508 or 800/728–1963* ⊕*www.goosecovelodge.com* ⇗*2 rooms, 7 suites, 13 cottages* ⌂*In-room: no a/c, no phone, no TV. In-hotel: 2 restaurants, beachfront, no-smoking rooms* ▤*D, MC, V* ⊗*All but 3 units closed mid-Oct.–mid-May* ⊺⊙*BP.*

$$–$$$$ ✕⊡ **Pilgrim's Inn.** A four-story gambrel-roof house, this inn dates from ★ about 1793. Wing chairs and Oriental rugs fill the library; a down-stairs taproom has a huge brick fireplace and pine furniture. Individu-ally furnished guest rooms—each filled with quilts, some with exposed beams and supports, others with canopy frames overhead—overlook a mill pond and harbor. Three cottages—Rugosa Rose, Ginny's One, and Ginny's Two—are perfect for families. The dining room ($$$–$$$$) is rustic yet elegant with exposed beams, hardwood floors, and French oil lamps. Try an appetizer of ouzo-flamed gulf shrimp with black olives and feta or a warm salad of spinach, smoked mussels, goat cheese, and pine nuts. For the main course, you can try traditional boiled Maine lobster, or go for something entirely different like sautéed venison with shiitake mushrooms. Be sure to save room for desserts like the mocha mousse. **Pros:** Memorable architecture and early-American interior, an oasis of fine cuisine. **Cons:** Creaky floors, squeaky bedsprings, and only adequate bathrooms. ⊠*20 Main St., 04627* ☎*207/348–6615 or 888/778–7505* ⊕*www.pilgrimsinn.com* ⇗*12 rooms, 3 cottages* ⌂*In-room: no a/c, no phone, no TV. In-hotel: restaurant, bicycles, no-smok-ing rooms, some pets allowed, no elevator* ▤*AE, D, MC, V* ⊗*Closed mid-Oct.–mid-May* ⊺⊙*BP.*

SPORTS & THE OUTDOORS

Famous landscape architect Frederick Law Olmsted once owned **Barred Island Preserve** (⊠*Goose Cove Rd., Deer Isle* ☎*No phone* ⊠*Free* ⊙*Daily dawn–dusk*). His grandniece, Carolyn Olmsted, donated it to the Nature Conservancy in 1969. The island is accessible only at low tide. The mile-long trail leading to the island offers great views of Penobscot Bay. Pick up a brochure at the Deer Isle–Stonington Cham-ber of Commerce for a map of the islands you can see from the area. The parking area fills quickly, so arrive early. While enjoying miles of woodland and shore trails at the **Edgar M. Tennis Preserve** (⊠*Tennis Rd. off Sunshine Rd., Deer Isle* ☎*No phone* ⊠*Free* [tours] ⊙*Daily dawn–dusk*), you can look for hawks, eagles, and ospreys, and wander among old apple trees, fields of wildflowers, and ocean-polished rocks. For picnics, bird-watching, or launching kayaks and canoes, visit **Mariners Memorial Park** (✉*Fire Rd. 501 off Sunshine Rd., Deer Isle* ☎*No phone* ☎*Free* ☉*Daily dawn–dusk*), overlooking secluded Long Cove. A mixture of hard- and soft-wood trees, including birch, oak, maple, and white pine, make an excellent habitat for songbirds at **Shore Acres Preserve** (✉ *Greenlaw District Rd. off Sunshine Rd., Deer Isle* ☎*No phone* ☎*Free* ☉*Daily dawn–dusk*) on the eastern edge of Deer Isle. On a 1½-mi walking trail you can see native plants like juniper, blueberry, and cranberry, as well as mushrooms, mosses, and ferns. You might even spot a fox, a red squirrel, or a hawk.

TAKE A TOUR

Registered guide Captain Walt Reed takes a maximum of four passengers on boat tours around Deer Isle. Guided Island Tours (✉*27 Seabreeze Ave., Stonington 04681* ☎*207/348-6789* ⊕*www.guidedislandtours.com*). For cruising the outer islands around Isle au Haut and Acadia National Park, check with the Isle Au Haut Company (✉*27 Seabreeze Ave., Stonington 04681* ☎*207/367-5193* ⊕*www.isleauhaut.com*).

One- and two-person canoes and kayaks are available at **Finest Kind Canoe & Kayak Rentals** (✉*70 Center District Crossroad, near Rtes. 15 and 15A, Deer Isle* ☎*207/348-7714* ⊕*www.finestkindenterprises.com*). The company offers free delivery and pickup. It also rents mountain bikes by the day or by the week.

SHOPPING

Blue Heron Gallery (✉*49 Sand Beach Rd.* ☎*207/367-2623* ⊕*www.blueherondeerisle.com*) sells work by the artists from the Haystack Mountain School of Crafts. Meet the artists at receptions from 3 to 5 PM every other Sunday in June and August. Purchase a handmade quilt from **Dockside Quilt Gallery** (✉*33 Church St.* ☎*207/348-2849 or 207/348-2531* ⊕*www.docksidequiltgallery.com*). If you don't see anything you like, you can commission a custom-designed quilt. **Harbor Farm** (✉*29 Little Deer Isle Rd. [Rte. 15], Little Deer Isle* ☎*207/348-7737* ⊕*www.harborfarm.com*) carries wonderful products for the home, such as pottery, linens, and folk art. **Nervous Nellie's Jams and Jellies** (✉*598 Sunshine Rd.* ☎*207/348-6182 or 800/777-6825* ⊕*www.nervousnellies.com*) sells jams and jellies, operates the Mountain View café, and has a sculpture garden with work by Peter Beerits. **Old Deer Isle Parish House Antiques** (✉*7 Church St.* ☎*207/348-6841*) is a great place for poking around in piles of old kitchenware, glassware, books, and linens. **Turtle Gallery** (✉*61 N. Deer Isle Rd.* ☎*207/348-9977* ⊕*www.turtlegallery.com*) exhibits contemporary painting, sculpture, and crafts.

STONINGTON

7 mi south of Deer Isle.

Stonington is rather isolated, which has helped retain its small-town flavor. The boutiques and galleries lining Main Street cater mostly to

Stonington Granite

CLOSE UP

Although you can see almost no sign of it today, the granite industry used to be a vital part of Stonington's economy. The first quarry was established in the 1860s, when the area known as Green's Landing had a population of approximately 300 people. From 1869 to 1969, area granite was used to build the Brooklyn Bridge, the Boston Museum of Fine Arts, the Smithsonian Institution, and other well-known sites. Demand was so high during the late 1800s that the town welcomed a wave of immigrants from Italy and Sweden, swelling the population to more than 5,000 people.

In 1897 Green's Landing split from Deer Isle and became known as

Stonington. Since no bridge connected the area to the mainland until 1939, the community had to be completely self-sufficient. The boom was short-lived, however. With the rediscovery of concrete in the early 20th century, the granite industry ground to a sudden halt. Although one quarry reopened in the 1960s to fashion the granite blocks used in the Kennedy Memorial, it was unable to remain profitable. Today, Stonington's year-round population totals less than 1,200. The only remaining active quarry is on Crotch Island, just off the coast of Stonington. Its granite is shipped to Rhode Island, where it is cut for countertops and building facades.

out-of-towners, but the town remains a fishing community at heart. The principal activity is at the waterfront, where boats arrive overflowing with the day's catch. The sloped island that rises to the south is Isle au Haut, which contains a remote section of Acadia National Park; it's accessible by mail boat from Stonington.

WHAT TO SEE

The tiny **Deer Isle Granite Museum** documents Stonington's quarrying tradition. The museum's centerpiece is an 8- by 15-foot working model of quarrying operations on Crotch Island and the town of Stonington at the turn of the last century. ⊠ *51 Main St.* ☎ *207/367–6331* ⊠ *Free* ⊘ *Memorial Day–Labor Day, Mon.–Sat. 10–5, Sun. 1–5.*

Once a busy mine employing hundreds of men, **Settlement Quarry** closed in the 1980s. Visit the grounds for the panoramic views and easy walking trails. ⊠ *Off Oceanville Rd.* ⊠ *Free* ⊘ *Daily.*

OFF THE BEATEN PATH

Off-Shore Islands. Many of the uninhabited islands near Deer Isle and Stonington are open for public use. One of the most popular is Green Island, which has an old quarry that is perfect for swimming. Some are for day-use only, while others allow overnight camping. All of these islands operate on a "leave no trace" basis, meaning that you must stay on marked trails and carry out what you carry in. For more information, contact **Island Heritage Trust** (⊠ *3 Main St.,* ✉ *Box 42, Deer Isle 04627* ☎ *207/348–2455*) or the **Maine Island Trail Association** (⊠ *328 Main St., Box C, Rockland 04841* ☎ *207/596–6456* ⊕ *www.mita.org*).

WHERE TO EAT & STAY

$$–$$$ ✗ **Maritime Café.** Specializing in ★ seafood, with crepes and espresso for clients taking in the view but not necessarily dining, this harborside terrace restaurant is an ideal, if slightly pricey, perch for watching the Stonington fishing port in action while also enjoying some of its freshest produce. The crab cakes are excellent. ✉ *27 Main St.* ☎ *207/367–2600* ▭ *MC, V.*

$–$$ ✗ **Lily's.** Homemade baked goods, delicious sandwiches, and fresh ★ salads are on the menu at this friendly café. Try the Italian turkey sandwich, which has slices of oven-roasted turkey and Jack cheese on homemade sourdough bread. The dining room's glass-top tables reveal the seashells and various treasures inside. A produce stand behind the restaurant sells some of the same organic foods used by the chefs here. ✉ *Corner of Rte. 15 and Airport Rd.* ☎ *207/367–5936* ▭ *MC, V.*

$$ ⌂ **Inn on the Harbor.** From the front, this inn made up of four century-old Victorian buildings is as plain and unadorned as the town in which it is located. But in the rear is an expansive deck over the harbor—a pleasant spot for morning coffee or afternoon cocktails. Rooms on the harbor side have lovely views, and some have fireplaces and private decks. One room is wheelchair accessible. **Pros:** Lovely harbor views, a sense of partaking in the life at the fishing port. **Cons:** Lobster boat traffic jams at 5 AM can be disruptive, street-side rooms are noisy at night. ✉ *45 Main St., Box 69, 04681* ☎ *207/367–2420 or 800/942–2420* ⊕ *www.innontheharbor.com* ⇋ *12 rooms, 2 suites* ⌂ *In-room: no a/c, dial-up. In-hotel: no kids under 12, no-smoking rooms, no elevator* ▭ *AE, D, MC, V* ⦿ *CP.*

¢–$ ⌂ **Boyce's Motel.** This downtown motel offers simply furnished guest rooms with wall-to-wall carpeting. It also has apartment-style accommodations with full kitchens, separate sitting areas, and decks with views of the harbor. **Pros:** Central location in the middle of Stonington; walking distance from restaurants, the harbor, and the opera house. **Cons:** Rooms are not spacious, and some are only a few feet off Main Street. ✉ *44 Main St., 04681* ☎ *207/367–2421 or 800/224–2421* ⊕ *www.boycesmotel.com* ⇋ *4 rooms, 7 apartments* ⌂ *In-room: no a/c, kitchen (some). In-hotel: some pets allowed, no elevator* ▭ *AE, D, MC, V* ⦿ *BP.*

¢ ⛰ **Old Quarry Campground.** This oceanfront campground offers both open and wooded campsites with raised platforms for tents, table, chairs, and fire rings. Carts are available to tote your gear to your site. Another property, Sunshine Campground, is on Deer Isle. **Pro:** Campsites on the water with spectacular views. **Con:** Somewhat uproarious in the height of summer when fully booked. ✉ *130 Settlement Rd., off Oceanville Rd., 04681* ☎ *207/367–8977* ⊕ *www.oldquarry.com* ⇋ *10 tent sites* ⌂ *Flush toilets, drinking water, guest laundry, showers, public telephone, general store, swimming* ▭ *MC, V* ⦿ *Closed Nov.–Apr.*

SPORTS & THE OUTDOORS

Old Quarry Ocean Adventures (✉*130 Settlement Rd.* ☎*207/367–8977* ⊕*www.oldquarry.com*) rents bicycles, canoes, and kayaks, and offers guided tours of the bay. Captain Bill Baker's three-hour boat tours take you past Stonington Harbor on the way to the outer islands. You can see Crotch Island, which has the area's only active stone quarry, and Green Island, where you can take a dip in a water-filled quarry. Tours cover the region's natural history, the history of Stonington, and the history of the granite industry. Sunset cruises are also available.

SHOPPING

Art and antiques are for sale at the **Clown** (✉*6 Thurlow's Hill* ☎*207/367–6348*), as well as specialty foods and wine. Facing the harbor, **Dockside Books & Gifts** (✉*62 W. Main St.* ☎*207/367–2652*) stocks an eclectic selection of books.

ISLE AU HAUT

14 mi south of Stonington.

Isle au Haut thrusts its steeply ridged back out of the sea south of Stonington. French explorer Samuel D. Champlain discovered Isle au Haut—or "High Island"—in 1604, but heaps of shells suggest that native populations lived on or visited the island prior to his arrival. The island is accessible only by mail boat, but the 45-minute journey is well worth the effort. As you pass between the tiny islands of Merchants Row, you might see terns, guillemots, and harbor seals. The ferry makes two trips a day between Stonington and the Town Landing from Monday to Saturday, and adds a Sunday trip from mid-May to mid-September. From mid-June to mid-September, the ferry also stops at Duck Harbor, located within Acadia National Park. The ferry will not unload bicycles, kayaks, or canoes at Duck Harbor, however.

Except for a grocery store and a natural-foods store, Isle au Haut does not have any opportunities for shopping. The island is ideal for daytrippers intent on exploring its miles of trails, or those seeking a night or two of low-key accommodations and delicious homemade meals.

★ Half of Isle au Haut is part of beautiful **Acadia National Park** (⇨*See* Chapter 6). More than 18 mi of trails wind through quiet spruce woods, along beaches and seaside cliffs, and over the spine of the central mountain ridge. The park's small campground, with five lean-tos, is open from mid-May to mid-October and fills up quickly. Reservations are essential. You can access Acadia from the Town Landing. If you turn right when you arrive at the dock, the ranger station is a short walk or bike ride away. Public rest rooms are here, as is the trailhead for the Duck Harbor Trail. ✉*Isle au Haut* ☎*207/288–3338* ⊕*www. nps.gov/acad.*

WHERE TO EAT & STAY

$$$$ 🏠**Inn at Isle au Haut.** This sea captain's home from 1897 retains its architectural charm. On the eastern side of the island, the seaside inn has views of sheep roaming around distant York Island and Cadillac

Mountain. Comfortable wicker furniture is scattered around the porch, where appetizers are served when the weather is good. Downstairs, the dining room has original oil lamps and a model of the sea captain's boat (which sank just offshore). Breakfast includes granola and a hot dish like a spinach, tomato, and cheese frittata. Dinner is an elaborate five-course meal usually incorporating local seafood. One night a week the inn has a lobster bake on the shore. The first-floor Captain's Quarters, the only room with a private bath, has an ocean view, as do two of the three upstairs rooms. All have colorful quilts and frilly canopies. **Pros:** Nonpareil views and first-class dining. **Cons:** Shared baths, thin walls. ⊠ *78 Atlantic Ave., Box 78, 04645* ☎ *207/335–5141* ⊕ *www. innatisleauhaut.com* ⇨ *4 rooms, 1 with bath* ⇘ *In-room: no a/c, no phone, no TV. In-hotel: bicycles, no-smoking rooms, no elevator* ⊟ *No credit cards* ⊙ *Closed Oct.–May* ⊚ *MAP.*

$$$$ ⌂ **Keeper's House.** Hidden by thick woods, this converted lighthouse keeper's home is an ideal spot to unwind. The ecofriendly inn has a reverse-osmosis system that purifies the drinking water, and solar-power and wind-power generators. There's no electricity in the guest rooms, however, so in the evening you can dine by candlelight and read by kerosene lantern. The spacious rooms are filled with painted wood furniture and decorated with local crafts. Breakfast features pancakes, granola with fresh fruit, eggs Benedict with smoked salmon, and other delicious dishes. Dinner emphasizes locally raised meats and freshly caught fish, like the haddock used for the delicious seafood stew. The inn also packs bag lunches for you to take with you when exploring the trails of Acadia National Park. **Pros:** A magical escape from the routine of daily life, esthetically and ecologically perfect. **Con:** Spaces in the garret room are a bit constricted. Caveat: At the time of this writing, the inn was for sale, so it may or may not be operating as an inn in 2008. ⊠ *Lighthouse Rd., Box 26, 04645* ☎ *207/460–0257* ⊕ *www. keepershouse.com* ⇨ *4 rooms, 2 with bath; 1 cottage* ⇘ *In-room: no a/c, no phone, no TV. In-hotel: bicycles, no-smoking rooms, no elevator* ⊟ *No credit cards* ⊙ *Closed mid-Oct.–mid-May* ⊚ *MAP.*

NEED A BREAK? For an eclectic potpourri of goods ranging from seafaring hero Linda Greenlaw books to homemade quilts, drop by the Sea Urchin (⊠ ⊹ *From boat landing, turn right on town road and walk ½ mi* ☎ *207/335–2021*).

SPORTS & THE OUTDOORS

There's no place to rent bicycles on Isle au Haut. If you want to bike around the island, head to **Old Quarry Ocean Adventures** (⊠ *130 Settlement Rd., Stonington* ☎ *207/367–8977* ⊕ *www.oldquarry.com*). The mainland company can transport you and your bikes to Isle au Haut.

THE BLUE HILL PENINSULA ESSENTIALS

To research prices, get advice from other travelers, and book travel arrangements, visit www.fodors.com.

TRANSPORTATION

BY AIR

Trenton's Hancock County–Bar Harbor Airport is near the Blue Hill Peninsula, but only one commuter airline—Colgan Air, a subsidiary of US Airways, flies here to and from Boston. The Boston–Bar Harbor flight offers, on a clear day, bird's-eye views of the Maine Coast, but bad weather often makes arrivals and departures uncertain. Most travelers to the peninsula prefer Bangor International Airport, an hour's drive away, into which American, Continental, Delta, Midwest Express, Northwest, and US Airways fly.

Airports **Bangor International Airport** (⊠ *287 Godfrey Blvd., Bangor* ☎ *207/947–0384* ⊕ *www.flybangor.com*). **Hancock County–Bar Harbor Airport** (⊠ *Rte. 3, Trenton* ☎ *207/667–7329* ⊕ *www.bhbairport.com*).

BY BUS

Bus routes travel to Bangor and a few other cities along Route 1. (⇨ *See* Transportation section in Maine Essentials in the back of the book.)

BY TRAIN

Portland is the closest city to the Blue Hill Peninsula with train service. From Portland, it takes approximately three hours by car to reach the peninsula. (⇨ *See* Portland Essentials in Chapter 2 for train details.)

CONTACTS & RESOURCES

EMERGENCIES

In an emergency, dial 911.

Police In Stonington, call ☎207/667–7575 for police emergencies.

24-Hour Medical Care **Blue Hill Memorial Hospital** (⊠ *57 Water St., Blue Hill* ☎ *207/374–2836* ⊕ *www.bhmh.org*). **Island Medical Center** (⊠ *Airport Rd. near Rte. 15, Stonington* ☎ *207/367–2311*).

MEDIA

NEWSPAPERS & MAGAZINES The weekly *Castine Patriot* provides news and features for the villages of Castine and Penobscot. *The Weekly Packet* serves Blue Hill, Brooklin, Brooksville, Sedgwick, and Surry. News about Deer Isle, Stonington, and Isle au Haut can be found in the weekly *Island Ad-Vantages*. The *Bangor Daily News* is the regional daily newspaper.

TELEVISION & RADIO Community radio station WERU (89.9 FM) in Blue Hill has eclectic programming, playing country, classical, folk, jazz, and reggae. The local National Public Radio affiliate is 90.9 FM. Channel 2 is the NBC affiliate, channel 7 is the ABC affiliate, and channel 5 is the CBS affiliate. Channel 12 is the Maine Public Broadcasting affiliate.

VISITOR INFORMATION

Contacts **Blue Hill Peninsula Chamber of Commerce** (⊠ *28 Water St., Blue Hill 04614* ☎ *207/374–3242* ⊕ *www.bluehillpeninsula.org*). **Deer Isle-Stonington Chamber of Commerce** (⊠ *Rte. 15, Deer Isle 04627* ☎ *207/348–6124* ⊕ *www.deerisle.com*).

Acadia National Park & Mount Desert Island

WORD OF MOUTH

"I've been going to Mount Desert Island every year for the past 25 years. It's a wonderful place; it always feels new. We never run out of things to do."

—tico

By Lelah Cole

Updated by
Stephen Allen

WITH SOME OF THE MOST DRAMATIC and varied scenery on the Maine Coast, and home to Maine's one and only national park, Mount Desert Island (pronounced "Mount Dessert" Island by locals), it's no wonder this is Maine's most popular tourist destination, attracting more than 2 million visitors a year. Much of the approximately 12-mi-long by 9-mi-wide island belongs to Acadia National Park. The rocky coastline rises starkly from the ocean, appreciable along the scenic drives. Trails for hikers of all skill levels lead to the rounded tops of the mountains, providing views of Frenchman and Blue Hill bays, and beyond. Ponds and lakes beckon you to swim, fish, or boat. Ferries and charter boats provide a different perspective on the island and a chance to explore the outer islands, all of which are a part of Maine but not a part of Mount Desert. A network of old carriage roads lets you explore Acadia's wooded interior, filled with birds and other wildlife.

Mount Desert Island has four different townships, each with its own personality. The town of Bar Harbor is on the northeastern corner of the island, and includes Bar Harbor and the little villages of Hulls Cove, Salisbury Cove, and Town Hill. The town of Mount Desert comprises the southeastern corner of the island and parts of the western edge, and includes Mount Desert and the little villages of Somesville, Hall Quarry, Beech Hill, Pretty Marsh, Northeast Harbor, Seal Harbor, and Otter Creek. As its name suggests, the town of Southwest Harbor is on the southwestern corner of the island, although the town of Tremont is at the southernmost tip of the west side. This area includes the villages of Southwest Harbor, Manset, Bass Harbor, Bernard, and Seal Cove. The island's major tourist destination is Bar Harbor, which has plenty of accommodations, restaurants, and shops. Less congested are the smaller communities of Northeast Harbor, Southwest Harbor, and Bass Harbor. Mount Desert Island is a place with three personalities: the hustling, bustling tourist mecca of Bar Harbor, the "quiet side" of the island composed of the little villages, and the vast natural expanse that is Acadia National Park.

EXPLORING ACADIA NATIONAL PARK & MOUNT DESERT ISLAND

Shaped like an upside-down "U"(some have likened it to the look of a lobster claw), Mount Desert Island is relatively easy to navigate. It may, however, take longer to reach some of the more distant points than you might expect. Somes Sound, the only fjord on the East Coast, runs up the middle of the island, requiring drivers at the ends of the "U" to drive quite a long distance to reach a town that is actually quite close as the crow flies. Beyond the geographical barriers, summer traffic can slow your progress and make finding a parking space, especially in Bar Harbor, nearly impossible. To combat this problem, Acadia National Park has created a free bus system called the Island Explorer. The system, which operates during the high season (Memorial Day through Labor Day), links the island's villages and campgrounds. These propane-propelled buses, which are air-conditioned and outfitted with bike racks, are kinder to the environment than most cars. (⇨ *See By Bus*

GREAT ITINERARIES

IF YOU HAVE 3 DAYS

If you have three days on Mount Desert Island, stay in **Bar Harbor**. There's plenty of things in this popular resort town to keep you occupied on your first day—from bustling boutiques to interesting museums. On Day 2, stop at the Hulls Cove Visitor Center to pick up information about special events, then head to Acadia National Park. A drive around **Park Loop Road** is a great way to learn the lay of the land. Stop along the way—a lot of the scenic overlooks have informational signs you may find interesting. Finish up the Park Loop Road journey by driving to the top of **Cadillac Mountain** to enjoy the sunset. On Day 3, rent a bike and explore the network of carriage roads that crisscross the island. Take in the spectacular view of **Jordan Pond** from the observation deck of

the Jordan Pond House, a restaurant known for its massive popovers with lots of strawberry jam. For the afternoon's entertainment, hike the South Bubble Mountain (easier) or Penobscot Mountain (more challenging). As an alternative to the above, you may want to consider a one-day excursion to Nova Scotia via The CAT, if it's running that day (⇨ *See listing in Bar Harbor section*).

IF YOU HAVE 5 DAYS

Follow the three-day itinerary above. On Day 4, drive to **Northeast Harbor,** the summer home of many of the country's wealthiest families. Take in the Asticou Azalea Garden and Thuya Gardens. On your last day, take a sightseeing cruise in the morning. In the afternoon, head to Bass Harbor Head Lighthouse, taking in **Somesville** and **Southwest Harbor** along the way.

in the Essentials section at the end of this chapter for Island Explorer contact information.)

Acadia's Park Loop Road provides an excellent overview of the island, but to get a feel for the island's natural beauty, you must leave your car behind. Instead, seek as many opportunities as you can for hiking, biking, and boating.

WHEN TO GO

Memorial Day and Labor Day mark the official beginning and end of high season on Mount Desert Island. The reality, however, is that there is no reason you have to visit during this narrow window. Temperatures often begin to rise in April or May. You may have to contend with minor irritants such as ice and snow on the trails through Acadia National Park, but the crowds are smaller during these months.

By September, the heat and humidity of summer begin to taper off, making it one of the most enjoyable months to visit. Autumn foliage peaks between the end of September and the middle of October, enhancing the already spectacular views. Although many seasonal businesses close their doors after Columbus Day, the island does not shut down entirely. You can still find some good restaurants and a small number of lodging options throughout the winter months.

Regardless of when you decide to go, you will enjoy your visit to the island more if you book your accommodations in advance, especially if you have a particular type of lodging in mind or if you'll be visiting on a holiday weekend. Although it's possible to find last-minute lodging during the summer months, it may take several phone calls. From November to April, your challenge shifts from finding an open room to finding an open hotel, motel, or bed-and-breakfast. Call ahead.

ABOUT THE RESTAURANTS

With some of the nation's wealthiest families making Mount Desert Island their summer residence, a handful of restaurants cater to those seeking an upscale dining experience. These restaurants offer carefully prepared dishes, extensive wine lists, and impressive service. Like most of the coast, the area is also home to many restaurants specializing in hamburgers and other typical American fare. You won't see fast-food chains, but you will find good food at reasonable prices. Many area restaurants carry locally produced microbrews on draft or by the bottle. If you like pale ales, brown ales, or stouts, you should be able to find something to tempt the palate. **Note:** In accordance with Maine state law, smoking is not allowed in any place that serves food, be it a restaurant or a bar.

ABOUT THE HOTELS

Mount Desert Island offers a range of accommodations to suit every budget. Whether you are looking for campgrounds, bed-and-breakfasts, or resort hotels, there are lodging options to meet your needs. Bar Harbor is the island's most well-known community, and it's a good choice for being close to shopping and nightlife, but the other villages offer accommodations that are equally—or even more—enticing, especially if you want a quieter lodging experience. If you drive along Route 3, you can spot a number of roadside motels and cabin-style accommodations that fall into lower price categories. Some bed-and-breakfasts can also be quite reasonable. Those looking to stay in a sprawling resort hotel or a beautifully appointed seaside inn should be prepared for prices in the top categories. Acadia National Park offers two wooded campgrounds but no cabins nor lodges.

The high-season rates go into effect during the second half of June and don't drop again until after Labor Day. Rates often dip significantly in spring and autumn. Winter rates are the lowest.

WHAT IT COSTS					
	¢	$	$$	$$$	$$$$
RESTAURANTS	under $7	$7–$10	$11–$17	$18–$25	over $25
HOTELS	under $60	$60–$99	$100–$149	$150–$200	over $200

Restaurant prices are for a main course at dinner, excluding sales tax of 7%. Hotel prices are for two people in a standard double room in high season, excluding service charges and 7% tax.

GATEWAYS TO MOUNT DESERT ISLAND

Ellsworth and Trenton are unlikely to be focal points during your vacation, but you can't avoid them if you're traveling to Mount Desert Island. Ellsworth is a good place to pick up supplies for your journey, while Trenton's best offering is the view you see when crossing the bridge to the island. On clear days, the sunlight sparkles off the ocean, and the bald peaks of Acadia's mountains stand out starkly against the rich forests of conifers and evergreens. The beauty of it is overwhelming.

ELLSWORTH

140 mi northeast of Portland, 28 mi south of Bangor.

Ellsworth is the storm's eye through which all vehicles traveling to Mount Desert Island must pass. As such, the few short miles of U.S. 1 that pass through the city can be fraught with frustration in summer. Traffic can back up for miles as cars wait to pass through the four traffic lights along High Street. Despite the congestion, Ellsworth is a good spot for refueling—literally and figuratively. With two supermarkets, several good restaurants, and a range of shops, the city has nearly anything you need. The main shopping roads are High Street, where you find two malls; and Main Street, home to distinctive shops set in attractive brick buildings.

Stanwood Homestead Museum & Wildlife Sanctuary. At this 130-acre attraction, look for birds along the trails and visit the museum, an 1850 Cape Cod–style house. Cordelia Stanwood, born in 1856, was one of Maine's earliest ornithologists. ✉ *Rte. 3* ☎ *207/667–8460* ⊕ *www.birdsacre.com* 🎫 *Free* ⊙ *Trails daily sunrise–sunset; museum mid-May–mid-Oct., daily 10–4.*

Woodlawn Museum. Between 1824 and 1828, Colonel John Black built an elegant Federal-style house on an 180-acre estate of fields and woods. Inside are an especially fine elliptical flying staircase and period artifacts from the three generations of the family that lived here. Outside, Woodlawn has 2 mi of walking trails that Colonel Black used as a bridle path. As a visitor, you can wander through several different gardens. The formal garden, enclosed by a lilac hedge, features flowers popular in the 19th century, including iris, daylilies, and phlox. The Woodlawn Museum is also the home of the increasingly popular Ellsworth Antiques Show, which takes place in mid-August. ✉ *19 Black House Rd.* ☎ *207/667–8671* ⊕ *www.woodlawnmuseum.org* 🎫 *$7.50, free access to gardens and grounds* ⊙ *May–Oct., Tues.–Sat. 10–5, Sun 1–4.*

WHERE TO EAT & STAY

$$–$$$ ✕ **Luna Rosa.** Formerly called Turriglio's Italian Restaurant, this excellent eatery is now in the hands of Luigi Del Conte. The menu offers traditional fare such as fettuccine Alfredo and stuffed manicotti, as well as more unusual entrées such as *aragosta alla pescatora,* a medley of lobster, scallops, shrimp, and mussels tossed with linguine and a

mildly spicy marinara sauce. Also available are early-bird specials, for guests who want to partake of slightly smaller portions at cheaper prices. ✉*59 Franklin St., Ellsworth* ☎*207/667–0202* ⊟*MC, V* ⊘*Closed Mon. No lunch.*

$–$$$ ✕**Cleonice.** Locals rave about this ★ place—and with good reason. Chef and owner Rich Hanson is a lover of tapas, and he will probably make you love them as well. Tapas are small portions of delicious little things to eat, which can be very appealing to those who like to eat light. The theme is Mediterranean, and the menu is unusual and interesting, with full-plate dishes on hand in addition to the tapas. Try the Paella Cleonice, which, like the restaurant, is named after the chef's mother. ✉*112 Main St.* ☎*207/664–7554* ⊕*www.cleonice.com* ⊟*AE, MC, V.*

¢–$$ ✕**Jordan's Snack Bar.** This take-out restaurant with a roll-up-your-sleeves atmosphere has some of the best fried clams around. Locals will wait more than an hour on opening day to order the delicious fried seafood. The menu also has burgers and fries. Choose between the indoor seating area and the outdoor picnic tables. To find this place, turn left where U.S. 1 splits from Route 3 and continue for about a mile. ✉*200 Down East Rd., Ellsworth* ☎*207/667–2174* ⊟*MC, V* ⊘*Closed Nov.–early Mar.*

¢–$$ ✕**Riverside Café.** The only thing better than the food at this popular eatery is the staff's camaraderie. The employees are fast, friendly, and frequently banter back and forth across the restaurant. Open early for breakfast, the café offers everything from French toast and blueberry pancakes to omelets and breakfast burritos. On Sunday, the menu expands to include raspberry-stuffed French toast and pumpkin pancakes with maple cream. For lunch you can choose among sandwiches, quiches, and salads. The baked goods, including muffins and biscuits, are baked on the premises. Works by a different area artist are displayed each month. ✉*151 Main St.* ☎*207/667–7220* ⊟*AE, MC, V* ⊘*No dinner Sun.–Wed..*

¢–$ ✕**Frankie's Café.** This small eatery serves fresh sandwiches, wraps, and soups, which you can eat in or take out. There are also a few hot dishes that rotate daily, including stuffed ravioli, fajitas, lasagna, and quiche. ✉*40 High St.* ☎*207/667–7701* ⊟*MC, V.*

$$–$$$ ▦**Comfort Inn.** Open throughout the year, this chain hotel has simply decorated rooms with some nice touches like hair dryers and irons. It sits adjacent to the L.L. Bean factory outlet and several eateries. Four rooms are handicapped accessible, and 10 are available to smokers. Service animals are okay, but otherwise no pets are allowed. **Pros:**

MOUNT DESERT ISLAND TOP 5

■ Take the circle drive through Acadia National Park.

■ Hike—or drive—to the 1,532-foot top of Cadillac Mountain for a spectacular view.

■ Climb down the rocks to the edge of the ocean to shoot the most photographed lighthouse in Maine, Bass Harbor Head Light.

■ Hop a ride on The CAT (high-speed catamaran) from Bar Harbor to Nova Scotia, Canada.

Breakfast included; there's a nice restaurant, Jasper's, within walking distance. **Con:** High Street can get noisy at night. ⊠ *130 High St., 04609* ☎ *207/667–1345* ⊕ *www.comfortinn.com* ➱ *63 rooms* ⌂ *In-room: refrigerator (some), Wi-Fi. In-hotel: gym, no-smoking rooms, no elevator* ⊟ *AE, DC, MC, V* ⎮◎⎮ *CP.*

$–$$$ ⚠ **Patten Pond Camping Resort.** This is a huge and attractive RV camp-ground with a lot of amenities, including full hookups, wireless access, and areas for swimming, boating, and fishing on a 740-acre lake. Boats—canoes, motorboats, paddleboats, and kayaks—and bikes are available for rent. In addition to the RV and tent sites, there are rental cabins (with fire ring and bathroom outside) and one cottage (with kitchen and bath inside). Tent sites run $20–$28 per night, while RV site rates are $25–$44. Cabins are $50–$85 per night, and cottages are a weekly rate of $1,100. Weekends bring live entertainment and blue-berry-pancake breakfasts on Saturday morning. **Pros:** Full-service and fun activities like ice-cream socials and hayrides. **Con:** If you like to dine out for dinner, you will need to drive. **Note:** Patten Pond is affili-ated with Bar Harbor Camping Resorts, which opened Narrows Too campground and RV park in 2007. It also is full-service with a host of activities and amenities. It is located at 1150 Bar Harbor Road, but uses the same phone number and Web site as Patten Pond. ⊠ *1470 Bucksport Rd. (U.S. 1), 04605* ☎ *207/667–7600* ⊕ *www.pattenpond. com* ➱ *90 RV sites, 30 tent sites* ⌂ *Flush toilets, portable toilets, full hookups, partial hookups, dump station, drinking water, guest laundry, showers, fire grates, picnic tables, electricity, public telephone, gen-eral store, play area, swimming, Wi-Fi* ⊟ *DC, MC, V* ⊘ *Closed mid-Oct.–mid-May.*

NIGHTLIFE & THE ARTS

A local landmark, the **Grand Auditorium** (⊠ *165 Main St.* ☎ *207/667–9500* ⊕ *www.grandonline.org*) opened as a movie theater in 1938. It fell into disrepair, sitting vacant from the '50s to the '70s. The the-ater reopened in 1975 and since then has staged plays, concerts, and shown films.

SPORTS & THE OUTDOORS

Bar Harbor Bicycle Shop (⊠ *193 Main St.* ☎ *207/667–6886* ⊕ *www. barharborbike.com* ⊘ *Daily*) rents road bikes plus recreational and high-performance bikes. It is closed Monday and November–March. Though the name is "Bar Harbor," the company has a shop in both Bar Harbor and Ellsworth.

SHOPPING

GIFTS The **Grasshopper Shop** (⊠ *124 Main St.* ☎ *207/667–5816* ⊘ *Daily*) sells fun and unique gifts. You can find books, candles, linens, jewelry, and women's clothing and shoes. Most of the lower level is dedicated to items for children. With a selection of organic and natural foods, **John Edwards Market** (⊠ *158 Main St.* ☎ *207/667–9377* ⊘ *Daily*) is a pleas-ant alternative to the supermarket when you're stocking up on supplies. Downstairs is a wine cellar and an art gallery that showcases works by area artists. The special lighting throughout is designed to help the many plants thrive and grow. You can find everything for your kitchen

IF YOU LIKE

CARRIAGE ROADS

Roads and cars often go hand in hand, but this is not always true in Acadia National Park. Between 1913 and 1940, John D. Rockefeller Jr. designed and funded the construction of more than 40 mi of carriage roads. Rockefeller, a summer resident of Mount Desert Island, wanted to maintain a way for horse-drawn carriages to safely travel the island after the arrival of automobiles.

Today, the carriage roads provide hours of enjoyment to walkers, joggers, and bikers. The roads wind through fields and forests, past lakes, ponds, and swamps, and around hills and mountains. You can admire the Canadian mayflowers and young, curled ferns in spring; nibble at blueberries that grow among the granite boulders in summer; collect the fallen crimson leaves of sugar maples in autumn; or enjoy the solitude of the winter landscape on snowshoes or cross-country skis. The network of roads offers excursions of varying length and difficulty, so be sure to pick up a map to plan your best routes.

GORGEOUS GARDENS

When Beatrix Farrand, one of the country's first well-known female landscape gardeners, was preparing to retire in the 1950s, she offered her own estate to Bar Harbor as a public park. Since she had designed plant-filled retreats for everywhere from the College of the Atlantic to the White House, she assumed the town would jump at the chance.

Instead, the town politely declined Farrand's offer, saying that the property taxes for the site would be too high. She decided to dismantle the garden and gave her friends a year to come and collect any plants they desired. Her friend Charles Savage, also a landscape designer, retrieved several of Farrand's rhododendrons and azaleas and used them when he created the Asticou Azalea Garden and Thuya Gardens in Northeast Harbor. Some of her beloved blooms remain in the gardens today.

ON THE WATER

With its dramatic coastline, Mount Desert Island is a great spot for sea kayaking. There are shops all over the island that are happy to provide you with gear, offer expert instruction, and give tips on possible routes. Along the way you'll see cormorants and other birds, and you might catch a glimpse of harbor seals.

If you're an angler, stop by the Hulls Cove Visitor Center to find out which species thrive in the dozens of ponds and lakes scattered around the island. Some are popular in the warmer months, while others are better for ice fishing. You can rent canoes in Bar Harbor and other towns. Most of the lakes and ponds have well-marked public access points, making boating even easier. If you are planning on using a motorized watercraft anywhere besides the ocean, check with the park rangers first—many lakes and ponds don't allow motorboats or may restrict the size of the engine.

6

at **Rooster Brothers** (⌧*29 Main St.* ☎*207/667–8675* ⊘*Mon.–Sat.*), including nonstick cookware and bamboo steamers, as well as wines, cheese, and freshly ground coffee. The second floor has a lot of whimsical stuff.

SPORTING One of the best sporting goods stores in the state, **Cadillac Mountain**
GOODS **Sports** (⌧*34 High St.* ☎*207/667–7819* ⊕*www.cadillacmountainsports.com* ⊘*Daily*) has developed a following among locals and visitors alike. A branch of the original store in Bar Harbor, this location carries top-quality bicycles, canoes, kayaks, cross-country skis, and a selection of hiking and camping equipment. If you need a pair of hiking boots, some running shoes, a bike helmet, or a warmer jacket, this is the place to stop (they do not rent equipment).

TRENTON

5 mi south of Ellsworth via Rte. 3.

Like Ellsworth, Trenton is a town that everyone traveling to Mount Desert Island must pass through. The town offers little in the way of dining or lodging options, but it does have the closest airport to the island, which is filled with private jets in summer. Sightseeing flights by plane or glider are popular. Carroll's Supermarket usually has the cheapest gas around—and often the longest lines at the pumps.

⟳ In its fields and woods, the **Acadia Zoo** shelters about 45 species of wild and domestic animals, including reindeer, alligators, wolves, and a moose. A converted barn serves as a rain-forest habitat for monkeys, birds, reptiles, and other Amazon creatures. Having a one-on-one encounter with a moose or a wolf in this exotic animal rescue facility is mostly on an advance-notice basis. ⌧*446 Bar Harbor Rd.* ☎*207/667–3244* ⊕*www.acadiazoo.com* ⌧*$10* ⊘*May–Dec., daily 9:30–dusk.*

SPORTS & THE OUTDOORS

About 8 mi from Route 3, the seaside **Lamoine State Park** (⌧*23 State Park Rd., Lamoine* ☎*207/667–4778 or 207/941–4014* ⊕*www.campwithme.com* ⌧*Park $3, camping sites $15–$20* ⊘*Apr.–Oct., except cross-country skiing in season*) offers a quiet respite from the crowds on Mount Desert Island. During the day you can stroll along the pebble beach, eat lunch on one of the picnic tables, or even camp in the park. There also is a fishing area.

The **Bar Harbor Golf Course** (⌧*51 Jordan River Rd., intersection of Rtes. 3 and 204, Trenton* ☎*207/667–7505*) is an 18-hole golf course open to the public. If you want to practice your swing, **Vokes Driving Range** (⌧*10 Bar Harbor Rd.* ☎*207/667–9519* ⊘*8 AM–7 PM, weather permitting*) has a driving range. There's also a miniature golf course.

⟳ **Seacoast Fun Park** (⌧*50 Bar Harbor Rd.* ☎*207/667–3573* ⊘*May–Sept., daily 10–9*) has go-karts, two waterslides, a 32-foot climbing wall, bungee trampolines, and a miniature golf course.

BAR HARBOR

160 mi northeast of Portland, 22 mi southeast of Ellsworth.

A resort town since the 19th century, Bar Harbor is the artistic, culinary, and social center of Mount Desert Island. It also serves visitors to Acadia National Park with inns, motels, and restaurants. The island's unique topography was shaped by the glaciers of the most recent Ice Age. Around the turn of the last century—before the days of air-conditioning—the island was known as the summer haven of the very rich because of its cool breezes; lavish mansions were built throughout the island. Many of them were destroyed in a great fire that devastated the island in 1947, but many of those that survived have been converted into businesses. Shops are clustered along Main, Mount Desert, and Cottage streets. Take a stroll down West Street, a National Historic District, where you can see some fine old houses.

The island and its surrounding Gulf of Maine are home to a great variety of wildlife: whales, seals, eagles, falcons, ospreys, puffins (probably the most unusual-looking birds in the world), and denizens of the forest, such as moose, deer, foxes, coyotes, and black bears.

∫ TO SEE

❷ Abbe Museum. This is the only museum devoted solely to Maine's American Indian heritage, with a collection of artifacts spanning thousands of years. Open since 2001, the museum has permanent and changing exhibitions. A good time to visit this museum would be during the annual Native American Festival, at the nearby College of the Atlantic (Route 3) the first week in July. (Note: Don't confuse this museum with the one in Acadia National Park.) ⊠26 *Mount Desert St.* ☎207/288–3519 ⊕*www.abbemuseum.org* ☞*$5* ⊗*Mid-May–mid-Oct., daily 9–5.*

❼ Atlantic Brewing Company & Bar Harbor Cellars Farm Winery. Near Bar Harbor in the village of Town Hill, this microbrewery has free tastings. It's also the home of America's first blueberry ale. Tours at 2, 3, and 4 PM last approximately 45 minutes. A barbecue restaurant, Mainely Meat, is also on the premises. ⊠15 *Knox Rd., off Rte. 3, Town Hill* ☎207/288–2337 ⊕*www.atlanticbrewing.com* ☞*Free* ⊗*May–late Oct., daily 10–5.*

❶ Bar Harbor Historical Society Museum. The museum displays photographs of Bar Harbor from the "Gilded Age" of 1880 to 1930. Other exhibits document the great fire that devastated the town and its surrounding areas in 1947. ⊠33 *Ledgelawn Ave.* ☎207/288–3807 or 207/288–0000 ☞*Free* ⊗*Mid-June–mid-Oct., Mon.–Sat. 1–4.*

❸ Bar Harbor Whale Museum. Learn about the history of whaling, the anatomy of whales, and how biologists are working to gain more information about these massive creatures at this interesting museum. All proceeds from the gift shop benefit Allied Whale, a nonprofit organization that conducts marine mammal research. ⊠52 *West St.* ☎207/288–0288 ⊕*www.barharborwhalemuseum.org* ☞*Free* ⊗*Daily, June, 9–10, July and Aug., 9–9.*

❹ Ethel Blum Gallery. This art museum at the College of the Atlantic hosts exhibits throughout the year on painting, sculpture, photography, and other media. ⊠105 *Eden St.* ☎207/288–5015 ☞*Free* ⊗*Tues.–Sat. 10–4.*

❺ George B. Dorr Museum of Natural History. This small museum at the College of the Atlantic displays the natural history of Maine through a human perspective. It has wildlife exhibits, a hands-on discovery room, interpretive programs, and summer field studies for children. ⊠105 *Eden St.* ☎207/288–5395 or 207/288–5015 ⊕*www.coa.edu/nhm* ☞*$4* ⊗*Mid-June–Labor Day, Mon.–Sat. 10–5; Labor Day–mid-Nov. and mid-Jan.–mid-June, Fri. and Sun. 1–4, Sat. 10–4.*

❻ Mount Desert Oceanarium & Lobster Hatchery. The oceanarium will tell you everything you ever wanted to know about lobsters. There also are exhibits on the fishing and sea life of the Gulf of Maine. ⊠Rte. 3, Salisbury Cove, Bar Harbor ☎207/288–5005 ⊕*www.theoceanarium.com* ☞*$9* ⊗*Mid-May–late Oct., Mon.–Sat. 9–5.*

FIDDLING WITH FIDDLEHEADS

As you head toward Mount Desert Island, it's common to see vendors on the side of the roadways selling produce from the back of a pickup truck. In spring, you're likely to see signs offering CLEAN FIDDLEHEADS. Unknown to many Americans, the fiddlehead fern is one of nature's true delicacies. Fiddleheads are the tightly coiled tips of newly emerging fronds, and are about the size of two or three quarters stacked on top of each other.

Fiddleheads come from different varieties of ferns. The best fiddleheads come from ostrich ferns, which, unlike most ferns, have hairless casings. You can also eat the fiddleheads from cinnamon ferns but they have a fuzzier casing. You shouldn't fiddle with some ferns, however. The bracken fern is similar to the ostrich fern, but it's hairy and can give you quite a stomachache.

It can be difficult to identify ferns, but if you are determined to forage, you can identify the type of fern by examining the dead stalks from the previous year. Often these stalks will hold firmly to the plant even after a winter of heavy snow and ice.

Even the best fiddleheads require a good cleaning, and should be thoroughly cooked. If you pick some fiddleheads, be sure to boil them for 10 to 15 minutes. The best method is to boil them for about 7 minutes in one pot, then discard the water and boil them in fresh water until they are tender. Fiddleheads have a distinct flavor that aficionados say is somewhere between asparagus and spinach. Many area restaurants will offer them as a side dish, toss them with pasta, or add them to other dishes. Be sure to give them a try if you are visiting in springtime.

WHERE TO EAT

$$$–$$$$
Fodor's Choice
★
✕**Reading Room at the Bar Harbor Inn & Spa.** This elegant waterfront restaurant serves mostly Continental fare. Look for Maine specialties such as lobster pie and Indian pudding. There's live music nightly. When the weather is nice, what could be more romantic than dining out under the stars at the inn's Terrace Grille with the ships of beautiful Bar Harbor right at your feet? The natural thing to order here would be the Maine lobster bake with all the fixings. For something different, you might try the lobster stew, which is served in a bread bowl. The restaurant is also famous for its Sunday brunch, 11:30–2:30. ⊠*Newport Dr., 04609* ☎*207/288–3351 or 800/248–3351* ⊕*www.barharborinn.com* ⚲*Reservations essential* ☐*AE, DC, MC, V* ⊘*Closed late Nov.–late Mar.*

$$–$$$$
★
✕**Guinness & Porcelli's.** This well-respected restaurant used to be in the Queen City of Bangor and now it's in Bar Harbor. Here's an explanation of the name: delicious Italian food but with "Irish hospitality." Some recommendations are the Penne alla Rustico, which contains wild boar Italian sausage, and the Veal Saltimbocca alla Guinness. Or dig into a pizza. ⊠*191 Main St.* ☎*207/288–0030* ⊕*www.guinnessporcellis.com* ☐*AE, DC, MC, V* ⊘*No lunch.*

$$–$$$$
★
✕**Havana.** As you would expect from the name, this is dining with a Latin flair. Soft jazz playing in the background sets the tone at this storefront restaurant on the edge of downtown Bar Harbor. The pumpkin-color

walls and wood floors lend an air of sophistication. The Latin-influenced menu emphasizes local ingredients and changes weekly. Lobster? Of course, but it's Latin-style. The menu also includes selections like Manchego-Crusted Halibut, Havana Tuna, and Argentian Hanger Steak. On the huge wine list, there are more than 500 choices. ⊠*318 Main St.* ☎*207/288–2822* ⊕*www.havanamaine.com* ⚄*Reservations essential* ▤*MC, V* ☺*Closed Oct.–mid-May. No lunch.*

$$–$$$$ ✕**Quarterdeck.** If you would like to dine while enjoying a view of the colorful harbor, head here. The majority of menu items are seafood— a good choice is the baked stuffed lobster. If you like your seafood uncooked, take a look at the raw bar, which overflows with oysters. ⊠*1 Main St.* ☎*207/288–1161* ⊕*www.quarterdeckbarharbor.com* ▤*AE, DC, MC, V.*

$$$ ✕**Burning Tree.** Local art adorns the walls in the two dining rooms and
★ on the porch at this restaurant in Otter Creek. The ever-changing menu emphasizes freshly caught seafood, and seven species of fish are offered every day, all from the Gulf of Maine. Entrées include pan-sautéed monkfish, oven-poached cod, and gray sole. There are always two or three vegetarian choices. ⊠*Rte. 3, Otter Creek* ☎*207/288–9331* ▤*DC, MC, V* ☺*Closed Tues. and mid-Oct.–mid-June.*

$$–$$$ ✕**Carmen Verandah.** Who would name a restaurant/nightspot "Carmen Verandah"? Probably the same kind of people who would name a restaurant "Rupununi," and the same people own both restaurants, which are right next door to each other. Carmen has a loyal following for dishes that range from Lobster Fra Diavolo to Asian Marinated Hanger Steak. It also has a huge beer and wine selection, plus certain nights of the week bring live music, dancing, and karaoke. ⊠*119 Main St. (upstairs)* ☎*207/288–2766* ⊕*www.carmenverandah.com* ▤*DC, MC, V* ☺.

$$–$$$ ✕**Mache Bistro.** Painted with muted earth tones and decorated with flickering candles, this restaurant's low-key ambience allows for the food to take center stage. The menu changes weekly, but always begins with freshly baked bread. Choose from appetizers such as seared scallops and fiddlehead ferns tossed with penne and Alfredo sauce. Entrées include a seared salmon fillet with ginger and basil, and panfried tofu with apricots. The seafood stew is highly recommended. There's also a cheese course featuring local blue cheese and chèvre. Choose from a short but thoughtfully selected wine list and be sure to save room for one of the homemade desserts—the lemon tart is excellent. ⊠*135 Cottage St.* ☎*207/288–0447* ⊕*www.machebistro. com* ▤*MC, V* ☺*Closed Mon. No lunch.*

$$–$$$ ✕**Rupununi.** Named after a river in Brazil, the Rup also calls itself "An American Bar & Grill." It's hugely popular with the collegiate crowd and Bar Harbor young people. They like the good, inexpensive food and the generous drinks. For something different, try the "Sea Balls." The decor is signs, pictures, and "things" from all over the world. When it comes to wines, beers, and microbrews, the choices are many, and the price is reasonable. ⊠*119 Main St.* ☎*207/288–2766* ⊕*www. rupununi.com* ▤*AE, DC, MC, V* ☺*Closed Nov.–mid-Apr.*

$–$$$ ✕**Galyn's.** Open throughout the year, this casual eatery serves items such as a Cajun pork sandwich or a chicken focaccia sandwich for lunch. For dinner, the emphasis switches to lobster dishes, steak, and seafood, with options such as garlic shrimp tossed with linguine. The Indian pudding is delicious. ⊠*17 Main St.* ☎*207/288–9706* ⚲*Reservations essential* ▤*AE, DC, MC, V* ⊘*Closed Nov.–Mar.*

$–$$$ ✕**McKay's Public House.** If the name sounds like this could be a fun place, you're right: it is. Low lighting and glowing candles set the right mood for relaxed but elegant dining. The pub menu includes familiar favorites such as fish-and-chips, but also more-unusual options such as lamb burgers, corned beef and cabbage, and that olde English favorite, bangers and mash. The restaurant also emphasizes fresh seafood, with crab cakes, porcini halibut, and seared scallops among the offerings. The Duck Two Ways is especially recommended. Key lime pie, crème brûlée, cheesecake, and other desserts will tempt your palate. ⊠*231 Main St.* ☎*207/288–2002* ⊕*www.mckayspublichouse.com* ▤*AE, MC, V.*

$$ ✕**Eden Vegetarian Café.** You'll find artfully prepared vegetarian meals at this restaurant near the harbor. Start with an appetizer of baby bok choy kimchi, chilled melon gazpacho, or grilled artichoke with a citrus-béarnaise sauce. Choose from entrées such as rigatoni with roasted garlic, broccoli, fresh tomatoes, and pesto. Vegetables here are organic and come from local farms. ⊠*78 West St.* ☎*207/288–4422* ▤*D, MC, V* ⊘*Closed Sun.*

¢–$ ✕**Geddy's.** Geddy's is a legendary Bar Harbor pub/restaurant with fun food and fine nightly entertainers, such as Grammy-winning jazz musician Wynton Marsalis and folk singer Arlo Guthrie. If you're looking for an easy-to-find place with inexpensive food and a refreshing atmosphere, this is it. A warning, however, about the menu: the owner apparently has a sense of humor. Among the choices on the menu are "Ba Haba Gull Wings," deep-fried guppies, and "Spam on the Half Shell." ⊠*19 Main St.* ☎*207/288–5077* ▤*MC, V.*

WHERE TO STAY

$$$$ ⌂**Balance Rock Inn.** This grand summer cottage built in 1903 commands
★ a prime waterfront location. An expansive lawn and gardens full of annuals lead down to the ocean. Even if your room doesn't have an ocean view, you can enjoy it from a wicker chair on the porch. Rooms are spacious and meticulously furnished with reproduction pieces—four-poster and canopy beds in guest rooms, crystal chandeliers and a grand piano in common rooms. All rooms have whirlpool tubs, and some have fireplaces. A buffet-style breakfast is served each morning. **Pros:** A lovely, old-fashioned place with a good breakfast. **Con:** A little on the pricey side. ⊠*21 Albert Meadow, 04609* ☎*207/288–2610 or 800/753–0494* ⚲*info@balancerockinn.com* ⊕*www.balancerockinn. com* ⌂*6 rooms, 3 suites* ♿*In-room: DVD, dial-up. In-hotel: bar, pool, gym, concierge, no elevator, no-smoking rooms* ▤*AE, D, MC, V* ⊘*Closed late Oct.–early May* ⏀*BP.*

$$$$**   Harborside Hotel & Marina. One of Bar Harbor's newest lodgings, this Tudor-style hotel has a prime location next to the harbor. The guest rooms are elegantly decorated in soft yellows and greens; the baths are tiled in marble. Most rooms have balconies, many have water views. Suites have high-definition televisions and surround-sound stereo; penthouse suites have a full kitchen, dining room, hot tub, and fireplace. A spa is on the premises. The inn's restaurant, the Pier ($$-$$$), is open to the public for lunch and dinner and specializes in fresh seafood, including lobster and jumbo scallops. **Pro: Great views of the harbor and surrounding islands. **Con:** Definitely not an "economy" accommodation for those on a tight budget. ⊠*55 West St., 04609* ☎*207/288–5033 or 800/328–5033* ⊕*www.theharborsidehotel.com* ⤴*187 rooms* ⚸*In-room: kitchen (some), dial-up. In-hotel: 3 restaurants, tennis court, pools, gym, spa, laundry service, no-smoking rooms* ▤*AE, DC, MC, V* ⵄ*CP.*

$$$–$$$$
Fodor'sChoice
★   Bar Harbor Inn & Spa. Originally established in the late 1800s as a men's social club, this waterfront inn has rooms spread out over three buildings on well-landscaped grounds. Most rooms have gas fireplaces and balconies with great views. Rooms in the Oceanfront Lodge have private decks overlooking the ocean. Many rooms in the main inn have balconies overlooking the harbor. Should you need more room, there are also some two-level suites. A relatively new addition to the inn is a luxury spa, which offers everything from massages and mud wraps to aroma therapy and facials. The inn is a short walk from town, so you're close to all the sights, and a terrific restaurant, the Reading Room, is on-site *(⇨ see Where to Eat)*. **Pros:** This is one of those resort hotels that truly seems to meet every need, plus it's right at the harbor. **Con:** Not as close to Acadia National Park as some other Bar Harbor properties, though still just a short drive. ⊠*Newport Dr., 04609* ☎*207/288–3351 or 800/248–3351* ⊕*www.barharborinn.com* ⤴*138 rooms, 15 suites* ⚸*In-room: safe, refrigerator, DVD. In-hotel: 2 restaurants, pool, gym, no-smoking rooms* ▤*AE, DC, MC, V* ⵁ*Closed late Nov.–late Mar.* ⵄ*CP.*

$$$–$$$$
★   Bass Cottage Inn. This elegant and refreshing inn, dating from 1885 but renovated in 2004, respects its Victorian history—without the stuffy Victorian decor. All rooms have their own character—each was designed by the owner with a family member or friend in mind. Light-color walls, hardwood floors, and gas fireplaces give them a comfortable, contemporary feel. Although the inn does not have ocean views, it is a short walk from most Bar Harbor attractions. Wine and hors d'oeuvres are served each evening, and a full gourmet breakfast is available in the atrium each morning. You can relax on the sun porch, in the parlor, or in the reading room by the fireplace. The club-style lounge is filled with puzzles and games. Appointments with a licensed massage therapist are available. **Pros:** A full breakfast is served in the morning; wine and hors d'oeuvres in the evening. **Cons:** No ocean views, and you may wish to drive for dinner. ⊠*14 The Field, 04609* ☎*207/288–1234 or 866/782–9224* ⊕*www.basscottage.com* ⤴*10 rooms* ⚸*In-room: DVD. In-hotel: public Internet no-smoking rooms* ▤*AE, MC, V* ⵁ*Closed Nov.–mid-May* ⵄ*BP.*

$$$–$$$$
Fodor'sChoice
★
🏨**Ullikana.** Inside the stucco-and-timber walls of this traditional Tudor cottage, antiques are juxtaposed with contemporary country pieces; vibrant color with French country wallpapers; and abstract art with folk creations. The combination not only works—it shines. Though the property is small, rooms are large with ample windows; many have fireplaces, and some have decks. Breakfast is an elaborate multicourse affair. The popular "A Yellow House" across the drive has six additional rooms decorated in traditional old Bar Harbor style.**Pro:** Lovely setting. **Con:** No views from rooms. ⊠*16 The Field, 04609* ☎*207/288–9552* ⊕*www.ullikana.com* ⇱*16 rooms* ⌂*In-room: no a/c (some), no phone, no TV. In-hotel: no-smoking rooms* ▤*MC, V* ⊗*Closed Nov.–mid-May* ⌐⃝*BP.*

$$–$$$$
🏨**Bar Harbor Grand Hotel.** The look and the feeling of this hotel is that of turn-of-the-century 1900s—and yet it was recently built, in 1994. Located in the heart of Bar Harbor, it is a short walk to the waterfront and to the downtown. Comfortable guest rooms have thoughtful additions such as coffeemakers and refrigerators. Meal plans at another hotel, the Bar Harbor Inn, can be arranged. Nearby, a shuttle service takes you to Acadia National Park. **Pro:** Good location for easy walking to restaurants. **Con:** Not right on the water (but close to it).. ⊠*269 Main St., 04609* ☎*207/288–5226 or 888/766–2529* ⊕*www.barharborgrand.com* ⇱*70 rooms* ⌂*In-room: refrigerator, DVD. In-hotel: pool, laundry facilities, public Wi-Fi, gym, no-smoking rooms* ▤*AE, DC, MC, V* ⊗*Closed mid-Nov.–mid-Apr.* ⌐⃝*CP.*

$$–$$$$
🏨**Bluenose Inn–Bar Harbor Hotel.** This resort is perched on the top of a hill overlooking Frenchman Bay. Most of the guest rooms have excellent views, and all of them have gas fireplaces. After touring Acadia National Park, you can relax in the hotel's hot tub or steam room, or swim a few laps in the indoor or outdoor pool. Fine dining is provided at the Rose Garden restaurant ($$$$), which features seafood and beef entrées on the three-course prix fixe and five-course tasting menus. To start, try the strudel filled with asparagus or the Maine lobster bisque. For the main entrée, order North Atlantic salmon, Maine lobster, rack of lamb, or the pan-seared venison steak. Finally, choose from desserts such as a warm apple tart, vanilla-bean crème brûlée, or flourless chocolate cake. **Pros:** Spectacular views of the bay and outer islands, wonderful on-site dining. **Con:** A bit of a hike to town (you'll probably want to drive). ⊠*90 Eden St., 04609* ☎*207/288–3348 or 800/445–4077* ⊕*www.bluenoseinn.com* ⇱*97 rooms, 1 suite* ⌂*In-room: safe, refrigerator. In-hotel: 2 restaurants, bar, pools, gym, public Internet* ▤*AE, D, DC, MC, V* ⊗*Closed Nov.–late Apr.*

$$–$$$
☾
🏨**Acadia Inn.** The Acadia in downtown Bar Harbor is one of area's newer hotels and has standard hotel décor. A gift shop is on the grounds. **Pros:** A lavish Continental breakfast, only 300 yards from The CAT high-speed boat to Nova Scotia. **Cons:** First-floor rooms don't have much of a view, rooms are not individualized like those in a bed-and-breakfast. ⊠*98 Eden St. (Rte 3), 04609* ☎*207/288–3500 or 800/638–3636* ⊕*www.acadiainn.com* ⇱*95 rooms* ⌂*In-room: refrigerator, Wi-Fi. In hotel: pool, laundry, public Internet* ▤*AE, DC, MC, V* ⌐⃝*CP.*

6

$$-$$$$ **Bar Harbor Regency (Holiday Inn).** Formerly the Bar Harbor Regency, this is another big hotel that's spread over a lot of ground, and many of the rooms have balconies and lovely views of the sea. Each room includes a coffeemaker and hair dryer. **Pros:** Several amenities, and one of the best lobster restaurants in town: Stewman's. **Con:** A large property, so you may not feel as cozy as you would at a B&B. ⊠*123 Eden St. (Rte. 3), 04609* ☎*207/288–9723 or 800/23–HOTEL (800/234–6835)* ⊕*www.barharborregency.com* ⌗*200 rooms* ♿*In-room: refrigerator. In-hotel: gym, tennis courts, laundry facilities, pool* ⊟*AE, DC, MC, V* ⊗*Closed Nov.–Apr.* ⦿*CP.*

$–$$$ **Wonder View Inn & Suites.** They've got the right name for this place. A lot of vacationers come to Bar Harbor looking for a view, and they've got it here, since the inn is high on a hill, overlooking Frenchman Bay. The Wonder View is spread out over 14 acres, so if you like to walk, this is the place. The property is pet-friendly. **Pros:** An excellent restaurant, the Rinehart Dining Pavilion, is right on the premises, so you don't have to drive to dinner. **Con:** If you want to do some shopping, you probably will want to drive to downtown. ⊠*50 Eden St. (Rte. 3), 04609* ☎*207/288–3358 or 888/439–8439* ⊕*www.wonderviewinn. com* ⌗*79 rooms* ♿*In room: refrigerator. In-hotel: pool, some pets allowed* ⊟*AE, DC, MC, V* ⊗*Closed Nov.–Apr.* ⦿*CP.*

$–$$ **Cromwell Harbor Motel.** If you like flowers, you will love this blossom-bedecked motel. Less than a mile from downtown Bar Harbor, this clean and pleasant motel is set amid pretty gardens. From here you can walk to a quiet section of Acadia National Park. **Pros:** Clean and modestly priced, with a choice of one, two, or three bedrooms. **Con:** You probably will have to drive to dinner. ⊠*359 Main St., 04069* ☎*207/288–3201 or 800/544–3201* ⊕*www.cromwellharbor.com* ⌗*26 rooms* ♿*In-room: refrigerator (some). In-hotel: pool, no-smoking rooms* ⊟*AE, D, MC, V.*

$–$$ **Seacroft Inn.** It's an easy walk to Bar Harbor or the shore path from this rambling, multigable inn. The property has seven efficiency units, including one two-bedroom unit that is a good choice for families. A breakfast basket is delivered to your room each morning.**Pro:** Breakfast in bed. **Con:** No on-site restaurant for dinner. ⊠*18 Albert Meadow, 04609* ☎*207/288–4669 or 800/824–9694* ⊕*www.seacroftinn.com* ⌗*6 rooms, 1 2-bedroom unit* ♿*In-room: refrigerator. In-hotel: no-smoking rooms* ⊟*MC, V* ⊗*Closed mid.-Nov.–May* ⦿*CP.*

¢–$$ **Maine Street Motel.** This is a relatively small accommodation a little off the beaten track, but you can't beat the price, and the location is convenient as well. There are rooms for smokers as well as nonsmokers. **Pro:** Reasonable price. **Con:** Not a lot of amenities. ⊠*315 Main St., 04609* ☎*207/288–3188 or 800/333–3188* ⊕*www.mainestreet-motel.com* ⌗*44 rooms* ♿*Wi-Fi, no-smoking rooms* ⊟*DC, MC, V* ⊗*Closed Nov.–Apr.*

$ **Eden Village Motel & Cottages.** Children can learn to fish at the pond on this 25-acre property, 5 mi from downtown Bar Harbor. Although the furnishings are not new, the rooms certainly are comfortable and most have views of the top of Cadillac Mountain. A back porch that extends the length of the building has picnic tables and grills. Cottages vary in size, but all have working fireplaces, barbecue grills, and scree porches. A mile-long nature trail passes by blueberry bushes, and cherry and apple trees. It's a good place for outdoorsy types. One small dog per cabin is allowed; no cats. **Pros:** An inexpensive motel in a friendly setting. **Cons:** Somewhat rustic and remote. ✉986 Rte. 3, 04609 ☎207/288–4670 ✐info@edenvillage.com ⊕www.edenvillage.com ⤴10 rooms, 11 cottages �б In-room: no a/c (some), kitchen (some). In-hotel: some pets allowed, no-smoking rooms ▭DC, MC, V ⊗Closed Nov.–Apr.

NIGHTLIFE & THE ARTS

Although Bar Harbor is known for its beautiful scenery, its wonderful harbor, and its first-class accommodations and restaurants, it is not especially known for its nightlife. Perhaps people are just too tired from their day's activities and boating by then. However, there are some goings-on in town if you look.

★ The **Arcady Music Festival** (☎207/669–4225 ⊕www.arcady.org) schedules classical concerts at locations around Mount Desert Island throughout the year. The **Bar Harbor Music Festival** (✉59 Cottage St. ☎207/288–5744) hosts jazz, classical, and pop concerts by young professionals from July to early August at the Criterion Theater. It has recently started including one opera every season and has done *La Bohème* and *La Traviata*. Bizet's *Carmen* is the expected opera for 2008. The art deco–style **Criterion Theater** (✉35 Cottage St. ☎207/288–3441) offers movies and stages concerts, plays, and other live performances. **ImprovAcadia** (✉15 Cottage St., 2nd fl. ☎207/288–2503) is one of the most interesting and entertaining places in town. As the name would imply, it's an improv comedy theater. The **Reel Pizza Cinerama** (✉33-B Kennebec Pl. ☎207/288–3811) shows first-run movies.

If you want to shoot some pool or throw some darts, try the **Carmen Verandah** (✉119 Main St. ☎207/288–2766 ⊕www.carmenverandah. com). The upstairs bar has live music and dancing.

SPORTS & THE OUTDOORS

AIR TOURS

There are few places in America as beautiful to see from the air as the
★ Mount Desert Island and Acadia National Park areas. **Scenic Biplane & Glider Rides Over Bar Harbor** (✉968 Bar Harbor Rd. [Rt. 3], Trenton ☎207/667–7627 ⊕www.acadiaairtours.com.) is a part of Acadia Air Tours and provides exactly what the name suggests: biplane and glider rides over Bar Harbor and Acadia National Park. It also offers helicopter tours.

BICYCLING

Acadia Bike Rentals (✉48 Cottage St. ☎207/288–9605 or 800/526–8615) rents mountain bikes good for negotiating the trails in Acadia National Park. The **Bar Harbor Bicycle Shop** (✉141 Cottage St. ☎207/288–3886 or 800/824–2453) rents bikes by the half or full day.

FODOR'S FIRST PERSON

Mike Nalepa
Fodor's Associate Editor

When my wife Sharon and I visited Acadia National Park, we joined the throngs at most of the typical views—the scenic overlooks along the Park Loop Road, Eagle Lake, and the Cadillac Mountain summit. But none of these vistas were as phenomenal as seeing the park *from* the water. We ventured out with National Park Sea Kayak Tours, and it was one of our trip highlights.

We'd gone kayaking back home in New Jersey a few times, but paddling on the ocean (OK, technically a bay) was a completely different experience. Our little canal back home doesn't have currents, waves, and wind—thus it doesn't provide such an exciting ride. We had the wind at our back for most of the trip, so it always felt like we were moving at a nice clip. At certain points when we caught a wave, it felt like we were surfing.

Despite the rocky conditions on the water, our kayak never felt unstable (they rarely flip—our guide said that he hadn't had a customer go in for a drink all year). The boat's skirts kept us warm and dry as we paddled, and there were ample opportunities for snapping photos along the way (they even provide a waterproof gear bag for your camera during the trip).

The best part of the tour, though, was the scenery. During our four-hour paddle we saw a soaring bald eagle and a swimming seal, and visited two gorgeous islands (one uninhabited, the other inhabited by the Rockefellers). We covered about 6 nautical miles of shimmering, deep blue water surrounded by craggy coastlines, towering forests, and picture-perfect bays and inlets. And we got a nice workout to boot (full disclosure: we are *not* in very good shape; anyone with a moderate fitness level would be able to handle a trip like this).

Caution: Riding a bike around Bar Harbor is fun, but be careful; the town is full of gawking tourists, and many of the streets are narrow.

BIRDING

Down East Nature Tours (✎ *Box 521, Bar Harbor 04609* ☎ *207/288–8128*) leads excursions for individuals and small groups. You can learn the basics of birding, including how to identify a particular species.

BOATING

Acadia Outfitters (✉ *106 Cottage St.* ☎ *207/288–8118*) rents canoes and sea kayaks. **Coastal Kayaking Tours** (✉ *48 Cottage St.* ☎ *207/288–9605 or 800/526–8615*) conducts tours of the rocky coastline led by registered guides. **National Park Sea Kayak Tours** (✉ *39 Cottage St.* ☎ *207/288–0342 or 800/347–0940*) leads guided kayak tours.

The **Bar Harbor Ferry** (✉ *Bar Harbor Inn Pier* ☎ *207/288–2984* ⊕ *www.barharborferry.com*) travels six times daily between Bar Harbor and Winter Harbor, home to Acadia National Park's Schoodic Peninsula. Along the way passengers are treated to great views of the mountains and a few lighthouses. A free bus shuttle from the ferry terminal goes to Winter Harbor, Schoodic Point, Birch Harbor, and Prospect Harbor. You can bring a bike along.

The CAT. Surely, the best boat excursions out of Bar Harbor must be the rides on "The CAT," North America's fastest international ferry. This is a high-speed (55 mph) catamaran that, in season, jets from Bar Harbor across the Gulf of Maine to Yarmouth, Nova Scotia, and back. You can do it all in one day, or you can take one of the one- or two-night package trips that include tours. The CAT can whisk you to Nova Scotia in a mere 2¾ hours You can have lunch at a waterside restaurant, do a little shopping, and come back the same day. On board, you will find a café for food, a bar for drinks, and a duty-free gift shop. The morning departure is around 7:45, and the returns are at 1 and 8:30 PM. ⊠ *12 Eden St.* ☎*888/249–7245* ⊕*www.catferry.com.*

Fodor$Choice ★

> FARMERS MARKETS
>
> Farmers' markets, in which a portion of a street is blocked off once a week so that farmers may set up stands and carts selling their fresh-from-the-farm wares, are becoming increasingly popular in Maine. On Sunday there is one in Bar Harbor, next to the YMCA; on Thursday, in Northeast Harbor, across from the Kimball Terrace Inn; and on Friday, in Southwest Harbor, near the elementary school.

The big 151-foot four-masted schooner **Margaret Todd** (⊠ *Bar Harbor Inn Pier* ☎*207/288–4585* ⊕*www.downeastwindjammer.com*) operates 1½- to 2-hour trips three times a day among the islands of Frenchman's Bay from mid-May to October. The sunset sail is the most popular. The schooner *Rachel B. Jackson* (⊠ *Harborside Hotel & Marina* ☎*207/288–2216*) offers three-day cruises and sunset cruises.

If you are curious about what's lurking in the deep, set sail on *The Seal* (⊠ *Bar Harbor Inn Pier* ☎*207/288–3483* ⊕*www.divered.com*). While "Diver Ed" is exploring the sea bottom with his underwater video camera, you can see what he finds by watching an LCD screen on the boat; also get an up-close look at the creatures he brings back.

GOLF

One of Maine's best courses, the **Kebo Valley Golf Club** (⊠ *Eagle Lake Rd.* ☎*207/288–3000* ⊕*www.kebovalleygolfclub.com*) is a classic links-style 18-hole course. Peak season greens fees are $75. You can play 9 or 18 holes of miniature golf at **Pirates Cove Adventure Golf** (⊠ *Rte. 3* ☎*207/288–2133*).

ROCK CLIMBING

On an island with steep rock faces, mountain climbing is—not surprisingly—a popular outdoor activity. The **Acadia Mountain Guides Climbing School** (⊠ *198 Main St.* ☎*207/288–8186 or 888/232–9559* ⊕*www. acadiamountainguides.com*) has private and group instruction for rock and ice climbing. In summer the school sponsors weeklong camps for teens. The **Atlantic Climbing School** (⊠ *24 Cottage St.* ☎*207/288–2521* ⊕*www.acadiaclimbing.com*) offers instruction for climbers of all skill levels. It can tailor its climbs for families or groups.

6

WHALE-WATCHING

There are two truly unique experiences you can have at Bar Harbor, and both of them are ideal for family outings. One is a trip on the fast CAT boat to Nova Scotia. The other, also at sea, is whale-watching. ★ **Bar Harbor Whale Watch Co.** (⊠*1 West St.* ☎*207/288–2386 or 800/ WHALES–4 (800/942–5374)* ⊕*www.whalesrus.com*) merged with the Acadian Whale Watcher to make one big company with four boats, one of them a 138-foot jet-propelled catamaran with spacious decks. In season, the outfit also offers lobsters and seals cruises, a nature cruise, and puffins cruises. How likely are you to actually see a whale? Very. In fact, the company can practically guarantee it—they apparently have some sort of arrangement with the whales.

SHOPPING

Bar Harbor is a shoppers paradise, but it is not for people who are looking for Wal-Mart–type bargains. Tourism shoppers not only come from the land, they also come from the sea, since some very large steamships, including the *Queen Elizabeth,* have made this a destination. (Imagine how delighted the store owners are to see her arrive, with thousands of passengers!)

GALLERIES

Fodor's Choice ★ Paint your own pottery or piece together a mosaic at **All Fired Up** (⊠*101 Cottage St.* ☎*207/288–3130* ⊕*www.acadiaallfiredup.com*). The gallery also sells glass sculptures, pendants, paintings, and decorative pottery. The **Alone Moose Fine Crafts** (⊠*78 West St.* ☎*207/288–4229*) is the oldest made-in-Maine gallery on the island. It offers bronze wildlife sculpture, jewelry, pottery, and watercolors. The **Eclipse Gallery** (⊠*12 Mount Desert St.* ☎*207/288–9048*) carries handblown glass, ceramics, and wood furniture. **Island Artisans** (⊠*99 Main St.* ☎*207/288–4214*) sells basketry, pottery, fiber work, and jewelry created by more than 100 of Maine's artisans. The gallery is a co-op owned and operated by the artists. **Native Arts Gallery** (⊠*99 Main St.* ☎*207/288–4474* ⊕*www. nativeartsgallery.com*) sells American Indian silver and gold jewelry.

GENERAL

One of the best sporting-goods stores in the state, **Cadillac Mountain Sports** (⊠*28 Cottage St.* ☎*207/288–4532* ⊕*www.cadillacmountain-sports.com*), has developed a following of locals and visitors alike. You can find top-quality climbing, hiking, and camping equipment. In winter you can rent cross-country skis, ice skates, and snowshoes. For one-hour photo developing, visit **First Exposure** (⊠*156 Main St.* ☎*207/288–5868*). The shop also stocks camera equipment. **Michael H. Graves Antiques** (⊠*10 Albert Meadow* ☎*207/288–3830*) specializes in maps and books focusing on Mount Desert Island. **Songs of the Sea** (⊠*47 West St.* ☎*207/288–5653*) specializes in folk music. It sells handcrafted Irish and Scottish musical instruments.

ACADIA NATIONAL PARK ESSENTIALS

Admission Fee: A user fee is required if you are anywhere in the park. The fee is $20 per vehicle for a seven-consecutive-day pass. Or use your National Park America the Beautiful Pass, which allows entrance to any national park in the United States. See www.nps.gov for details.

Admission Hours: The park is open 24 hours a day, year-round, though the roads often are closed in winter because of snow. Operating hours are 8 AM–4:30 PM April 15–October and until 6 PM. in July and August

Camping: There are more than 500 campsites in the park. Ask for a guide at the Hulls Cove Visitor Center. Blackwoods Campground has 16 wheelchair-accessible sites. There are no hook-ups, though some sites can fit RVs.

Pets: Pets are allowed at all park locations, but they must be on leashes no longer than six feet.

Visitor Information: ⌂ *Acadia National Park, Box 177, Bar Harbor 04609* ☎ *207/288–3338* ⊕ *www.nps.gov/acad.*

TREATS

Ben and Bill's Chocolate Emporium (✉ *66 Main St.* ☎ *207/288–3281*) is a chocolate lover's nirvana. It also has more than 20 flavors of ice cream, including the popular KGB (Kahlua, Grand Marnier, and Bailey's).

6

ACADIA NATIONAL PARK

4 mi northwest of Bar Harbor.

With more than 30,000 acres of protected forests, beaches, mountains, and rocky coastline, Acadia National Park is the second-most-visited national park in America (the first is the Great Smoky Mountains National Park). According to the national park service, more than 2.2 million people visit Acadia each year. The park holds some of the most spectacular scenery on the eastern seaboard: a rugged coastline of surf-pounded granite, and an interior graced by sculpted mountains, quiet ponds, and lush deciduous forests. Cadillac Mountain (named after an American Indian, not the car), the highest point of land on the Eastern Coast, dominates the park. Although it's rugged, Acadia National Park also has graceful stone bridges, horse-drawn carriages, and the elegant Jordan Pond House restaurant.

The 27-mi Park Loop Road provides an excellent introduction, but to truly appreciate the park, you must get off the main road and experience it by walking, biking, sea kayaking, or taking a carriage ride. If you get off the beaten path, you can find places you can have practically to yourself. Mount Desert Island was once the site of summer homes for the very rich (still is for some), and, because of this, Acadia is the only national park in America that was largely created by the donations of private land. A small part of the park is on the Isle au Haut, which is out in the ocean and more than 10 mi away.

WHAT TO SEE

HISTORIC SITES & MUSEUMS

Abbe Museum at Sieur de Monts Spring. The original Abbe Museum (a larger one is in Bar Harbor) has exhibits on the history of the Abbe people who once inhabited this area. The museum is on the National Register of Historic Places. ✉ *26 Mt. Desert St., Sieur de Monts Spring exit from Rte. 3 or Park Loop Rd.* ☎ *207/288–3519* ⊕ *www.abbe-museum.org* 🎫 *$2* ⊙ *Memorial Day–mid-Oct., daily 10–4.*

★ **Bass Harbor Head Light.** Originally built in 1858, this lighthouse is one of the most photographed in Maine. The light, now automated, marks the entrance to Blue Hill bay. The grounds and residence are Coast Guard property, but two trails around the facility provide excellent views. ■ **TIP**➡ **The best place to take a picture of this small but beautiful lighthouse is from the rocks below—but watch your step, they can be slippery.** ✉ *Rte. 102, halfway between Tremont and Manset Bass Harbor* 🎫 *Free* ⊙ *Daily 9–sunset.*

SCENIC DRIVES & STOPS

★ **Cadillac Mountain.** At 1,532 feet, this is the first place in America to see the sun's rays at break of day. It is the highest mountain on the eastern seaboard north of Brazil. Dozens of visitors make the trek to see the sunrise or, for those less inclined to get up so early, sunset. From the smooth summit you have an awesome 360-degree view of the jagged coastline that runs around the island. Decades ago a train took visitors to a hotel at the summit. Today a small gift shop and some rest rooms are the only structures at the top. The road up the mountain is generally closed from the end of October through March because of snow.

Jordan Pond. The water source for the village of Seal Harbor, Jordan Pond is best seen from the observation deck next to the Jordan Pond House restaurant. Rising above the water are the Bubbles, two mountains of similar size and shape. Maps and other items are available at the information booth beside the restaurant. Many people leave their cars in the overflow parking lots north of the restaurant's parking lot when setting off on biking or hiking trips along the carriage roads that converge here.

⊙ **Park Loop Road.** This 27-mi road provides a perfect introduction to the
★ park. You can do it in an hour, but allow at least half a day or more for the drive so that you can explore the many sites along the way. Traveling south on Park Loop Road toward Sand Beach, you'll reach a small ticket booth, where, if you haven't already, you will need to pay the park's good-for-seven-consecutive-days $20 entrance fee (the fee is not charged from November through April). Traffic is one-way from the Route 233 entrance to the Stanley Brook Road entrance south of the Jordan Pond House. The section known as Ocean Drive is open year-round.

Sand Beach. This small stretch of pink sand is one of the few sandy beaches on the island. A lifeguard is on duty from Memorial Day through Labor Day. Although people do swim here, the water tem-

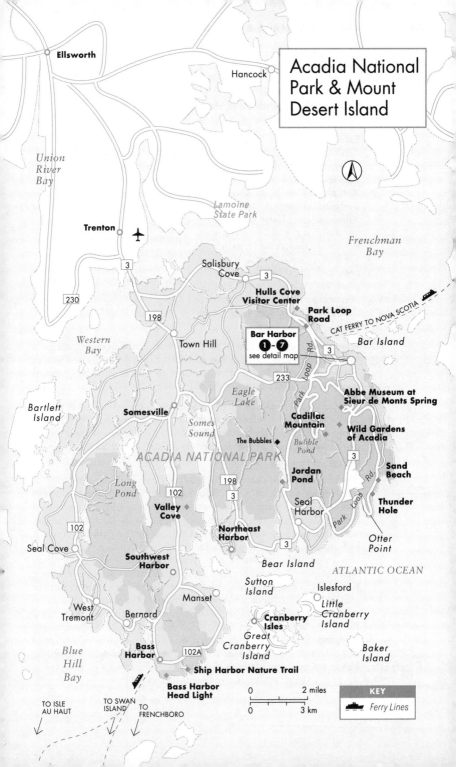

perature rarely exceeds 55°F. Rest rooms and changing facilities are available. You may recognize this beach from the movie *The Cider House Rules.* **Caution:** the water here is *cold.*

Thunder Hole. The ocean "thunders" into this natural seaside cave, spraying water all the way up to the viewing area. This is a popular stop along Park Loop Road, especially on stormy or windy days. Although the closest view of this attraction is reached by a stairway, a wheelchair-accessible path provides fairly good views. A parking area and gift shop are across the road. This is best seen at high tide; at low tide, it's not all that impressive. Check the *Bangor Daily News* for tide times.

> **TAKE A TOUR**
>
> Acadia National Park Tours operates a 2½-hour bus tour of Acadia National Park, narrated by a naturalist, from May to October, and 2½-hour narrated trolley tours. Columbia Air Services, at Hancock County Airport between Ellsworth and Bar Harbor, rents aircraft and flies seven aerial sightseeing routes from spring to fall.
>
> **Tour Information Acadia National Park Tours** (☎ *207/288–3327* ⊕ *www.acadiatours.com*). **Columbia Air Services** (☎ *207/667–5534* ⊕ *www.columbiaairservices.com*).

Valley Cove. A parking area tucked away near Fernald Point Road leads to a carriage road accessing scenic Valley Cove. Along Somes Sound, Valley Cove offers hiking trails that lead to Acadia and Flying mountains. ⊠ *Southeastern end of Fernald Point Rd.*

Wild Gardens of Acadia. Adjacent to Sieur de Monts Springs, several gardens display well-labeled plants that are representative of the island's many habitats. ⊠ *Off Rte. 3 or Park Loop Rd. (Sieur de Monts Spring exit), about 1 mi from Bar Harbor* ☎ *207/288–3400* ☑ *Free.*

VISITOR CENTER

At the Hulls Cove entrance to Acadia National Park, northwest of Bar Harbor on Route 3, the **Hulls Cove Visitor Center,** operated by the National Park Service, is a great spot to get your bearings. A large relief map of Mount Desert Island gives you the lay of the land, and you can watch a free 15-minute video about everything the park has to offer. Pick up guidebooks, maps of hiking trails and carriage roads, schedules for naturalist-led tours, and recordings for drive-it-yourself tours. Don't forget the *Acadia Beaver Log,* the park's free newspaper detailing guided hikes and other ranger-led events. Junior-ranger programs for kids, nature hikes, photography walks, tide-pool explorations, and evening talks are all popular. The visitor center is off Route 3 at Park Loop Road. ⊠ *Park Loop Rd., Hulls Cove* ☎ *207/288–3338* ⊕ *www.nps. gov/acad* ⊙ *Mid-June–Aug., daily 8–6; mid-Apr.–mid-June, Sept., and Oct., daily 8–4:30.* The **Acadia National Park Headquarters** is on Route 233 in the park not far from the north end of Eagle Lake. It serves as the park's visitor center during the off-season.

SPORTS & THE OUTDOORS

The best way to see Acadia National Park is to get out of your vehicle and explore by foot, bicycle, or boat. There are more than 40 mi of carriage roads that are perfect for walking and biking in the warmer months, and cross-country skiing and snowshoeing in winter. There are more than 115 mi for hiking, numerous ponds and lakes for canoeing or kayaking, two beaches for swimming, and steep cliffs for rock climbing.

> ### BOOK A CARRIAGE RIDE
>
> If you would like to take a horse-drawn carriage ride down one of these roads, from mid-June to mid-October, you can do so by making a reservation with Wildwood Stables (☎ 207/276–3622). Two of their carriages can accommodate two wheelchairs each.

BICYCLING

The more than 40 mi of carriage roads that crisscross the island are open to bicycles. Originally designed and funded by John D. Rockefeller to facilitate carriage travel after automobiles were introduced, these well-maintained gravel roads provide a range of terrains for bikers of all levels. Even during the busiest months you can find quiet stretches where you can get close-up looks at the native ferns, mosses, and trees. You may also spot chipmunks, birds, or even deer.

The two most popular places to start your ride are Eagle Lake and Jordan Pond. Eagle Lake has a small parking lot that fills up quickly, so don't be surprised if you have to park on the roadside. The 6-mi carriage road around Eagle Lake is popular with families. It meets up with other carriage roads along the way. Jordan Pond has a larger parking lot and a number of different trails. You may want to bike from Eagle Lake to Jordan Pond, where you can stop for tea and popovers at Jordan Pond House restaurant. Perhaps the most challenging route is the Around the Mountain Trail, an 11-mi loop with an extended climb up the northwest side of Parkman Mountain. Other places to start your ride—with less parking—are the Gate House and Parkman Mountain in Northeast Harbor.

Remember that horses and carriages still use these roads—in fact, you can ride a horse along this road, too (though you must bring your own horse). It is best to yield to horses when they approach and to warn the rider when approaching from behind. Although it is not nearly as peaceful, you can bike along Park Loop Road. You must follow the traffic on the one-way section between the Route 233 entrance and the Stanley Brook Road entrance. If you want to bike the entire loop, ride clockwise. Biking is not allowed on any of the hiking trails.

Although the carriage roads are marked at most intersections, it's a good idea to carry a map. With so many side roads and loops, it is easy to extend or shorten your trip. You can pick up trail maps at the Hulls Cove Visitor Center.

BOATING

Mount Desert Island has numerous lakes and ponds that attract canoers and kayakers. Motorboats are permissible, but Eagle Lake, Jordan Pond, Lower Hadlock Pond, and Upper Hadlock Pond have a 10-horsepower limit. Motorboats are most often seen on the ocean, which gives you a great view of this and neighboring islands. Public launching areas are available at each town pier.

> **CAUTION**
>
> A couple of people a year fall off one of the park's trails or cliffs and are swept out to sea. There is a lot of loose, rocky gravel along the shoreline, and sea rocks can often be slippery—so watch your step. Don't bring a sudden end to your visit by trying to get that "impossible" photo op.

CROSS-COUNTRY SKIING

When the snow falls on Mount Desert Island, the more than 40 mi of carriage roads used for biking and hiking during the rest of the year are transformed into a cross-country skiing paradise. With so few visitors on the island at this time of year, you can ski or snowshoe for miles without seeing anyone else. Be sure to bring a carriage road map with you. Snowshoe tracks are usually to the right of or between the ski trails.

FISHING

Several lakes and ponds throughout Acadia National Park attract anglers. Maine residents 16 and older and non-Maine residents 12 and older must have a license to fish in freshwaters. Fishing licenses can be purchased at town halls and at some stores. Fishing licenses are not required for ocean fishing.

HIKING

Acadia National Park maintains more than 120 mi of hiking paths, from easy strolls around lakes and ponds to rigorous treks with climbs up rock faces and scrambles along cliffs. Although most hiking trails are on the east side of the island, the west side also has some scenic trails. For those wishing for a long climb, try the trails leading up Cadillac Mountain or Dorr Mountain. Another option is to climb Parkman, Sargent, and Penobscot mountains. Most of the hiking is done from mid-May to mid-October. Snow falls early in Maine, so from late October to the end of March, cross-country skiing and snowshoeing replace hiking.

■ **TIP**→ The Hulls Cove Visitor Center and area bookstores have trail guides and maps and will help you match a trail with your interests and abilities. You can park at one end of any trail and use the free shuttle bus to get back to your starting point.

Distances for trails are given for the round-trip hike.

EASY **Cadillac Summit.** The ½–mi trail around the summit is mostly level and offers panoramic views of Bar Harbor, Frenchman Bay, and the outer islands. ⊠ *Cadillac Summit parking lot.*

Carriage Roads. A treasure because of their historical significance and scenic vistas, the park's carriage roads make for an easy walk. There are several to choose from; distances vary. ✉*Throughout the park.*

Jordan Pond Nature Trail. This 1-mi trail loops through a forest setting. ✉*Jordan Pond parking lot.*

★ **Ocean Patch Trail.** This 3.6-mi, easily accessible trail runs parallel to the Loop Road from Sand Beach to Otter Point. It has some of the best scenery in Maine: the cliffs and boulders of pink granite at the ocean's edge, the twisted branches of the dwarf jack pines, and ocean views that stretch to the horizon. ✉*Sand Beach or Otter Point parking area.*

> **ACADIA LEAF PEEPING**
>
> The fall foliage in Maine can be spectacular. Because of the moisture, the fall foliage comes later along the coast than it does in the interior of the state. In the interior, it's usually the last week of September, whereas along the coast, it's usually around the middle of October. The best way to catch the colors along the coast is travel on the Acadia National Park Loop Road. In fall 2007, the National Park Service placed Acadia National Park on its fall foliage list of "The 10 Best Places in the U.S. to Take Photographs." For up-to-date information, go online to www.mainefoliage.com.

6

Ship Harbor Nature Trail. Located on the southwestern side of the island, just beyond Seawall, this mostly flat, 1.3-mi trail winds through the woods and along the seashore. The nearby Wonderland Trail offers a similar walk. ✉*Ship Harbor parking area.*

MODERATE **Bowl Trail.** Beginning 100 feet north of Sand Beach, this 1.4-mi trail goes through forest and includes granite ledges and a pond. ✉*Sand Beach parking area.*

Bubble Rock Trail. The 1-mi trail through the forest includes views of Jordan Pond. ✉*Bubble Rock parking area.*

Jordan Pond Shore Trail. This 3.3-mi loop follows the water's edge; there are some rocky sections. ✉*Jordan Pond parking area.*

DIFFICULT **Acadia Mountain Trail** This is the king of the trails. The 2½-mi round-
★ trip climb up Acadia Mountain is steep and strenuous—but the payoff is grand: views of Somes Sound and Southwest Harbor. If you want a guided trip, look into the ranger-led hikes for this trail. ✉*Acadia Mountain parking area, on Rte. 102.*

Beehive Trail This 0.8-mi hike is a steep climb from woods to exposed cliffs. ✉*100 ft north of Sand Beach parking area.*

Cadillac Mountain South Ridge Trail Only for the experienced hiker, this 7.4-mi trail ascends gradually from a beautiful forest setting to granite. ✉*100 ft south of Blackwoods Campground.*

Pemetic Mountain Trail This 2.4-mi trail packs a punch with its array of terrain: forest, ocean, and lake views. ✉*Bubble Pond parking area.*

Precipice Trail This 1.6-mi, nearly 1,000-foot vertical climb is the most challenging trail and is only for the most experienced and the most physically fit. Watch for peregrine falcons along the way. ⊠*Schooner Head parking area of the Park Loop Rd.*

HORSEBACK RIDING

Acadia National Park does not have its own horseback riding program, but you can arrange for carriage rides or board your own horse at **Wildwood Stables** (⊠*Park Loop Rd., Seal Harbor* ☎*207/276–3622 or 859/356–7139* ⊕*www.acadia. net/wildwood*). With more than 40 mi of carriage roads, the park is an excellent place to ride your horse at a slow, comfortable pace. The stables, which do not rent horses, are ½ mi south of the Jordan Pond House restaurant.

> **THE EARLY BIRD GETS THE SUN**
>
> During your visit to Mount Desert, pick a day when you are willing to get up very early, such as 4:30 or 5 AM. Drive with a friend to the top of Cadillac Mountain in Acadia National Park. Stand on the highest rock you can find there and wait for the sun to come up. When it does, have your friend take a photo of you looking at it from behind. Then you can label the photo something like: "The first person in America to see the sun come up on June 1, 2008."

ROCK CLIMBING

Acadia National Park has plenty of rock faces to challenge both novice and advanced climbers. Otter Cliffs and Champlain Mountain are popular for face climbing, and Gorham Mountain offers good boulder climbing.

SNOWMOBILING

Once the snow falls, most of Park Loop Road closes to cars, and snowmobiles take over. Except for a few well-marked places, snowmobiles are not allowed on the carriage roads. The speed limit for snowmobiles is 35 mph.

SWIMMING

The park has two beaches that are perfect for swimming, Sand Beach and Echo Lake Beach. Sand Beach, along Park Loop Road, has changing rooms, rest rooms, and a lifeguard on duty from Memorial Day to Labor Day. The water temperature here rarely reaches above 55°F. Echo Lake Beach, on the western side of the island just north of Southwest Harbor, has much warmer water. There are changing rooms, rest rooms, and a lifeguard on duty throughout summer.

WHERE TO EAT & STAY IN ACADIA

Jordan Pond House is the only restaurant in the park, but there are many excellent places around the Loop Road to have a picnic, and bathrooms are available (including handicapped accessible) at the Fabbri, Thompson Island, and Seawall picnic areas.

Acadia National Park does not have its own hotel, and there are no cabins or lodges. But 500 campgrounds within the park for RVers and tenters are available. There are also five primitive sites on the part of the park on the Isle au Haut, out to sea 10 mi away. Visitors with RVs do need to be warned, however, that facilities at both of the Acadia National Park campgrounds are deliberately kept minimal. There are no hookups. So if you are used to and like a lot of facilities, you may wish to opt for campgrounds outside the park. Both campgrounds within the park are wooded, and both are within a 10-min. walk of the ocean, but neither is located right on the ocean.

WHERE TO EAT

$–$$$ ✕ **Jordan Pond House.** Oversize popovers with strawberry jam or home-made ice cream are a century-old tradition at this restaurant overlooking Jordan Pond. Dine outside on the tea lawn or the brick patio, or inside an enclosed porch or dining room. The lunch menu emphasizes sandwiches and salads, while the dinner menu includes seafood as well as beef and chicken. With two satellite parking lots, the restaurant makes an ideal base for hiking or biking along the nearby carriage roads. You can also use the adjacent boat launch for canoeing or kayaking on Jordan Pond. The gift shop sells bottled water, juices, and sodas from 9 to 9. ⊠*Park Loop Rd. at Jordan Pond* ☎*207/276–3316* ☰*AE, D, MC, V* ☉*Closed late Oct.–Apr.*

WHERE TO STAY

¢ ⚠ **Blackwoods Campground.** One of only two campgrounds located inside inland Acadia National Park, Blackwoods is open throughout the year (though restrictions apply for winter camping; call ahead for details). Reservations are handled by the National Recreation Reservation Service ☎877/444–6777, not by the park. Reservations for high season (May–Oct.) can be made up to six months in advance. During the off-season, a limited number of campsites are available for primitive camping, and a camping permit must be obtained from the park headquarters. Rates drop by 50% for the shoulder season (April and November). ⊠*Rte. 3, 5 mi south of Bar Harbor, Otter Creek* ☎*207/288–3274 or 800/365–2267* ⌂*35 RV sites; 198 tent sites* ⚴*no hookups or utilities; bathrooms, water, showers, picnic tables, fire pits, shuttle bus* ☰*DC, MC, V.*

¢ ⚠ **Seawall Campground.** On the "quiet side" of the island, this campground does not accept reservations, but offers space on a first-come, first-served basis, starting at 8 AM. Seawall is open from late May to late September. Walk-in tent sites are $14 per night, while drive-in sites for tents and RVs are $20. ⊠*Rte. 102A, 4 mi south of Southwest Harbor, Manset* ☎*207/244–3600* ⌂*42 RV sites; 163 tent sites* ⚴*No hookups or utilities; bathrooms, showers, fire pits, picnic tables* ☰*MC, V* ☉*Closed late Sept.–late May.*

AROUND MOUNT DESERT ISLAND

While Bar Harbor is the best-known town on Mount Desert Island, there's plenty to see and do around the entire island. Take a scenic drive along Sargent Drive for spectacular views of Somes Sound—the only fjord on the East Coast. Visit the villages of Northeast Harbor, Somesville, and Southwest Harbor, each with its own unique character. The west side of the island—also known as the "back side" or the "quiet side"—has its own restaurants and accommodations. To get a unique perspective of the island, take a cruise. Away from the crowds and traffic, you'll have plenty of time to discover some of the island's less-obvious charms.

NORTHEAST HARBOR

12 mi south of Bar Harbor via Rtes. 3 and 198 or Rtes. 233 and 198.

The summer community for some of the nation's wealthiest families, Northeast Harbor is a quiet place to stay. The village has one of the best harbors on the coast, and fills with yachts and powerboats during peak season. It's a great place to sign up for a cruise around Somes Sound or to the Cranberry Islands. Other than that, there isn't much to hold your attention for long. There's a handful of restaurants, boutiques, and art galleries on the downtown streets.

WHAT TO SEE

With many varieties of rhododendrons and azaleas, the Japanese-style **Asticou Azalea Garden** is spectacular from the end of May to the middle of June. Even when the pink, white, and blue flowers are not in full bloom, you can find plenty to admire. Originally designed by Charles Savage, the gardens contain many plants from landscape gardener Beatrix Farrand's Bar Harbor garden. Both Asticou and Thuya Gardens are now part of the Mount Desert Land and Garden Preserve. ⊠ *Rtes. 198 and 3* ⊕ *www.asticou.com/gardens.html* ⊡ *$1* ⊙ *Daily.*

The official repository for the records of the Town of Mount Desert, the **Northeast Harbor Library** hosts an always-changing exhibit in the Patterson Room. ⊠ *1 Joy Rd.* ☎ *207/276-3333* ⊙ *Mon.–Sat. 10–5.*

Hidden atop a hill on Peabody Drive, **Thuya Gardens** was once the summer home of Boston architect Joseph Henry Curtis. Today the site is a peaceful and elegant spot to take in formal perennial gardens. Designed by Charles Savage and named for the property's majestic white cedars, *Thuja occidentalis,* the garden is filled with colorful blooms throughout summer. Walk the immaculately groomed grass paths or enjoy the view from a well-placed bench. You'll find delphiniums, daylilies, dahlias, heliotrope, snapdragons, and other types of vegetation. If you have time, take a look inside the Curtis home, which has a large collection of books compiled by Savage. To get to the gardens, park in the small lot near the Asticou Inn and climb the footpath across the road. Alternately, continue down Peabody Drive and make a left on Thuya Drive. ⊠ *Peabody Dr.* ☎ *207/276-5130* ⊕ *www.gardenpreserve.org* ⊡ *$1* ⊙ *Daily.*

WHERE TO EAT & STAY

$$$–$$$$ ✕ **Abel's Lobster Pound.** You can watch the sun set and the cooks steam your lobster from the panoramic windows of this restaurant, situated a stone's throw from Somes Sound. If you want a slight variation on the famed crustacean, try the Lobster Newburg. ⊠ *Rte. 198 south of junction of Rtes. 198 and 233, Mount Desert* ☎207/276–5827 ▤*MC, V* ⊘*Closed Labor Day–mid-June.*

$–$$$ ✕ **Colonel's Delicatessen.** Known around town simply as "The Colonel's," this restaurant serves up simple fare for breakfast, lunch, and dinner. In front, the bakery turns out delicious breads, rolls, croissants, turnovers, and muffins, as well as cookies, cakes, Maine's famous whoopie pies, and other sumptuous desserts. Try one of the glazed doughnut twists, with or without chocolate drizzled over the top. The adjacent deli offers a range of premium meats. At the restaurant in the rear, you can eat in the dining room or take your food outside to the deck. The kitchen serves seafood specials, as well as burgers and pizza. ⊠*143 Main St.* ☎207/276–5147 ▤*No credit cards* ⊘*Closed mid-Oct.–mid-May.*

$–$$$ ✕ **The Docksider.** As its name suggests, this roll-up-your-sleeves restaurant sits just above the Northeast Harbor Marina. If you're looking for a lobster dinner with a minimum amount of fuss, this is the place. There are also hamburgers and other quick bites. Finish off with an ice-cream cone or a milk shake. Eat inside, on the deck, or take it with you. ⊠*14 Sea St.* ☎207/276–3965 ▤*MC, V* ⊘*Closed mid-Oct.–May.*

¢–$$$ ✕ **Tan Turtle Tavern.** Owner Rob DeGennaro was sailing on the Gulf of Maine one day when he saw a tan turtle floating on the surface of the water. And that's how the restaurant got its name (why not?). The family-oriented menu here is HUGE and includes seafood, ribs, steaks, pasta, and sandwiches. Especially recommended are the Ultimate Seafood Combo and the Lobster and Shrimp Curry. Bread is baked on the premises, and if you arrive between 9 and 11 AM you can get free coffee and a muffin. ⊠*151 Main St.* ☎207/276–9898 ▤*AE, MC, V.*

$–$$ ✕ **Bass Cocina de Tapeo.** If you like Mediterranean food, particularly those little tapas (like appetizers) from Spain, then this is the place for you. But in fact, the food of 17 countries is offered. ⊠*3 Old Firehouse La.* ☎207/276–0555 ▤*MC, V.*

$$$$ ✕▦ **Asticou Inn.** Established in 1883, this grand inn overlooking Northeast Harbor has some of the best views you'll find. The attractively furnished guest rooms have hardwood floors, hand-braided rugs, and brass beds. The restaurant ($$–$$$$) is open to the public for breakfast and dinner, as well as lunch in July and August. You can eat in the dining room or outside on the deck overlooking the harbor. The baked stuffed lobster is among the most popular dishes, but the kitchen also does great things with salmon and halibut. The extensive wine list includes more than 100 wines. The inn is close to Acadia National Park's hiking trails and carriage roads. One room is handicapped accessible; all rooms are no smoking and no pets. **Pro:** You don't have to look around for a place to go for dinner. **Con:** The inn is on the pricey side. ⊠*15 Peabody Dr., 04662* ☎207/276–3344 or 800/258–3373 ⊕*www.asticou.com* ⊅*24 rooms, 24 suites* ⌕*In-room: no a/c (some),*

TV (some). In-hotel: restaurant, tennis court, pool, no-smoking rooms ⊟*MC, V* ☉*Closed mid-Oct.–mid-May* ⊠*CP.*

$$$–$$$$ ⊡ **Northeast Harbor Inn.** (Includes Maison Suisse Inn and the Peregrine Lodge.) A bit removed from the hustle and bustle of Main Street, this inn—at least the Maison Suisse section of it—dates back to the late 1800s. Surrounded by gardens, the main building has sunny common areas where guests congregate. The guest rooms, each individually decorated, are filled with antiques, and some have beautiful silk-screened wallpaper. Many of the rooms have terraces and private porches. Peregrine Lodge has five additional rooms, each with a fireplace. One suite with full kitchen is perfect for families. All rooms are no smoking. **Pro:** This is a truly lovely place that will make you feel like you are in a private home in Europe. **Con:** You will have to drive to dinner. ⊠*144 Main St., 04662* ☎*207/276–5223 or 800/624–7668* ⊕*www.maison-suisse.com* ⤶*11 rooms, 5 suites* ♿*In-room: no a/c (some). In-hotel: no-smoking rooms, no elevator, public Wi-Fi* ⊟*AE, MC, V* ☉*Closed late Nov–Apr.* ⊠*BP.*

$$$ ⊡ **Kimball Terrace Inn.** Overlooking Northeast Harbor, this lodging offers clean, comfortable accommodations. Many of the guest rooms have views of the marina or the surrounding mountains. A short distance from the center of the village, the inn is close enough to walk to shops and galleries, but far enough away to feel a bit secluded. Adjacent to the inn, the Main Sail restaurant serves breakfast, lunch, and dinner. Dine inside or out on the deck. Two rooms are handicapped accessible and two are available to smokers—but no pets. **Pros:** Nicely kept with good views of the harbor. **Con:** Not near downtown shopping. ⊠*10 Huntington Rd., 04662* ☎*207/276–3383 or 800/454–6225* ⊕*www. kimballterraceinn.com* ⤶*70 rooms* ♿*In-hotel: restaurant, bar, pool. In-hotel: no-smoking rooms* ⊟*AE, DC, MC, V.*

$$–$$$ ⊡ **Harbourside Inn.** Built in 1888 by noted architect Fred Savage, this hillside inn is tucked into the edge of the woods. It's easy to get to Acadia National Park, as trails begin in the backyard. A unique collection of maps hangs in the public rooms, including one of the United States dating back to 1860. Rooms have hardwood floors, Oriental rugs, and flowers plucked from the surrounding gardens. Some 19th-century furnishings add to the period feel. Most bathrooms have marble sinks and wonderful tubs for soaking. Some of the rooms have real wood-burning fireplaces, and some have small kitchenettes. One room and one suite are handicapped accessible. **Pro:** If you're looking for a bargain, this inn is it. The inn has been in a Maine family for years, and they don't run it to make a profit. **Con:** No credit cards—just checks, debit cards, and, of course, cash. ⊠*Harborside Rd., 04662* ☎*207/276–3272* ⊕*www.harboursideinn.com* ⤶*11 rooms, 3 suites* ♿*In-room: no a/c, kitchen (some), no TV. In-hotel: no-smoking rooms, no elevator* ⊟*No credit cards* ☉*Closed mid-Sept.–mid-June* ⊠*CP.*

SPORTS & THE OUTDOORS

BEACH   Only a few miles from Northeast Harbor, **Seal Harbor Beach** (⊠*Rte. 3, Seal Harbor*) gives those daring enough to brave the cold water a chance to swim in the ocean. There's ample parking across the street, where you can also find public rest rooms.

BOATING A number of different boat charter companies operate tours out of Northeast Harbor. The desk near the harbormaster's office has information about the different companies. Boat charters and tours usually begin on Memorial Day weekend and run through Columbus Day, but schedules vary depending on the weather. Call ahead if you're visiting at the beginning or the end of the season. **Cranberry Isles Mail Boat Ferry Service** (⊠*Northeast Harbor* ☎*207/244–3575*) is the easiest way to travel to Little or Great Cranberry Island. The boat departs from the Northeast Harbor marina every two hours during the day, seven days a week, and stops at both islands. The company also has boats available for excursions around the area. Departing from Northeast Harbor or Southwest Harbor, the *Delight* (☞*Available in summer only* ☎*207/244–5724*) takes you on tours or transports you to other ports. Specializing in photography charters and picnic charters, **MDI Water Taxi** (☎*207/244–7312*) can transport you to an outer island or provide private charter services for sightseeing tours. The boat departs from Northeast Harbor or Southwest Harbor. The same company also operates **Downeast Sloop Charters** (☎*207/266–5210* ⊕*www.sailacadia. com*). *The Sea Princess* (⊠*Northeast Harbor* ☎*207/276–5352*) offers two different nature cruises, a sunset dinner cruise, and a trip around Somes Sound. These naturalist-narrated tours will introduce you to the wildlife you may encounter in the inland waters. The nature cruises include a stop at Little Cranberry Island, where you will have time to visit the Islesford Historical Museum *(*⇨*see full listing in the Outer Islands section of this chapter).* The sunset cruise stops here for dinner at the Islesford Dock Restaurant.

GOLFING The **Northeast Harbor Golf Club** (⊠*15 Sargeant Dr.* ☎*207/276–5335* ☉*Mid-May–mid-Nov.*) has an 18-hole course originally built in 1895. Peak-season greens fees are $85 to walk and $109 to ride. The club may close to the public during holiday weekends.

SHOPPING

You won't find Northeast Harbor's main street lined with T-shirt and souvenir shops. Instead, the town has many upscale stores selling jewelry, clothing, and fine art. A smaller version of the Bar Harbor shop, **Island Artisans** (⊠*119 Main St.* ☎*207/276–4045* ⊕*www.islandartisans.com*) sells work by area artists, including pottery, tiles, jewelry, and clothing. The **Kimball Shop** (⊠*135 Main St.* ☎*207/276–3300* ⊕*www.kimballshop.com*) carries fine china, glassware, and cookware. There are also soaps and candles that make nice gifts. You can find unique ornaments at **Shaw Jewelry** (⊠*100 Main St.* ☎*207/276–5000* ⊕*www.shawjewelry.com*). These pieces are designed by more than 100 nationally recognized artists. **Smart Studio** (⊠*Main St.* ☎*207/276–5152* ☉*June–Oct.*) was the first gallery in Northeast Harbor, but soon other galleries followed. They have two floors of showroom space with works by Maine artists. They also have a similar gallery in Boca Grande, Florida.

EN ROUTE

The best way to see Somes Sound—the only fjord on the East Coast of North America—is to take the scenic **Sargeant Drive**, which branches off Route 198. A long stretch of the roadway is edged by granite cliffs on one side and the shore on the other. Along the way you can take in views of Valley Cove and Hall Quarry. In summer you can watch sailboats and large yachts cruising the fjord. In winter, the ice masses that form on the cliffs create a spectacular show. The road is a bit narrow and is closed to large vehicles.

SOMESVILLE

7 mi northwest of Northeast Harbor via Rtes. 198 and 102.

Most visitors pass through Somesville on their way to Southwest Harbor, but this well-preserved village, the oldest on the island, is more than a stop along the way. Originally settled by Abraham Somes in 1763, this was once a bustling commercial center with shingle, lumber, and wool mills; a tannery; a varnish factory; and a dye shop. Today, Route 102, which passes through the center of town, takes you past a row of white clapboard houses with black shutters and well-manicured lawns. Designated a historic district in 1975, Somesville has one of the most-photographed spots on the island: a small house with a footbridge that crosses an old mill pond. Get out your camera. In spring, summer, or fall, this scene will remind you of a Thomas Kinkade painting. Maybe even in winter, too.

WHAT TO SEE

A few miles off Route 102, the **Beech Hill Farm** grows several acres of organic produce for area markets. Operated by the College of the Atlantic, the vegetable and flower garden are open to the public four days a week. ⊠*307 Beech Hill Rd.* ☎*207/244–5204* ☉*July–Oct., Tues., Wed., Thurs., and Sat. 8–5.*

Maintained by Acadia National Park, the **Pretty Marsh Picnic Area** is a secluded spot well suited for a picnic lunch, an afternoon barbecue, or a lobster bake. There are fire pits, picnic tables, and rest rooms. ⊠*4 mi from Somesville, Rte. 102A, Pretty Marsh* ⊠*Free* ☉*May–Oct.*

★ Open since 1964, the **Seal Cove Auto Museum** has around 100 immaculately maintained vehicles from the "Brass Era," which ran from the beginning of auto production until about 1915. There are also 35 antique motorcycles. See gasoline, steam, and electric vehicles and some interesting rarities. Each car has a sign detailing its history. This one-of-a-kind museum is worth a visit, even if you aren't normally interested in antique cars. ⊠*Rte. 102, Seal Cove* ☎*207/244–9242* ⊕*www.sealcoveautomuseum.org* ⊠*$5* ☉*June 1–Sept. 15, daily 10–5.*

Operated by the Mount Desert Island Historical Society, the **Somesville Museum** has exhibits depicting the island's long history. You can also purchase a booklet with a self-guided walking tour of the village here. The historical society also operates the **Old School House & Museum** at the intersection of Routes 3 and 198. ⊠*2 Oak Hill*

Rd. ☎207/276–9323. ⊕www.mdihistory.org ✉Donations accepted ⊙Mid-June–Sept., Tues.–Sat. 1–4

WHERE TO STAY

¢ △**Mount Desert Campground.** Near the village of Somesville, this campground has one of the best locations imaginable. It lies at the head of Somes Sound, the only fjord on the East Coast. The campground prefers tents, so vehicles longer than 20 feet are not allowed. Many sites are along the waterfront, and all are tucked into the woods for a sense of privacy. Rest rooms and showers are placed sensibly throughout the campground and are kept meticulously clean. Canoes and kayaks are available for rent, and there's a dock with access to the ocean. The Gathering Place has baked goods in the morning, and ice cream and coffee in the evening. **Pro:** A lovely location for sightseeing. **Con:** Fills up quickly during peak season. ⊠*516 Sound Dr., Mount Desert 04660* ☎*207/244–3710* ⊕*www.mountdesertcampground.com* ↩*150 sites* △*Flush toilets, drinking water, showers, fire pits, food service, swimming (ocean)* ⊟*MC, V* ⊙*Closed mid-Sept.–mid-June.*

NIGHTLIFE & THE ARTS

Across the road from the Somesville Fire Station, the **Acadia Repertory Theatre** (⊠*Rte. 102* ☎*207/244–7260* ⊕*www.acadiarep.com*) produces plays for both adults and children throughout summer. This small, informal theater is an excellent place to spend a summer evening.

SPORTS & THE OUTDOORS

At the south end of Echo Lake, **Echo Lake Beach** (⊠*Rte. 102*) has a sandy beach where many people brave the icy waters. Lifeguards are on duty in summer. Look for the sign just before you reach Southwest Harbor. **Long Pond** (⊠*Pretty Marsh Rd.*) is the largest body of freshwater on the island. It's a great spot for canoeing, kayaking, and swimming. Several feet from Long Pond, the largest pond on Mount Desert Island, is **National Park Canoe & Kayak Rentals** (⊠*Pretty Marsh Rd.* ☎*207/244–5854 or 877/378–6907* ⊕*www.acadia.net/canoe*). You can be in the water in minutes.

SHOPPING

Port in a Storm Bookstore (⊠*Rte. 102* ☎*207/244–4114* ⊕*www.portinastormbookstore.com* ⊙*Mon.–Sat. 9–6*) stocks a well-chosen selection of books. The atmosphere, with soaring ceilings and comfy chairs, is conducive to browsing.

SOUTHWEST HARBOR

5 mi south of Somesville via Rte. 102 S.

On what is known as the "quiet side" of the island, Southwest Harbor has fewer attractions than other towns. It can still be quite busy in summer, however. This working port is home to well-known boatbuilding companies, a major source of employment in the area. To reach the harbor from Route 102, make a left onto Clark Point Road.

WHAT TO SEE

The **Mount Desert Oceanarium** has exhibits on the fishing and sea life of the Gulf of Maine, a live-seal program, and hands-on exhibits such as a touch tank. ■TIP➔ **The museum closes at 5, but you should get there no later than 4 if you want to see everything.** ⊠ *Clark Point Rd.* ☎207/244–7330 ⊕*www.the-oceanarium.com* 🎟*$10* ⊙*Mid-May–late Oct., Mon.–Sat. 9–5.*

The **Wendell Gilley Museum** showcases bird carvings by Gilley, has carving demonstrations and workshops, and exhibits wildlife art. Bird carvings are to scale, and include the ruffed grouse, upland sandpiper, American goldfinch, Atlantic puffin, and loon. ⊠ *4 Herrick Rd.* ☎207/244–7555 ⊕*www.wendellgilleymuseum.org* 🎟*$5* ⊙*July and Aug., Tues.–Sun. 10–5; June, Sept., and Oct., Tues.–Sun. 10–4; May, Nov., and Dec., Fri.–Sun. 10–4.*

WHERE TO EAT & STAY

$$$–$$$$ ✕ **Deck House Restaurant & Cabaret Theater.** A beautiful view of Southwest Harbor isn't the only reason to come to this harborside restaurant. Beginning around 7:45 PM, the servers sing, dance, and play musical instruments when they aren't serving your dinner. All guests pay a $10 show fee in addition to the meal. ⊠ *Great Harbor Marina* ☎207/244–5044 ▤*AE, DC, MC, V* ⊙*Closed Mon. and mid-Sept.–mid-June.*

$$$–$$$$ ✕ **Red Sky.** Whether you're dressed for a night on the town or have
★   just tied your boat up at the pier, you feel comfortable at this downtown restaurant. Start with a salad of locally grown greens topped with chunks of blue cheese, caramelized pears, and balsamic vinaigrette, or the baby lamb chops with a bittersweet-chocolate-and-cider-mint reduction. For an entrée, choose from among delicious dishes like lobster risotto with asparagus and porcini mushrooms, and maple-glazed baby back ribs. The restaurant has more than 110 wines by the bottle and 10 wines by the glass. Save room for the cheese course. ⊠ *14 Clark Point Rd.* ☎207/244–0476 ⊕*www.redskyrestaurant.com* ▤*AE, DC, MC, V* ⊙*Closed Mar.*

$$–$$$$ ✕ **Fiddler's Green.** Perhaps the most difficult part of dining at this harborside restaurant is selecting just one entrée. It's hard to choose between dishes such as pan-seared yellowfin tuna with wasabi-and-tamari sauce or scallops with asparagus, spinach, tomato, pancetta, and grilled polenta. Everything here is fresh, including the locally grown organic produce. The desserts—including vanilla-bean crème brûlée and Grand Marnier bundt cake—make for hard decisions. Choose a bottle from a wine list that regularly includes 130 selections and has as many as 180 at the height of summer. ⊠ *411 Main St.* ☎207/244–9416 ⊕*www.fiddlersgreenrestaurant.com* ▤*AE, DC, MC, V* ⊙*Closed mid-Oct.–late-May, Mon. in July and Aug., and Mon.–Wed. late May–June and Sept.–mid-Oct.*

$-$$$ ✕**Beal's Lobster Pier.** You can watch lobstermen hauling in their catch at this working lobster pound. Lobster, clams, and other seafood make up most of the menu. You can eat your meal outside on the picnic tables. If you want to organize your own lobster bake, order the critters to go. ⊠*182 Clark Point Rd.* ☎*207/244–7178* ⊕*www.bealslobster.com* ⊟*AE, MC, V* ⊗*Closed mid-Oct.–mid-May.*

$-$$ ✕**XYZ Restaurant.** Unlike the proverbial rose, a restaurant with a name like XYZ is just as sweet as it'd be with a an easier-to-understand name. The popular restaurant is named after Xalapa, Yucatan, and Zacatecas, three Mexican towns. Try the Seven-Chile Chili and a margarita. ⊠*Bennett La.* ☎*207/244–5483* ⊟*MC, V* ⊗*Closed Labor Day–Memorial Day.*

$-$$ ✕**Café 2/Eat-A-Pita.** Fresh vegetables are the focus of the menu at this downtown eatery. Offering two kinds of pita bread, a hefty list of crisp veggies, and other fillings, this restaurant is a good bet for lunch. Try a whole-wheat pita stuffed with chickpeas, tomatoes, leaf lettuce, cucumbers, shredded carrots, alfalfa sprouts, green onions, bell peppers, and marinated chicken drizzled with honey-mustard dressing. At night, the restaurant turns into Café 2, which features salmon, lamb, and other heartier fare. ⊠*326 Main St.* ☎*207/244–4344* ⊟*MC, V* ⊗*Closed mid-Oct.–May.*

$-$$ ✕**Little Notch Pizzeria.** Delicious pizzas are on the menu here. Try a pie with prosciutto, ricotta, and artichoke hearts. The restaurant also serves salads, sandwiches, and other light fare, as well as delicious breads. ⊠*340 Main St.* ☎*207/244–3357.*

$$$-$$$$ ▥**Harbour Cottage Inn.** Elegant but casual, this lodging is close to the harbor. Built in 1870 as part of the island's first summer hotel, the inn has tastefully decorated rooms that are named after different kinds of boats. All have private bathrooms, most with steam showers or whirlpool tubs. A carriage house is also available. The nearby oceanfront property, Pier One, has four suites and one cottage rented by the week. **Pros:** Good location, easy walk to the harbor, the suite is handicapped accessible. **Con:** Breakfast is early (between 8 and 9 AM). ⊠*9 Dirigo Rd., 04679* ☎*207/244–5738 or 888/843–3022* ⊕*www.harbourcottageinn.com* ⇨*8 rooms, 3 suites* ⚬*In-room: no a/c (some). In-hotel: bar, no-smoking rooms* ⊟*MC, V* ⊗*Closed Nov.–mid-Apr.* ⦿*BP.*

$$-$$$$ ▥**Kingsleigh Inn.** It's the details that make the difference at this inn in Southwest Harbor. In your guest room you'll find fresh flowers, bottles of port, and divine homemade chocolate truffles, and in the bath there are fluffy robes and slippers. Originally built in 1904, the inn is decorated with period furnishings. Guest rooms have atmospheric additions like ceiling fans. Several rooms have balconies with harbor views. The third-floor suite has hardwood floors, a wood-burning fireplace, and a telescope for stargazing or watching boats travel in and out of the harbor. You can relax by the fireplace in the living room or take in the fresh sea air from the wraparound porch.**Pros:** Bend-over-backwards customer service, an excellent four-course gourmet breakfast. **Con:** Most breakfasts don't include meat. ⊠*373 Main St., 04679* ☎*207/244–5302* ⊕*www.kingsleighinn.com* ⇨*8 rooms, 1 suite* ⚬*In-room: no*

6

a/c (some), no phone, no TV. In-hotel: no-smoking rooms ▤*AE, MC, V* ⊘ *Closed Nov.–Apr.* ⍾○⍾*BP.*

$$–$$$$ ⌘**Lindenwood Inn.** If you're looking for something other than Victoriana, try the accommodations at this harborside inn. The sunny rooms are decorated with art from around the world. The penthouse has a deck with an outdoor hot tub. A separate bungalow has a downstairs bedroom, a sleeping loft, and a kitchen.**Pro:** This place has a variety of accommodation choices. **Con:** You will probablyneed to drive to dinner. ⊠*118 Clark Point Rd., Box 1328, 04679* ☎*207/244–5335 or 800/307–5335* ⊕*www.lindenwoodinn.com* ⇝*5 rooms, 3 suites, 1 bungalow* ⌂*In-hotel: pool, no-smoking rooms* ▤*MC, V* ⊘ *Closed Jan.–Mar.* ⍾○⍾*BP.*

$$–$$$ ⌘**Island House.** This B&B on the "quiet side" of the island has two simple and bright rooms in the main house and one suite in the carriage house. Perfect for families, the carriage-house suite has a living area and a kitchenette.**Pro:** A nice quiet setting. **Con:** No views. ⊠*36 Freedman Ridge Rd., Box 1006, 04679* ☎*207/244–5180* ⊕*www.islandhousebb.com* ⇝*2 rooms, 1 suite* ⌂*In-room: no a/c, no phone, kitchen, no TV. In-hotel: no kids under 5, no-smoking rooms* ▤*MC, V* ⍾○⍾*BP.*

¢   ⌂**Smuggler's Den Campground.** Whether you're camping in a tent or sleeping in a recreational vehicle, Smuggler's has everything you need. Located in a wooded area, the campground has amenities such as basketball and volleyball courts and a heated pool. There are hot showers, a coin laundry, and a camp store for any last-minute needs. The simple cabins can accommodate up to five people. Campsites are available for any length of time, while cabins are rented by the week. They have 100 sites for RVs and tents. **Pro:** A good array of amenities. **Con:** The sites fill up quickly during peak season. ⊠*Rte. 102, 04679* ☎*207/244–3944 or 877/244–9033* ⊕*www.smugglersdencampground.com* ⇝*4 cabins, 100 RV and tent sites* ⌂*Flush toilets, full hookups, drinking water, showers, fire pits, picnic tables, public telephone, general store, play area, swimming (heated pool)* ▤*MC, V.*

SPORTS & THE OUTDOORS

BICYCLING   **Southwest Cycle** (⊠*370 Main St.* ☎*207/244–5856*) rents bicycles by the day or week.

GOLF   If you want to hit the links, there's a 9-hole golf course at **Causeway Club** (⊠*Fernald Point Rd., Southwest Harbor* ☎*207/244–7220*).

WATER SPORTS   The **Maine State Sea Kayak Guide Service** (⊠*254 Main St., Southwest Harbor* ☎*207/244–9500 or 877/481–9500* ⊕*www.mainestatekayak. com*) offers half-day sea kayak tours for up to six people. Tours are tailored to suit both beginning and experienced paddlers. If you want to explore on your own, **Mansell Boat & Marine** (⊠*Rte. 102A, Manset* ☎*207/244–5625*) rents small powerboats and sailboats. **Manset Yacht Service** (⊠*Shore Rd., Manset* ☎*207/244–4040*) charters powerboats and sailboats. Specializing in photography tours, **MDI Water Taxi** (⊠ ☎*207/244–7312*) can transport you to the outer islands. The boat departs from the docks at Southwest Harbor or Northeast Harbor.

Next to the Coast Guard Station, **Vagabond Fishing** (✉ *Clark Point Rd.* ☎ *207/244–5385*), formerly called the Masako Queen Fishing Company, has half-day fishing trips and full-day deep-sea fishing excursions. Each passenger is assigned a lobster trap and can keep any legal lobsters caught in that trap. These trips fill up fast, so reservations are recommended.

SHOPPING

Aylen & Son (✉ *320 Main St.* ☎ *207/244–7369* ⊙ *Mon.–Sat.*) sells fine jewelry using stones from local, national, and international sources. All pieces are in sterling silver or 18-karat gold. The **Moody Mermaid** (✉ *366 Main St.* ☎ *207/244–3121*) sells clothing, sandals, and athletic footwear. You can find a superb selection of wines, olives, and cheeses at **Sawyer's Specialties** (✉ *353 Main St.* ☎ *207/244–3317*).

BASS HARBOR

4 mi south of Southwest Harbor via Rte. 102 or Rte. 102A

Bass Harbor is a tiny lobstering village with a relaxed atmosphere and a few accommodations and restaurants. If you're looking to get away from the crowds, consider using this hardworking community as your base. Although Bass Harbor does not draw as many tourists as other villages, the Bass Harbor Head Light in Acadia National Park is one of the region's most popular attractions and is undoubtedly the most-photographed lighthouse in Maine. (The best picture is taken from the rocks below, but be careful: they can be slippery.) From Bass Harbor you can hike on the Ship Harbor Nature Trail or take a ferry to Frenchboro.

WHERE TO EAT & STAY

$–$$$ ✕**Seafood Ketch.** You can watch lobster boats in the harbor while you enjoy fresh seafood on the deck or in the dining room at this family-owned restaurant. If you're looking for fried clams or steamed lobster dinners with all the fixings, you can find them here. ✉ *McMullin Ave.* ☎ *207/244–7463* ▭ *DC, MC, V* ⊙ *Closed Nov.–Apr.*

¢–$$ ✕**Thurston's Lobster Pound.** On the peninsula across from Bass Harbor, Thurston's is easy to spot because of its bright yellow awning. You can buy fresh lobsters to go or sit at outdoor tables. Order everything from a grilled cheese sandwich to a boiled lobster served with clams or mussels. ✉ *1 Thurston Rd., at Steamboat Wharf, Bernard* ☎ *207/244–7600* ▭ *MC, V* ⊙ *Closed Columbus Day–Memorial Day.*

$$$ ⊞**Bass Harbor Gables.** For all the comforts of home, step into one of the two-level apartments or the cottage at this lodging near the water. The upstairs rooms of both apartments have ocean views. North Gables, the smaller of the two, has a cozy living room, a full kitchen, and two bedrooms. Grand Gables has hardwood floors and a spiral staircase leading to a master bedroom with cathedral ceilings and two other bedrooms. The cottage has a separate living room with a pullout sofa, a full kitchen, and sliding-glass doors opening out to two decks with views of the water. No smoking is allowed and they're not handicapped accessible, but they are pet-friendly. **Pro:** A lot of different kinds of

accommodations can be found here. **Con:** They don't take credit cards. ✉*10 Earl's Way, 04653* ☎*207/244–3699* ⊕*www.bhgables.com* ⏎*2 apartments, 1 cottage* ♿*In-room: no a/c, no phone, DVD, VCR. In-hotel: some pets allowed.* ▭*No credit cards* ☾*Closed Nov.–Apr.*

$–$$ ⌂**Bass Harbor Inn.** If you're looking for someplace away from the crowds, consider this lodging near the harbor. Originally built in 1870, the inn has a relaxed atmosphere. Two of the ground-floor rooms lead out to sunny decks. The third-floor studio has cathedral ceilings, a kitchenette, and views of the ocean.Pros: Great location, reasonable rates. **Con:** Away from the action. ✉*28 Shore Rd., 04653* ☎*207/244–5157* ⊕*www.bassharborinn.com* ⏎*6 rooms, 1 studio* ♿*In-room: no a/c, no phone, no TV. In-hotel: no-smoking rooms,* ▭*AE, MC, V* ☾*Closed Nov.–Apr.* ⦿*CP.*

SPORTS & THE OUTDOORS

At Little Island Marina, **Island Cruises** (✉*Shore Rd.* ☎*207/244–5785*) offers a lunch cruise to Frenchboro and an afternoon nature cruise through Blue Hill bay. These popular cruises are scheduled from mid-June to late September.

The **Maine State Ferry Service** (☎*207/244–3254*) operates a ferry carrying both passengers and vehicles to Swans Island and Frenchboro.

SHOPPING

E.L. Higgins (✉*Bernard Rd., Bernard* ☎*207/244–3983* ⊕*www.anti-quewicker.com*) carries antique wicker, furniture, and glassware.

THE OUTER ISLANDS

If your schedule permits, take the time to visit one or more of the islands off Mount Desert Island. You're likely to see seals and other wildlife, as well as unobstructed views of Mount Desert Island's mountains. Each island has its own unique character, and some offer more amenities than others. Explore on foot or by bicycle.

CRANBERRY ISLES

1–5 mi south of Mount Desert Island via boat.

Off the southeast shore of Mount Desert Island lie the five Cranberry Isles—Great Cranberry, Islesford (also frequently called Little Cranberry), Baker Island, Sutton Island, and Bear Island. Ferry trips to Great Cranberry, Islesford, and Baker Island are a great way to escape the crowds on Mount Desert Island. Consider bringing a bike to Great Cranberry and Islesford. Be sure to look for the beautiful lighthouse on Bear Island, located just before the entrance to Northeast Harbor.

WHAT TO SEE

Baker Island, the remotest of the Cranberry Isles, looks almost black from a distance because it is covered by a thick spruce forest. The Islesford Ferry from Northeast Harbor conducts a 4½-hour narrated tour, during which you are likely to see ospreys, cormorants, and harbor seals. Because Baker Island has no natural harbor, you ride in a fishing dory to get to shore.

The **Great Cranberry Island Historical Society** has a collection of artifacts from the island that includes baskets, photographs, and even old report cards. ⊠*Great Cranberry* ☎*207/244–9055* ⊕*www.gcihs.org* ✉*Free* ☉*Late June–mid-Sept., Mon.–Sat. 10:30–4.*

Of the Cranberry Islands, Islesford has the closest thing to a village. You can find a cluster of houses, a church, a market, and a fishermen's co-op near the ferry dock.

The **Islesford Historical Museum,** run by Acadia National Park, has displays of ship models, dolls, tools, and other artifacts that document the island's history. ⊠*Islesford* ☎*207/244–9224* ✉*Free* ☉*Mid-June–late Sept., daily 10–noon and 12:30–3.*

WHERE TO EAT

$–$$$ ✕**Islesford Dock Restaurant.** You can't ask for a better seaside atmosphere than at this restaurant. Overlooking the harbor, this casual eatery has great views of the ocean and Mount Desert Island. You can dine on traditional seafood fare or opt for steaks. An added plus is that most of the vegetables and herbs are grown on the premises. ⊠*Islesford* ☎*207/244–7494* ▭*DC, MC, V* ☉*Closed Labor Day–mid-June. No lunch Sun. and Mon.*

SPORTS & THE OUTDOORS

Sailing from Northeast Harbor, the **Beal & Bunker Mail Boat Ferry Service** (☎*207/244–3575*) serves Great Cranberry, Islesford, and Sutton Island. The **Cranberry Cove Boating Company** (☎*207/244–5882* ⊕*www. barharborferry.com*) runs from Southwest Harbor to Great Cranberry, Islesford, and Sutton Island. There are six trips daily in peak season.

Explore the Cranberry Isles in two-person kayaks from **Joy of Kayaking** (⊠*Islesford* ☎*207/244–4309*). Life jackets, laminated maps, and compasses are provided. Make sure to reserve a day or two ahead.

SHOPPING

Established in 1987, **Islesford Artists** (⊠*Mosswood Rd., Islesford* ☎*207/244–3145*) displays works by island artists.

FRENCHBORO

8 mi south of Bass Harbor via boat.

The popular catchphrase "You can't get there from here" applies to the island of Frenchboro. You *can* get to Frenchboro, but only on certain days of the week. The ferry service runs two round-trip voyages to Frenchboro on Friday, and one-way voyages on Wednesday, Thursday, and Sunday. Some charter services also will take you to Frenchboro. A bed-and-breakfast has opened on the island, but Frenchboro is really better for just a day trip. You won't find streets lined with galleries and boutiques here, but if you want to see an authentic fishing community, this is the place.

WHAT TO SEE

You can find local memorabilia at the **Frenchboro Historical Society Museum.** The museum has a gift shop with locally made crafts and a cookbook compiling recipes from island residents. Stop here to pick up a map detailing the island's walking trails. ⊠*Frenchboro* ☎*207/334–2932* ✉ ⊙*Memorial Day–Labor Day, noon–5.*

If you're traveling in the region around the beginning of August, check out the annual **Frenchboro Lobster Festival.** A tradition for half a century, the festival is always held the second Saturday of August. Round-trip ferry service is available.

WHERE TO EAT

$–$$$ ✕ **Lunt's Deli.** Popular among visitors to the island, this dockside restaurant serves up lobster rolls, seafood chowder, sandwiches, and salads. ⊠*Frenchboro Dock* ☎*207/334–2922* ⊙*Closed Sun. and Oct.–June.*

SPORTS & THE OUTDOORS

The **Maine State Ferry Service** (⊠*Bass Harbor* ☎*207/244–3254 or 800/491–4883* ⊕*www.state.me.us/mdot/opt/ferry/ferry.htm*) operates round-trip passenger ferry service between Frenchboro and Bass Harbor from April to October.

ACADIA NATIONAL PARK & MOUNT DESERT ISLAND ESSENTIALS

To research prices, get advice from other travelers, and book travel arrangements, visit www.fodors.com.

TRANSPORTATION

BY AIR

Although Trenton's Hancock County–Bar Harbor Airport offers the closest airport to the Mount Desert Island region, only one commuter airline, Colgan Air (operated by US Airways Express), services the airport. It flies to Boston and Rockland. Most people prefer Bangor International Airport, an hour's drive from the island. Direct flights are available to and from Boston, New York LaGuardia, Philadelphia, Cincinnati, Detroit, and Albany. Major car-rental companies also are found at the airport. (⇨ *See Transportation in Maine Essentials in the back of the book.*)

Airports Bangor International Airport (⊠ *287 Godfrey Blvd., Bangor* ☎ *207/947–0384* ⊕ *www.flybangor.com*). **Hancock County–Bar Harbor Airport** (⊠ *Rte. 3, Trenton* ☎ *207/667–7171 or 800/428–4322* ⊕ *www.bhbairport.com*).

BY BIKE

Although Acadia National Park is a bicycle-friendly area, traveling along the island's major thoroughfares can be challenging. Bike lanes are narrow or nonexistent on many stretches of road, leaving bikers the choice of biking in roadside gravel, which can be soft when wet, or sharing the road with vehicle traffic. In summer, when traffic is heavy and many drivers are distracted by the scenery, it's a good idea to avoid the main roads.

BY BOAT

Many huge and famous steamships, such as the *Queen Elizabeth II,* occasionally visit the port of Bar Harbor, and there are a lot of smaller ferries going to places like the outer islands. But other than a few windjammers, such as the *Margaret Todd,* the only other major boat going to and from the island is The CAT, traveling to Nova Scotia (⇨ *see Bar Harbor section for both).*

BY BUS

The free Island Explorer shuttle service circles the entire island from the end of May to September, with limited service continuing through mid-October. Buses, which are equipped with racks for bicycles, service the major campgrounds, Acadia National Park, and Trenton's Hancock County–Bar Harbor Airport. They also run from Bar Harbor to Ellsworth. Concord Trailways operates shuttle service from Bangor International Airport to Bar Harbor, with stops along the way in Bangor and Ellsworth. Concord Trailways also operates a twice-daily coastal bus service from Bangor to Boston. Vermont Transit runs between Bangor and Bar Harbor. If the bus isn't delayed by traffic, it takes about an hour. Downeast Transportation operates buses from Ellsworth to various locations on Mount Desert Island. Greyhound Bus Lines services Bangor. West's Coastal Connection is a public bus operated by the Maine Department of Transportation. You can take the bus from the Bangor International Airport to Ellsworth, where you can transfer to another bus to the island.

Bus Lines **Concord Trailways** (☎ *207/942–8686 or 888/741–8686* ⊕ *www. concordtrailways.com).* **Greyhound** (☎ *207/772–6587 or 800/231–2222* ⊕ *www. greyhound.com).* **Island Explorer (Downeast Transportation)** (☎ *207/667–5796* ⊕ *www.exploreacadia.com).* **Vermont Transit** (☎ *207/772–6587 or 800/231–2222* ⊕ *www.vermonttransit.com).*

BY CAR

From the gateway towns of Ellsworth and Trenton, Route 3 leads to Mount Desert Island. When you reach the island, Route 3 continues to Bar Harbor. Route 102 heads toward Somesville and Southwest Harbor. In summer, traffic can slow considerably, especially in the afternoon. If Northeast Harbor is your first destination when arriving on the island, take Route 102 to Somesville, then turn onto Route 198.

In Acadia National Park, the 27-mi Park Loop Road is accessible from Hulls Cove (visitor center entrance), Otter Creek (Sieur de Monts Spring entrance), and Seal Harbor (Jordan Pond House entrance). You can also access the Park Loop Road from Bar Harbor (Cadillac Mountain entrance).

BY TRAIN

Portland is the closest city to the Mount Desert Island region with train service (⇨ *see Greater Portland Essentials in Chapter 2.)*

CONTACTS & RESOURCES

DISABILITIES & ACCESSIBILITY

America leads the pack in accommodations and restaurants when it comes to providing for people with disabilities. By Maine state law, any new accommodations or restaurants must provide handicapped access. Older facilities, such as historical B&Bs, can be "grandfathered in" because making the necessary changes could adversely affect the architectural integrity of the property. When you call about "handicapped accessibility," make sure the person you are talking to knows what that phrase means: the building is accessible, the room or restaurant is accessible, and the bathroom is accessible.

EMERGENCIES

In case of an emergency, call 911.

Hospitals **Eastern Maine Medical Center** (✉ *489 State St., Bangor* ☎ *207/973–8000*). **Maine Coast Memorial Hospital** (✉ *50 Union St., Ellsworth* ☎ *207/664–5311* ⊕ *www.mainehospital.org*). **Mount Desert Island Hospital** (✉ *10 Wayman La., Bar Harbor* ☎ *207/288–5081*). **Northeast Harbor Clinic** (✉ *Kimball Rd., Northeast Harbor* ☎ *207/276–3331*). **Southwest Harbor Medical Center** (✉ *45 Herrick Rd., Southwest Harbor* ☎ *207/244–5513*).

MEDIA

The major daily newspaper distributed in the area is the *Bangor Daily News,* but at convenience stores or supermarkets you also can buy copies of the *Boston Globe, New York Times,* and *Portland Telegram.* Weekly papers include the *Bar Harbor Times, Ellsworth American, Ellsworth Weekly,* and the *Islander.* Community radio station WERU 89.9 FM in Blue Hill has eclectic programming featuring reggae, jazz, blues, oldies, folk, and other music. WMEH 90.9 is the local National Public Radio affiliate. WLBZ, channel 2, is the NBC affiliate. WVII, channel 7, is the ABC affiliate. WABI, channel 5, is the CBS affiliate. WMEB, channel 12, is the Maine Public Broadcasting affiliate.

VISITOR INFORMATION

Contacts **Acadia National Park** (✍ *Box 177, Bar Harbor 04609* ☎ *207/288–3338* ⊕ *www.nps.gov/acad*). **Bar Harbor Chamber of Commerce** (✉ *93 Cottage St.* ✍ *Box 158, Bar Harbor 04609* ☎ *207/288–3393, 207/288–5103, or 800/288–5103* ⊕ *www.barharborinfo.com*). **Bar Harbor Merchant's Association** (✍ *Box 431, Bar Harbor 04609* ⊕ *www.barharbormerchants.com*) is a good place to call if you're planning to come during any of the off-seasons—spring, fall, and winter. **Ellsworth Area Chamber of Commerce** (✉ *163 High St., Ellsworth 04605* ☎ *207/667–5584* ⊕ *www.ellsworthchamber.org*). **Mount Desert Chamber of Commerce** (✉ *Sea St., Northeast Harbor 04662* ☎ *207/276–5040* ⊕ *www.mountdesertchamber. org*). **Southwest Harbor/Tremont Chamber of Commerce** (✉ *Main St.* ✍ *Box 1143, Southwest Harbor 04679* ☎ *207/244–9264 or 800/423–9264* ⊕ *www. acadiachamber.com*).

Way Down East

WORD OF MOUTH

"Gorgeous area, pristine views—enjoyed the ride up Route 1 with stops for ice cream, seafood, views."

—Escargot

By Mary Ruoff

SLOGANS SUCH AS "THE REAL MAINE" ring truer Way Down East. The raw, mostly undeveloped coast in this remote region is more accessible than it is farther south. Pleasure craft don't crowd out lobster boats and draggers in small harbor towns the way they do in other coastal towns. Even in summer here you're likely to have rocky beaches and shady hiking trails to yourself. The slower pace is as calming as a sea breeze.

One innkeeper relates that visitors who plan to stay a few days often opt for a week after learning more about the region's offerings, which include national wildlife refuges, state parks, historic sites and preserves, and increasingly, conservancy-owned public land. Cutler's Bold Coast, with its dramatic granite headlands, is protected from development. Waters near Eastport have some of the world's highest tides. Lakes perfect for canoeing and kayaking are sprinkled inland. Rivers snake through marshland as they near the many bays. Boulders are strewn on blueberry barrens. Rare plants thrive in coastal bogs and heaths. Dark-purple-and-pink lupines line the roads in late June.

The Downeast Heritage Museum in Calais helps visitors learn about the wilderness areas Way Down East. It's just one example of how ecotourism is offering economic hope in a region that remains one of the poorest in the state. Residents often work a series of seasonal jobs, and many hope to siphon tourist dollars, as you might guess from the signs beckoning you to stop at homestead galleries, roadside stands, and quiet inns.

EXPLORING WAY DOWN EAST

Way Down East covers roughly a fourth of the state's coast, at least as the crow flies. A car is essential for exploring this vast swath of land. You can take a bus from Bangor that stops in towns along U.S. 1 and rent a car in Calais and Machias or just south of the region in Ellsworth. U.S. 1, usually following the coast slightly inland, is the main transportation spine. Towns highlighted are along this highway or nearby on the area's many bays and peninsulas, where cell-phone reception may be spotty at best (Canadian cell towers pick up calls in Lubec, Eastport, and Calais). The inland countryside is sprinkled with lakes and rolling with hills, so consider returning via an inland route.

WHEN TO GO
Reservations are recommended in July and August, although it's usually possible to find last-minute rooms. The exception is during one of the popular summer festivals, when you may find hotels are booked solid, even in neighboring towns. Temperatures in summer average about 70°F during the day. Nights are cool, so be sure to bring a light jacket. Fog is likely this time of year—and more common than in the south—so come prepared to appreciate its haunting beauty. Many establishments are open from Memorial Day weekend to Columbus Day. Winter-sports outfitters are rare, but folks trickle in for winter getaways—the scenery never disappoints.

ABOUT THE RESTAURANTS

You won't find fast-food chains Way Down East except for a few in Calais and Machias. If you don't have time to stop at a restaurant, you can grab a sandwich or slice of pizza at most convenience stores. Your only choice for a sit-down meal is often one of the many family establishments serving breakfast, lunch, and dinner. All of these places have massive menus heavy on the seafood (it's not all fried), and many have added items like wraps and Cobb salads. Save room for the desserts, often made right on the premises. Upscale dining establishments serving more creative cuisine are scattered throughout the region; Machias has an impressive cluster. Don't be surprised if you find that the best restaurant is in the inn where you're staying.

ABOUT THE HOTELS

In the villages and along the back roads you can find wonderful bed-and-breakfasts run by innkeepers eager to share Way Down East's laid-back charms. Some are cozy places where you might feel you're staying in a friend's country house, while others are grand mansions where the rooms are filled with antiques. Hardly any have air conditioning—with cooling sea breezes you don't need it. Don't write off anything called a cottage; many in this region are lovely. Inns often charge less than you might think; upscale establishments that would command $150 a night or more in Bar Harbor often have rooms for about $100 here. What you won't find Way Down East are chain hotels, though there are some inexpensive roadside motels, most of them in larger towns.

WHAT IT COSTS					
	¢	$	$$	$$$	$$$$
RESTAURANTS	under $7	$7–$10	$11–$17	$18–$25	over $25
HOTELS	under $60	$60–$99	$100–$149	$150–$200	over $200

Restaurant prices are for a main course at dinner, excluding sales tax of 7%. Hotel prices are for two people in a standard double room in high season, excluding service charges and 7% tax.

EASTERN HANCOCK COUNTY

As you drive east from Ellsworth, Mount Desert Island rises across Frenchman Bay. Eastern Hancock County attracts people who come to visit Acadia National Park and busy Bar Harbor, but want a respite from the crowds. With dramatic seaside scenery, tucked-away fishing villages, and artists in droves, lots of folks come just to stay put.

HANCOCK

9 mi north of Ellsworth via U.S. 1.

A small triangular green with a Civil War monument marks the center of Hancock. Not far away are the summer cottages at Hancock Point where stunning views await, especially at sunset, across Frenchman

WAY DOWN EAST TOP 5

■ **Hike Cutler's Bold Coast:** The open ocean views are stupendous, but what also makes hiking here so memorable is peering down at coves below the cliffs, or at wild cranberries between the rocks at your feet.

■ **Meet the innkeepers:** Some offer rooms with shared baths without apology, others pride themselves on private baths with spa tubs, but all share a passion for the area and will give you pamphlets galore.

■ **Savor chocolate at the end of the road:** Way up the Maine Coast in Lubec there are not one but two scrumptious chocolatiers. Continue on to Calais, where it's a short walk across the bridge downtown to the Chocolate Museum in St. Stephen, New Brunswick.

■ **Explore Campobello Island:** Roosevelt Campobello International Park is a must-see, but there are other gems on this Canadian island, like the wide sand beach at Herring Cove and the village of Wilson's Beach, where the water views are like unfurling ribbons en route to East Quoddy Head Lighthouse.

■ **Mingle with artisans:** Artists selling fine paintings and crafters offering less-pricey wares all have stories to tell, about themselves and the region and why they are here.

Bay. You can pick up items for an impromptu picnic in Hancock or across the bridge in Sullivan, where you'll find another town green and more mountain-framed views.

☼ **Willowbrook Garden.** Beside their homestead gallery, Paul and Ann Breeden painstakingly created this whimsical, nationally profiled half-acre shade garden. Below tall trees, paths wend past water-lily pools, perennial beds, wild plants, sculpture—even a teahouse and a toy-stocked playhouse. ☒ *19 Willowbrook La., Sullivan* ☎ *207/422–3007* ⊕ *www.willowbrookgarden.com* ☒ *Free* ☉ *May–Oct., daily 9–5.*

WHERE TO EAT & STAY

$$–$$$$ ✕**Tidal Falls Lobster Restaurant.** This lobster stand overlooks one of New ★ England's best-known reversing falls, a phenomenon created when the current "reverses" from the bay to the harbor. White water roils from an hour before to an hour after low or high tide, but the falls always put on a good show. Besides lobster and fried seafood, the menu includes wood-smoked barbecue dishes. Look for sides such as garlic bread and crab dip. You can eat outdoors or inside a screened room. Bring your own wine (glasses and openers are provided). The restaurant is seasonal, but the grounds, owned by the Frenchman Bay Conservancy, are open daily, year-round. ☒ *71 Tidal Falls Rd.,* ✛ *turn on East Side Rd. from U.S. 1* ☎ *207/422–6457* ⊕ *www.frenchmanbay.org* ☒ *MC, V* ☉ *Closed Labor Day–mid-June.*

$–$$$ ✕**Ruth & Wimpy's.** Identifiable by the giant statue of "Wilbur the Lob-☼ ster," this is a popular stop for families. Eat in the large dining room or outside beside a wood-fired cooker. The menu includes more than 25 lobster dishes, including fried lobster, lobster Newburg, and lobster with haddock. You can order sandwiches and fish and chicken baskets at dinner. Get steamed lobsters, clams, and mussels to go at the rustic

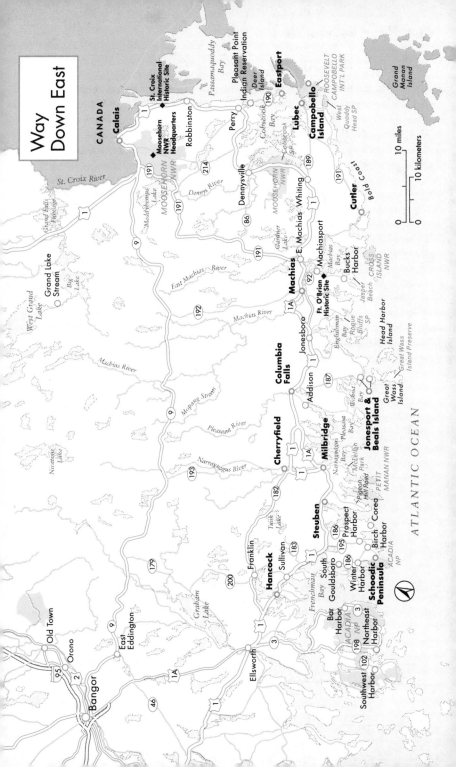

Way
Down East

CANADA

St. Croix River

Grand Falls Flowage

Meddybemps Lake

MOOSEHORN NWR

Calais

St. Croix International Historic Site

Moosehorn NWR Headquarters

Robbinston

Denny River

Passamaquoddy Bay

Pleasant Point Indian Reservation

Perry

Deer Island

Eastport

ROOSEVELT CAMPOBELLO INT'L PARK

Grand Manan Island

Cobscook Bay

Lubec

West Quoddy Head SP

Campobello Island

Denrysville

Whiting

E. Machias

MOOSEHORN NWR

Gardner Lake

Cutler

Bold Coast

Grand lake Stream

West Grand Lake

Big Lake

Grand Lake

East Machias River

Machias

Ft. O'Brian Historic Site

Machiasport

Machias Bay

Bucks Harbor

CROSS ISLAND NWR

Jasper Beach

Machias River

Machias River

Megang Stream

Jonesboro

Roque Bluffs SP

Englishman Bay

Head Harbor Island

Great Wass Island Preserve

Nicatous Lake

Columbia Falls

Addison

Pleasant River

Cherryfield

Narraguagus River

Milbridge

Jonesport & Beals Island

Great Wass Island

PETIT MANAN NWR

Tunk Lake

Steuben

Prospect Harbor

Birch Corea Harbor

Pigeon Hill Road

Franklin

Sullivan

Hancock

South Gouldsboro

Winter Harbor

Schoodic Peninsula

ACADIA NP

Graham Lake

Bar Harbor

ACADIA NP

Northeast Harbor

Old Town

Orono

Bangor

East Eddington

Ellsworth

Southwest Harbor

ATLANTIC OCEAN

10 miles

10 kilometers

IF YOU LIKE

PUFFIN CRUISES

Set sail from Cutler or Jonesport on a cruise to Machias Seal Island, the state's largest puffin colony. Many people come Way Down East just to visit this treeless, rocky isle 10 mi off the coast, a summer home puffins share with scores of other seabirds, including razorbills, common terns, arctic terns, common murres, black guillemots, and common eiders. With clownish ways and a "stuffed toy" look—white breasts beneath jet-black coats, goggle-like eyes, and blue bands on red-orange beaks—thousands of puffins steal the show. Canada and the United States dispute ownership of the migratory bird sanctuary, but tour operators cooperate with the Canadian Wildlife Service to control access. Weather can prevent boat landings, as there is no pier, but if you go ashore, you can walk on boardwalks and grassy paths to closetlike blinds where four people can stand comfortably as puffins court, clatter, and nuzzle. Bring layers: temperatures in July and August can drop to 50°F.

SEA KAYAKING

Since much of the coastline of Way Down East remains undeveloped, it's no surprise that paddlers—novice and experienced—love it here. The glacier-carved topography makes this a top kayaking destination. Many fjordlike bays offer stunning scenery on both sides of the boat. Islands near the mainland entice paddlers to explore. Pink granite ledges are common in the southern half of the region. North of Jonesport the coast changes, and these smooth rocks are replaced with jagged shorelines. Here in Machias Bay you can see where American Indians left their mark on the landscape: this region is home to what some consider the most significant petroglyph sites on the East Coast. Two are easy to reach by sea kayak. Paddle out to see carvings of a caribou, a walrus, and humans adorned with antlered headdresses.

lobster shack. ⊠792 U.S. 1 ☎207/422–3723 ⊟D, MC, V ☉Closed mid-Dec.–Mar., and Sun. Apr.–early Dec.

$$$ ✕☒ **Le Domaine Inn & Restaurant.** In the French country–style dining room ($$$$), opened in 1946, you can order the five-course prix fixe dinner ($35) or select from a changing menu with dishes like filet mignon with bordelaise sauce and veal sweetbreads and truffle sauce on microgreens. The poultry is almost always duck or quail. An extensive wine list (French and California vintages) accompanies the French cuisine. The popular Sunday brunch always includes crab cakes. Le Domaine is known primarily for its food, but the French-influenced guest rooms are also inviting. They open onto private decks overlooking the perennial gardens. A pair of suites have fireplaces to keep out the chill. The former owner's mother was from Provence, so the decor is quite authentic. **Pros:** Wide decks, cathedral ceilings in suites. **Con:** Close to road. ⊠1513 U.S. 1, 04640 ☎207/422–3395 or 800/554–8498 ⊕www.ledomaine.com ⇩3 rooms, 2 suites ♻In-room: no TV, Wi-Fi. In-hotel: restaurant, no elevator, public Wi-Fi, some pets allowed, no-smoking rooms ⊟AE, D, MC, V ☉Closed late Oct.–May. Restaurant closed Mon. No lunch Tues.–Sat. ❘⊙❘CP.

$$–$$$ ✕⊞ **Crocker House Inn.** Set amid towering fir trees, this shingle-style
★ lodging was built in 1884. The inn holds comfortable rooms decorated
with authentic antiques and country-style furnishings. The accommodations in the carriage house, where there is a den for all inn guests,
are perfect for families. The inn's restaurant ($$$–$$$$) draws din-
ers from Bangor and beyond with dressed-up versions of traditional
New England fare. The signature dish is scallops sautéed in white wine
and topped with garlic, lemon, mushrooms, scallions, and tomatoes.
Pros: Only lodging on exclusive Hancock Point, hot tub off den, piano
music in parlor most Friday and Saturday evenings. **Con:** No water
views. ⊠*967 Point Rd., 04640* ☎*207/422–6806 or 877/715–6017*
⊕*www.crockerhouse.com* ⤴*11 rooms* ⌂*In-room: no a/c (some), no
TV, Wi-Fi. In-hotel: restaurant, bicycles, no elevator, public Internet,
public Wi-Fi, some pets allowed, no-smoking rooms* ▤*AE, D, MC, V*
⊗*Closed Jan.–mid-Mar., and Mon.–Wed. late Mar.–Apr. and Nov.–
Dec. No lunch.* ⦿*BP.*

$$ ⊞ **Island View Inn.** Built in the late 1880s as a summer "cottage" for
wealthy owners, this spacious shingled house is filled with original
furnishings. Steps lead from the manicured lawn to a private beach,
where the views extend directly across Frenchman Bay to Mount Desert Island. Padded rocking chairs line the wraparound porch. All rooms
have water views and open onto shared porches. The massive living
room has an antique game table and built-in seats beside a fieldstone
fireplace with an exposed chimney rising through an atrium-like space.
Pros: Large rooms, wide lawn. **Con:** Right below busy U.S. 1. ⊠*12
Miramar Ave., Sullivan 04664* ☎*207/422–3031* ⊕*www.maineus.
com/islandview* ⤴*4 rooms* ⌂*In-room: no a/c, no phone, no TV. In-
hotel: beachfront, water sports, some pets allowed, no-smoking rooms,
no elevator* ▤*D, MC, V* ⊗*Closed mid-Oct.–May* ⦿*BP.*

$$ ⊞ **Three Pines Bed & Breakfast.** The owners' impeccable saltbox on Sul-
☾ livan Harbor is connected to a two-story guesthouse by a covered
walkway. You can enjoy the lacto-ovo vegetarian breakfast on the
screened porch, in the dining room, or in your room. A path along the
shore looks toward Cadillac Mountain, while trails traverse the mostly
wooded 40 acres. There's also a small organic farm. **Pros:** Farm away
from lodging, kids love the animals. **Con:** Long dirt drive. ⊠*274 East
Side Rd., 04640* ☎*207/460–7595* ⊕*www.threepinesbandb.com* ⤴*2
rooms* ⌂*In-room: no a/c, no phone, DVD (some), VCR (some), no TV.
In-hotel: water sports, bicycles, no elevator, no-smoking rooms, some
pets allowed* ▤*AE, D, MC, V* ⦿*BP.*

SPORTS & THE OUTDOORS

You can paddle on open water in Frenchman Bay or follow the shores
of Taunton Bay on kayak excursions with **Hancock Point Kayak Tours**
(⊠*58 Point Rd.* ☎*207/422–6854* ⊕*www.hancockpointkayak.com*).
The company also arranges overnight kayaking and backpacking trips,
and cross-country skiing and snowshoeing trips.

SHOPPING

FOOD   Touting freshly made "good foods to go" such as Thai peanut noodles, Provençal roasted vegetables, and organic chicken, color-splashed **Mano's Market** (✉*1517 U.S. 1* ☎*207/422–6500*) also has a café and stocks wine, cheese, and packaged specialty foods. The **Sullivan Harbor Farm Smokehouse** (✉*1545 U.S. 1* ☎*207/422–2209 or 800/422–4014* ⊕*www.sullivanharborfarm.com*) cold-smokes salmon and other seafood in the traditional Scottish manner. Watch workers through the inside window in the shop, where you can buy wood tips and pans for smoke-flavored grilling and crackers and sauces to complement the seafood. Load up for a picnic—insulated bags are available.

GALLERIES   Acclaimed regional artist Philip Barter's boldly hued paintings of Down East scenes dominate at **Barter Family Gallery** (✉*318 S. Bay Rd.,* ✛ *off U.S. 1 in Sullivan, Franklin* ☎*207/422–3190* ⊕*www.barterfamilygallery*). This playful gallery near Sullivan also showcases sculpture, woolen rugs, and other art by talented family members. Barter is open June 15 to October 15 or by appointment. Heron-patterned dinnerware is one of the specialties at **Hog Bay Pottery** (✉*245 Hog Bay Rd., Franklin* ☎*207/565–2282* ⊕*www.hogbay.com*), which also sells handwoven wool rugs with geometric designs. The potter fires his wood-burning kiln three times a year; his wife makes the rugs. It's open May through October or by appointment. Walkways connect Japanese-style pavilions at **Lunaform** (✉*66 Cedar La., Sullivan* ☎*207/422–0923* ⊕*www.lunaform.com*), which makes large, hand-turned concrete urns and planters for gardens and homes. It is open year-round. Human figures fuse with animals and the natural world in Russell Wray's sculpture, etchings, and engravings, sold at **Raven Tree Gallery** (✉*536 Point Rd.* ☎*207/422–8273* ⊕*www.raventreegallery.com*), which also carries the artist's jewelry. Raven Tree is open June through October and by appointment.

★   Ann and Paul Breeden's **Spring Woods Gallery** (✉*19 Willowbrook La., Sullivan* ☎*207/422–3007* ⊕*www.springwoodsgallery.com*), nestled between their home and a large shade garden for visitors, is illuminated by a tall arched window. Local farm animals appear often in her colorful, playful oil paintings. His strikingly realistic acrylic paintings capture the intensity of the Maine Coast. The gallery is open May through October and by appointment. Eagles and bears sawed from pine-tree trunks tower along the roadside at **"Wild Mountain Man" Art Gallery** (✉*742 U.S. 1* ☎*207/565–3377* ⊕*www.thewildmountainman.com*), where "chainsaw sawyer artist" Ray Murphy's folk art also includes smaller figures and wall plaques.

NIGHTLIFE & THE ARTS

At Ray Murphy's **Chainsaw Sawyer Art Stage Show** (✉*734 U.S. 1* ☎*207/565–3377* ⊕*www.chainsawentertainer.com* ☎*$10* ☉*Mid-June–early Oct., daily at 7 PM*), the nationally profiled sawyer creates 15 works in five minutes and saws numbers on a toothpick. Shows are in a large building with bleachers next to his "Wild Mountain Man" Art Gallery (⇨*see Shopping*).

Heading north on U.S. 1, the **Schoodic National Scenic Byway** starts at the Hancock-Sullivan bridge. By spring 2008 displays are to be installed at a rest area here and at spots along the way detailing the region's history, culture, and natural resources. The byway turns south on Route 186 en route to the Schoodic section of Acadia National Park, but you don't have to wait until then for awesome views of Cadillac Mountain across Frenchman Bay. One of the best is 1½ mi north of the bridge. On the **State Route 182 Maine Scenic Byway,** overhanging trees create a tunnel of color come fall. From U.S. 1, take Route 182 to Franklin, a quaint town where the 13-mi scenic drive begins. Take in the scenery at Tunk Lake, about 6 mi from Franklin. The byway ends in Cherryfield, where you can return to U.S. 1.

SCHOODIC PENINSULA

16 mi southeast of Hancock via U.S. 1 and Rte. 186, 25 mi east of Ellsworth.

The landscape of Schoodic Peninsula makes it easy to understand why the overflow from Bar Harbor's wealthy summer population settled in Winter Harbor. The craggy coastline, the towering evergreens, and views over Frenchman Bay are breathtaking year-round. A drive through the well-to-do summer community of Grindstone Neck shows what Bar Harbor might have been like before so many mansions there were destroyed in the Great Fire of 1947. Artists and artisans have opened galleries in and around Winter Harbor. Anchored at the foot of the peninsula, Winter Harbor was once part of Gouldsboro, which wraps around it.

WHAT TO SEE

Within Gouldsboro on the Schoodic Peninsula are several small coastal villages. You drive through **Wonsqueak** and **Birch Harbor** after leaving the Schoodic section of Acadia National Park. Near Birch Harbor you can find **Prospect Harbor,** a small fishing village nearly untouched by tourism. There's also **Corea,** where there's little to do besides watch the fishermen at work, wander along stone beaches, or gaze out to sea—and that's what makes it so special.

Fodor'sChoice
★
The only section of **Acadia National Park** (⇨ *see Chapter 6*) that sits on the mainland is at the southern side of the Schoodic Peninsula. A few miles east of Winter Harbor, the park has a scenic 6-mi one-way loop that edges along the coast and yields views of Grindstone Neck, Winter Harbor, and Winter Harbor Lighthouse. At the tip of the point, huge slabs of pink granite lie jumbled along the shore, thrashed unmercifully by the crashing surf (stay away from water's edge), and jack pines cling to life amid the rocks. Fraser Point at the beginning of the loop is an ideal place for a picnic. Work off lunch with a hike up Schoodic Head for the panoramic views up and down the coast. A free bus called the Island Explorer (☎207/288–4573 [late June–Columbus Day] or 207/667–5796 ⊕*www.exploreacadia.com*) takes passengers from Prospect Harbor, Birch Harbor, and Winter Harbor and drops

them off anywhere in the park. In Winter Harbor you can get off at the ferry to Bar Harbor. The $10 park admission fee is generally not charged when you're just visiting Schoodic. ✉ *Rte. 186, Winter Harbor* ☎ *207/288–3338* ⊕ *www.nps.gov/acad* ☒ *$10* ⊙ *Year-round, 24/7.*

WHERE TO EAT

$$$–$$$$ ✕ **Bunker's Wharf.** On a narrow harbor that is home to an 18-boat lobster fleet and opens onto the ocean, this restaurant sits near Acadia National Park. Enjoy the views from the stone patio or from the large windows in the blond-wood dining room. Some seats in the bar face the water. The setting—quintessential Maine—isn't all that keeps locals coming back. Lobster (served with roasted corn-bread pudding) is bought off boats in the harbor. The restaurant is also known for generous portions and scrumptious fare, from fried clams on a baguette at lunch to baked haddock with focaccia-bread stuffing at dinner. ✉ *260 E. Schoodic Dr., Birch Harbor* ☎ *207/963–2244* ⊕ *www.bunkerswharfrestaurant.com* ▭ *MC, V* ⊙ *Closed some days Sept.–June; call for hours.*

$–$$$ ✕ **Chase's Restaurant.** The orange booths may remind you of a fast-food joint, but this family restaurant has a reputation for serving good, basic fare. In this region, that means a lot of fish. There are large and small fried seafood dinners and several more expensive seafood platters. Try the sweet-potato fries as a side. Lunch fare, sold all day, includes wraps and burgers with toppings like pesto and guacamole. It's also open for breakfast. ✉ *193 Main St. (Rte. 186), Winter Harbor* ☎ *207/963–7171* ▭ *AE, D, MC, V.*

$–$$ ✕ **J. M. Gerrish Provisions.** The store that opened here in the early 1900s was where locals and visitors alike went for ice cream. The name remains and part of the old marble counter, but this is now a deli and café where folks bustle in for fudge and coffee and linger at tables inside and on the porch. A simple menu has soups, salads, and savory sandwiches such as turkey and Jarlsberg cheese topped with peach salsa. The deli case offers salads and dishes such as scallops with roasted tomatoes. Baked goods crowd the counter, a building out back that's to open in 2008 will sell wine and beer, and, yes, you can still buy an ice cream. ✉ *352 Main St., Winter Harbor* ☎ *207/963–2727* ▭ *MC, V* ⊙ *Closed mid-Oct.–mid-May.*

WHERE TO STAY

$$–$$$ ▦ **Oceanside Meadows Inn.** This place is a must for nature lovers. Trail
⟳   maps guide you through a 200-acre preserve dotted with woods,
Fodor'sChoice   streams, salt marshes, and ponds. Inspired by the moose, eagles, and
★   other wildlife that thrive here, the innkeepers created the Oceanside Meadows Innstitute for the Arts & Sciences, which holds lectures, musical performances, art exhibits, and other events in the restored barn. Furnished with antiques, country pieces, and family treasures, and scented with flowers from the gardens, the inn has sunny, inviting living rooms with fireplaces and a separate guest kitchen. Guest rooms are spread between two white clapboard buildings fronting a private beach shaded by granite ledges. Breakfast is an extravagant multicourse affair that includes chilled fruit soup. **Pros:** One of the region's few sand beaches, many spacious rooms, handicapped-accessible room

GREAT ITINERARIES

IF YOU HAVE 3 DAYS

Head to the **Schoodic Peninsula**, where you can explore the tide pools on the surf-beaten ledges of Acadia National Park. Then amble about the downtown area of tranquil Winter Harbor—bustling Bar Harbor across the bay seems a world away. There are more shops to discover all around Schoodic Peninsula, where many artists have galleries beside their homes. Spend the night at a small inn in Gouldsboro, Corea, or Prospect Harbor. On Day 2, travel north to **Milbridge**, where you can enjoy the Milbridge Historical Museum, with displays on weir fishing and the town's shipbuilding heyday. In **Cherryfield**, follow the Narraguagus River while checking out the impressive Victorian homes. Next, tour historic Ruggles House in **Columbia Falls**. Continuing north, take the road to **Jonesport**. When you arrive, cross the bridge to **Beals Island** for a late-afternoon hike

at the Great Wass Island Preserve. Spend the night in Jonesport, or nearby in **Machias**. The next day, take a morning puffin cruise from Jonesport.

IF YOU HAVE 5 DAYS

Follow the three-day itinerary above. On Day 4, drive to **Lubec** and cross the bridge to New Brunswick's **Campobello Island**. Tour the Roosevelt Cottage at Roosevelt Campobello International Park and, if tides allow, walk out to East Quoddy Head Lighthouse. Then head to West Quoddy Head Light in Lubec to hike along the shore. Stay overnight in Lubec or on Campobello Island. On Day 5, visit downtown Lubec, checking out galleries and chocolate shops and taking a tour of the Historic McCurdy Smokehouse. Returning south on U.S. 1, visit the Burnham Tavern Museum in Machias. If time allows, take in the area's other historic sites or travel down to Roque Bluffs State Park for a hike or swim.

with water view. **Con:** Need to cross road to beach. ✉ *202 Corea Rd. (Rte. 195), Prospect Harbor 04669* ☎ *207/963–5557* ⊕ *www.oceaninn.com* ➷ *12 rooms, 3 suites* ♿ *In-room: no a/c, no TV, Wi-Fi. In-hotel: beachfront, no elevator, public Internet, public Wi-Fi, no-smoking rooms, some pets allowed* ☰ *AE, D, DC, MC, V* ⊗ *Closed Nov.–Apr.* ⦿ *BP.*

$$ 🛏 **Black Duck Inn.** The comfortable common areas and guest rooms at this B&B are tastefully furnished with antiques, including the owner's toy collection. The walls are decorated with works by artists who've stayed here. A beach-stone fireplace is the focal point of the cozy den. The first-floor guest room has a separate entrance and a private deck. Two tiny cottages are perched on the harbor. Salt marshes and a small bay are tucked along trails on the inn's 12 acres. **Pros:** Spacious common areas, rent two rooms at special rate. **Con:** Near but not on water. ✉ *36 Crowley Island Rd., off Rte. 195* ⊕ *Box 39, Corea 04624* ☎ *207/963–2689* ⊕ *www.blackduck.com* ➷ *2 rooms, 1 suite, 2 cottages* ♿ *In-room: no a/c, no phone, no TV (some). In-hotel: no elevator, no kids between 2 and 7, no-smoking rooms* ☰ *D, MC, V* ⊗ *Closed mid-Oct.–mid-May* ⦿ *BP.*

$–$$ 🏠 **Bluff House Inn.** Combining the service of a hotel with the ambi-
☕ ence of a cozy lodge, this modern two-story inn on a secluded hillside
★ has expansive views of Frenchman Bay. You can see the bay's granite
shores from the inn's partially screened wraparound porches. There's
a picnic area with grill (a lobster pot is available for those who want
to boil their own dinner). A stone fireplace warms one of the knotty-
pine lounge areas. The individually decorated guest rooms have furnishings from around the state. **Pros:** Close to things but secluded,
apartment has two bedrooms. **Con:** Hill to water a bit steep. ✉ *57
Bluff House Rd., off Rte. 186, Gouldsboro 04607* ☎ *207/963–7805*
⊕ *www.bluffinn.com* ⌨ *8 rooms, 1 apartment* ♿ *In-room: no a/c, no
TV (some), kitchen (some), DVD (some). In-hotel: no elevator, no-
smoking rooms* ☐ *AE, MC, V* ⊙ *CP.*

NIGHTLIFE & THE ARTS

CONCERTS   Schoodic Arts for All presents local musicians at the 1904 **Hammond
Hall** (✉ *427 Main St.* ☎ *207/963–2569* ⊕ *www.schoodicarts.org*).
Classical and jazz music is featured during the Hammond Hall Renais-
sance Concert Series, held the second Friday of the month from May to
October. Local musicians take the stage for Last Friday Coffee House
on the last Friday of the month throughout the year.

FESTIVALS &   Afternoon and evening musical, poetry, puppet, magic and the-
EVENTS   ater performances, and speakers are part of the **Schoodic Arts Festival**
(☎ *207/963–2569* ⊕ *www.schoodicarts.org*), which takes place at venues throughout the peninsula during the first two weeks of August.
Schoodic Steel, a community steel pan band, drums up a lot of excite-
ment at its evening performance on the last weekend of the festival. An
art show is held on the second Saturday, and you can take workshops
in everything from dance to writing. Sculptors from around the world
bring their drills and blades to the biennial **Schoodic International Sculpture Symposium** (⊕ *www.schoodicsculpture.org*), next set for 2009. This
free event is held from late July to early September outdoors at the
Schoodic Education and Research Center in the Schoodic section of
Acadia National Park on Route 186 in Winter Harbor. Watch and listen—it's noisy!—as large public sculptures are made from Maine granite for area communities. Free musical concerts and lectures on topics
such as Maine's lobster fishery and the Ice Age's impact on the region
are held at **Oceanside Meadows Innstitute for the Arts & Sciences** (✉ *202
Corea Rd. [Rte. 195], Prospect Harbor* ☎ *207/963–5557*) from late
June through September. The Innstitute is housed in a restored barn
at Oceanside Meadows Inn, whose owners founded the organization.
Lobster boats from up and down the Maine Coast race in the **Winter Harbor Lobster Festival** (☎ *207/963–7658* ⊕ *www.acadia-schoodic.
org*) on the second Saturday of August. The free event also includes a
parade, an arts-and-crafts fair, an art show, a pancake breakfast, and a
lobster dinner that draws hundreds.

SPORTS & THE OUTDOORS

KAYAKING   Registered Master Maine Guides lead all-day, half-day, and overnight
sea kayaking and hiking trips to the region's less visited islands and
trails for **Ardea EcoExpeditions** (✉ *242 S. Gouldsboro Rd., Goulds-*

boro [Rte. 186] ☎207/460–9731 ⊕www.ardea-ecoexpeditions.com). Learning is part of the fun on these ecotourism adventures. The company also offers sunrise birding and sunset kayaking tours, expeditions that lend a hand to ecological research and conservation projects, and cross-country skiing and snowshoeing trips.

GOLFING You can see the ocean from every green at the 9-hole **Grindstone Neck Golf Course** (✉106 *Grindstone Ave., Winter Harbor* ☎207/963–7760 ⊕*www.grindstonegolf.com*), one of Maine's oldest courses. Greens fees are $20 to $45.

SHOPPING

ANTIQUES & Hand-cast bronze doorbells and wind bells are among the items sold at
MORE **U.S. Bells** (✉56 *W. Bay Rd. (Rte. 186), Prospect Harbor* ☎207/963–7184 ⊕*www.usbells.com*). You can also buy finely crafted quilts, wood-fired pottery, and wood and bronze outdoor furniture, all made by family members of the foundry owner. Tours of the foundry are given frequently. The shop is open June through December and by appointment. Children appear in many of the watercolor, pastel, and Asian ink paintings of Down East landscapes by Wendilee Heath O'Brien, the friendly artist-owner of **whopaints** (✉316 *Main St., Winter Harbor* ☎207/963–2076 ⊕*www.whopaints.com*); the artist's studio-gallery is beside her home. You're welcome to listen in if she's teaching a class. Open year-round. In three buildings fronted by gardens, **Winter Harbor Antiques & Works of Hand** (✉424-426 *Main St., Winter Harbor* ☎207/963–2547) stocks antiques and local arts and crafts, from wool scarves to paintings to stained glass. Author-signed Maine books and antique linens are a specialty. It's open June through Columbus Day and by appointment. Step back in time at **Winter Harbor 5 & 10** (✉349 *Main St., Winter Harbor* ☎207/963–7927 ⊕*www.winterharbor5and10.com*), a tried-and-true dime store with a big selection of local T-shirts and sweatshirts. Open year-round.

ART GALLERIES Handcrafts by area artisans, including jewelry and wool items, and the owner's colorful hooked rugs with animal and nature themes are sold in an old school at **Chapter Two** (✉611 *Corea Rd. [Rte. 195], Corea* ☎207/963–7269) You can enjoy a cup of tea, and you might catch a hooking group or class in action. Art of the Schoodic Peninsula is sold in the house-turned-gallery next door, and the garage is stocked with used books.Glass wildlife sculptures, flowers, goblets, and beads are for sale at **Gypsy Moose Glass Co.** (✉20 *Williamsbrook Rd., off Rte. 186, Gouldsboro* ☎207/963–2674 ⊕*www.gypsymoose.com*), whose owner gives glassblowing demonstrations. It's open March to December. Window panes are fused in a kiln at **Lee Fusion Art Glass Studio** (✉679 *S. Gouldsboro Rd. [(Rte. 186], Gouldsboro* ☎207/963–7280) to create unusual glass dishware. Colorful enamel accents depict birds, lighthouses, flowers, and designs made from doilies. The studio is open June through October. Stoneware and porcelain sinks and dishware are the mainstay at **Maine Kiln Works** (✉115 *S. Gouldsboro Rd. [Rte. 186], Gouldsboro* ☎207/963–5819 ⊕*www.waterstonesink.com*), but you can also buy pressed flower lamp shades. Watch the potter hard at work in this former general store. It's open early April through mid-

October and by appointment. Born in Winter Harbor, M. Louise Shaw worked as an artist and graphic designer in Connecticut for many years and now sells her oils and watercolors of local scenes at the small but charming **Maloué Gallery** (⊠ *355 Main St., Winter Harbor* ☎ *207/963–5558*), open mid-June through mid-October and by appointment.

FOOD   The wines sold at **Bartlett Maine Estate Winery** (⊠ *175 Chicken Mill Rd., off U.S. 1, Gouldsboro* ☎ *207/546–2408* ⊕ *www.bartlettwinery.com*) are produced from locally grown apples, pears, blueberries, and other fruit. Ask the vintners what foods to pair them with while sampling different wines in the tasting room. It's open late May through mid-October and by appointment. A pioneering organic grower on West Bay, **Darthia Farm** (⊠ *51 Darthia Farm Rd., off Rte. 186, Gouldsboro* ☎ *207/963–7771 or 800/285–6234* ⊕ *www.darthiafarm.com*) operates a store from June through September where you can buy produce and herbs, along with preserves, hand-spun yarn, knitted items, and other handcrafts. The farm is open late May through mid-October. Salmon pâté and smoked salmon, mussels, and cheese are among specialty foods sold at **Grindstone Neck of Maine** (⊠ *311 Newman St. [Rte. 186], Winter Harbor* ☎ *207/963–7347 or 866/831–8734* ⊕ *www. grindstoneneckofmaine.com*), which gives tours of its smokehouse. You can also watch workers through the inside picture window. Load up for a picnic—coolers are sold and loaned out for a deposit. Open year-round. Along with mostly organic local produce, **Winter Harbor Farmers' Market** (⊠ *10 Main St. [Rte. 186], Winter Harbor* ☎ *207/963–2984*) sells goat cheese, beef and chicken, hand-spun yarn, knitted items, and maple syrup, chutney, and preserves. The market operates on Tuesday mornings from late June to early September.

STEUBEN TO CHERRYFIELD

Towns in the southwestern corner of Washington County seem more like one community than those off at the ends of necks and peninsulas farther Down East. Though it's less well known as a destination, the area's wildlife refuge, charming architecture, salmon-filled river, and historical museums make this a path to beat.

STEUBEN

17 mi north of Hancock via U.S. 1.

Steuben is the first town in Washington County if you're heading north on U.S. 1. The village is east of the highway, largely hidden by trees. At the least, drive through (there's a second turnoff if you miss the first one). Settled in the 1760s, Steuben was named for a Revolutionary War general at the suggestion of Jacob Townsley, an aide-de-camp to General George Washington. Townsley's 1785 Federal-style manse still stands on a hill across from the town center. Steuben has a lost-in-time feel. The 1850s Greek Revival Steuben Union Church beside the village green is a classic. The handsome Henry D. Moore Parish House next door, built in 1910, is a public library.

SPORTS & THE OUTDOORS

Visitors are welcome at **Petit Manan National Wildlife Refuge,** a 2,166-acre sanctuary of fields, forests, and rocky shorefront at the tip of a peninsula. The wildlife viewing and bird-watching are renowned. In August the park is a popular spot for picking wild blueberries. You can explore the refuge on two walking trails; the shore trail looks out on sand-color Petit Manan Lighthouse, Maine's second-tallest light. ⊠ *Pigeon Hill Rd.* ☎ *207/546–2124* ⊕ *www.fws.gov/northeast/mainecoastal* ⊠ *Free* ☉ *Daily, sunrise–sunset.*

MILBRIDGE

22 mi north of Hancock via U.S. 1.

Lumbering spurred the shipbuilding that thrived here in the 1800s, and Milbridge is still a commercial center. As you enter town, you pass a Christmas wreath wholesaler and blueberry packager's headquarters.

WHAT TO SEE

The facade of the **Milbridge Historical Museum** may lack period charm, but the interior more than makes up for it. Permanent exhibits document maritime industries past and present: shipbuilding, sardine canning, weir fishing, and lobstering. There are also displays about blueberry production and a lighthouse in nearby Addison. Changing exhibits occupy about a third of the display space, and the meeting room doubles as an art gallery—local artists are on a waiting list. ⊠ *83 Main St.* ☎ *207/546–4471* ⊕ *www.milbridgehistoricalsociety. org* ⊠ *Free* ☉ *June–early Sept., weekends 1–4; July and Aug., Tues. and weekends 1–4.*

WHERE TO EAT

$–$$$ ✕ **44 Degrees North Restaurant & Pub.** With dishes like grilled swordfish and seafood lasagna, the menu here isn't heavy on fried seafood. Lobster is boiled or baked with seafood stuffing. On Friday and Saturday nights, locals come for prime rib. Order wraps and sandwiches from the lunch menu anytime. The dining room has a dessert case and booths, and there's a big-screen TV in the pub. ⊠ *17 Main St.* ☎ *207/546–4440* ☰ *AE, MC, D, DC, V.*

NIGHTLIFE & THE ARTS

The town's largest annual event is the **Milbridge Days Celebration** (☎ *207/546–2422* ⊕ *www.milbridgedays.com*), held each year on the last weekend of July. There's a blueberry-pancake breakfast, clam-and-lobster bake, parade, crafts show, and most famously, a codfish relay race. There's only one screen at **Milbridge Theatre** (⊠ *26 Main St.* ☎ *207/546–2038*), but it's a large one and the price is right—$4.50. The owner of the only movie theater between Ellsworth and Calais is likely to greet you in the little lobby—he hasn't missed a show since opening the place in 1978. If you're lucky, you'll catch one of the player-piano performances. The theater is open daily Memorial Day through early January and weekends in April and May.

SPORTS & THE OUTDOORS

The town may be small, but it has 75 mi of coastline spread about several peninsulas and bays that are waiting to be explored. You can hike along the shore and enjoy views of the islands dotting Narraguagus Bay at the 10-acre **McClellan Park.** Rounded boulders swathe the shore, and smaller stones form a gray- and black-hue beach near the waterfront picnic area. A dozen campsites accommodate tents and small to medium recreational vehicles. For more information on camping, contact the town office (☎207/546–2422). There are no electrical hookups. ⊠356 *Tom Leighton Pt. Rd. from U.S. 1 turn on Wyman Rd.* ☉ *May–Oct., daily.*

WHALE-
WATCHING
& OTHER
CRUISES

Departing from Milbridge Marina in a six-passenger lobster boat, **Robertson Sea Tours Adventures** (☎207/483–6110 or 207/461–7439 ⊕*www.robertsonseatours.com*) runs sightseeing excursions and lobster dinner cruises (you can haul a few of the captain's traps), and puffin-watching trips to Petit Manan Island. Prices start at $50 per person. Whale-watching tours are to start in 2008. The company operates from mid-May to mid-October.

SHOPPING

You can buy more than local, mostly organic produce at the **Milbridge Farmers' Market** (⊠*Main St.* ☎207/546–2395), including soap, goat cheese, baked goods, and hand-spun wool items. In a parking lot set back from Main Street, the market operates from 9 to noon on Saturday, from June to mid-October.

CHERRYFIELD

6 mi north of Milbridge via U.S. 1.

Up the Narraguagus River from Milbridge, Cherryfield was a lumbering center in the 1800s. The river was once lined with lumber mills. Now this stretch is a lovely waterway (with native salmon) overlooked by a gazebo in a small town park. The industry's legacy remains in the surprising number of ornate Victorian homes, unusual for a small New England village. The town has 52 buildings on the National Historic Register in such styles as Colonial Revival, Greek Revival, Italianate, and Queen Anne. The historic district runs along U.S. 1 and the handful of side streets. You can pick up a guide to the district at the town office (⊠*12 Municipal Way off U.S. 1*). Today, Cherryfield is known as the "Blueberry Capital of the World." Maine's two largest blueberry plants sit side by side on Route 193. To see the area's wild blueberry barrens, head north past the factories and take a right onto Ridge Road. The best way to explore this hilly landscape is by bicycle.

Cherryfield-Narraguagus Historical Society Museum. Overlooking the Narraguagus River, this museum has exhibits on logging and local history in an 1840s homestead. A pine blanket chest from the 1750s belonged to the area's first settler. The society sponsors a historic home tour in July. ⊠*88 River Rd.* ☎*No phone* ⊠*Free* ☉*July and Aug., Fri. 1–4 or by appointment.*

Don't miss the **William M. Nash House,** on the River Road. This lavishly embellished Second Empire mansion perched high on a hill was considered as a location for one of the *Addams Family* movies.

WHERE TO STAY

$ ⚏ **Englishman's Bed & Breakfast.** Built in 1793 by a prominent early settler, this large, historic Federal home has matching front and back "scissors" stairs in the central hall and decorative moldings in the parlor. Breakfast is served beside the original cooking hearth with baking oven. Enjoy a cup of tea (the innkeepers sell fine teas as a sideline) on the L-shape deck, lulled by the rush of the tidal Narraguagus River. A charming guesthouse beside the deck sleeps four. **Pros:** See artifacts found in restoration, screened gazebo. **Con:** Room with half bath. ✉ *122 Main St. 04622* ☎ *207/546–2337* ⊕ *www.englishmansbandb. com* 🛏 *2 rooms, 1 suite* ♿ *In room: no a/c, no room phones, kitchen (some), VCR (some), Wi-Fi. In hotel: no elevator, public Wi-Fi, no-smoking rooms* ▤ *MC, V* ⦿ *BP.*

COLUMBIA FALLS TO CUTLER

It's hard to tell where one bay ends and another begins among the points and peninsulas of this section of Way Down East. Above Jonesport the granite shores become more jagged. Fishing villages here retain their centuries-old culture even as more tourists trickle in.

7

COLUMBIA FALLS

48 mi north of Ellsworth via U.S. 1, 74 mi west of Calais.

Founded in the late 18th century, Columbia Falls is a pretty village along the Pleasant River. True to its name, a waterfall tumbles into the river in the center of town. Once a prosperous shipbuilding center, Columbia Falls still has a number of stately homes dating from that era. U.S. 1 used to pass through the center of town, but now it passes to the west. It's worth driving through even if you don't have time to stop.

WHAT TO SEE

Downeast Salmon Federation. Check out the salmon in the fish tank, then head for the deck out back, where a staff person will explain the depletion of native river salmon and the federation's efforts to restore them. Overlooking a defunct fish ladder below falls on the Pleasant River and the marshlands beyond, it's the perfect spot to hear this intriguing fish tale. See the hatchery in action from January through March. ✉ *187 Main St.* ☎ *207/483–4336* ⊕ *www.mainesalmonrivers.org* ✉ *Free* ⊙ *Weekdays 9–5.*

★ **Ruggles House.** Judge Thomas Ruggles, a wealthy lumber dealer, store owner, postmaster, and justice of the Court of Sessions, built this home about 1820. The house's distinctive Federal architecture, flying staircase, Palladian window, and intricate woodwork were crafted over three years by Massachusetts wood-carver Alvah Peterson. ✉ *146*

Main St. ☎207/483–4637 ⊕*www.ruggleshouse.org* ☒*$5* ⊙*June– mid-Oct., Mon.–Sat. 9:30–4:30, Sun. 11–4:30.*

$–$$$ ✕**White House Restaurant & Pub.** Deep-fried, sautéed, or broiled seafood dinners are the draw at this longtime favorite. If you love lobster but don't want to do all the work, the "lazy man's lobster" is shelled for you. The Friday-night special is boiled haddock with egg sauce. The corned-beef hash served at breakfast is beloved by locals. Eat in the pub room or in the dining room with blueberry-color booths and photographs of the local blueberry and cranberry harvest. ☒*532 U.S. 1, Jonesboro* ☎207/434–2792 ☐*AE, D, MC, V.*

¢–$ ⊞**Blueberry Patch Motel.** Midway up the coast from Bar Harbor and convenient to Machias and Jonesport, this tidy lodging has motel rooms with two doubles and queens in a building near the road. Tiny but classic roadside cabins from the 1930s and a few larger, newer units are set back where the highway used to be. **Pro:** Next to White House Restaurant & Pub. **Con:** Older baths in vintage cabins. ☒*550 U.S. 1* ✆*Box 36, Jonesboro 04648* ☎207/434–5411 ⤴*10 rooms, 9 cabins* ♿*In room: refrigerator (some), kitchen (some), Wi-Fi. In hotel: pool, no elevator, public Wi-Fi, no-smoking rooms* ☐*AE, D, MC, V* ⊙*Closed mid-Oct.–May.*

¢–$ ⊞**Pleasant Bay Bed & Breakfast.** This Cape Cod–style inn takes advan-
🕐 tage of its riverfront location. Stroll the nature paths on the 110-
★ acre property, which winds around a peninsula and out to Pleasant Bay—you can even take one of the inn's llamas along for company. A screened porch and deck overlook the Pleasant River, and the suite has a private deck. The country-style rooms, all with water views, are decorated with antiques, as are the roomy common areas. A library with a fireplace is tucked away from the family room. **Pros:** Fireplace at one of three waterfront picnic areas, river mooring, extra bed or pullout couch in most quarters. **Con:** Just a Continental breakfast for late risers. ☒*386 West Side Rd., Box 222, Addison 04606* ☎207/483–4490 ⤴*3 rooms, 1 with bath; 1 suite* ♿*In-room: no a/c, no phone (some), kitchen (some), TV (some), Wi-Fi. In-hotel: no elevator, public Wi-Fi, no-smoking rooms* ☐*MC, V* ⦿*BP.*

GOLFING Blueberry barrens border the 9-hole **Barren View Golf Course** (☒*1354 U.S. 1, Jonesboro* ☎207/434–6531 ⊕*www.barrenview.com*), which also has a driving range and clubhouse. Greens fees are $18 to $40.

Next door to historic Ruggles House, **Columbia Falls Pottery** (☒*150 Main St.* ☎207/483–4075 ⊕*www.columbiafallspottery.com*) carries owner April Adams's hand-thrown earthenware pottery. Her work is decorated with local flora (blueberry, columbine, and bunchberry are popular), ships, and lighthouses. It's open June through October and by appointment. Yes, the deep-blue geodesic dome housing **Wild Blueberry Land** (☒*1067 U.S. 1* ☎207/483–2583) is supposed to resemble a giant blueberry. In addition to foods filled with blueberries and all sorts of blueberry-themed gifts, you can watch a video about the local cash

CLOSE UP

Wild for Blueberries

There's no need to inquire about the cheesecake topping if you dine out in August when the wild blueberry crop comes in. Anything but blueberries would be unthinkable.

Way Down East, wild blueberries have long been a favorite food—and a key ingredient in cultural and economic life. Maine produces about a third of the commercial harvest, which totals about 70 million pounds annually, with Canada supplying virtually all the rest. Washington County yields 65% of Maine's total crop, which is why the state's largest blueberry processors are here: Cherryfield Foods' predecessor and Jasper Wyman & Son were founded shortly after the Civil War.

Wild blueberries, which bear fruit every other year, thrive in the region's cold climate and sandy, acidic soil. Undulating blueberry barrens stretch for miles in Deblois and Cherryfield—"the Blueberry Capital of the World"—and are scattered throughout Washington County. Look for tufts among low-lying plants along the roadways. In spring, fields shimmer as the small-leaf plants turn myriad shades of mauve, honey orange, and lemon yellow. White flowers appear in June. Fall transforms the barrens into a sea of red.

Amid Cherryfield's barrens, a plaque on a boulder lauds the late J. Burleigh Crane for helping advance an industry that's not as wild as it used to be. Honeybees have been brought in to supplement native pollinators. Fields are irrigated. Barrens are burned and mowed to rid plants of disease and insects, reducing the need for pesticides. Most fields are owned by the large blueberry processors.

About 80% of Maine's crop is now harvested with machinery. That requires moving boulders, so the rest continues to be harvested by hand with blueberry rakes, which resemble large forks and pull the berries off their stems. Years ago, year-round residents did the work. Today migrant workers make up two-thirds of this seasonal labor force.

Blueberries get their dark color from anthocyanins, believed to provide their antioxidant power. Wild blueberries have more of these antiaging, anticancer compounds than their cultivated cousins. Smaller and more flavorful than cultivated blueberries, wild ones are mostly used in packaged foods. Less than 1% of the state's crop—about 500,000 pints—is consumed fresh, mostly in Maine. Look for fresh berries (sometimes starting in late July and lasting until early September) at roadside stands, farmers' markets, and supermarkets.

Wild Blueberry Land in Columbia Falls sells everything blueberry, from muffins and ice cream to socks and books. Find farm stores, stands, and markets statewide, many selling blueberries and blueberry jams and syrups, at www.getrealgetmaine.com, a Maine Department of Agriculture site that promotes Maine foods.

—Mary Ruoff

7

crop. A retired manager of the state blueberry research farm and his wife run this unusual shop. It's open from June through December.

JONESPORT & BEALS ISLAND

12 mi northeast of Columbia Falls via U.S. 1 and Rte. 187, 20 mi southwest of Machias.

The birding is superb around Jonesport and Beals Island, a pair of fishing communities joined by a bridge over the harbor. A handful of stately homes is tucked away on Jonesport's Sawyer Square, where Sawyer Memorial Congregational Church's exquisite stained-glass windows are illuminated at night. But the towns are less geared to travelers than those on the Schoodic Peninsula. Lobster traps are still piled in the yards, and lobster-boat races near Moosabec Reach are the highlight of the community's annual Independence Day celebration.

At the tip of Beals Island, the Nature Conservancy's **Great Wass Island Preserve** (⊠ *Beals Island* 🕾 *207/729–5181* ⊕ *www.nature.org* 🖃 Free, dawn to dusk ⊙ *Daily*) is a 1,540-acre preserve where you can find stunted pines and raised peat bogs. Trails lead through the woods and emerge onto the undeveloped coast, where you may spot gray seals as you make your way among the rocks and boulders. Parking is limited. No pets are allowed. If it's been raining it may be too wet for hiking here.

WHERE TO EAT & STAY

$–$$$ ✕ **Tall Barney's.** Salty accents add plenty of flavor at this down-home restaurant, which serves breakfast, lunch, and dinner (some nights). Reserved for fishermen, the "liar's table" near the entrance is about as legendary as the namesake. The breakfast menu tells of Tall Barney, a brawny fisherman who left truly tall tales in his wake. Your server may be among his multitudinous descendants. The menu includes five types of seafood stew, grilled as well as fried seafood, and over-size desserts such as molasses cookies, a local favorite. ⊠ *52 Main St.* 🕾 *207/497–2403* ⊕ *www.tallbarneys.com* ▤ *MC, V* ⊙ *Closed Feb. Closed Sun.–Tues. late Oct.–Jan. and March and April. No dinner Sun.–Tues. May–Mid-Oct.*

$$ 🏨 **Harbor House on Sawyer Cove.** The two spacious rooms on the third
★   floor of this harbor-front building have big windows overlooking the water. Both have separate sitting areas and are tastefully furnished with Victorian flourishes such as cabbage-rose wallpaper and handwoven rugs. Breakfast is served on the enclosed porch. You can relax on the lawn, which is flanked by beach roses. Don't miss the telegraph office in an original storefront, now the inn's antiques and gift shop. **Pros:** Nice yard with picnic table, private entrance to rooms. **Con:** No common parlor. ⊠ *27 Sawyer Sq., Box 468, Jonesport 04649* 🕾 *207/497–5417* ⊕ *www.harborhs.com* 🛏 *2 rooms* ⌂ *In-room: no a/c, no phone, Wi-Fi. In-hotel: no elevator, public Wi-Fi, no kids under 12, no-smoking rooms* ▤ *D, MC, V* ⊙*BP.*

SPORTS & THE OUTDOORS

In business since 1940, **Norton of Jonesport** (☎*207/497–5933* ⊕*www.machiassealisland.com*) takes passengers on day trips to Machias Seal Island, where thousands of puffins nest. Arctic terns, razorbill auks, common murres, and many other seabirds also nest on the rocky island. Trips, which cost $100 per person, are offered from late May through August. Mistake Island is a highlight of trips offered by **Coastal Cruises** (☎*207/497–3064*). A six-passenger boat traverses island-strewn waters, spotting seabirds, eagles, and seals. On the island, a boardwalk leads to 72-foot Moose Peak Light. Prices start at $45 per person. The season runs from late June to early September.

SHOPPING

Antique ship bells, old maritime prints, authentic sextants, compasses, and ship wheels are among the treasures at **Jonesport Nautical Antiques** (⊠*6 Cogswell St. [intersection with Main St.]* ☎*207/497–5655* ⊕*www.nauticalantiques.com*). It's open May through October and by appointment. Years ago, many Down East fishermen hunted sea ducks to help feed their families, and the area's decoy-carving tradition lives on at **Nelson Decoys** (⊠*13 Cranberry La.* ☎*207/497–3488*), whose owner carves and paints black ducks, puffins, and other waterfowl, as did her late husband. The store, in an old elementary school, also carries works by other Maine artists, including watercolor paintings and sea-glass sculptures. The shop is open May to mid-December or by appointment.

You often catch the artist at work at **Pierce-Kettering Gallery** (⊠*344 Main St.* ☎*207/497–2874*), where there's a salon feel to parlors hung with oil and acrylic paintings of animals and local landscapes. Relax on the sofa with a cup of tea or enjoy the gardens and porch, which show the artist's touch. It's open June through October and by appointment.

MACHIAS

20 mi northeast of Jonesport.

The Machias area—Machiasport, East Machias, and Machias, the Washington County seat–lays claim to being the site of the first naval battle of the Revolutionary War, which took place in what is now Machiasport. Despite being outnumbered and outarmed, a small group of Machias men under the leadership of Jeremiah O'Brien captured the armed British schooner *Margaretta*. That battle, fought on June 12, 1775, is now known as the "Lexington of the Sea." The Margaretta Days Festival on the second weekend in June commemorates the event with a Colonial dinner, period reenactors, and a parade. The town's other claim to fame is wild blueberries. On the third weekend in August, the annual Machias Wild Blueberry Festival is a community celebration complete with parade, crafts fair, concerts, and plenty of blueberry dishes.

WHAT TO SEE

★ The **Burnham Tavern Museum**, housed in a building dating from 1770, details the colorful history of Job Burnham and other early residents of the area. It was in this tavern that the men of Machias laid the plans that culminated in the capture of the *Margaretta* in 1775. Period furnishings show what life was like in Colonial times. ⊠ *98 Main St. (Rte. 192 section)* ☎ *207/255–6930* ⊕ *www.burnhamtavern.com* ✉ *$5* ◷ *Early June–Fri. before Labor Day, weekdays 9–5, or by appointment.*

> **LOOK UP!**
>
> With no large cities, stargazing is great Way Down East. But if you want a great show on a dark night, paddle a canoe on a lake and look down. Bioluminescent organisms in the water light up as you churn your paddle. But don't forget to look up, too.

At the head of Machias Bay, **Fort O'Brien State Historic Site** looks toward the waters where a naval battle was waged in 1775. This was an active fort during the Revolutionary War, the War of 1812, and the Civil War. ⊠ *Rte. 92, just south of village center, Machiasport* ☎ *207/941–4014* ⊕ *www.state.me.us/doc/parks* ◷ *Memorial Day–Labor Day, 9–sunset.*

Built in 1810, the **Nathan Gates House** is home to the Machiasport Historical Society. The museum contains an extensive collection of old photographs, period furniture, housewares, and other memorabilia. There's also a genealogical library. The Marine Room highlights the area's seafaring and shipbuilding past. A model schoolroom and post office and a large collection of carpentry tools occupy the adjacent Cooper House, a utilitarian building constructed in 1850. ⊠ *344 Port Road (Rte. 92), Machiasport* ☎ *207/255–8461* ✉ *Free* ◷ *Late June–early Sept., Tues.–Fri. 12:30–4:30.*

▌ **NEED A BREAK?**   **Bad Little Falls Park**, at the intersection of Rte. 92 and U.S. 1, is a great picnic stop with a bridge over the falls on the Machias River. A trail leads to O'Brien Cemetery, the final resting place for many of Machias's early settlers.

WHERE TO EAT & STAY

$$$–$$$$ ✗ **Artist's Café.** In an old house across from the University of Maine, this restaurant has garnered a strong local following. The white-wall dining rooms provide a simple backdrop for the eye-catching works by the chef-owner and the palate-pleasing dishes. The menu changes weekly, but a beloved appetizer called Horses Standing Still—hand-rolled Thai dumplings filled with chicken and shrimp and served with a dipping sauce—is almost always available. There are always four entrées, including a vegetarian dish. You might find the Mex, a stack of spicy tortillas, on the menu. Lunch has Italian, French, and Thai influences. ⊠ *3 Hill St.* ☎ *207/255–8900* ▭ *MC, V* ◷ *Closed mid-Oct.–mid-Apr. No lunch Sat.*

$–$$$ ✗ **Blue Bird Ranch.** Family restaurants dominate Way Down East, and this is a favorite of people throughout the region. The Blue Bird Ranch is known for its home-style cooking and reasonable prices. The dining rooms are large and the staff is chipper. The menu includes everything from Cobb salad to fried, boiled, or sautéed fish dinners. ✉*3 E. Main St.* ☎*207/255–3351* ⊟*AE, D, DC, MC, V.*

$ ✕⬛**Riverside Inn & Restaurant.** A bright yellow exterior invites a stop at ★   this delightful inn perched on the banks of the Machias River. Inside you can find hammered-tin ceilings and lots of hand-carved wood. The spacious guest rooms have antique furnishings and colorful quilts. The upstairs suite in the coach house has a private balcony overlooking the river. The restaurant ($$$–$$$$) has maintained its excellent reputation. The chef brings a special flair to traditional dishes such as pork served with a pistachio crust. His signature dish is salmon stuffed with crabmeat and shrimp. In summer the menu includes an updated take on the chef salad. Try pairing it with standout appetizers like hake cakes and red tuna wontons. Ask for a table in the intimate sunroom. **Pros:** Suites a good value, garden overlooks river, walk to riverside park. **Con:** Small grounds. ✉*608 Main St. (U.S. 1),* ⬠*Box 373, East Machias 04630* ☎*207/255–4134 or 888/255–4344* ⊕*www. riversideinn-maine.com* ⥯*2 rooms, 2 suites* ♿*In-room: no a/c (some), no phone, kitchen (some), refrigerator (some). In-hotel: no elevator, restaurant, no-smoking rooms* ⊟*AE, MC, V* ☾*Closed Jan.–early Feb. Restaurant closed Mon.–Wed. mid-Feb.–May and Nov. and Dec. No lunch* ⲑ*BP.*

$–$$ ⬛**Broadway Inn.** On a residential street near downtown Machias, this inn has rooms that are named for favorite New England authors such as Robert Frost and Edith Wharton. Furnished with antiques such as an oaken bed and an unusual pair of wood wing chairs, the guest rooms are inviting and comfortable. **Pros:** Two rooms with electric fireplaces, sittings rooms on both floors. **Con:** Some smallish rooms. ✉*14 Broadway, 04654* ☎*207/2558551 or 207/255–4447* ⊕*www. broadwayinn.us* ⥯*5 rooms, 1 with bath* ♿*In-room: no a/c, no phone, no TV, Wi-Fi. In-hotel: no elevator, public Wi-Fi, no-smoking rooms* ⊟*MC, V* ⲑ*BP.*

$ ⬛**Captain Cates Bed & Breakfast.** The main portion of this Victorian home was built in 1865. On a bright morning or afternoon, you can relax in the two parlors or on the covered swing on the front lawn, overlooking a wide stretch of the Machias River. Rooms are furnished with antiques, and most have water views. **Pros:** Lower rate with three-night minimum, two $75 one-person rooms. **Con:** Smallish rooms. ✉*309 Port Rd., (Rte. 92) Machiasport 04655* ☎*207/255– 8812* ⊕*www.captaincates.com* ⥯*6 rooms without bath* ♿*In-room: no a/c, no phone, no TV, Wi-Fi. In-hotel: no elevator, no-smoking rooms, public Wi-Fi* ⊟*MC, V* ⲑ*BP.*

$ ⬛**Micmac Farm.** You can launch a kayak or canoe on the Machias ★   River at this wonderfully secluded 50-acre property. Grouped along the river are three spacious cabins with pine interiors, kitchenettes, and decks. The historic cape house B&B has an antiques-filled parlor and a "keeping room" that looks much as it did when the home was built in 1776. The single guest room here is off the parlor in a modern addition with river-view deck and a whirlpool bath. **Pros:** Hiking trail, sweeping river views, whirlpool bath in B&B. **Con:** Cabins close together. ✉*47 Micmac La., Machiasport 04655* ☎*207/255–3008*

⊕*www.micmacfarm.com* ⤷*1 room, 3 cabins* ⚇*In-room: no a/c, no phone, kitchen (some), no TV (some). In-hotel: no elevator, some pets allowed, no-smoking rooms* ▤*MC, V* ⊗*Closed late Oct.–mid May* ⦿*CP (B&B only).*

NATURAL DIAPERS

A peat bog formed in Lubec after the ocean receded there thousands of years ago. Good thing for American Indian moms: They used the super-absorbent sphagnum moss that grows in this acidic environment as diapers.

NIGHTLIFE & THE ARTS

Although small, the **Art Galleries at the University of Maine** (⊠*9 O'Brien Ave.* ☎*207/255–1200*) have a strong selection of paintings by John Marin and other regional artists. Two galleries showcase rotating exhibitions of works from the permanent collection. Don't miss the William Zorach sculpture just outside the front door. In July and early August the **Machias Bay Chamber Concert Series** (⊠*7 Centre St.* ☎*207/255–3889* ⊕*www.centrestreetchurch.org* ✉*$12*) is held on Tuesday at 7:30 PM at Centre Street Congregational Church. Head to the vestry afterwards for punch and to see work by local artists.

SPORTS & THE OUTDOORS

ⓒ Down East's rock- and fir-bound shores give way to a crescent-shape pebble beach at **Roque Bluffs State Park.** Just beyond the beach you can find a freshwater pond that's ideal for swimming. The park has changing areas, rest rooms, a picnic area with grills, and a playground. Miles of trails traverse woods, apple orchards, and blueberry fields. The trail head is just before the park entrance at Roque Bluffs Community Church. ⊠*145 Schoppee Point Rd., follow signs from U.S. 1 in Jonesboro or Machias, Roque Bluffs* ☎*207/255–3475 or 207/941–4014* ⊕*www.state.me.us/doc/parks* ✉*$3* ⊗*Staffed May 15–Oct. 15., daily 9–half hour before sunset.*

KAYAKING **Sunrise Canoe & Kayak** (⊠*Hoyttown Rd., off U.S. 1, Machias* ☎*207/255–3375 or 877/980–2300* ⊕*www.sunrisecanoeandkayak. com*) offers sea-kayaking day trips to petroglyphs (many 1,500 to 3,000 years old) carved on slate ledges in Machias Bay. The company also outfits canoes and leads overnight sea-kayaking and canoe trips, including trips on the Machias River. If you prefer to go solo, there are bike, kayak, and canoe rentals; drop-off service is available.

SHOPPING

ARTS & CRAFTS High-fire porcelain dinnerware and housewares in abstract designs, decorative raku pieces, and colorful tile backsplashes and tables are for sale at **Connie's Clay of Fundy Pottery** (⊠*Main St. [U.S. 1], 1 mi north of village center, East Machias* ☎*207/255–4574 or 888/255–8131* ⊕*www.clayoffundy.com*). The owner gives demonstrations in the attached studio and invites visitors to relax on the deck. Open year-round. Art of all kinds can be found at the congenial **Woodwind Gallery** (⊠*Dublin St. [U.S. 1]* ☎*207/255–3727*). Exhibitors range from a self-taught watercolor painter to a leading pastel artist. This gallery is also headquarters of the Maine Black Fly Breeders Association, a charitable tongue-in-cheek group that sells funny souvenirs. Open year-round.

FOOD   Stock up on fresh fruits and vegetables at **Machias Valley Farmers' Market** (✥*South end of U.S. 1 causeway* ☎*207/255–8556*), held early May through October on Saturday from 8 to noon. The market is occasionally open on a Wednesday or a Friday. Get organic produce and other picnic picks at **Whole Life Natural Market** (✉*80 Main St. [Rte. 192 section]* ☎*207/255–8855* ⊕*www.wholelifemarket.com*)or call ahead for a box lunch. Fresh, organic food to go, from Indonesian rice salad to spanakopita, can also be eaten at the window-side tables, or relax there with a coffee or tea. Open year-round.

CUTLER

13 mi southeast of East Machias via Rte. 191.

There's just one small shop in this fishing hamlet—Cutler's natural beauty is what makes it worth exploring. Puffin cruises depart from the protected harbor, which opens like a keyhole onto the ocean and is known as Little River because of its shape. The Bold Coast, as the towering headlands flanking the harbor entrance are called, has some of Maine's best shoreline trails.

Hike in the state preserve in Cutler (➪ *see Sports & the Outdoors*) for views of **Little River Lighthouse** (☎*207/259–3638* ⊕*www.lighthousefoundation.org*), facing the ocean on a tiny, wooded island at the harbor's mouth. You can also paddle to its shores. The island is always open, and Friends of Little River Lighthouse give free tours by appointment. By summer 2008, the group plans to have set hours and offer overnight stays from July through mid-October.

WHERE TO EAT & STAY

$–$$ 🏚**Little River Lodge.** Built in the 1880s to house guests arriving by steamship, this small inn no longer has its elegant three-story tower. The interior is relaxed but retains a sense of grandeur, however, with lovely woodwork and fireplaces in the living and dining rooms. Guest rooms are decorated with nautical antiques, maritime art, and old books. If you are intent on exploring the area, the innkeepers are happy to pack you a picnic or bag lunch. **Pros:** Walk to waterfront, picture windows overlook harbor. **Con:** Some small rooms. ✉*2656 Cutler Rd. [Rte. 191]), Box 251, 04626* ☎*207/259–4437* ⊕*www.cutlerlodge.com* ⚓*5 rooms, 2 with bath* ⚒*In-room: no a/c, no TV, no phone, Wi-Fi. In-hotel: no elevator, public Wi-Fi, no-smoking rooms* ▭*No credit cards* ⊘*Closed mid-Oct.–Apr.* ⏸*BP.*

SPORTS & THE OUTDOORS

★   The beautiful coastal trails at **Cutler Coast Public Reserved Land** (✉*Rte. 191, 17 mi from East Machias* ☎*207/827–1818* ⊕*www.state.me.us/doc/parks* ⛶*Free* ⊘*Daily*) are likely to take your breath away. The 12,000-acre state preserve northeast of Cutler Harbor includes 4½ mi of the undeveloped Bold Coast between Cutler and Lubec. Although much of Maine's coast is chiseled with large bays and coves, here a wall of steep cliffs—some 150 feet tall—juts below ledges partially forested with spruce and fir. Look for whales, seals, and porpoises while taking in views of cliff-ringed Grand Manan Island and the Bay of Fundy. Climb down the log ladders to reach the pebble beaches. Revealing the area's unusual terrain, the two hiking trails loop inland, passing peat bogs, salt marshes, blueberry barrens, swamps, and meadows. The trail from the parking area to the coast is 1½ mi; the longer hiking trails are 6 and 10 mi long. There are three primitive campsites here.

Maine Coast Heritage Trust's **Western Head Preserve** (⊠ *End of Destiny Bay Rd.* ☎ *207/729–7366* ⊕ *www.mcht.org* ✉ *Free* ☉ *Daily, dawn to dusk*) flanks the coast southeast of Cutler Harbor. This pristine 247-acre preserve is known for its awesome views. Along the steep cliffs, wind and salt spray have sculpted spruce and fir trees into odd, stunted shapes. Cranberries, iris, and juniper grow from rock ledges. There are beaches here.

SHOPPING

Picturesque labels, including one of Cutler's harbor, adorn the canned mussels, clams, lobster meat, chowders, and bisques packed in small batches at **Look's Gourmet Seafood** (⊠ *1112 Cutler Rd. [Rte. 191]* ☎ *207/259–3341* ⊕ *www.barharborfoods.com*). Buy them at the small shop at the plant, which also carries baked beans and Indian pudding, both New England favorites, and sauces and dips. It is open year-round.

EN ROUTE After dipping to Cutler from East Machias, Route 191 loops toward Lubec. Mounded, treeless terrain is found along this lonely stretch. Heaths and bogs form a subarctic ecosystem where rare plants thrive in the acidic soil.

COBSCOOK & PASSAMAQUODDY BAYS

Distances can be confusing in this part of the region. It's only a mile or so by boat from Lubec, on Cobscook Bay, to Eastport, facing Passamaquoddy Bay, while the circuitous land route is nearly 40 mi. The area's huge tides are as high as 28 feet, and the largest whirlpool in the Northern Hemisphere, called "Old Sow," swirls off Eastport. Canadian islands, including Campobello, can be seen directly across the water. In summer you can take the ferry from Campobello to Canada's Deer Island and on to Eastport. Or take the "Quoddy Loop," ferrying to the Canadian mainland from Deer Island and returning by land. Calais, upriver from where the St. Croix River widens into Passamaquoddy Bay, is across from St. Stephen, Canada.

LUBEC

28 mi northeast of Machias via U.S. 1 and Rte. 189.

Lubec is the first town in the United States to see the sunrise. A popular destination for outdoor enthusiasts, there are plenty of opportunities for hiking and biking, and the birding is renowned. It's a good base for day trips to New Brunswick's Campobello Island, reached by a bridge—the only one to the island—from downtown Lubec. The village is perched at the end of a narrow strip of land, so you often can see water in three directions.

WHAT TO SEE

Small buildings clustered on piers on the downtown waterfront are what remain of the nation's last herring smokehouse, which operated here from the 1890s until 1991. Restoration is ongoing, but the skinning and packing sheds at the **Historic McCurdy Smokehouse** have exhibits about the smoking operation and the local fisheries industry. The property is on the National Register of Historic Places. ⊠ *Water St. next to Lubec Landmarks, 50 Water St.* ☎ *207/733-1095* ⊠ *Free* ☉ *Memorial Day weekend–Labor Day, Fri.–Sun. 10–4, or by appointment.*

★ The easternmost point of land in the United States, **Quoddy Head State Park,** is marked by candy-striped West Quoddy Head Light. In 1806 President Thomas Jefferson signed an order authorizing construction of a lighthouse on this site. You can't climb the tower, but the former light keeper's house has a museum with a video showing the interior. The museum also has displays on Lubec's maritime past and the region's marine life. A gallery displays lighthouse art by locals. A mystical 2-mi path along the cliffs here, one of four trails, yields magnificent views of Canada's cliff-clad Grand Manan island. Whales can often be sighted offshore. The 540-acre park has a picnic area. ⊠ *S. Lubec Rd., off Rte. 189* ☎ *207/733–0911 or 207/941–4014* ⊕ *www.state.me.us/doc/parks* ⊠ *$2* ☉ *May 15–Oct. 15, 9–sunset.*

WHERE TO EAT & STAY

$-$$$ ✕**Uncle Kippy's Restaurant.** There isn't much of a view from the picture windows, but locals don't mind—they come here for the satisfying seafood. There's one large dining room with a bar beside the main entrance. The menu includes seafood dinners and combo platters, and the fresh-dough pizza is popular. A take-out window and ice-cream bar are open spring through fall. ⊠ *170 Main St.* ☎ *207/733–2400* ⊕ *www.unclekippys.com* ▭ *MC, V* ☉ *Generally closed Mon. Sept. and Oct.; Mon. and Tues. Apr.–June, Nov., and Dec.; and Mon.–Wed. Jan.–Mar.*

¢-$$ ✕**Atlantic House Coffee & Deli Shop.** From this restaurant's two small decks you can gaze past the old smokehouses to the Lubec Narrows. Enjoy favorites such as spanakopita or opt for pizza or a sandwich on homemade bread. For a sweet treat there's ice cream, doughnuts, and yummy pastries made on the premises. It also sells breakfast sandwiches. ⊠ *52 Water St.* ⊕ *www.atlantichouse.net* ☎ *207/733–0906* ▭ *No credit cards* ☉ *Closed Nov.–Apr.*

$-$$ ✕⬚ **Home Port Inn.** A Colonial-style house perched high atop a hill, this grand lodging dating from 1880 has generously sized guest rooms, some with water views. All are furnished with family antiques, including several stately beds. Warm up by the fireplace in the large cherry-red living room's two sitting areas. The elegant restaurant ($$–$$$), one of the best in town, opens onto a deck overlooking Cobscook Bay. The menu emphasizes seafood, but the steak au poivre is a favorite among the locals. Lobster is served in a casserole with drawn butter, sherry, and bread crumbs, pan-seared over linguine, or in a salad with artichoke hearts and a creamy tarragon dressing. **Pros:** Restaurant has private entrance, large yard has sitting area. **Con:** No off-street parking. ✉*45 Main St., 04652* ☎*207/733–2077 or 800/457–2077* ⊕*www. homeportinn.com* ➟*7 rooms* ☐*In-room: no a/c, no phone, no TV, Wi-Fi. In-hotel: restaurant, no elevator, public Wi-Fi, no-smoking rooms* ▭*AE, D, MC, V* ⊗*Closed mid-Oct.–Apr. Restaurant closed mid-Sept.–mid-June. No lunch* ✶❘*CP.*

$–$$ 🔲**Peacock House.** Five generations of the Peacock family lived in this
★ white clapboard house before it was converted into an inn. With a large foyer, library, and living room, the 1860 sea captain's home has plenty of places where you can relax. Minglers are drawn to the sunroom, which opens to the deck and has a handsome bar with glasses for your wine or spirits. The best of the rooms has a separate sitting area and a wet bar and gas fireplace. **Pros:** Piano in library, lovely garden off deck, handicapped accessible suite. **Con:** Only one off-street parking space. ✉*27 Summer St., 04652* ☎*207/733–2403 or 888/305–0036* ⊕*www.peacockhouse.com* ➟*5 rooms, 2 suites* ☐*In-room: no a/c, no phone, refrigerator (some), VCR (some), no TV (some), Wi-Fi. In hotel: no elevator, public Wi-Fi, no-smoking rooms* ▭*MC, V* ⊗*Closed Nov.–Apr.* ✶❘*BP.*

NIGHTLIFE & THE ARTS

Offering free classical and jazz performances, the **Mary Potterton Memorial Concert Series** has performances on Wednesday evenings from June to August at the Congregational Christian Church (✉*3 Church St. (intersection with Main St.)*). The series is sponsored by SummerKeys (☎*207/733–2316* ⊕*www.summerkeys.com*), which offers summer "music vacation" workshops.

SHOPPING

ARTS & CRAFTS Housed in a red cape, **Downeast Artisans** (✉*60 Washington St.* ☎*207/733–8811* ⊕*www.downeastartisans.com*) carries works by more than 30 area artists and artisans. Iron dinner bells, traditional wood toys, and jewelry are some of the many items sold here. It's open late May to mid-October. Changing exhibits of local art are shown at **Lubec Landmarks** (✉*50 Water St.* ☎*No phone*), in the old Mulholland Bros. Market building. Open Memorial Day weekend through Labor Day.

FOOD Sampling is encouraged at **Bayside Chocolates** (✉*37 Water St.* ☎*207/733–8880 or 888/816–8880* ⊕*www.baysidechocolates.com*), where quality chocolate is made in small batches. You can order an espresso after perusing shelves of wrapped and boxed delights like dipped blueberries and chocolates with lemon zest nougat centers. Open year-round. Pick up a six-pack—of smoked salmon kabobs—at **Bold Coast Smokehouse** (✉*224 County Rd.* ☎*207/733–8912 or 888/733–0807* ⊕*www.bold-coastsmokehouse.com*). Other offerings include trout and smoked lobster pâté and salt-cured salmon from Scandinavia. Open year-round. Parlors in an old home just beyond downtown are artfully arrayed with scrumptious boxed and wrapped chocolate at **Monica's Chocolates** (✉*56 Pleasant St.* ☎*866/952–4500* ⊕*www.monicaschocolates.com*), where bonbons (70 flavors), toffee "Sea Urchins," and other delights use a filling from the owner's native Peru. The large selection also includes blueberry clusters and needhams, a Maine tradition, with a coconut and potato filling. Open year-round.

GIFTS Loaded with local souvenirs such as moose T-shirts, **Puffin Pines Country Gift Store** (✉ *U.S. 1, Whiting* ☎*207/733–9782* ⊕*www.puffinpines. com*) also has a well-stocked information center. Open April through December and by chance January through March.

SPORTS & THE OUTDOORS

The Registered Maine Guides who own **Cobscook Hikes and Paddles** (✉*13 Woodcock Way, Robbinston* ☎*207/454–2130 or 207/726– 4776* ⊕*www.cobscookhikesandpaddles.com*) lead lake and sea kayaking, canoeing, hiking, and snowshoeing day trips.

On educational tours by **Tours of Lubec and Cobscook** (✉*24 Water St.* ☎*207/733–2997 or 888/347–9302* ⊕*www.toursoflubecandcobscook. com*) you can visit historic locales and lighthouses, walk the shoreline to learn about the area's high tides and tide pools, tour a ninth-generation farm on Cobscook Bay, explore a bog, and visit artist galleries.

CAMPOBELLO ISLAND, CANADA

28 mi east of Machias.

A popular excursion from Lubec, New Brunswick's Campobello Island has two fishing villages, Welshpool and Wilson's Beach. The only bridge is from Lubec, but in summer a car ferry shuttles passengers from Campobello Island to Deer Island, where you can continue on to the Canadian mainland. U.S. citizens need a passport or other federal government–approved ID when traveling to Canada.

Stop at the information center (open mid-May to mid-October) after passing customs for an update on tides—specifically, when you will be able to walk to **East Quoddy Head Lighthouse** (✉*East end of Rte. 774, Wilson's Beach*). On a tiny island off the eastern end of Campobello, this distinctive lighthouse is marked with a large red cross and is accessible only at and around low tide, but it's worth a look no matter the sea level. You may spot whales in the island-dotted waters off the small park on the rock-clad headland across from the light.

★ A joint project of the American and the Canadian governments, **Roosevelt Campobello International Park** is crisscrossed with interesting hiking trails. Eagle Hill Bog has a wooden walkway and signs identifying rare plants. Neatly manicured Campobello Island has always had a special appeal for the wealthy and famous. It was here that President Franklin Roosevelt and his family spent summers. The 34-room Roosevelt Cottage was presented to Eleanor and Franklin as a wedding gift, and the wicker-filled structure looks essentially as it did when the family was in residence. A visitor center has displays about the Roosevelts and Canadian-American relations. ■TIP➔ **Note that the Islands are on Atlantic Time, which is an hour later than EST.** ✉*459 Rte. 774, Welshpool, New Brunswick, Canada* ☎*506/752–2922* ⊕*www.nps. gov/roca* ▤*Free* ☉*House, Memorial Day weekend–Columbus Day,*

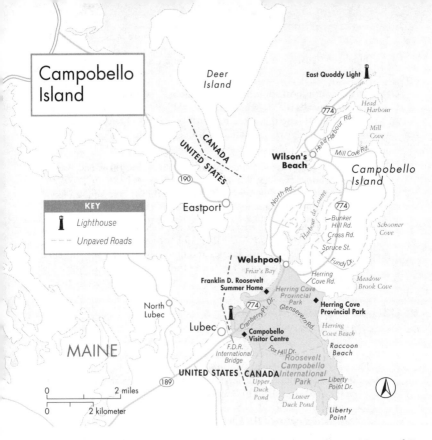

Campobello Island

Deer Island

East Quoddy Light

Head Harbour

Wilson's Beach

Mill Cove

Campobello Island

Eastport

Bunker Hill Rd.
Crass Rd.
Spruce St.

Schooner Cove

KEY

🗼 Lighthouse

--- Unpaved Roads

Welshpool

Friar's Bay

Franklin D. Roosevelt Summer Home

Herring Cove Rd.

Meadow Brook Cove

North Lubec

Herring Cove Provincial Park

Herring Cove Provincial Park

MAINE

Lubec

Campobello Visitor Centre

Herring Cove Beach

Raccoon Beach

F.D.R. International Bridge

UNITED STATES | **CANADA**

Roosevelt Campobello International Park

Liberty Point Dr.

Upper Duck Pond

Lower Duck Pond

Liberty Point

0 — 2 miles

0 — 2 kilometer

---

daily 10–6. Grounds, year-round 24/7. Visitor Center, Memorial Day weekend–Oct.

Many visitors to Campobello Island don't venture beyond Roosevelt Campobello International Park, but for those who do, much awaits at the adjacent **Herring Cove Provincial Park.** There's a golf course and restaurant, 88 campsites (40 with electric hookups), playgrounds, and six trails, including a carriage road that traverses log bridges and spruce forests. Don't miss the mile-long black-sand beach at the namesake cove, with sea-smoothed stones in mesmerizing hues at low tide. ⊠*Herring Cove Rd. off Rte. 774* ☎*506/752–7010* 💲*Free* ⊗*Daily, 24/7.*

WHERE TO EAT & STAY

$–$$$ ✕**Family Fisheries.** Seafood lovers know that fried fish doesn't have to be greasy. That's why people keep heading across the bridge to eat at this family restaurant in Wilson's Beach. The freshest seafood is delivered to the restaurant and the adjoining fish market. Order fried haddock, scallops, shrimps, or clams alone or as part of a seafood platter. Lobsters are cooked outside. Eat in the large dining room or in a screened room beside the playground. ⊠*1977 Rte. 774, Wilson's Beach* ☎*506/752–2470* ▤*MC, V* ⊗*Closed mid-Nov.–Mar.*

$–$$ ✕ **Sweet Time Bakery and Restaurant.** Grab some freshly baked goodies or stop for breakfast, lunch, or dinner at this popular eatery in Welshpool. Sandwiches, salads, and seafood dishes are on the menu. For breakfast try Cindy's Pick, with eggs, toast, and fish cakes and chowchow, a pickled sweet green tomato spread. ⊠ *1001 Rte. 774, Welshpool* ☎ *506/752–2428* ⊟ *No credit cards* ⊘ *Closed late Dec.–Jan. 1.*

$–$$ ✕⊞ **Lupine Lodge.** Next to Roosevelt Campobello International Park, this inn was originally a Roosevelt cousin's summer home. One of three log buildings houses a water-view restaurant ($$–$$$) warmed by a two-sided fireplace. The menu includes specialties such as pollack with mustard onions. Rooms are the same cedar-walled sleeping quarters used years ago. Some have huge baths with original tile and clawfoot tubs. **Pros:** Park trails border property, suite has fireplace. **Con:** A few rooms are a bit dark. ⊠ *610 Rte. 774, Welshpool, New Brunswick, Canada E5E 1A5* ☎ *506/752–2555 or 888/912–8880* ⊕ *www.lupinelodge.com* ⇆ *10 rooms, 1 suite* ⟂ *In-room: no a/c, no phone, no TV. In-hotel: no elevator, public Wi-Fi, no-smoking rooms* ⊟ *MC, V* ⊘ *Closed mid-Oct.–mid-May.*

$$–$$$ ⊞ **Owen House.** Built in 1835 by an admiral, this large, handsome
★ seaside home has an unusual two-sided staircase. A spinning wheel and horsehair couch are among the many furnishings dating back to the 19th century. Quilts add a homey touch to the historic property. Relax in the two sitting rooms and wainscoted sunporch, admire the owner's art in the gallery, or stroll about the expansive lawn. Breakfast is shared around the dining room table. **Pros:** Path to secluded point with benches, wall map of island-hopping ferry route to points north, near ferry landing. **Con:** Some third-floor rooms. ⊠ *11 Welshpool St., Welshpool, New Brunswick, Canada E5E 1G3* ☎ *506/752–2977* ⊕ *www.owenhouse.ca* ⇆ *8 rooms, 6 with bath; 1 suite* ⟂ *In-room: no a/c, no phone, no TV. In-hotel: no elevator, no kids under 6 (Aug. only), no-smoking rooms* ⊟ *MC, V* ⊘ *Closed late Oct.–mid-May* ⦁⦁ *BP.*

SPORTS & THE OUTDOORS

Spot whales and other creatures from a 20-passenger lobster boat operated by **Island Cruises** (⊠ *1 Head Harbour Wharf Rd., Wilson's Beach* ☎ *506/752–1107 or 888/249–4400*). It operates daily from July to September. Cruises cost $48 and depart from Head Harbour Wharf.

EN ROUTE Fingers of land extend into Whiting Bay and Broad and Burnt coves at the 888-acre **Cobscook Bay State Park** (⊠ *S. Edmunds Rd., off U.S. 1 Edmunds Township* ☎ *207/726–4412* ⊕ *www.state.me.us/doc/parks* ⊟ *$3* ⊘ *May 15–Oct. 15, daily 9–sunset [day use]*), a great place to spend the afternoon. You won't be disappointed if you arrive at low tide—the islands rising from the mud flats after the water has receded have an ethereal beauty. A short hiking trail to a rock crest with views of Whiting Bay links with a longer trail. There are 106 primitive campsites.

EASTPORT

39 mi northeast of Lubec via Rte. 189, U.S. 1, and Rte. 190; 109 mi north of Ellsworth via U.S. 1 and Rte. 190.

Connected by a granite causeway to the mainland at Pleasant Point Reservation, Eastport has wonderful views of the nearby islands. Known for its diverse architecture, the island city was one of the nation's busiest seaports in the early 1800s. In the late 19th century, 14 sardine canneries operated here. The industry's decline in the 20th century left the city economically depressed, but now the town has set its sights on salmon, shipping, and tourism. The weekend after Labor Day, the Maine Salmon Festival attracts large crowds with boat tours of salmon pens, architecture and cemetery tours, arts and crafts shows, and dinners featuring the local delicacy. On the same weekend, the Eastport Pirate Festival brings folks out in pirate attire for a ship race, parade, and other events.

Get downtown early to secure a viewing spot for Maine's largest July 4th parade. Canadian bagpipe bands make this an event not to be missed. The day culminates with fireworks over the bay. On the second weekend in August, locals celebrate Sipayik Indian Days at the Pleasant Point Reservation. This festival of Passamaquoddy culture includes canoe races, dancing, drumming, fireworks, and traditional dancing.

WHAT TO SEE

Anchoring downtown Eastport is the **National Historic Waterfront District,** which extends from the Customs House down Water Street to Bank Square and the Peavey Memorial Library. Spanning such architectural styles as Federal, Victorian, Queen Anne, and Greek Revival, the district was largely built in the 19th century. A cannon sits on the lawn at the Romanesque Revival library, one of the many interesting structures. Take the waterfront walkway to watch the fishing boats and freighters. The tides, among the highest in the world, fluctuate as much as 28 feet. That explains the ladders and steep gangways necessary to access boats.

The **Quoddy Crafts and Quoddy Dam Museum** shows a local history video and has the large concrete model used for a tidal power project aborted soon after it was begun in the 1930s. The gift shop is a craft cooperative where you can buy painted furniture, sweaters, and jewelry. ⊠*69–71 Water St.* ☎*207/853–6630* 🖃*Free* ☉*Memorial Day weekend–mid-Sept., daily 10–6.*

As you enter town, the yellow trim on **Raye's Mustard Mill** makes it hard to miss. This is the only remaining stone mill in the U.S., producing only stone-ground mustard. This historic property once served the sardine-packing industry. You can tour the mill and purchase mustards made on the premises at its Pantry Store, which also stocks Maine-theme gifts. A small café serves light fare at lunch and sweet treats throughout the day. ⊠*83 Washington St.* ☎*207/853–4451 or 800/853–1903* ⊕*www. rayesmustard.com* 🖃*Free* ☉*Jan.–late May, weekdays 9–4, Sat. 10–4; Memorial Day weekend–Dec., weekdays 8:30–5, weekends 10–5.*

Housed in a former bank, the **Tides Institute & Museum of Art** exhibits works depicting the Passamaquoddy Bay area from the 1800s through the present. With tall windows letting in lots of light, the main room is ideal for viewing photos of fishermen or a dreamy painting of Grand Manan Island's towering cliffs. Changing exhibits show photography, paintings, and prints. ⊠*43 Water St.* ☎*207/853–4047* ⊕*www.tides-institute.org* ✉*Free* ☉*Mid-June–mid-Sept., Tues.–Sun. 10–4; mid-Sept.–mid-June, Wed.–Sat. 10–4.*

WHERE TO EAT

$$–$$$$ ✕**Eastport Chowder House.** Just north of downtown Eastport, this expansive waterfront eatery sits on the pier next to where the ferry docks. Built atop an old cannery foundation, it has original details such as wood beams and a stone wall. Eat in the downstairs pub, upstairs in the dining room, or on the large deck. This place is hopping in summer, when families turn out for fried and baked seafood dishes. The house specialties include a smoked fish appetizer and seafood pasta in a wine-and-cheese sauce. ⊠*167 Water St.* ☎*207/853–4700* ⊟*D, MC, V* ☉*Closed mid-Oct.–mid-May.*

$–$$$ ✕**WaCo Diner.** You can find out about everything happening in and around Eastport at this favorite local spot. Beyond the old-fashioned counter and booths there's a modern dining room with fireplace overlooking the water and a deck that's open in warmer weather. Lobster rolls, haddock sandwiches, and fish-and-chips are some of the most popular dishes, and there's no scrimping on the ice cream served with the homemade pies. ⊠*47 Water St.* ☎*207/853–4046* ⊕*www.waco-diner.com* ⊟*AE, D, DC, MC, V* ☉.

¢ ✕**Rosie's Hot Dog Stand.** Frankfurters, french fries, onion rings, and chili are on the menu at this hot dog stand on the Eastport Breakwater. Opened in the 1960s, it is an Eastport institution. ⊠*Shore end of Eastport Breakwater* ☎*No phone* ⊟*No credit cards* ☉*Closed Oct.–Apr.*

WHERE TO STAY

$$–$$$ ☷**Chadbourne House Bed and Breakfast.** With two fireplaces and comfortable armchairs and couches, the large double parlor is inviting in this 1821 Federal-style home. There are antiques and paintings of local landscapes; the feel is elegant and uncluttered. A large third-floor room has a sitting area, TV, skylights, a king bed, and a twin bed. **Pros:** Gas fireplaces in two rooms, large yard with gardens. **Con:** Two-night minimum on weekends June through October. ⊠*19 Shackford St., Box 191, 04631* ☎*207/853–2727 or 888/853–2728* ⊕*www.chadbournehouse.com* ⇆*4 rooms* ⌂*In room: no a/c, no phone, DVD (some), no TV (some), Wi-Fi. In hotel: no elevator, public Wi-Fi, no kids under 16, no-smoking rooms* ⊟*AE, MC, V* ⥿*BP.*

$$ ☷**Motel East.** These rooms with a view also happen to be a good value. All the spacious accommodations at this three-level waterfront motel on the edge of downtown look across Passamaquoddy Bay to Campobello Island. Furnishings such as wing chairs are a step above those found at most motels. Rooms have balconies or terraces. The adjacent cottage has a deck and its own yard. **Pros:** Easy walk to sites, helpful staff. **Con:** Awkward stone steps to waterfront. ⊠*23A Water St.,*

7

04631 ☎📠*207/853–4747* 🌐*www.eastportme.info/moteleast.html* 🛏*14 rooms, 1 cottage* 👍*In-room: no a/c, kitchen (some), refrigerator (some), Wi-Fi. In-hotel: no elevator, public Wi-Fi, no-smoking rooms, some pets allowed* 💳*AE, D, DC, MC, V.*

$ **Todd House.** This pre–Revolutionary War home has changed little over the years. Latched plank doors, wood floors, a hearth, and a two-sided "good morning" staircase are all original. Antiques and artifacts add to the feeling of having stepped back in time. Two parlors downstairs have been converted into guest rooms. Two upstairs rooms share a bath, while a pair of large, modern rooms in an addition have private baths. **Pros:** Grill on outside deck, water views from most rooms. **Con:** Common den is small. ✉*1 Capen Ave., 04631* ☎*207/853–2328* 🛏*6 rooms, 4 with bath* 👍*In-room: no a/c, no phone, kitchen (some), refrigerator (some). In-hotel: no elevator, some pets allowed, no-smoking rooms* 💳*No credit cards* 🍽*BP July–Sept. only.*

$ **Weston House.** A Federal-style home built in 1810, this antiques-filled inn overlooks Passamaquoddy Bay. The Weston Room epitomizes the home's comfortable elegance, with crimson walls, tasteful works of art, and a fireplace decorated with a fleur-de-lis and flanked with small pillars. Naturalist John James Audubon slept in the room decorated with bird prints and his books. The three rooms share two baths, but they allow plenty of privacy. The deck and patio lead to a large garden with fanciful sitting areas. A lavish breakfast is served in the formal dining room, one of several spacious common rooms. **Pros:** Afternoon sherry or tea, bathrobes, one block to downtown. **Con:** One smaller room. ✉*26 Boynton St., 04631* ☎*207/853–2907 or 800/853–2907* 🌐*www.westonhouse-maine.com* 🛏*3 rooms without bath* 👍*In-room: no a/c, no phone. In-hotel: no elevator, no-smoking rooms* 💳*No credit cards* 🍽*BP.*

Fodor's Choice ★

NIGHTLIFE & THE ARTS

A summer concert series and plays by community theater company Stage East are performed at **Eastport Arts Center** (✉*36 Washington St.* ☎*207/853–4650* 🌐*www.eastportartscenter.com*).

SPORTS & THE OUTDOORS

From the short trail that begins behind Washington County Community College, **Shackford Head State Park** (✉*Deep Cove Rd.* ☎*207/941–4014* 🌐*www.state.me.us/doc/parks* 🎫*Free* 🕓*Daily*) has wonderful views of Cobscook Bay and over Passamaquoddy Bay to Campobello Island. From here you can see the pens for Eastport's salmon-farming industry. Side trails lead to a pebble beach and a rock promontory with caves and arches at its base. Retrace your steps or return on a loop trail around the undeveloped peninsula that's home to this 90-acre park.

WHALE-WATCHING & FISHING

Operated by a family that's plied local waters for five generations, **Eastport Windjammers/Harris Whale Watching & Fishing** (✉*104 Water St.* ☎*207/853–2500 or 207/853–4303* 🌐*www.eastportwindjammers.com*) offers whale-watching and sunset cruises on the 49-passenger *Sylvina W. Beal,* a schooner built in 1911. You can help hoist the red sails on the windjammer, which docks downtown. Deep-sea fishing trips are available on the 35-passenger *Quoddy Dam,* which in July and August takes folks to SummerKeys concerts across the water in Lubec. The *Halie Matthew* is to offer overnight cruises in 2008. Eastport Windjammers operates from June to mid-October. Sunset cruises are $25, and whale-watching trips are $35. Reservations are recommended.

SHOPPING

Bird lovers flock to **Crow Tracks** (⊠*11 Water St.* ☎*207/853–2336* ⊕*www.crowtracks.com*), a gallery that sells the owner's vividly painted carvings of all sorts of fowl, including some on driftwood. It's open April through September and by appointment. Giant bowls, vases and garden sculptures catch your eye at **Earth Forms** (⊠*5 Dana St.* ☎*207/853–2430* ⊕*www.earthforms.biz*), but there are many more manageable sizes as well. The friendly owner uses his own constantly changing glaze recipes to create cleverly banded designs. The shop is open March to December and by appointment. Displaying works by artists who live in the area, **Eastport Gallery** (⊠*74 Water St.* ☎*207/853–4166* ⊕*www.eastportgallery.com*) is open mid-June to mid-October.

Adirondack-style furnishings on the veranda draw people to the **45th Parallel** (⊠*U.S. 1, Perry* ☎*207/853–9500* ⊕*www.fortyfifthparallel.com*). This large store stocks a fun mix of antiques, gifts, jewelry, nautical decorations, and home furnishings. It's open May to December. **Quoddy Wigwam** (⊠*1015 U.S. 1, Perry* ☎*207/853–4812*) sells handcrafted Quoddy Trail Moccasins made at the factory next door as well as Passamaquoddy baskets and other American Indian crafts. The store is open Thursday to Sunday mid-June through October or by appointment. Bowls made from gourds and tree burls, silk jackets, Passamaquoddy baskets, and glass-bead jewelry are some of the items found at the **Shop-At-The-Commons** (⊠*51 Water St.* ☎*207/853–4123* ⊕*www.thecommonseastport.com*), which represents more than 60 area artists and artisans. Open year-round.

Selling nautical supplies since 1818, the nation's oldest ship chandlery, **S. L. Wadsworth & Son** (⊠*42 Water St.* ☎*207/853–4343*) is still run by the same family. An interesting pamphlet details its history. Check out the nautical maps and old photos of Eastport's waterfront. Open year-round. Load up on farm-fresh eggs, locally grown produce, and fresh flowers at **Sunrise County Farmers' Market** (⊠*63 Washington St.* ☎*287/454–3896*). The market is held on Thursday from 10 to 2, from late June to early October in the Eastport Framing parking lot.

EN ROUTE

Much of U.S. 1 to Calais is a scenic drive that cruises along the St. Croix River, which enters Passamaquoddy Bay in Robbinston. The river often resembles the elongated bays along the coast and can be just as breathtaking. Don't miss the overlook in Robbinston across from a Greek Revival mansion. Keep an eye out for the 12 granite milestones between Robbinston and Calais, erected in the late 1800s by a wealthy Calais lumberman, abolitionist, author, and diplomat who liked to pace his horses between the river city and his summer estate.

CALAIS

28 mi north of Eastport via Rte. 190 and U.S. 1.

The St. Croix River is tidal from Passamaquoddy Bay to Calais. Tides here can surge more than 30 feet, the highest in the continental United States. France's settlement of North America started on St. Croix Island; its 400th anniversary was the cause of much celebrating in 2004. A shipbuilding and lumbering center in the 1800s, Calais struggled economically in the late 20th century, but tourism is beginning to change the tide. The opening of the Downeast Heritage Museum on the waterfront was part of the settlement commemorations. There is a riverfront park with a walkway; one of the nation's oldest wildlife refuges is nearby.

St. Stephen, in New Brunswick, shares a border crossing with Calais. Traffic delays at the downtown bridge can last an hour or longer in summer, but walking from downtown to downtown takes only a few minutes. A bridge north of downtown is less busy; a third bridge is to open in 2008. U.S. citizens need a passport or other federal government-approved ID when traveling to Canada.

WHAT TO SEE

Ⓒ Treat yourself to free samples at the **Chocolate Museum,** in downtown St. Stephen, New Brunswick. The museum tells the story of one of Canada's leading candy companies, Ganong Bros., the first in North America to sell chocolates in heart-shape boxes. Housed in Ganong's original factory, the museum has interactive exhibits and a delightful collection of candy boxes. Acadian heroine Evangeline, Ganong's marketing symbol for years, is carved in chocolate. You can buy hand-dipped chocolates at the store next door. ✉ *73 Milltown Blvd., St. Stephen, New Brunswick* ☎ *506/466–7848* ⊕ *www.chocolatemuseum.ca* 🖼 *$5 (CAN)* ⊙ *Early Mar.–late June, weekdays 10–5; late June–early Sept., Mon.–Sat. 9:30–6:30, Sun. 11–3; early Sept.–late Sept., Mon.–Sat. 10–4; late Sept.–late Nov., weekdays 10–4.*

Ⓒ **Downeast Heritage Museum.** Housed in a three-level brick-and-glass building on the waterfront, the center has information about the region's natural wonders. You can use touch screens to search out places of interest. Exhibits tell the history of the Passamaquoddy Indians and early French settlement and how Mainers have made a living in the woods and from the sea. There's a touch tank filled with sea creatures, and a state visitor center is in the lobby. ✉ *39 Union St.* ☎ *207/454–7878 or 877/454–2500* ⊕ *www.downeastheritage.org* 🖼 *Free* ⊙ *Memorial Day weekend–Columbus Day, daily 10–5.*

Fodor's Choice
★

Statues of French settlers and Passamaquoddy Indians grace the path at the mainland section of **St. Croix Island International Historic Site,** 8 mi south of downtown Calais. It looks out at the small island in the St. Croix River where France's settlement of the New World began. An accompanying text tells the story of the American Indians who came to the aid of French settlers after ice floes trapped them on the now uninhabited island, which they abandoned for the mainland after a harsh winter. A pavilion shelters a model of the 1604 settlement based on a drawing by Samuel Champlain, who explored this region. Rangers offer programs from mid-June through August. ⊠ *76 St. Croix Dr.* ⌖ *off U.S. 1* ☎ *207/454–3871 in season, 207/288–3338* ⊕ *www.nps. gov/sacr* ⊒ *Free* ⊙ *May–Oct., daily 8–dusk.*

WHERE TO EAT & STAY

$$–$$$$ ✕**Chandler House.** Tables covered with red tablecloths are scattered among several rooms in this old homestead. Soft lighting gives the place a homey feel. Not everything on the extensive menu is fried. Many of the fish and seafood entrées are cooked in white wine or topped with sauces flavored with dill or pine nuts. Fish-and-chips and other smaller entrées are available at lunch. ⊠ *9 Chandler St.* ☎ *207/454–7922* ⊟ *AE, D, MC, V* ⊙ *Closed Mon.*

$$ ✕**Bernardini's Restaurant.** The woodwork in this popular storefront Italian restaurant was salvaged from a Catholic church slated for demolition. The owners say the recipe for the spicy spaghetti sauce was handed down by an ancestor who moved here from Italy. Veal is a specialty—try it lightly breaded, sautéed with mushrooms, or topped with crabmeat, asparagus, and hollandaise sauce. You can order smaller-size portions of pasta for lunch. ⊠ *257 Main St.* ☎ *207/454–2237* ⊕ *www. bernardinis.com* ⊟ *MC, V* ⊙ *Closed Sun.*

$ ✕⌂**Redclyffe Shore Motor Inn.** Overlooking the St. Croix River and Passamaquoddy Bay, this lodging has motel rooms with water views. The restaurant ($–$$$) is in a landmark 1863 Victorian Gothic with ornate gingerbread trim. The menu includes steak-and-seafood combos as well as veal, chicken, and duck dishes. **Pro:** Generous-size rooms. **Con:** Close to road. ⊠ *553 U.S. 1, in village center* ⌂ *Box 40, Robbinston 04671* ☎ *207/454–3270* ⊕ *www.redclyffeshoremotorinn.com* ⊳ *16 rooms* ⌂ *In-room: no a/c (some), refrigerator. In-hotel: no elevator, no-smoking rooms* ⊟ *AE, D, MC, V* ⊙ *Motel closed Nov.–Apr.; restaurant closed mid-Jan.–Apr. No lunch.*

¢–$ ✕⌂**Heslin's.** On the St. Croix River, this lodging has basic rooms, as well as cottages of varying size. Some cottages are on the water, and some motel rooms have water views. The lovely restaurant ($$–$$$$) has picture windows to ensure that every table has wonderful views. Try the lobster pie or the shrimp and scallops flavored with brandy and mustard. **Pro:** Newer cabin has deck. **Con:** Most quarters feel dated. ⊠ *26 Brogan Rd., 04619* ☎ *207/454–3762* ⊕ *www.heslinsmotel.com* ⊳ *11 rooms, 10 cottages* ⌂ *In-room: no a/c (some), no phone (some), kitchen (some), refrigerator (some). In-hotel: no elevator, no-smoking rooms* ⊟ *D, MC, V* ⊙ *Closed late Oct.–early May. No lunch.*

$$–$$$ ⌂**Brewer House B&B.** Built in 1828 by a sea captain where the St. Croix River flows into Passamaquoddy Bay, this eye-stopping property has rows of pillars on two facades and is on the National Register of Historic Places. Breakfast is served on one side of a double parlor with a Gothic-style fireplace. Some of the antique beds in the comfortable rooms have hand-carved headboards. **Pros:** Owner's art gallery next door, across from scenic rest area with boat launch. **Con:** Close to road. ⊠ *590 U.S. 1,* ⌂ *Box 88, Robbinston 04671* ☎ *207/454–2385* ⊕ *www.thebrewerhousebnb.com* ⊳ *4 rooms, 1 apartment* ⌂ *In-room:*

DVD (some), no TV (some), no phone, kitchen (some), In-hotel: no elevator, some pets allowed (apartment only), no-smoking rooms ⊟D, MC, V ⊗*Closed late Dec.–Mar.* ⍦⏢*BP.*

SPORTS & THE OUTDOORS

One of Down East's best birding spots is the **Moosehorn National Wildlife Refuge** (⊠*103 Headquarters Rd., turn off U.S. 1 on Charlotte Rd., Baring* ☎*207/454–7161* ⊕*www.fws.gov/northeast/moosehorn* ☒*Free* ⊗*Daily sunrise–sunset*). Spread across 29,000 acres, the refuge is home to game birds, songbirds, shorebirds, wading birds, and waterfowl. An observation deck overlooks platforms where bald eagles and osprey nest. Look for moose and other wildlife along 60 mi of roads and trails used for biking, hiking, and cross-country skiing. Several lakes and streams are open to fishing.

OUTFITTER   The Registered Maine Guides who own **Cobscook Hikes and Paddles** (⊠*13 Woodcock Way, Robbinston* ☎*207/454–2130 or 207/726–4776* ⊕*www.cobscookhikesandpaddles.com*) lead lake and sea kayaking, canoeing, hiking, and snowshoeing day trips.

SHOPPING

Maine books are handily arrayed at the front of **Calais Bookshop** (⊠*405 Main St.* ☎*207/454–1110*), where the inviting selection of used, rare, and new books includes many on American Indians. Open year-round. Maine-made handcrafts, from sweetgrass baskets to bath salts to driftwood mirrors, are sold at **Chmerto's** (⊠*283 Main St.* ☎*207/454–3300*). You also can pick up jams and chocolates produced Down East. Open year-round. Fill your picnic basket with local fruits, baked goods, and vegetables at **Sunrise County Farmers' Market** (⊠*15 Union St.* ☎*207/454–3896*), where you'll also find crafts. The market is open June through October, Tuesday 10 to 2.

EN ROUTE   The Grand Lake Stream region 50 mi west of Calais is a remote watershed of cove-lined lakes and flowages world-famous for fishing, especially for land-locked salmon and smallmouth bass. Classic fishing camps and lodges here also attract families who come to swim, canoe, hike, and kayak. The village of Grand Lake Stream, off U.S. 1 on West Grand Lake, was one of the world's largest tannery centers in the late 1800s. Today the tiny town is known for the Grand Laker, a square-end wood canoe built specifically for use on the oft-windy lakes in this region. On the last full weekend of July, the Grand Lake Stream Folk Arts Festival (☎207/796–8199 ⊕www.thecclc.org/glsfaf) attracts thousands of visitors with art, canoe, and antique quilt exhibits, and bluegrass, jazz, and folk music performances.

WHERE TO STAY

$$$$ ⌷ **Leen's Lodge.** Rustic cabins varying in size from one to four bedrooms are nestled on 23 wooded acres on West Grand Lake. All have wood-stoves or fireplaces and big windows to take in the views. A country-style breakfast and a hearty, home-style dinner are served in a central lodge, where you can also find a TV, card tables, books, and games. The lodge can arrange fishing trips, wildlife, or photographic trips.

Boat rentals are available. **Pro:** Right on water. **Con:** No cell phone amplifier to improve reception. ✉ *368 Bonney Brook Rd., Box 40, 04637* ☎ *207/796–2929 or 800/995–3367* ⊕ *www.leenslodge.com* ⇌ *10 cabins* ☆ *In-room: no a/c, no phone, kitchen (some), no TV, Wi-Fi (some). In-hotel: beachfront, no elevator, public Wi-Fi, some pets allowed* ⊟ *AE, MC, V* ⊙ *Closed Nov.–Apr.* ⦾ *AP.*

$$$$ 🏠 **Weatherby's.** Nicknamed "the fishermen's resort," Weatherby's is ideal for anglers who want to be in the center of the action. The cottages, each with a fireplace, surround the main lodge. Breakfast and dinner are served in the dining room, and boxed lunches are provided for guests exploring the area. **Pro:** Cell phone amplifier (improves reception) for guests. **Con:** Not on the water. ✉ *112 Millford Rd., Box 69, 04637* ☎ *207/796–5558* ⊕ *www.weatherbys.com* ⇌ *15 cottages* ☆ *In-room: no a/c, no phone, no TV, Wi-Fi (some). In-hotel: water sports, bicycles, public Wi-Fi, some pets allowed* ⊟ *D, MC, V* ⊙ *Closed Nov.–Apr.* ⦾ *FAP.*

WAY DOWN EAST ESSENTIALS

To research prices, get advice from other travelers, and book travel arrangements, visit www.fodors.com.

TRANSPORTATION

BY AIR

Hancock County–Bar Harbor Airport, 13 mi from the town of Hancock, is served by US Airways Express. However, most visitors traveling by air to this region use Maine's two major commercial airports in Bangor and Portland. Bangor International Airport is 99 mi from Calais. Portland International Jetport is 226 mi from Calais. *(⇨ See Transportation in Maine Coast Essentials in the back of the book.)*

BY BOAT & FERRY

East Coast Ferries provides ferry service between Eastport and Deer Island and Deer Island and Campobello from late June to mid-September. Ferries run on Atlantic time, which is one hour ahead of Eastern time. Bar Harbor Ferry provides passenger service between Bar Harbor and Winter Harbor from mid-May to early October.

Ferry Lines **Bar Harbor Ferry** (☎ *207/288–2984* ⊕ *www.barharborferry.com*). **East Coast Ferries** (☎ *506/747–2159* ⊕ *www.eastcoastferries.nb.ca*).

BY BUS

West's Coastal Connection provides bus service between Calais and Bangor via Ellsworth, stopping at towns en route on U.S. 1.

Information **West's Coastal Connection** (☎ *207/546–2823 or 800/596–2823* ⊕ *www.westbusservice.com*).

BY CAR

U.S. 1 is the primary coastal route in this region, with smaller roads leading to towns along the coast. Route 182 between Franklin and Cherryfield, a pleasant inland route, is a Maine Scenic Byway. The

Schoodic National Scenic Byway follows U.S. 1 through Sullivan, then turns south on Route 186 on its way to the Schoodic Peninsula. Route 1A shaves several miles off a coastal trip north of Milbridge but bypasses historic Cherryfield. The most direct route to Lubec is Route 189, but Route 191 between East Machias and West Lubec is a scenic coastal drive through Cutler. Coastal U.S. 1 winds its way to Calais, but the quickest route from Bangor is Route 9 (known as the "Airline" because it's so direct). Route 191 is a scenic route from the Calais area back Down East. From Machias take Route 192 to Route 9.

BY TRAIN

There is no rail service Way Down East. Amtrak operates between Boston and Portland ($\Rightarrow$ *see Greater Portland Essentials in Chapter 2*).

CONTACTS & RESOURCES

EMERGENCIES

In case of an emergency dial 911.

Hospitals **Calais Regional Hospital** (⊠ *24 Hospital La., Calais* ☎ *207/454–7521*). **Down East Community Hospital** (⊠ *Court St., Machias* ☎ *207/255–3356*).

MEDIA

The *Bangor Daily News* is published weekdays. Other weekly newspapers in the region include the *Calais Advertiser, Downeast Coastal Press* (Cutler), *Machias Valley News Observer,* and the twice-monthly *Quoddy Tides* (Eastport). WMEH 90.0 and WMED 89.7 are the local National Public Radio affiliates. WLBZ, channel 2, is the NBC affiliate. WVII, channel 7, is the ABC affiliate. WABI, channel 5, is the CBS affiliate. WMEB, channel 12, and WMED, channel 13, are the Maine Public Broadcasting affiliates.

VISITOR INFORMATION

Many chambers of commerce in the region distribute free copies of the pamphlet "Maine's Washington County: Just Off the Beaten Path." It's several cuts above the usual tourist promotion booklet.

Contacts **Campobello Island Tourism Association** (⊠ *1977 Rte. 774, Wilson's Beach, New Brunswick E5E 1J7 Canada* ☎ *506/752–2419* ⊕ *www.campobelloislandtourism.com*). **Cobscook Bay Chamber of Commerce** (✉ *Box 42, Whiting 04691* ☎ *207/733–2201* ⊕ *www.cobscookbay.com*). **Eastport Area Chamber of Commerce** (✉ *Box 254, Eastport 04631* ☎ *207/853–4644* ⊕ *www.eastport.net*). **Grand Lake Stream Chamber of Commerce** (✉ *Box 124, Grand Lake Stream 04637* ⊕ *www.grandlakestream.com*). **Machias Bay Area Chamber of Commerce** (⊠ *12 E. Main St., Box 606, Machias 04654* ☎ *207/255–4402* ⊕ *www.machiaschamber.org*). **Milbridge Area Merchants Association** (⊠ *Box 536, Milbridge 04658* ☎ *207/483–9770* ⊕ *www.milbridge.org*). **St. Croix Valley Chamber of Commerce** (⊠ *39 Union St., Calais 04619* ☎ *207/454–2308 or 888/422–3112* ⊕ *www.visitstcroixvalley.com*). **Schoodic Peninsula Chamber of Commerce** (✉ *Box 381, Winter Harbor 04693* ☎ *207/963–7658* ⊕ *www.acadia-schoodic.org*).

Maine Coast
Essentials

PLANNING TOOLS, EXPERT INSIGHT,
GREAT CONTACTS

There are planners and there are those who, excuse the pun, fly by the seat of their pants. We happily place ourselves among the planners. Our writers and editors try to anticipate all the issues you may face before and during any journey, and then they do their research. This section is the product of their efforts. Use it to get excited about your trip to Maine Coast, to inform your travel planning, or to guide you on the road should the seat of your pants start to feel threadbare.

GETTING STARTED

Fodors.com is a great place for trip planning. Scan Travel Wire for suggested itineraries, restaurant and hotel openings, and travel deals. Check out Booking to research prices and book plane tickets, hotel rooms, and rental cars. Head to Talk for on-the-ground pointers from travelers who frequent our message boards.

▮ RESOURCES

ONLINE TRAVEL TOOLS

ALL ABOUT THE MAINE COAST

Bed-and-Breakfasts Bed and Breakfast Inns Online (⊕ www.bbonline.com/me) breaks the Maine Coast into four regions in its comprehensive guide to fine lodging.

Media Each issue of *Down East: The Magazine of Maine* (⊕ *www.downeast. com*) has one to three stories on coastal destinations. *MaineToday.com: Exploring Maine* (⊕ *www.travel.mainetoday. com*) is a good online travel guide.

National & State Parks Maine Bureau of Parks and Lands (⊕ www.maine.gov/doc/ parks) has camping, hiking, and more information on Maine's state parks. **The National Park Service** (⊕ www.nps.gov) can provide information on Acadia National Park.

VISITOR INFORMATION

State Tourism Maine Tourism Association (⊠ 327 Water St., Hallowell, ME 04347 ☎ 207/623–0363 or 888/624–6345 ⊕ www. mainetourism.com).

▮ THINGS TO CONSIDER

GEAR

A cold foggy morning in spring can and often does become a bright, 60°F afternoon. A summer breeze can suddenly turn chilly, and rain often appears with little warning. It can go from comfortably warm to sweat-inducing humid in a matter of hours. Thus, the best advice on how to dress is to layer your clothing.

INSPIRING READS

Up Maine: 165 Recipes That Capture Authentic Down East Flavors includes local facts, recipes, and a food lover's travel guide. *A Seat on the Shore: Quietly Admiring the Maine Coast* features 90 images by local photographer Nance Trueworthy. In *Acadia: Visions and Verse*, broadcast journalist Jack Perkins, in poems and duo-tone photographs, tells the story of life on his small island near Maine's national park.

Showers are frequent, so pack a raincoat and umbrella. Even in summer bring long pants, a sweater or two, and a waterproof windbreaker; evenings can be chilly.

Casual sportswear, including walking shoes and jeans or khakis, will take you almost everywhere, but swimsuits and bare feet will not: shirts and shoes are required attire at even the most casual, beachside venues. Dress in restaurants is generally casual. Jeans are often frowned upon at upscale resorts, and these resorts will, at the very least, require men to wear collared shirts at dinner.

In summer bring a hat and sunscreen. Remember also to pack insect repellent to protect you from black flies, mosquitoes, and the tiny biting flies called no-see-ums (you'll-feel-um for sure, trust us). To prevent Lyme disease, you need to guard against ticks from early spring through summer.

PACKING FOR AIR TRAVEL

Be absolutely sure to follow the latest rules for what items can be carried on and checked in your baggage. (Check your airline's Web site for specifics.)

BOOKING YOUR TRIP

▌ ACCOMMODATIONS

Beachfront motels and historic-home B&Bs make up the majority of accommodation options along the Maine Coast. There are a few large luxury resorts, such as the Samoset Resort in Rockport or the Bar Harbor Inn in Bar Harbor, but most accommodations are simple and relatively inexpensive. Many properties close during the off-season—mid-October until mid-May; those that stay open drop their rates dramatically. There is a 7% state hospitality tax on all room rates.

The lodgings we list are the best in each price category. We always list the facilities that are available, but we don't specify whether they cost extra; when pricing accommodations, you may want to ask what's included and what's extra. Properties are assigned price categories based on the range between their least and most expensive standard double rooms at high season. Lodgings are indicated in the text by a house icon, 🏠 ; those marked ✕🏠 are lodgings whose restaurants warrant a special trip.

CATEGORY	COST
¢	Under $60
$	$60–$99
$$	$100–$149
$$$	$150–$200
$$$$	Over $200

All prices are for a standard double room in high season, based on the European Plan (EP) and excluding tax and service charges.

Reservations are always a good idea. Still, know the hotel's cancellation policy. Some places allow you to cancel without any kind of penalty—even if you prepaid to secure a discounted rate—if you cancel at least 24 hours in advance. Others require you to cancel a week in advance

10 WAYS TO SAVE

1. Call direct. You can sometimes get a better price if you call a hotel's local toll-free number (if available) rather than a central reservations number.

2. Look for weekend deals at business hotels. High-end chains catering to business travelers are often busy only on weekdays; to fill rooms, they often drop rates dramatically on weekends.

3. Know when to go. If your destination's high season is April through October and you're trying to book, say, in late October, you might save money by changing your dates by a week or two. If your dates straddle peak and nonpeak seasons, a property may still charge peak-season rates for the entire stay, so ask when rates go down.

4. Check online. Check hotel Web sites, as well as online travel sites.

5. Look for specials. Always inquire about packages and corporate rates.

6. Look for guaranteed rates. With your rate locked in you won't pay more.

7. Ask about taxes. Taxes could add 20% or more to your bill, so ask if it's included in the quoted rate.

8. Read the fine print. Watch for add-ons, including resort fees, energy surcharges, and "convenience" fees.

9. Join "frequent guest" programs. You may get preferential treatment in room choice and/or upgrades.

10. Weigh your options. A hotel may be cheaper because it's out of the way, but weigh transportation time and cost against the savings of staying there.

or penalize you the cost of one night. Small inns and B&Bs are most likely to require you to cancel far in advance. Most hotels allow children under a certain age to stay in their parents' room at no extra charge, but others charge for them as extra adults.

■ TIP➔ **Assume that hotels operate on the European Plan (EP, no meals) unless we specify that they use the Breakfast Plan (BP, with full breakfast), Continental Plan (CP, Continental breakfast), Full American Plan (FAP, all meals), Modified American Plan (MAP, breakfast and dinner) or are all-inclusive (AI, all meals and most activities).**

APARTMENT & HOUSE RENTALS
Seasonal apartments and houses for rent are common along the Maine Coast, but they are also popular and expensive. The following are some of the best property-rental agencies along the coast.

Local Agents Entire Coast: **A1 Vacations** (⊕ *www.A1vacations.com*). **Cottage Connection of Maine** (☎ *800/823–9501* ⊕ *www. cottageconnection.com*). **Find Vacation Rentals** (⊕ *www.findvacationrentals.com*). **Great Rentals** (⊕ *www.greatrentals.com*). **Vacation Rentals by Owner** (⊕ *www.vrbo.com*). Belfast area: **Green-Keefe** (☎ *207/338–3500*). Camden area: **Camden Accommodations** (⊕ *www.camdenac.com*). **Camden Real Estate** (☎ *207/236–6171*). Mid-Coast area: **Jaret and Cohn** (⊕ *www.jaretcohn.com*). Mount Desert Island: **Hinckley Real Estate** (☎ *207/244–7011*).

BED & BREAKFASTS
The B&Bs of Maine offer some of the region's most distinctive lodging experiences. Many are in historic homes, have beautiful views of the ocean, and provide full American-style breakfasts.

Reservation Services **Bed & Breakfast.com** (☎ *800/462–2632* ⊕ *www.bedandbreakfast. com*) also sends out an online newsletter. **Bed & Breakfast Inns Online** (☎ *800/215–7365* ⊕ *www.bbonline.com*). **BnBFinder.com** (☎ *888/547–8226* ⊕ *www.bnbfinder.com*).

HOME EXCHANGES
With a home exchange you stay in someone else's home while they stay in yours.

Exchange Clubs **HomeExchange.com** (☎ *800/877–8723* ⊕ *www.homeexchange. com*); $99.95 for a one-year online listing. **HomeLink International** (☎ *800/638–3841* ⊕ *www.homelink.org*); $90 yearly for Web-only membership; $140 includes Web access and printed directories. **Intervac Home Exchange** (☎ *800/756–4663* ⊕ *www.intervacus.com*); $78.88 for Web-only membership; $126 includes Web access and a catalog.

HOTELS
The Maine Coast is liberally supplied with small, independent motels, which run the gamut from the tired to the tidy. Don't overlook these mom-and-pop operations; they frequently offer cheerful, convenient accommodations at lower rates than the chains. If you stay at a motel located directly on U.S. 1, request a room in the back to avoid noise caused by traffic. Keep in mind that many motels shut down from mid-October until mid-May.

Most hotels and motels will hold your reservation until 6 PM; call ahead if you plan to arrive late. All will hold a late reservation for you if you guarantee your reservation with a credit-card number.

Information **Maine Innkeepers Association** (☎ *207/865–6100* w *www.maineinns.com*). **The Unofficial Maine State Lodging Directory** (⊕ *www.visitmaine.net*).

▌ RENTAL CARS

A car is essential in most parts of the Maine Coast (⇨ see *Transportation: By Car*). All the major car-rental agencies have counters at the airports. Rental rates average about $38 per day, or $175 per week, for a compact car. Many towns also have at least one car-rental firm, but often they are not open weekends. To rent a car at most agencies, you must be at least 21 years of age and have a major credit card.

When you reserve a car, ask about cancellation penalties, taxes, drop-off charges (for one-way rentals), and surcharges (for being under or over a certain age, for additional drivers, or for driving across state or country borders or beyond a certain mileage). All these things can add substantially to your costs. If you want car seats and extras such as GPS, request them when you book.

Rates are sometimes—but not always— better if you book in advance or reserve through a rental agency's Web site. There are other reasons to book ahead, though: for popular destinations, during busy times of the year, or to ensure that you get certain types of vehicles.

■TIP➔ Make sure that a confirmed reservation guarantees you a car. Agencies sometimes overbook, particularly for busy weekends and holiday periods.

CAR-RENTAL INSURANCE

Everyone who rents a car wonders whether the insurance that the rental companies offer is worth the expense. No one, including us, has a simple answer. It depends on how much regular insurance you have, how comfortable you are with risk, and if money is an issue.

If you own a car and carry comprehensive car insurance for both collision and liability, your personal auto insurance will probably cover a rental, but read your policy's fine print to be sure. If you don't have auto insurance, then you should probably buy the collision- or loss-damage waiver (CDW or LDW) from the rental company. This eliminates your liability for damage to the car.

Some credit cards offer CDW coverage, but it's usually supplemental to your own insurance and rarely covers SUVs, vans, luxury models, and the like. If your coverage is secondary, you may still be liable for loss-of-use costs from the car-rental company (again, read the fine print). Credit-card insurance is valid only if you use that card for *all* transactions, from reserving to paying the final bill.

You may also be offered supplemental liability coverage; the car-rental company is required to carry a minimal level of liability coverage insuring all renters, but it's rarely enough to cover claims in a really serious accident if you're at fault. Your own auto-insurance policy will protect you if you own a car; if you don't, you have to decide whether you are willing to take the risk.

U.S. rental companies sell CDWs and LDWs for about $15 to $25 a day; supplemental liability is usually more than $10 a day. The car-rental company may offer you all sorts of other policies, but they're rarely worth the cost. Personal accident insurance, which is basic hospitalization coverage, is an especially egregious rip-off if you have health insurance.

■TIP➔ You can decline the insurance from the rental company and purchase it through a third-party provider such as Travel Guard (www.travelguard.com)—$9 per day for $35,000 of coverage.

■ GUIDED TOURS

Guided tours are a good option when you don't want to do it all yourself. You normally travel with a group, stay in prebooked hotels, eat with your fellow travelers (the cost of meals are sometimes included in the price of your tour, sometimes not), and follow a schedule.

Not all guided tours are an if-it's-Tuesday-this-must-be-Belgium experience. A knowledgeable guide can take you places that you might never discover on your own, and you may be pushed to see more than you would have otherwise. Tours

10 WAYS TO SAVE

1. Beware of cheap rates. Those great rates aren't always so great when you add in taxes, surcharges, and insurance. Such extras can double or triple the initial quote.

2. Rent weekly. Weekly rates are usually better than daily ones. Even if you only want to rent for five or six days, ask for the weekly rate; it may very well be cheaper than the daily rate for that period of time.

3. Don't forget the locals. Price local companies as well as the majors.

4. Look beyond the airports. Airports often add surcharges, which you can sometimes avoid by renting from an agency whose office is just off airport property.

5. Enlist a wholesaler's help. Investigate wholesalers, which don't own fleets but rent in bulk from firms that do, and which frequently offer better rates (note that you must usually pay for such rentals before leaving home).

6. Find rate guarantees. With your rate locked in, you won't pay more.

7. Pump it yourself. Don't buy the tank of gas that's in the car when you rent it unless you plan to do a lot of driving.

8. Fill up farther away. Avoid hefty refueling fees by filling the tank at a station well away from where you plan to turn in the car.

9. Get all your discounts. Find out whether a credit card you carry or organization or frequent-renter program to which you belong has a discount program. And confirm that such discounts really are a deal. You can often do better with special weekend or weekly rates offered by a rental agency.

10. Check out packages. Adding a car rental onto your air/hotel vacation package may be cheaper than renting a car separately.

aren't for everyone, but they can be just the thing for trips to places where making travel arrangements is difficult or time-consuming.

Whenever you book a guided tour, find out what's included and what isn't. Some tours, for example, include all your travel within the destination, but not flights to and from. In most cases prices in tour brochures don't include fees and taxes. Also, you'll be expected to tip your guide (in cash) at the end of the tour.

SPECIAL-INTEREST TOURS

ART

Contact **Smithsonian Journeys** (☎877/338–8687 ⊕ www.smithsonian-journeys.org).

BIKING

Contact **Summerfeet Maine Coast Cycling Adventures** (☎207/828–0342 or 866/857–9544 ⊕ www.summerfeet.net).

ECO TOURS

Contact **Voyage of the Wanderbird** (☎207/338–3088 or 866/732–2473 ⊕ www.wanderbirdcruises.com).

MOTORCYCLE

Contact **Maine Coast Motorcycle** (☎207/354–6500 or 866/439–2453 ⊕ www.mainecoastmotorcycle.com).

SAILING

Contacts **Maine Adventure Sails** (☎888/300–3377 ⊕ www.maineadventure-sails.com). **Schooner Mary Day** (☎800/992–2218 ⊕ www.schoonermaryday.com).

SEA KAYAKING

Contact **Carpe Diem Kayaking Company** (www.carpediemkayaking.com ☎207/669–2338).

WALKING

Contact **Boundless Journeys** (☎800/941–8010 ⊕ www.boundlessjourneys.com).

TRANSPORTATION

TRAVEL TIMES FROM PORTLAND TO . . .	BY AIR	BY CAR
Acadia National Park/Bar Harbor	½ hour	2¾ hours
Boston	½ hour	1½ hours
Montreal	4 hours	5½ hours
New York City	1½ hours	6 hours
Quebec City	4¾ hours	5 hours

The two main hubs to access the Maine coast are the cities of Portland and Bangor, approximately 133 mi from one another. Both can be reached by the Maine Turnpike, and each one is served by an airport. Once in the state, travel along the coast is best enjoyed by car, enabling you to take as relaxed a pace as you wish while reserving the right to follow whatever country road you choose. Unless you visit in the dead of winter, there are no particular impediments to driving, though local traffic can be heavy during rush hour.

■ TIP → The Maine Turnpike is rather boring, but the various routes that follow the coast, especially Route 1, pass through one picturesque town after another.

■ BY AIR

AIRPORTS

The two primary airports serving the Maine Coast area are Portland International and Bangor International. Manchester Airport, in New Hampshire, is only 45 mi from the beginning of the Maine Coast and is becoming an increasingly popular airport because of the number of discount airlines, such as Southwest, that fly there. (Boston is about 65 mi (a roughly 90-minute drive) from the southern end of the Maine Coast; Boston's Logan International is the closest major international airport.)

Airport Information Bangor International (BGR) (✉287 Godfrey Blvd., Bangor, ME ☎207/992-4600 ⊕www.flybangor.com).

Logan International (BOS) (☎800/235-6426 ⊕www.massport.com/logan). **Manchester-Boston Regional Airport (MHT)** (✉1 Airport Rd., Manchester, NH ☎603/624-6556 ⊕www.flymanchester.com). **Portland International (PWM)** (✉1001 Westbrook St., Portland, ME ☎207/874-8877 ⊕www.portlandjetport.org).

Air Travel Resources in Maine Office of the Maine Attorney General (⊕www.maine.gov/ag) is a good place to file any air-travel or airline-related complaints.

Air Travel Security Issues Transportation Security Administration (⊕www.tsa.gov) has answers for almost every question that might come up.

GROUND TRANSPORTATION

Portland is small enough that getting to and from Portland International is simple and quick. Downtown is less than 20 minutes away in traffic, and the Maine Turnpike is right next to one of the airport's entrances. The same ease goes for Bangor International. Taxi fare to or from downtown Portland or Bangor runs about $15. Both airports are also served by local buses, limousines, and hotel shuttles.

FLIGHTS

Portland International and Bangor International airports are both served by Delta, American, Northwest, Continental, and US Airways. Portland is also served by United, AirTran, and jetBlue. Southwest serves Manchester, New Hampshire.

Airline Contacts AirTran Airways (☎800/247-8726 ⊕www.airtran.com). **American Airlines** (☎800/433-7300

⊕ www.aa.com). **Continental Airlines** (☎ 800/523–3273 for U.S. and Mexico reservations, 800/231–0856 for international ⊕ www.continental.com). **Delta Airlines** (☎ 800/221–1212 for U.S. reservations, 800/241–4141 for international ⊕ www.delta.com). **jetBlue** (☎ 800/538–2583 ⊕ www.jetblue.com). **Northwest Airlines** (☎ 800/225–2525 ⊕ www.nwa.com). **Southwest Airlines** (☎ 800/435–9792 ⊕ www.southwest.com). **United Airlines** (☎ 800/864–8331 for U.S. reservations, 800/538–2929 for international ⊕ www.united.com). **US Airways** (☎ 800/428–4322 for U.S. and Canada reservations, 800/622–1015 for international ⊕ www.usairways.com).

▌ BY BOAT

Maine State Ferry Service provides ferry service to the islands of Monhegan, Mantinicus, Vinalhaven, North Haven, and Islesboro. The CAT is a swift catamaran ferry that goes between Bar Harbor, on Mount Desert Island, and Yarmouth, Nova Scotia. You can bring your car on The CAT and the ferries to Islesboro, Vinalhaven, North Haven, and Mantinicus. The Monhegan Island ferry is passengers-only.

Casco Bay Lines connects the city of Portland with the islands of Casco Bay. The best way to experience island life is by foot or by bike, but if you must bring your car, make sure to reserve a spot on one of the car ferries.

Information Casco Bay Lines (☎ 207/774–7871 ⊕ www.cascobaylines.com). **The CAT** (☎ 888/249–7245 ⊕ www.catferry.com). **Maine State Ferry Service** (☎ 207/596–2202 or 800/491–4883).

▌ BY BUS

Greater Portland's Metro runs several bus routes in Portland, including to the airport. The fare is $1.25; exact change is required. Buses run from 5:30 AM to 11:45 PM. The Portland Explorer has express shuttle service to the Old Port from Portland International. The shuttle runs hourly, seven days a week, from noon to 7 PM. Fare is $2.

Long-distance bus travel is available within the state of Maine and neighboring New England states. Concord Trailways offers service to Boston's Logan Airport, Boston, and points within coastal Maine. Vermont Transit Company services towns throughout Maine and northern New England, including Portland's Greyhound stop.

Bus Information Concord Trailways (☎ 800/639–3317 ⊕ www.concordtrailways.com). **Greyhound** (☎ 207/772–6587 [Portland], 207/945–3000 [Bangor] ⊕ www.greyhound.com). **Metro Greater Portland Transit District** (☎ 207/774–0351 ⊕ www.gpmetrobus.com). **Portland Explorer** (☎ 207/774–9891 ⊕ www.transportme.org). **Vermont Transit** (☎ 800/642–3133 ⊕ www.vermonttransit.com).

▌ BY CAR

The Maine Coast is best explored by car. It's generally pretty easy to get there from here (though a good map always helps), you can drive at your own pace, and you can check out any country road or fishing village on a whim. Just be sure to watch for deer and even moose crossing the road, especially at night.

GASOLINE

There are numerous gas stations along the Maine Coast, but in smaller locales many close at 6 PM. Irving stations are among those open 24 hours; they have a convenience store, and pride themselves on the cleanliness of their rest rooms. Nearly all gas stations are self-service, and allow you to pay with a credit card at the pump. At this writing, gas was $2.75 a gallon.

PARKING

Outside major cities, parking along the Maine Coast is neither difficult nor expensive. Many of the more-picturesque towns don't even bother with parking meters. In Portland, metered on-street parking is available at 25¢ per half hour, with a two-hour maximum. Parking lots and garages can be found downtown, in the Old Port, and on the waterfront; most charge $1 per hour or $8–$12 per day. If you're shopping or dining, remember to ask local vendors if they participate in the Park & Shop program, which provides an hour of free shopping for each participating vendor visited. If your meter runs over, you may be surprised to return to your car and find that the ticket on your windshield is nothing more than a friendly reminder, complete with map, of where downtown's free and fee municipal parking lots are located.

ROAD CONDITIONS

Most principal roads in Maine are well maintained, and plowed and graveled in winter before things get too messy. Secondary roads are another matter; beware of potholes and frost heaves. Watch out for deer and moose on the road; the number of accidents caused by moose is astonishingly high.

U.S. 1 is a well-paved and maintained highway, but it's only two lanes wide for much of its distance and can be quite slow. To get more quickly to a destination like Bar Harbor, take I–95.

RULES OF THE ROAD

The speed limit on the Maine Turnpike or the interstate is 65 mph. The speed limit on secondary roads is 35 to 50 mph. If you see a car passing in the opposite direction flashing its lights at you, slow down and keep an eye out for a state trooper or policeman aside the road.

Maine has zero tolerance for driving under the influence of alcohol—the legal limit is .08—and penalties are severe. Car radars are legal, as are right turns on a red light. Although you are not required by law to stop and get off the road when using a cell phone, Maine state police suggest that it is a good practice to do so. Pedestrians have the right of way at all marked crossings; you have to stop for them. Always strap children under age four or under 40 pounds into approved child-safety seats.

▎ BY TRAIN

Amtrak's *Downeaster* connects Portland with Boston. The train makes four daily runs to and from Boston, with eight stops along the way. The fare is $22 each way.

Contact Amtrak Downeaster (☎ *207/780–1000* ⊕ *www.thedowneaster.com*).

ON THE GROUND

■ CAMERAS & PHOTOGRAPHY

The Maine Coast is a photographer's dream. The changing weather often makes for dramatic pictures, whether due to fog, snow, or clouds that reflect all colors imaginable from the setting sun. Quintessential subject matter includes lighthouses (especially Portland Head Light), fall foliage, and all things lobster, especially lobster fishing—boats, buoys, and traps. If you haven't yet, switch to digital so you'll never run out of film again.

EQUIPMENT PRECAUTIONS

Don't pack film or equipment in checked luggage, where it is much more susceptible to damage. X-ray machines used to view checked luggage are extremely powerful and therefore are likely to ruin your film. Try to ask for hand inspection of film, which becomes clouded after repeated exposure to airport X-ray machines, and keep videotapes and computer disks away from metal detectors. Better still, consider switching to digital photography; the convenience and quality are outstanding, and you won't have to worry about airport scanners harming the media cards that store the images you make. Always keep film, tape, and computer disks out of the sun. Carry an extra supply of batteries, and be prepared to turn on your camera, camcorder, or laptop to prove to airport security personnel that the device is real.

■ CHILDREN IN MAINE

Perhaps the most extensive guide for what to do with your children when visiting Maine, *Maine-ly Fun!: Great Things to Do with Kids in Maine*, published by Down East, features almost 800 things to do and places to visit. The book's 20 chapters are arranged by topics, such as "Beaches," "Things to Cook," and "Great Ideas from Famous Maine Folks."

For a host of activities and exhibits all in one location, visit the Children's Museum of Maine, situated next to the Portland Museum of Art. Preregistration is required for Parent's Night Out, during which you can drop off your children for an evening of pizza and fun.

Want a quick and easy idea to occupy the kids? Head to any of Maine's beaches for a few hours of beachcombing and tidal-pool exploring.

■TIP→ If you are renting a car, don't forget to arrange for a car seat when you reserve. For general advice about traveling with children, consult Fodor's FYI: Travel with Your Baby (available in bookstores).

LODGING

Most hotels in Maine allow children under a certain age to stay in their parents' room at no extra charge, but others charge for them as extra adults; be sure to find out the cutoff age for children's discounts. Bed-and-breakfasts usually have tighter age restrictions; some allow only children above a certain age.

SIGHTS & ATTRACTIONS

Places that are especially appealing to children are indicated by a rubber-duckie icon (☽) in the margin.

■ COMMUNICATIONS

INTERNET

Complimentary high-speed Internet service, wireless or otherwise, is increasingly available at most lodging options along the coast, and coffee shops with free Wi-Fi connections are becoming common in the larger towns and cities. Libraries are also a good bet for free Internet, though there is usually a time limit for surfing.

Contact Cybercafes (⊕ *www.cybercafes.com*) lists more than 4,000 Internet cafés worldwide.

▌DISABILITIES & ACCESSIBILITY

General information for travelers with disabilities visiting Maine can be obtained from the Committee for Accessible Leisure, Arts & Recreation. Most hotels, motels, restaurants, and ferries are reasonably accessible to those in wheelchairs. B&Bs are another matter. Many of them are in historic homes in which the owners cannot violate the integrity of the property by adding something like a ramp or an elevator. It's best to call first.

Local Resources **Committee for Accessible Recreation, Arts & Leisure** (⊕ *www.maine. gov/portal/travel/accessrec/index.html*).

LODGING

Despite the Americans with Disabilities Act, the definition of accessibility differs from hotel to hotel. Some properties may be accessible by ADA standards for people with mobility problems but not for people with hearing or vision impairments. Typically, B&Bs have limited access; elevators are a rarity, and bathrooms are not always updated.

If you have mobility problems, ask for the lowest floor on which accessible services are offered. If you have a hearing impairment, check whether the hotel has devices to alert you visually to the ring of the telephone, a knock at the door, and a fire/emergency alarm. Some hotels provide these devices without charge. Discuss your needs with hotel personnel if this equipment isn't available, so that a staff member can personally alert you in the event of an emergency.

If you're bringing a guide dog, get approval ahead of time and write down the name of the person who approved it.

RESERVATIONS

When discussing accessibility with an operator or reservations agent, ask hard questions. Are there any stairs, inside *or* out? Are there grab bars next to the toilet *and* in the shower/tub? How wide is the doorway to the room? To the bathroom? For the most extensive facilities meeting the latest legal specifications, opt for newer accommodations. If you reserve through a toll-free number, consider also calling the hotel's local number to confirm the information. Get confirmation in writing when you can.

SIGHTS & ATTRACTIONS

Many popular attractions along the Maine Coast are fairly accessible by wheelchair. The Portland Museum of Art is accessible, for example, as are buses, some horse-drawn carriages, and sites such as Thunder Hole at Acadia National Park. Some paths at many public beaches are made of asphalt and wheelchair-friendly. Most public parking facilities and public rest rooms are accessible as well.

TRANSPORTATION

Public transportation is generally easily accessible to travelers with disabilities, including the ferries that connect the mainland with outlying islands. Drivers can use their out-of-state windshield cards in Maine, so long as they're easily visible.

The U.S. Department of Transportation Aviation Consumer Protection Division's online publication *New Horizons: Information for the Air Traveler with a Disability* offers advice for travelers with a disability, and outlines basic rights.

Information **Americans with Disabilities Act** (☎ *800/514–0301* ADA information line, *800/514–0383* TTY ⊕ *www.ada.gov*). **Departmental Office of Civil Rights** (☎ *866/355–2629, 617/494–3472* TTY ⊕ *www.dotcr.ost. dot.gov*). **U.S. Department of Transportation Hotline** (☎ *800/778–4838* or *800/455–9880* TTY for disability-related air-travel problems ⊕ *www.disabilityinfo.gov*).

▌EATING OUT

The one signature dinner on the Maine Coast is, of course, the lobster dinner, or as some restaurants call it, the Shore Dinner. It generally includes boiled lobster, a clam or seafood chowder, corn on the cob, and perhaps a salad. Lobster prices vary from day to day; most restaurants list "market price" next to the lobster dinners on their menus. Generally, a full lobster dinner should cost around $25; without all the add-ons, about $18.

For guidelines on tipping see Tipping.

MEALS & MEALTIMES

Many breakfast spots along the coast open as early as 6 AM to serve the going-to-work crowd. Lunch generally runs 11–2:30; dinner is usually served 5–9. Only in the larger cities will you find full dinners being offered much later than 9, although you can usually find a bar or bistro serving a limited menu late into the evening in all but the smallest towns.

Many restaurants in Maine are closed Monday, though this isn't true in resort areas in high season. However, resort-town eateries often shut down completely in the off-season. Unless otherwise noted, restaurants in this guide are open daily for lunch and dinner.

Credit cards are accepted for meals throughout Maine in all but the most modest establishments.

RESERVATIONS & DRESS

It's a good idea to make a reservation if you can. In our listings, we only mention them specifically when reservations are essential (there's no other way you'll ever get a table) or when they are not accepted. For popular restaurants, book as far ahead as you can (often 30 days), and reconfirm as soon as you arrive. (Large parties should always call ahead to check the reservations policy.) We mention dress only when men are required to wear a jacket or a jacket and tie.

WINES, BEER & SPIRITS

The drinking age in Maine is 21, and a photo ID must be presented to purchase alcoholic beverages. Most bars and taverns are open until 2 AM. Beer and wine are sold at convenience stores, and hard alcohol is available at the large supermarkets, generally from 9 AM to 9 PM. There are a number of good local microbreweries along the Maine Coast, a couple of them in the Camden area.

No matter what you might see in the local parks, drinking alcohol in public parks or on the beaches is illegal. It is also illegal to have open containers of alcohol in motor vehicles.

❚ HEALTH

Maine seems to have more doctors than most states, but if you have an emergency, there are four hospitals on the mid and upper Maine Coast, one near Camden, one in Belfast, and two in Bangor. Portland has two (see individual chapters for contact information).

Maine is famous in late spring and summer for its black flies, and the farther inland you go, the worse they seem to get. Packing a good insect repellent is recommended if you are going to be outside. For some reason, they are not as bothersome along the coast as they are inland. An old salt told us: "The flies don't like the salt air." Maybe he's right.

Maine's other greatest insect pest is the mosquito. Mosquitoes can be a nuisance just about everywhere in summer—they're at their worst following snowy winters and wet springs. The best protection against both pests is repellent containing DEET. A particular pest of coastal areas, especially salt marshes, is the greenhead fly. Their bite is nasty; repel them with a liberal application of Avon Skin So Soft.

Coastal waters attract seafood lovers who enjoy harvesting their own clams and mussels; permits are required, and casual harvesting of lobsters is strictly forbidden. Amateur clammers should be aware that Maine shellfish beds are periodically visited by red tides, during which microorganisms can render shellfish poisonous.

To keep abreast of the situation, inquire when you apply for a license (usually at town halls or police stations) and watch for red-tide postings.

▌ HOURS OF OPERATION

In general, banks are open from 9 to 4; post offices from 8 to 5. Most large grocery stores or supermarkets are open from 9 AM to 9 PM; Hannaford Supermarkets are usually open from 7 AM to 11 PM daily. Some convenience stores, such as the Irving chain, where you also can get gas, are open 24/7.

Most museums in Maine are open from 9 to 5, some close on Sunday, and many of them, such as the Penobscot Marine Museum in Searsport, close during the off-season, mid-October to mid-May.

Most shops are open from 9 to 5, seven days a week. Those that cater to the tourism business, in Camden for example, are often open until 9 PM in the high season but close down completely between mid-October and mid-May.

▌ MONEY

Prices throughout this guide are given for adults. Substantially reduced fees are almost always available for children, students, and senior citizens.

CREDIT CARDS

Most major credit cards are accepted throughout the coast; some restaurants and accommodations do not accept American Express or Diners Club. Throughout this guide, the following abbreviations are used: **AE**, American Express; **D**, Discover; **DC**, Diners Club; **MC**, MasterCard; and **V**, Visa.

It's a good idea to inform your credit-card company before you travel, especially if you're going abroad and don't travel internationally very often. Otherwise, the credit-card company might put a hold on your card owing to unusual activity—not

a good thing halfway through your trip. Record all your credit-card numbers—as well as the phone numbers to call if your cards are lost or stolen—in a safe place, should you need them.

Reporting Lost Cards **American Express** (☎ 800/992-3404 in the U.S. ⊕ *www. americanexpress.com*). **Diners Club** (☎ 800/234-6377 in the U.S. ⊕ *www.diners-club.com*). **Discover** (☎ 800/347-2683 in the U.S. ⊕ *www.discovercard.com*). **MasterCard** (☎ 800/622-7747 in the U.S. ⊕ *www.master-card.com*). **Visa** (☎ 800/847-2911 in the U.S. ⊕ *www.visa.com*).

TRAVELER'S CHECKS & CARDS

Some consider this the currency of the caveman. It's true that fewer establishments accept traveler's checks these days, and Maine has plenty of cash machines from which to withdraw funds. Nevertheless, traveler's checks are a cheap and secure way to carry extra money, particularly on trips to urban areas. Both Citibank (under the Visa brand) and American Express issue traveler's checks in the United States, but Amex is better known and more widely accepted; you can also avoid hefty surcharges by cashing Amex checks at Amex offices. Keep track of all the serial numbers in case the checks are lost or stolen.

American Express now offers a stored-value card called a Travelers Cheque Card, which you can use wherever American Express credit cards are accepted, including ATMs. The card can carry a minimum of $300 and a maximum of $2,750, and it's a very safe way to carry your funds. Although you can get replacement funds in 24 hours if your card is lost or stolen, it doesn't really strike us as a very good deal. There's a high initial cost ($14.95 to set up the card), plus $5 each time you "reload"). The maximum load is the most you can carry for any 14-day period. Further, each time you use the card in an ATM you pay a transaction fee of $2.50 on top of the 2% transaction fee for the conversion—add it all up and it can be considerably more than you would pay when simply using your own ATM card. Regular traveler's checks are just as secure and cost less.

Contact **American Express** (☎ 888/412–6945 in the U.S. ⊕ www.americanexpress.com).

▮ SAFETY

Maine is for the most part a safe place to travel, even when walking about at night, but standard precautions are still applicable. Always lock your car and room doors, for example, and be discreet when using cash machines and credit cards. You're probably safe wearing jewelry, though ostentatious displays will stand out in this down-to-earth state.

▮ SENIOR-CITIZEN TRAVEL

To qualify for age-related discounts, mention your senior-citizen status up front when booking hotel reservations (not when checking out) and before you're seated in restaurants (not when paying the bill). Be sure to have identification on hand. When renting a car, ask about promotional car-rental discounts, which can be cheaper than senior-citizen rates.

Educational Programs **Elderhostel** (☎ 877/426–8056, 978/323–4141 international callers, 877/426–2167 TTY ⊕ www. elderhostel.org).

▮ SHOPPING

There's a lot to shop for in Maine. Opportunities run the gamut from large regional malls to small boutiques; from name-brand outlet stores to the tackiest of tourist traps that peddle cheap T-shirts and lobsters emblazoned on everything you could think of. Some of the best finds are located off the beaten path; stores that sell artisan wares such as local pottery, paintings, and one-of-a-kind jewelry. Many small-town Main streets have been revitalized with such stores.

KEY DESTINATIONS

Maine shopping is best known for the numerous outlet stores in Freeport, which include the world headquarters of L.L. Bean. Though Main Street is chockablock with stores (and hundreds of shoppers), the city has the kind of strict zoning in place that required McDonald's to locate within a white Victorian building and forego a drive-through and its prominent golden arches. Farther south along the coast in Kittery are additional outlets, though the experience is nothing near that of Freeport.

The Maine Mall in South Portland is the state's largest, with almost 120 stores, restaurants, and kiosks.

SMART SOUVENIRS

Candy made from Maine maple sugar is a delicious and uncommon treat outside Maine. Buy it at some of the nicer shops that target tourists in downtown Portland. Cool as a Moose has stores in Portland, Freeport, and Bar Harbor; it sells funky fun shirts, hats, pants, and more that feature the likeness of the large animal that symbolizes Maine.

▮ SPORTS & OUTDOORS

No visit to the Maine Coast is complete without some outdoor activity–be it generated by two wheels, two feet, two paddles, or by pulling a bag full of clubs.

BICYCLING

Bicycling is an ideal (and healthy) way to explore the coast of Maine, with Acadia National Park a special favorite among road bikers. The Bicycle Coalition of Maine and Explore Maine by Bike are both excellent sources for trail maps and other riding information, including where to rent bikes.

Information **Bicycle Coalition of Maine** (☎ 207/623–4511 ⊕ www.bikemaine.org). **Explore Maine by Bike** (☎ 207/624–3250 ⊕ www.exploremaine.org/bike).

GOLF

A round or two of golf is more enjoyable with the ocean as your backdrop and sea breezes to energize you. The Maine State Golf Association is a center of information for amateur golfers and schedules of events. Check out the Golf Maine Association to locate golf schools and find courses.

Information Maine State Golf Association (☎ 207/846-3800 ⊕ www.mesga.org). **The Golf Maine Association** (☎ 877/553-4653 ⊕ www.golfme.com).

HIKING

Exploring the Maine coast by foot is a quick way to acclimate to the relaxed pace of life here. Healthy Maine Walks has comprehensive listings for quick jaunts and more involved hikes alike.

Information Healthy Maine Walks (⊕ www. healthymainewalks.com).

KAYAKING

Nothing gets you literally off the beaten path like plying the salt waters in a graceful sea kayak. Beginners can find guides and instructors through the Maine Association of Sea Kayaking Guides and Instructors, while more seasoned paddlers can get maps of Maine's famous sea trails system at the Maine Island Trails Association.

Information Maine Association of Sea Kayaking Guides and Instructors (⊕ www. maineseakayakguides.com). **Maine Island Trails Association** (☎ 207/761-8225 ⊕ www. mita.org).

▌ STUDENTS IN MAINE

Most major attractions in the region offer discount admissions to students.

IDs & Services STA Travel (☎ 800/781-4040 24-hr service center ⊕ www.sta.com). **Travel Cuts** (☎ 800/592-2887 in the U.S. ⊕ www. travelcuts.com).

▌ TAXES

Maine state sales tax is 5% and applies to all purchases except prepackaged food. Maine's hospitality tax is 7%, and applies to all lodging and restaurant prices.

▌ TIME

Maine is in the Eastern Standard Time zone; it observes daylight saving time.

▌ TIPPING

At restaurants, a 15% tip is standard for waiters; up to 20% is expected at more-expensive establishments. The same goes for taxi drivers and hairdressers. Tip bartenders $1 to $5 per round of drinks. Coat-check operators usually expect $1 to $2; bellhops and porters should get $1 to $5 per bag; hotel maids should get about $1 to $3 per day of your stay. Hotel concierges should be tipped if you utilize their services; the amount varies widely depending on the nature of service. On package tours, conductors and drivers usually get $10 per day from the group as a whole; check whether this has already been figured into your cost. For local sightseeing tours, you may tip the driver-guide 10%, depending on the length of the tour, the number of people in your party, and if he or she has been helpful or informative.

▌ TRANSPORTATION AROUND MAINE

If you plan to travel along the coast of Maine, a car is a *must*. Rail connections exist only along Amtrak's *Downeaster* line from Portland to Boston, and regional travel by air is expensive. Concord Trailways runs a luxury bus several times a day from Orono, near Bangor, to Logan International Airport, in Boston, and makes stops at major towns along the way, but schedules are often inconvenient. (⇨ see *Transportation*).

INDEX

PHOTO CREDITS

Inside back cover: *James Ingram/Alamy.* 6, *Jeff Greenberg/Alamy.* 7 (left), *Stock Connection Blue/Alamy.* 7 (right), *Jerry Whaley/age fotostock.* 8, *Peter Arnold, Inc./Alamy.* 9, *Joy Brown/Shutterstock.* 10, *Rubens Abboud/Alamy.* 11 (left), *NA/Alamy.* 11 (right), *Sandy Macys/Alamy.* 12, *Michael S. Nolan/age fotostock.* 17, *Jeff Greenberg/age fotostock.* 18, *Jeff Greenberg/Alamy.* **Chapter 1: The Southern Coast:** 53, *Nancy Trueworthy/Aurora Photos.* **Chapter 3: The Mid-Coast Region:** 138, *Christina Tisi-Kramer/Shutterstock.* **Chapter 4: Penobscot Bay:** 154, *David McLain/Aurora Photos.* **Chapter 7: Way Down East:** 277, *Skip Caplan/Alamy.*

ABOUT OUR WRITERS

Stephen and Neva Allen have written extensively about travel for many newspapers and magazines. They moved to the Mid-Coast of Maine in 2000 and are devoted to the beautiful area they've come to call home.

Though based in Salt Lake City, Utah, **John Blodgett** still goes home to Maine— the place he spent much of his first 22 years. The lobster roll at Gilbert's Chowder House in Portland's Old Port alone is worth the airfare, but he also misses sitting next to the booming foghorn at Two Lights State Park, listening to the clang of buoys bobbing in Casco Bay, and simply sitting on a lawn chair under the shelter of his parents' garage while watching the rain.

After living in Massachusetts, Connecticut, and Illinois, **Sherry Hanson** and her husband moved to the beautiful coast of Maine in 1992. As a writer, Sherry covers everything from the Civil War to how to kayak with a dog and brew beer at home. Her poetry has appeared in many journals as well as her own poetry book, a collection titled *A Cab to Stonehenge*, published in 2006. When not working, reading, or creating poetry, Sherry's pursuits include biking, kayaking, skiing, hiking, inline skating, archery, and identifying constellations in the winter night sky.

As a Maine-based freelance writer, **Mary Ruoff** has enjoyed writing articles about Maine travel among other topics. A graduate of the University of Missouri School of Journalism, she began her writing career as a newspaper reporter. Mary is married to a Mainer, Michael Hodsdon, and spends as much time as she can at their family land "Way Down East," where Michael's grandfather was a fisherman.

Laura V. Scheel has spent a good portion of her years in Maine driving and exploring the state's numerous back roads and small towns. History and travel are two of her favorite subjects, and she has written frequently for Fodor's. In September 2007, she welcomed baby Cole William to the world.

George Semler has been coming to Maine's Blue Hill Peninsula since the summer before he was born. A frequent writer for Fodor's (France, Spain, Cuba, Morocco, Andalusia, Barcelona-to-Bilbao, and Barcelona) as well as for Saveur, Sky, Forbes, and other publications, Semler writes about the outdoors, food, travel, and culture.